Multi-Polar Capitalism

Robert Guttmann

Multi-Polar Capitalism

The End of the Dollar Standard

palgrave
macmillan

Robert Guttmann
Economics Department
Hofstra University
Hempstead, NY, USA

Centre d'Économie Paris Nord
(CEPN)
Université Sorbonne Paris Nord
Paris, France

ISBN 978-3-030-88246-4 ISBN 978-3-030-88247-1 (eBook)
https://doi.org/10.1007/978-3-030-88247-1

This Palgrave Macmillan imprint is published by the registered company Springer Nature Switzerland AG
The registered company address is: Gewerbestrasse 11, 6330 Cham, Switzerland

To Gina, Alexandre, and Maxine
With Love and Gratitude

Acknowledgments

Multi-Polar Capitalism is the fruit of years of discussion with colleagues who in the course of arguments have become close friends.

I want to thank Michel Aglietta, Luiz Carlos Bresser Pereira, Robert Boyer, Bruno De Conti, Benjamin Coriat, Eckhard Hein, Hans-Jôrg Herr, Annina Kaltenbrunner, Marty Kenner, Jan Kregel, Marc Lavoie, Jacques Mazier, Pascal Petit, Dominique Plihon, Daniela Prates, and Stephan Schulmeister for having put up with me and invested so much in guiding my work.

I wish Elmar Altvater, Eugenia Correa, Suzanne De Brunhoff, Alfred Eichner, Ernest Mandel, and Alfred Sohn-Rethel—all important sources of influence on my thinking—were still alive so that I could tell them how much they shaped me and how much I love them for it.

Contents

List of Tables

CHAPTER 1

International Money in Motion

Nowadays America's political divisions have become notorious. Many subjects of contention about the strengths or weaknesses of its society are hotly debated. Yet you rarely, if ever, hear anyone talk about a crucial pillar of America's global standing, the dominant role of the US dollar (USD) as world money in international cross-border transactions. After all, the USD has had that role for the last three quarters of a century, since January 1945 when the world adopted the so-called *Bretton Woods* agreement for a new postwar international economic order. This absence of any reference to the USD's world-money role in public discourse is all the more surprising, given how crucially important the dollar's international presence has been to how the US economy has operated during our lifetime. The very foundations of its organization have been shaped by having the USD function simultaneously as US currency and as primary international medium of exchange between countries in their cross-border transactions. For example, the US economy can run either budget deficits or trade deficits like no other country, because it can finance those by borrowing from abroad in its own currency which amounts to an open-ended, automatic financing capacity at extremely favorable terms. This is just one of several crucial advantages bestowed upon the United States by its currency's global standing, and we shall explore several others in the course of the book.

R. Guttmann, *Multi-Polar Capitalism*,
https://doi.org/10.1007/978-3-030-88247-1_1

Ignoring a factor inevitably breeds ignorance. The fact that nearly all Americans, from politicians to the broad electorate, do not think about the USD's international role leaves them not only unaware about what that implies, but also prone to misconceptions bearing possibly serious, if not tragic consequences. When Americans worry about the budget deficit or the national debt, concerns often raised among Republicans to justify opposing Democrats' spending plans, they are not only wrongly equating public debt with private debt as if those two were one and the same, but also failing to appreciate America's privileged position of being able to tap foreign savings like no other country can. Many Americans, especially those inclined to listen to ex-President Trump's musings, believe that trade is a game of winners and losers and that we tend to be the "suckers" in that "game," entirely ignoring here not only the win–win nature of trade in general but more specifically also the favorable terms of trade the United States gains from having its money dominate the world economy. US policy-makers may then end up having those false beliefs, rooted in a failure to appreciate the meaning of the dollar standard, motivate them to opt for fiscal austerity or launch trade wars when the opposite stance would have been called for. Such ignorance can easily leave us in the grip of painful policy mistakes.

But it is not just a question of policy context. We have been able to ignore the dollar standard, because we could take it for granted. When it works, it has an automaticity on its own that carries it forward through time. Yet we cannot take the dollar standard for granted. The international monetary system changes over time, even though those changes are typically a long time in the making. Sometimes, however, the typically slow nature of change concerning world money accelerates, may even shift dramatically. We may be facing precisely such a situation of deeper and faster change right now. Having ignored the dollar standard and its benefits for the United States for so long, Americans may not be well prepared to cope with its demise.

I shall argue here, in this book, that fundamental changes in the international monetary system do not arise arbitrarily, but follow certain patterns. Looking at those coalescing right now, a case can be made that we are finding ourselves precisely in such a context of structural change. We may very well face the end of the dollar standard, finding ourselves arguably already at the end of the beginning of its demise. As we move toward a multi-polar configuration, with the United States, the European Union, and China each using the international status of their respective currency to carve out regional zones of influence and propel forward a distinct global reach, Americans' perceptions will have to move beyond taking America's superpower status for granted and instead come to appreciate the complex new reality of cooperation, competition, and conflict with other powers reshaping the world economy. If we want to be prepared for that change in our circumstance, we better come to grips with the dollar standard and its possible transformation into a multi-currency system.[1]

1.1 Money as Good, Money as Asset

The lack of attention Americans typically pay to the dollar standard is mirrored by the economics profession itself not appreciating sufficiently the international monetary system as institutional framework structuring the world economy whose growth dynamic and distributional patterns it thereby greatly shapes. The open-economy macroeconomic model favored by mainstream economists looks at the international economy from the point of view of a national economy connected to the rest of the world through its balance of payments (trade, capital flows) and the exchange rate of its currency. Here the world economy is essentially viewed as "the sum of its parts," as agglomeration of all the national economies combined. This perspective of simply adding up the different countries by aggregation deprives the world economy of any determinant quality as something with its own supranational growth dynamic.

1.1.1 Mainstream View of Money as Good

Mainstream economists have yet another conceptual barrier to give the international monetary system its proper due. They just do not take money seriously enough as a social phenomenon. Their principal theoretical framework, the so-called Quantity Theory of Money, argues that

[1] It is tempting to refer to the emerging international monetary system, with its three pillars of US dollar, euro, and Chinese yuan, as a "triad." But ever since Mundell's (1960) argument of the impossibility of combining full cross-border mobility of capital, fixed exchange rates, and autonomy of national monetary policy, we have often framed his "trilemma" as an "impossible triad." Multi-currency system or multi-polar configuration are hence less confusing terms, also because other currencies beyond USD, EUR, and CNY may become more internationalized.

money is nothing but a "veil" leaving the real economy—output, employment, relative prices—unaffected. Changes in the money supply will affect absolute prices (i.e. inflation), but not "real" variables. This proposition, referring to the so-called "neutrality" of money, is as old as economics itself.[2] Key to this vision is analyzing money as a good, which exists as such separated from all the other goods as an exogenous stock variable whose size the central bank concerned can adjust at will. In this framework we have only national currencies, all of them of equal standing, differing in size proportional to their economies, connected to each other via exchange rates, but otherwise devoid of any international significance. As a matter of fact, the international dimension of the quantity-theory-of-money approach, known as the "monetary approach to the balance of payments," basically lines up the national money-supply stocks next to each other in their different currency denominations and then connects them to each other via their exchange rates which move in accordance with relative money-supply change differentials. That in a nutshell is the whole mainstream approach to the international monetary system.[3]

Yet one thing is for sure. Whatever form of money serves as international medium of exchange carries a special quality which strictly national currencies do not possess. That choice, presuming a broad-based consensus because of the prerequisite of general acceptability in the global realm, is neither accidental nor arbitrary. Instead we have to see that choice as a historic process. Once chosen and generally accepted, the international medium of exchange organizes a supranational space of economic activities across borders and geopolitical power relations between nation-states whereby the world economy gains its *sui generis* quality of being more than just the sum of its parts.

[2] See Patinkin and Steiger (1989) for a very meaningful analysis on the origins and foundations of the standard theory's notions of "money as veil" and "neutrality of money." These concepts are as old as economics itself, with the Quantity Theory of Money (from Hume, 1752 all the way to Friedman, 1956) shaping how mainstream economists have chosen to integrate money into their basically money-less "equilibrium" models.

[3] This so-called "monetary approach to the balance of payments" has been well elaborated in all its dimensions by Frenkel and Johnson (1976).

1.1.2 Keynesian View of Money as Asset

A more meaningful view of money, one that opens also the door for due consideration of the specificities of world money used between countries, arose with the revolution in economic thinking caused by the British economist John Maynard Keynes (1936). His key innovation of macroeconomic modeling aimed to explain why and how capitalist economies deviate from a balanced-growth path to show cyclical fluctuations and/or experience long periods of stagnation, both in response to corresponding variations in aggregate demand. This paradigm has a very different view of money, treating it as an asset competing with other financial assets, notably bonds.

What makes people want to hold money, even though it yields no interest or much lower interest than bonds, is the public's preference for liquidity which money embodies. Keynes' (1936) theory of liquidity preference led him to identify, beyond the standard transaction motive to pay for purchases, two additional money-demand motives. One is the precautionary motive for money demand when many actors become worried in reaction to signs of trouble ahead and so start storing cash to be better prepared. And the other is the speculative one which, broadly defined, prompts economic actors to store their wealth in money to be ready for future profit opportunities as they may arise.[4]

1.1.3 International Liquidity Preference

Keynes' theory of liquidity preference, with its different money-demand motives, can be meaningfully extended to the international sphere. A while back there were a few attempts to do so, notably among Post-Keynesian economists such as Paul Davidson (1982) and Sheila Dow (1999). When it comes to the transaction demand for money, the question arises which money might be used to pay for international trade in

[4] The discussion in Keynes (1936) of the transaction, precautionary, and speculative money-demand motives can be found for the most part in Chapter 15, meaningfully entitled "The Psychological and Business Incentives to Liquidity." Keynes (1937a, 1937b) proposed a so-called finance motive of money demand whereby businesses build up cash holdings in preparation for launching large-scale and correspondingly expensive investment projects, a pro-cyclical behavior which typically grips many producers around the same time when recovery is about to turn into a boom. For more on Keynes' rather complex "finance" motive, see Bibow (1995).

goods and services or cross-border investments in productive or financial assets. This is an issue of general acceptability. Each one of us accepts to get paid for our sales in a specific money form in the knowledge that we will be able to get rid of such money anytime, anywhere when paying for our purchases. National currencies, while generally accepted in domestic circulation within their respective countries of issue, do not necessarily find themselves in that position abroad. If, for example, Israel buys Volvos, the Swedish car maker may not accept to be paid in Israeli shekels, because those would only be useful for subsequent Swedish purchases of Israeli products. Nor would the Israelis find it easy to obtain Swedish kronor for payment unless they had earned some in preceding sales or were willing to acquire this thinly traded currency facing wide bid-offer spreads. Hence there has always been an innate and widespread desire, a universal inclination if you will, to settle on a single global money standard at the center of whatever international monetary system then in place—Constantinople's Bezant in medieval Europe, Spain's silver dollar taking hold across the globe in the sixteenth and seventeenth centuries, Britain's pound sterling from 1815 onward, the US dollar since 1945.

There have always been lesser alternatives in more limited international circulation—Florence's florin or Venice's ducat during the Middle Ages, the Dutch gulden from the mid-seventeenth century onward, Austria's Maria Theresa thaler after 1741, nowadays the euro—to complement the primary world-money form without putting its central status in question. The latter typically gained general acceptability across large swaths of whatever constituted then the world economy not only because of the strategic position of the issuing power (e.g. Spain's colonization drive, the emerging British empire), but also because of the highly reputed minting quality of the coins in question. Other countries often copied their own versions of the world-money coins, and these imitations exchanged with their widely traded counterparts at fixed rates derived from their respective relative weight differentials. Convertibility conditions, gradually widened beyond gold and silver coins to include government-issued paper currency and commercial bank notes or deposits (see Britain's Bank Charter Act of 1844 as an example), are a crucial institutional underpinning of money demand's transaction motive crystallized as the payments system.

The precautionary motive of money demand prompts economic actors to accumulate cash for protection against unforeseen circumstances or to meet contingencies. It manifests itself most figuratively in the foreign-exchange reserves which countries accumulate not least to withstand incidences of global financial instability like speculative attacks on their currencies. Of course, the desire to build up cash positions for protection in the face of heightened uncertainty grabs private actors as well. That is why internationally accepted monies have to provide large, deep, and highly liquid financial markets where a wide range of actors can park their excess cash safely and in easily accessible fashion. When the precautionary motive intensifies in periods of growing instability, there will be a rapidly spreading "flight to quality" during which frightened actors rush into monies carrying safe-haven status. Today this role falls still predominantly to the US dollar. But to a notable degree the Swiss franc or the Japanese yen, both well reputed for competent central bank management, low inflation, and exchange-rate strength, serve also as (at least regional) safe havens.

1.1.4 *The Eurocurrencies Market*

The speculative money-demand motive has by now acquired a complex international dimension. Until the second half of the 1960s speculative activity across borders was severely limited by prevailing arrangements—a binary choice of internationally accepted monies (gold, US dollars) linked to each other in an iron-clad fixed exchange rate, an official payments system controlled by central banks, and extensive capital controls. But this situation was not to last. From 1960 onward London-based banks had begun to offer dollar-denominated deposits and loans, so-called Eurodollars, which operated outside the jurisdiction of the Federal Reserve and so helped to circumvent regulatory restraints such as domestic interest-rate ceilings on bank deposits or capital controls. Those Eurodollars were then given their own global payments system, supported by an electronic fund-transfer system known as Clearing House Interbank Payments System (CHIPS) and an inter-bank communication network known as Society of Worldwide International Financial Telecommunications (SWIFT), whereby the world's leading banks gained a transnational presence beyond the regulatory reach of governments.[5]

That private payments system has since become the spearhead of globalization, the vector of global finance driving cross-border flows

[5] CHIPS and SWIFT are both electronic networks of supercomputers owned by consortiums of commercial banks, the first launched in 1970 and headquartered in New York and the second set up in 1973 while based in Brussels.

and supra-national organization of economic activity. At first this global banking network, the so-called *Eurocurrencies market* (also referred to as Euromarket or "offshore banking"), launched repeated speculative attacks on the overvalued dollar which forced US suspension of the dollar-gold convertibility at the heart of Bretton Woods in August 1971 and of fixed exchange rates in March 1973. Then it became a platform for currency diversification away from the US dollar as an explosion in the global volume of currency trading, which has risen from about $100 billion per day in 1973 to an average daily transaction volume exceeding $6.5 trillion today, turned money into a speculative object.

These Eurocurrencies—euro-denominated time deposits in London, yen-denominated floating-rate notes in Singapore, and so forth—have also spawned a growing variety of money-market and capital-market instruments through which the speculative money-demand motive extends nowadays beyond highly leveraged bets on anticipated exchange-rate movements to profitable exploitation of interest-rate differentials, interest arbitrage, carry-trade operations, and more effective protection against inflation. The international monetary system, having gained this privatized and primarily profit-driven dimension of global finance across the globe over the last half a century, has thus "normalized" speculation nowadays into a central activity of financial institutions, non-financial corporations, and wealthy individuals further motivated by tax evasion and/or money laundering. This gigantic high-speed cross-border flow activity can be for avoidance of losses as much as pursuit of gains.

1.2 Functions of International Money

Just as much as one can specify the international dimensions of liquidity preference giving world money a specific institutional context (see Sect. 1.1.3), so can we also identify the uniquely international aspects of world money's functions. These are in important respects different from the standard discussion of money's functions. For one, the emergence of a globally integrated banking system through the aforementioned Eurocurrencies market in the 1960s and 1970s established quite literally a private sphere of "stateless" near- and quasi-monies in international circulation beyond the direct regulatory reach of central banks. This private–public dichotomy is probably even more pertinent today, when the private dimension of cross-border activity—trade, global value chains combining the decentralization of production and centralization of cash-flow management, the digital economy, supranational inter-linking of financial markets, global diversification of investment portfolios, inter-bank lending and fund transfers, et cetera—has grown so dramatically to the point of dwarfing the public (i.e. central bank) sphere of international transactions. Already relatively early on, Paul Krugman (1984) elaborated a 2 × 3 matrix of international-money functions rooted in the three traditional money functions of medium of exchange, unit of account, and store of value, each of which has both a public as well as a private expression when applied to the international realm.

1.2.1 International Medium of Exchange

With regard to the public medium-of-exchange function of money, central banks use internationally accepted monies for interventions usually motivated by efforts to manage the exchange rates of their domestic currencies. For example, a central bank may defend its currency's exchange rate against downward pressure by buying up its currency for which it would have to sell dollars or euros out of its reserves. Incidentally, such a foreign-exchange sale has the same effect as an open-market sale in terms of draining bank reserves and may therefore have to be counteracted ("sterilized") by off-setting purchases of domestic government securities (i.e. so-called open-market purchases).

In the private sphere parties usually pay each other in an internationally accepted medium of exchange rather than in either the buyer's or seller's respective currencies. For example, going back to our earlier example when an Israeli firm buys a product from a Swedish firm (e.g. Volvo), it is not obvious that it will have Swedish krona (SEK) ready for payment. Nor may the Swedish firm accept being paid in Israeli shekels (ILS), since that currency is only useful if expended on future purchases from Israel. Neither ILS nor SEK have widespread circulation. On the other hand, USD circulates everywhere, as would to a somewhat lesser degree also the euro (EUR). It is their universal acceptability which makes these two key currencies more attractive to a large number of actors outside the United States or Eurozone. Such globally used money also serves as "vehicle" for exchanges of other currencies. It is thus rightfully characterized as "vehicle" currency when referring to its private medium-of-exchange function.

1.2.2 International Unit of Account

The unit-of-account function of money has to do with its ability to serve as standard of prices. In the public sphere comprising the actions of central banks this function manifests itself when stating the par value of the domestic currency in terms of USD or EUR which thus serve as "anchors" denominating the exchange rate. Central banks may fix the price of their domestic currency in terms of that anchor, when adopting a fixed exchange-rate regime known as a "peg."

As regards the private sphere, international money serves as unit of account when it comes to "invoicing," that is defining the monetary unit in which the prices of goods traded across borders are denominated. For example, many globally traded commodities, such as oil, are typically priced all over the world in terms of the dominant currency serving as world money, in this case the USD.

1.2.3 International Store of Value

When it comes to store of value, the public manifestation of that function in the international realm concerns the choice of monies central banks wish to hold their foreign-exchange reserves in. In this regard the most important currencies, notably the USD and to a lesser extent also the EUR, serve as "reserve" currencies. There has in recent years been some degree of diversification in terms of various central banks holding a growing variety of currencies as reserves, for example the Chinese yuan (CNY).

In the private sphere the store-of-value function expresses itself in terms of which key currencies non-financial actors keep their excess cash reserves in, whether in their bank accounts or in other types of highly liquid assets such as Treasuries. We may characterize this as the "banking" role of international money.

1.2.4 International Means of Payment

Throughout his wide-ranging and exhaustive analysis of capitalism Karl Marx (1867/1887, Chapter 3; 1894/1967, Chapter 36; 1910/1951, Chapter 17) stressed a fourth function, that of means of payment which in his theory of money refers to the settlement of payment obligations, notably debt. While often ignored in standard theory or conflated with money's medium-of-exchange function, we insist on including this function in its own right not least because we operate in a system of credit-money whose issue in the banking system is inexorably tied to taking on debt. In the international realm this function of money as means of payment is even more meaningful, because the currency used for settling debt owed to foreigners has important implications.[6]

When it comes to the public dimension of international money's means-of-payment function there are two issues worth taking note of. First, there is the challenge of a country's foreign debt and the need for servicing that debt by earning enough of the currency (or currencies) in which that debt is denominated. Excessively indebted countries find themselves sooner or later in crisis in which case they will need to impose drastic, often painful economic-policy changes and may even require debt restructuring. Second, there is the ability of the country issuing the primary form of world money, in this case the United States, to borrow from the rest of the world in its own currency and cope with associated foreign-debt-servicing charges simply by issuing more of its own currency transferred to foreign creditors, which basically delays actual settlement of foreign debts indefinitely. The United States owes the rest of the world $7.07 trillion (as of June 2020), and whatever portion of that debt is coming due simply gets rolled over for the most part. It is this curious characteristic of key currencies used as international medium of exchange allowing their issuers to escape proper settlement of their debts with the rest of the world which makes explicit consideration of the means-of-payments function of (international) money so relevant here.

In the private sphere foreign debts also raise the dangerous possibility of denomination mismatches, a problem which Barry Eichengreen et al. (2002) characterized as "original sin." Having your assets in local currency but your liabilities in a world-money currency (because you borrowed in international capital markets or from foreign banks) makes you much more vulnerable in case your domestic currency devalues or you are otherwise prevented from earning the international currency through exports. This vulnerability has in recent years dramatically intensified in the wake of so-called "carry trade" through which investors (banks,

[6] Kindleberger (1981), an eminent analyst of international monetary relations, refers to the same means-of-payments function evoked by Marx as "standard of deferred payment." As so often the case among mainstream economists, Krugman (1984, p. 263) rejects the idea of such a debt-settlement function deserving to stand alone.

Table 1.1 The matrix of international-money functions

Money function	*Public*	*Private*
Medium of exchange	Intervention	Vehicle
Unit of account	Anchor, peg	Invoicing
Store of value	Reserves	Banking
Means of payment	Sovereign debt, exorbitant privilege	Foreign debt, carry trade, original sin

funds) borrow cheaply in the international currency and then invest those funds in emerging-market economies where interest rates are higher.

Table 1.1 summarizes the eight different international-money functions as follows:

1.3 Currency Shares Per International-Money Function

Now that we have identified the 2 × 4 matrix of world-money functions, we can take a closer look at the respective currency shares per world-money function. Some of those are regularly measured in an official fashion by international monetary authorities (e.g. IMF) as part of their data-collection effort; others are harder to measure reliably. Either way, we get the same picture of a hierarchical structure.

1.3.1 The International Currency Pyramid

When looking at the currencies, which have some presence across their jurisdictional boundaries and thus international recognition, we can identify what looks like a pyramid, with several, clearly identifiable layers.[7] On top of that pyramid we can see the USD still dominating throughout while the EUR is clearly established second. The Japanese yen (JPY), British pound (GBP) and, to a lesser extent, the Swiss franc (CHF) form a third layer of widely traded currencies.

[7] The idea of a "currency pyramid," denoting the hierarchy of internationally accepted monies with the USD on top, was first elaborated by Cohen (1998, 2004) and subsequently refined by De Paula et al. (2017) as well as De Conti and Prates (2018).

Table 1.2 Internationalization of Commodity Currencies (daily currency trading volume, $ Billion)

Currency	*2001*	*2007*	*2010*	*2013*	*2016*	*2019*
CAD	56	143	210	244	260	332
AUD	54	220	301	463	349	447
NZD	7	63	63	105	104	137
BRL	6	13	27	59	51	71
MXN	10	44	50	135	97	114
RUB	4	25	36	86	58	72
CNY	0	15	34	120	202	285

Source Bank for International Settlements, Triennial Central Bank Survey

A fourth layer consists of so-called "commodity" currencies. We are talking here about the currencies of multi-commodity exporters with wide-open economies and solid financial systems such as Canada (CAD), Australia (AUD), and New Zealand (NZD). To a lesser degree this layer also includes the Brazilian Real (BRL), the South African Rand (ZAR), Scandinavian currencies such as the Swedish krona (SEK) or the Norwegian krone (NOK), the Russian ruble (RUB), and the Saudi Arabian riyal (SAR). The exchange rates of these currencies move in close correlation with the world-market prices of the commodities these countries specialize in exporting, as long as those commodity exports make up at least a quarter or more of their total export earnings. For example, the AUD's exchange rate will closely track iron ore prices, the RUB's exchange rate will closely track the price of crude, the Chilean peso or Peruvian nuevo sol will both closely track the price of copper, and so forth.[8] Commodity currencies depend for their internationalization to a significant degree on the commodity-price cycle, hence benefiting from the boom conditions during the 2000s and early 2010s but less so in recent years (see Table 1.2).

[8] The direct positive link between exchange-rates of the "commodity currencies" of commodity-exporting nations and the prices of commodities responsible for much of their export earnings has been well analyzed by Cashin et al. (2004) as well as Kohlscheen et al. (2016).

A fifth layer consists of currencies from emerging-market economies undergoing rapid industrialization and thus enjoying fast growth, especially those managing to play an increasingly strategic role as manufacturing platforms in global value chains. We may want to refer to those as "platform" currencies (my term!) which include the South Korean won (KRW), the Polish zloty (PLD), the Israeli shekel (ILS), and potentially over time a host of other emerging-market monies such as the Indian rupee (INR), the Vietnamese Dong (VND), or the Malaysian ringgit (MYR).

Given the dynamic of globalization, some commodity exporters are also trying hard to build up their domestic industrial base, which renders the distinction between commodity currency and platform currency less sharply drawn in the case of their currencies. This, for example, is the case of the Mexican peso (MXN). Mexico is a major exporter of crude oil and food products while also serving as platform in US global value chains so that the MXN may be classified as either a "commodity" currency or a "platform" currency. You may also mention the Brazilian real (BRL) in this context.

That layer of "platform" currencies would normally be led by the Chinese currency, the renminbi (RMB). But China's rapidly expanding global reach as a superpower in the making has over the last decade been accompanied by a complex internationalization process of its currency, a process which has already gained the "redback" a new international symbol as CNY for Chinese yuan or CNH when traded offshore in Hong Kong. China's RMB/CNY/CNH is for this reason a layer onto itself, one that may well sooner or later rival the two top layers USD and EUR, a prospect we shall analyze in greater detail below (see Sects. 4.2.3 and 6.2 for more).

The world's many other currencies are for the most part strictly local, circulating within their country of issue but not much, if at all, beyond those domestic boundaries. Many of these currencies are not even fully convertible with other currencies and have as a consequence informal exchange rates dominating official ones. It is not clear whether or not the many strictly local, more or less inconvertible monies should actually be considered part of the international currency pyramid.

1.3.2 World-Money Market Shares (by Function)

We will provide some market-share calculations pertaining to different world-money functions, both private and public, where data is easily available to illustrate the prevailing international currency hierarchy. For example, the Bank for International Settlements (BIS) conducts a so-called "Triennial Central Bank Survey of Foreign Exchange and OTC Derivatives Markets" (https://www.bis.org/publ/rpfx16.htm) the results of which are summarized every three years in the relevant year-end issue of the *BIS Quarterly Review*, the last one published in December 2019. The survey's collection of data on global trading patterns in the foreign-exchange markets can be used as proxy measure for the private medium-of-exchange function, in the process identifying which monies may serve as vehicle currency in cross-border transactions.

We should note that the shares in Table 1.3 add up to 200 percent, since each transaction involves two currencies. The USD's share has maintained its overwhelming dominance, notwithstanding a temporary post-crisis blip in 2007 and 2010. The EUR's share has been battered more persistently in the wake of its own systemic crisis(2009–2012). Quite notable has been the steady diversification into a variety of second-tier "commodity" (AUD, CAD, NZD, BRL) and "platform" currencies (MXN, KRW) over the last two decades. This trend extends to

Table 1.3 Currency distribution of global transactions in foreign exchange market

Currency	*1998*	*2001*	*2004*	*2007*	*2010*	*2013*	*2016*	*2019*
USD	86.6	89.9	88.0	85.6	84.9	87.0	87.6	88.3
EUR	–	37.9	37.4	37.0	39.1	33.4	31.3	32.3
JPY	21.7	23.5	20.8	17.2	19.0	23.0	21.6	16.8
GBP	11.0	13.0	16.5	14.9	12.9	11.8	12.8	12.8
AUD	3.0	4.3	6.0	6.6	7.6	8.6	6.9	6.8
CAD	3.5	4.5	4.2	4.3	5.3	4.6	5.1	5.0
CHF	7.1	6.0	6.0	6.8	6.3	5.2	4.8	5.0
CNY	0.0	0.0	0.1	0.5	0.9	2.2	4.0	4.3
MXN	0.5	0.8	1.1	1.3	1.3	2.5	2.2	1.7
KRW	0.2	0.8	1.1	1.2	1.5	1.2	1.6	2.0
NZD	0.2	0.6	1.1	1.9	1.6	2.0	2.1	2.1
BRL	0.2	0.5	0.3	0.4	0.7	1.1	1.0	1.1

Source BIS Triennial Central Bank Survey

many other currencies not listed in this table, such as Sweden's SEK, Norway's NOK, Turkey's TRY, Poland's PLN, Russia's RUB, India's INR, Malaysia's MYR, or South Africa's ZAR, all of whom went from 0 to 0.5 percent in 1998 to shares between 1 and 2 percent, respectively by 2016. The rise of China's CNY (previously abbreviated as RMB) has been especially pronounced.

Another well-documented world-money function is that of official foreign-exchange reserves held by central banks, as measured by the IMF's Currency Composition of Official Foreign Exchange Reserves (COFER), to be downloaded from www.data.imf.org/COFER (Table 1.4).

We can round out our data-collection exercise regarding currency shares as follows:

- The Society for Worldwide International Financial Telecommunications (SWIFT, 2018) concluded that in December 2017 the USD had a 39.8 percent share in its global inter-bank payment network, based on payment value, compared to a 35.7 percent share for the EUR, a 7.1 percent share for the GBP, and a 3 percent share for the JPY. At that point the CNY had reached a 1.6 percent share, exceeding the 1.3–1.6 percent shares reported for the CAD, AUD, and CHF respectively.
- The Bank for International Settlements (BIS, 2019) reported that of the $24.36 trillion stock of international debt securities outstanding in the first quarter of 2019 the USD had a 46.6 percent share, compared to a 38 percent share for the EUR (which during the first

Table 1.4 Composition of official foreign exchange reserves

Currency	*Q4 2000*	*Q4 2004*	*Q4 2008*	*Q4 2012*	*Q4 2016*	*Q1 2019*	*Q3 2020*
USD	71.1	65.6	63.8	61.2	65.4	61.7	60.5
EUR	18.3	24.7	26.2	24.2	19.1	20.7	20.5
JPY	6.1	4.3	3.5	4.0	4.0	5.2	5.9
GBP	2.8	3.5	4.2	4.0	4.3	4.4	4.5
CNY	0.0	0.0	0.1	0.8	1.1	1.9	2.1
CHF	0.3	0.2	0.1	0.3	0.2	0.2	0.2
Other	1.5	1.9	2.2	5.5	6.0	6.0	6.3

Source IMF's COFER, https://data.imf.org/?sk=E6A5F467-C14B-4AA8-9F6D-5A09EC4E62A4

half of the 2010s had exceeded that of the USD), an 8.2 percent share for the GBP, and a 1.9 percent share for the JPY.

- The International Monetary Fund (IMF, 2020) identified nearly one half of the 192 countries, 97 countries to be precise, as pursuing some sort of exchange-rate anchor, including currency boards, traditional pegs, crawling pegs, or managed floats, of which 38 were tied to the USD and 25 to the EUR.[9]

1.4 Why the US Dollar's World-Money Status Has Endured

Looking at the statistics, the USD is still dominant across the board. The EUR is a solid second. All the other currencies lag far behind in their international posture. While both of these key currencies suffered their own setbacks following financial crisis—the USD during the end of the 2000s and the EUR in the first half of the 2010s—they both have stood their ground since. We have also seen the relatively rapid advance of the CNY after 2008, once the Chinese authorities decided that they needed to diversify away from their excessive dependence on (and thus exposure to) the USD. What the data presented does not show the difficulties and setbacks which the ongoing internationalization of the CNY has encountered since 2015, a complicated stop–go process which we will ultimately discuss further below (in Sect. 4.2.3). Global finance has managed to engulf many more countries over the last quarter of a century, especially via the carry trade, and this has led to a whole lot more currencies gaining some degree of international circulation. Nonetheless, despite this evident diversification of the international monetary system, the USD still rules the roost.

1.4.1 Preference for a Single World-Money Standard

What then explains the continued dominance of the US dollar? One way to answer this question is to go back to an analysis of why private

[9] De Conti and Prates (2018) provide additional data on the respective market shares for key currencies in different segments of global finance, notably money markets, derivatives, and penetration of foreign currencies in local banking. Their findings by and large confirm the ranking established in our discussion so far, meaning the still-prevailing dominance of the USD, followed more or less closely by the EUR, persistent presence of key currencies JPY, GBP and CHF, rising role of commodity currencies CAD, AUD and NZD, and the rapid advance of the CNY from a near-zero base a decade ago.

economic actors demand money, in this case why a specific currency ends up being used so predominantly in cross-border transactions. This means, as we did already earlier in Sect. 1.1.1, extending John Maynard Keynes' (1936) theory of liquidity preference to the international realm, as has been done by Sheila Dow (1999). Going back to Keynes' trifecta of transaction, speculative, and precautionary money-demand motives, Professor Dow demonstrates how each of those leaves large numbers of actors with a clear preference for a single global monetary standard. It is much easier, from the point of view of the practicality of transacting with each other, to get paid in a currency that buyers have and sellers can spend immediately no matter where. There are obvious network externalities at work here, to the extent that the more widely this agreed-to international monetary standard is used, the more attractive it will be for each individual user. And these get coupled with considerable economies of scale in the international financial system which arise when conducting large volumes of business in the same currency, leading to lower transaction costs and less price risk. The issuer of the international monetary standard has large and deep financial markets, themselves boosted in size by that money's global use as vehicle currency. Profit-seeking actors will also keep large cash reserves in the key currency to take advantage of speculative opportunities that may arise or to prevent losses from exposure to marginal positions. Finally, the international monetary standard satisfies the precautionary money-demand motive in the face of heightened uncertainty by offering a safe haven when expectations turn nervous.

1.4.2 America's "Exorbitant Privilege"

Another crucial aspect surrounding the modus operandi of the vehicle currency, like the USD today, is the advantage it bestows upon its issuer who thus is inclined to defend that status. The issuer of the national currency serving as world money benefits from this position in a variety of ways. Widely recognized by mainstream economists in this regard is the so-called "seigniorage" benefit which refers to the profit the issuing country earns when it creates low-interest reserves held by the rest of the world (as its liabilities) while accumulating at the same time higher-yielding assets invested abroad. This rather narrowly conceived advantage earns the United States about $20 billion each year, as noted by Ben Bernanke (2016).

Paul Krugman (1993) has made the valid point that mainstream economists latch on to seigniorage so as to avoid asking themselves more difficult questions about the international monetary system. This comment also applies to the strategic advantages accruing to the issuer of world money which, when you think about it, go beyond the yield spread on the issuing central bank's balance sheet underpinning "seigniorage." The benefits a country enjoys from being the issuer of world money are significantly more profound than that. After all, the vehicle currency gets created within the domestic banking system and then has to be transferred into international circulation via net outflows from the issuing country to the rest of the world. In other words, the issuing country, in this case the United States, has to run chronic balance-of-payments deficits whereby such net outflows of USD get organized. The rest of the world automatically absorbs those deficit-induced net outflows of USD when using those for payments or as reserves. Another way of framing this advantage, often referred to as America's "exorbitant privilege," is to recognize that the United States can borrow from the rest of the world in its own currency as surpluses overseas get recycled as reserves held in US Treasuries or other US-issued debt.[10]

1.4.3 *The "Dollar Trap"*

The other side of that equation are other countries building up large dollar holdings over time. Such a build-up happens naturally on an ongoing basis to the extent that over half of all cross-border transactions are carried out in US dollars and two-thirds of all foreign exchange reserves of countries are denominated in US dollars. But the rest of the world's accumulation of USD shifted to a whole new level in the late 1990s. In the wake of a global currency crisis during the late 1990s, which engulfed a large number of emerging-market economies from Thailand to Argentina, many countries reacted by greatly increasing their USD-denominated reserves to protect against speculative attacks and capital flight. China built up a $4 trillion dollar hoard, and even Japan ended up with more than a trillion in dollar reserves. There were many other

[10] As pointed out by Eichengreen (2010) in his eponymous work analyzing the history of the USD as world money, the notion "exorbitant privilege" was coined by French President Charles De Gaulle's finance minister Valery Giscard D'Estaing in the late 1960s as applying to the United States' ability to borrow from others in its own currency.

emerging-market economies and industrial nations accumulating scores or even hundreds of billions in USD-denominated reserves, part of a broader phenomenon characterized by Ben Bernanke (2005) as a "global savings glut." Supplies of these funds into USD assets drove down long-term US interest rates to very low levels and in turn fueled recurrent asset bubbles in the United States—the internet (so-called "dot-com") bubble of 1997–2000, the housing bubble 2003–2007. Of course, this phenomenon coincided neatly with ever-larger US trade deficits due to overspending on the part of Americans in response to the positive wealth effects from these very asset bubbles. For example, during the real estate bubble of the 2000s US homeowners were able to obtain ever larger mortgages or home-equity loans on their rapidly appreciating homes when refinancing. Whatever the driving engine behind this mutually reinforcing dynamic, the rest of the world ended up having locked in huge sums into USD-denominated reserves.

Eswar Prasad (2014) has characterized this lock-in as a "dollar trap." Any sustained move out of the USD, resulting in a significant depreciation of the "greenback," would thus inflict major capital losses on the (predominantly dollar-denominated) foreign-exchange reserves of China, Japan, and others. In other words, any movement away from the USD's dominant international-money role carries large "switch" costs which in turn explains in part why that vehicle currency has sustained its large world-market share(s) for so long. Steve Johnson (2019) reports a proxy measure for this strong incumbency advantage, dividing the USD's share in global reserves by the US share in global output. In 2018 that ratio stood at 4.1 for the United States, compared to the Eurozone's 2.15, Great Britain's 1.96, Japan's 1.15, Switzerland's 0.49, and China's still negligible 0.07.[11]

1.5 Characteristics of World-Money Issuers

The continued dominance of the USD has also been rooted structurally in the relative strength of the United States as its issuer. This gets us to the

[11] Johnson's (2019) graph reveals the spectacular decline in the reserve share/output share ratio for the GBP from about 6 to just 0.5 between 1967 and 1975 and the similarly steep fall in said ratio for the CHF from 5.2 in 1980 to 0.8 in 1995. Prasad's "dollar trap" is evidenced by the USD-ratio's steady rise from 2.6 in 1991 to above 4 now.

important question what characteristics a country must possess to have a currency capable of acquiring and sustaining an important international presence. One crucial factor is obviously size. A currency is more likely to have international significance, the larger the economy of its issuer. In this regard the huge size of the US economy is a determinant factor, as is the size of the European Union's Eurozone (roughly the same as that of the United States). Long-standing deflationary shrinkage of its GDP notwithstanding, Japan still has a fairly large economy. And even Great Britain's economy ranks fifth in the world if measured by its nominal GDP (even though if measured on a purchasing-power-parity basis, ultimately a more accurate basis for international comparisons, China, India, Russia, and Indonesia would all have larger economies).

1.5.1 Financial and Geopolitical Dimensions of Power

The issuer's size is obviously not the only factor, because otherwise the CNY would be a lot more dominant given the scale of China's huge economy. Another factor is a country's insertion into the world economy. Once again, if measured in terms of trade links, China's emergence as a commercial juggernaut should have already yielded a larger international role for the CNY as has been the case for the EUR (even though more than half of its trade is intra-Eurozone). A more important measure of a key-currency issuer's integration into the world economy would be of a financial nature. This factor might be rooted in the size and global reach of its banking system, which incidentally would help explain the continued importance of Britain's GBP and the (at least until recently) outsized influence of the Swiss CHF. Or it might concern the scale and depth of its financial markets which we can measure as the size of that country's capital (i.e. bond and equity) markets as a share of its gross domestic product. In both regards of finance the United States still stands out. Not only are many of the leading transnational banks American, but the United States also possesses highly developed stock, corporate bond, and above all government bond markets.

However, the criteria for determining why certain countries issue key currencies dominating the international monetary system go beyond economics and finance. They also must include a geopolitical dimension, in other words the projection of military, diplomatic and strategic power.[12] And here once again the United States has until recently stood out. US military spending, which in 2019 amounted to $732 Billion, is larger than that of the next ten countries combined (i.e. China, India, Russia, Saudi Arabia, France, Germany, United Kingdom, Japan, South Korea, and Brazil spending together $726 Billion that year), and America's long-standing security commitments span the globe. It is not surprising, as noted by Barry Eichengreen, Arnaud Mehl, and Livia Chitu (2017), that countries substantially dependent on the United States for their security (e.g. Japan, Germany, Saudi Arabia) rely proportionately more on the USD for reserves than countries having independent nuclear forces (e.g. China, France, Russia).

1.5.2 The "Soft Power" of Multilateralism

From the end of World War II onward the United States built and then dominated the multilateral institutions exercising global governance, starting with the United Nations. In this regard America's influence over the International Monetary Fund, the World Bank, and the World Trade Organization has played a decisive role in shaping the international monetary system and its evolution. This outsized projection of geopolitical influence continued until the end of Barack Obama's second term, concluding with the Paris Climate Agreement in December 2015 and the Trans-Pacific Partnership in February 2016.

But then America's posture took a very dramatic turn in a different direction under Donald Trump, who systematically abrogated US diplomatic leadership in multilateral settings. Trump's isolationist "America First" stance basically implied abandoning the "soft power" posture needed to lead the world. It is also true that, apart from paralyzing or weakening crucial multilateral pillars of global governance such as the World Trade Organization or the World Health Organization, Trump ripped apart many of America's carefully nourished alliances. Here his extensive use of tariffs and other trade barriers did a lot of damage, notably because their tit-for-tat escalation led to trade "wars" with China and, to a slightly less virulent degree, also the European Union. At the

[12] Geopolitical aspects of a leading power's influence over the international monetary system in general, and the use of its currency as world money in particular, have also been highlighted by Kindleberger (1970), Kirshner (1995), and more recently Cohen (2015).

same time Trump aggressively pushed a hard-power strategy of sanctions, military pressure, and conflict. Even though he was able to get away with such a newly aggressive and unilateralist strategy during his term (2017–2021), Trump's highly controversial actions started to get other countries more interested in seeking alternative arrangements which would circumvent US power.

We may think of Trump's raucous presidency as an aberration, and it may turn out to have been just that. After all, he got voted out of office after only one term in favor of Joe Biden who embodies America's traditional "internationalism" that has guided its bipartisan policy consensus for decades now. And it is already obvious that, true to his word, Biden will use his presidency to return the United States to the fold of multilateralism. Still, much damage to America's standing has been done. Both the European Union and China have committed to making themselves less dependent on US leadership in general and the dollar standard in particular. They have both expressed a renewed interest in advancing, even accelerating, the international use of their currencies, the EUR and the CNY (see Chapter 6 for more). Most importantly, Trump's electoral base remains sizeable and vocal, committed to anti-immigrant and anti-trade "America First" isolationism. Even the Left of the Democrats, the so-called Progressives, are very doubtful, if not altogether opposed, to free trade and globalization. The Biden Administration will thus face opposition on both Right and Left to ambitious resumption of multilateralism. These political constraints remain, irrespective of Trump who captured those anti-globalist sentiments before anyone else all the way to his surprise victory in 2016. We need to understand these underlying political shifts as reflections of contradictory pressures and examine to what extent those might have anything to do with the United States as issuer of world money. Here we may return to an old paradox faced by the issuer of world money, first captured by Robert Triffin (1960) and henceforth known as the "Triffin Dilemma," and update that phenomenon to apply today.

1.6 The Triffin Dilemma Revisited

Triffin pointed in 1960 to an inherent contradiction of the Bretton Woods system endangering its viability over the long run, the inability of the United States to guarantee the automatic convertibility of US dollars held abroad with America's gold reserves on demand at a fixed rate of $35 per ounce of gold. That promise served as the anchor for a system of fixed exchange rates based on the respective gold weights of currencies. Triffin framed the problem he wanted to address as a "dilemma" for the US central bank, the Federal Reserve, inasmuch as it faced two incompatible policy objectives at the same time. The long-run survivability of Bretton Woods depended on continuous US-mobilized injections of dollars into international circulation via regular US balance of payments deficits resulting in the required net outflows. To the extent that such outflows would lead to global dollar supplies exceeding US gold reserves and so render the dollar unsustainably overvalued, worried central banks might want to swap their dollars for gold which would oblige the Fed to raise interest rates in order to reduce America's external deficits and/or slow conversions and outflows of gold. At the same time, the Fed's short-term policy objectives in the face of any recession, as may arise from the deflationary impact of foreign demand of US gold reserves thereby flowing out, would be to lower interest rates. The Triffin Dilemma thus pointed to the systemic difficulties which the issuer of world money may have to deal with when facing possibly incompatible national policy objectives and international commitments at the same time.

1.6.1 The 1960 Crisis

One reason why Triffin's argument resonated so strongly at the time was the fact that the US government had to deal precisely with such a policy dilemma for the first time just when he had raised that issue. It was, after all, in 1960 that the Federal Reserve's foreign liabilities, dollars in international circulation, exceeded its monetary gold reserves for the first time. In other words, the USD as world money was becoming de facto inconvertible. That prospect did indeed trigger a first crisis of confidence about the long-term prospects of Bretton Woods which had to be addressed. The US government feared a run by other governments on its dwindling gold reserves for arbitrage gains (since gold fetched at that point already $40 per ounce in the London-based open market due to its mounting shortage). Foreign governments in turn worried about a possible devaluation of the seemingly overvalued USD which would cause them losses on their USD reserves. In the midst of a tightly fought election campaign, the Democratic candidate John F. Kennedy had to address these fears by promising not to devalue the dollar, if elected. In return, European governments agreed to pool their gold reserves in support of US convertibility commitments, the so-called Gold Pool, and also enhance the lending capacity of the International Monetary Fund so that it could cope more effectively with currency crises to come. This step, giving rise to the Group of Ten (G-10), was known as the General Agreements to Borrow. The combination of Gold Pool and GAB stabilized Bretton Woods until 1968.[13]

In addition, the emerging Triffin Dilemma also affected US policy. With the US economy in recession since 1959, the Fed did indeed face the kind of policy dilemma Triffin had highlighted, a seeming clash between the need for higher interest rates to slow down dollar-gold conversions undermining Bretton Woods and the imperative for lower interest rates to fight the recession. The US central bank met this challenge in ingenious fashion, through an innovation in its open-market operations known as Operation Twist which it ran from 1961 to 1965. In this new two-step procedure the Fed sold Treasury bills, thereby driving up short-term interest rates (as sales lowered prices of the bills which move inversely with their yields), and used proceeds from the sales to buy longer-term Treasury bonds whose yields thereby fell (as its purchases drove up their prices) as a way to lower long-term interest rates with which to counteract the recession.[14]

1.6.2 America's Trade Deficits and Asset Bubbles

It is important to bring the Triffin Dilemma up to date. Nowadays, within the context of the contemporary dollar standard, the Triffin Dilemma no longer concerns itself with the gold-dollar convertibility conditions, since these became irrelevant after President Nixon suspended that guarantee at the heart of Bretton Woods on August 15, 1971. But the Triffin Dilemma still holds true in the broader sense of pointing to the difficulties and conflicts US policy-makers may face because of the US dollar's dual role as national currency and world money. During the Bretton Woods

[13] The G-10 members included Belgium, Canada, France, Germany, Italy, Japan, the Netherlands, Sweden, the United Kingdom and the United States, plus Switzerland as an associated member. Once formed as a network of the richest IMF members, these eleven countries met regularly for coordination purposes at the Bank for International Settlements (BIS) which they thereby helped to revive as an umbrella organization for the world's leading central banks. See here also Bank for International Settlements (2020).

[14] See Alon and Swanson (2011) on the Fed's Operation Twist and its measurable impact on flattening America's yield curve during the first half of the 1960s.

years (1945–1971) the needed dollar outflows from the United States to the rest of the world took the form of large net capital exports in excess of America's regular trade surpluses. But the post-Bretton Woods dollar standard emerging in the late 1970s and early 1980s has relied instead on chronic US trade deficits to supply the rest of the world with needed injections of USD into international circulation. Seemingly insatiable foreign demand for dollar reserves has recurrently put upward pressure on the USD's effective exchange rate and contributed to a chronic and ultimately very large US trade deficit, as we have seen play out from 1985 onward. Since these trade deficits have been automatically financed by foreigners holding and using these international dollars, they do not pose much of a problem for the United States from a financial point of view. Yet they have had a lasting effect on America's industrial structure by accelerating deindustrialization, greatly shrinking manufacturing, causing massive losses of well-paying jobs, and leaving key regions in the industrial heartland of America chronically depressed. Trump's electoral base stems in large degree from this reservoir of disaffected workers hurt by the changing nature of the US economy because of trade as well as labor-saving automation technologies.

These angry voters, ostensible victims of globalization, are also upset at the explosion of income inequality over the last four decades. While that trend has surely been accentuated by the decline of manufacturing polarizing the American employment structure toward both more lower-paying as well as more higher-paying jobs in various service sectors, it has been given additional impetus by a stratum of rich Americans enjoying sustained boosts of capital income in the form of interest, dividends and, above all, capital gains from booming financial markets. As we shall see later (in Sect. 3.3.4), America's continuous and large-scale access to international dollar supplies has kept its interest rates lower than they would have otherwise been for the last quarter of a century. The availability of cheap debt, while spurring more credit-financed spending overall, also has had the effect of making the US economy more prone to recurrent asset bubbles, be they in the stock market (as during the 1983–1987 boom, or the "dot-com" bubble of the late 1990s) or in real estate (as during the 2000s). Low-interest rates not only provide favorable conditions for leveraged financing of such asset bubbles, but also boost the valuation of targeted assets. Those three major asset bubbles, one per decade, have arguably helped enrich a burgeoning investor class whose increased income share has made them the biggest winners of financial globalization to the chagrin of many American wage-earners just scraping by.

The dollar standard's chronic US trade deficits and propensity for asset bubbles helped feed a process of political polarization toward anti-globalist fervor on both the Left (see Bernie Sanders' remarkable presidential campaigns in 2016 and 2020) as well as on the Right (see Donald Trump's successful exploitation of those sentiments in 2016). These political forces, the Progressives on the Left and the Trumpists on the Right, have managed to weaken the bipartisan consensus upon which the dollar standard's multilateralism has been based ever since the waning days of the Roosevelt Administration three quarters of a century ago.

1.6.3 The Triffin Dilemma as Structural Flaw

Such political polarization has its roots in structural changes transforming the US economy, and those have in turn been accentuated by the modus operandi of an international monetary system based on the USD as primary form of world money. That dollar standard thus has evidently had contradictory repercussions for the United States. It has brought tangible benefits, as through the automatic financing of its budget and trade deficits under perennially favorable funding conditions. But it has also hurt, as evidenced by the accelerated erosion of its manufacturing base or greater income inequality. And in the same vein it is fair to say that the dollar standard has produced winners as well as losers within the United States. Contradictory effects of the dollar standard also play out on the other side of the equation, the rest of the world using USD for cross-border transactions and as reserve asset. They may enjoy better export-led growth opportunities due to the dollar's overvaluation, but such dependence may also leave these surplus countries with imbalanced growth patterns that are vulnerable to rising exchange rates and/or interest rates. The contradictions affecting the United States and those potentially destabilizing the rest of the world are mutually feeding, mirror images of each other. America's "buyer of the last resort" trade deficits and surplus countries' supposed "savings glut" go hand in hand, one begetting the other, two sides of the same coin, with the "coin" here referring to a global growth pattern shaped by the prevailing dollar-dominated international monetary system to which its participants are subjected to.

The dilemma Triffin pointed to in 1960, albeit in its precise manifestation at that point focused on the durability of the dollar's convertibility with gold, still holds in more general terms. While there may be some who reject the idea that the Triffin Dilemma outlived the specificities of Bretton Woods, Triffin himself meant to focus our attention to what he termed "built-in destabilizers" when using a national currency as world money as is the case with the dollar standard.[15] There is *eo ipso* a structural flaw at hand when using a national currency as an international reserve asset. This is a problem of over-determination. If we have "n" countries with "n" currencies in a closed world-economy system, then we have only "n − 1" degrees of freedom in the international monetary system. This means that only "n − 1" autonomous policies are possible to achieve the payment objectives of the "n − 1" countries, and only "n − 1" exchange rates can be "independent" to the extent that the exchange rate measures the price of one money relative to another. A combination of network externalities and economies of scale will prompt the "n − 1" countries to pick ultimately which "nth" currency issued by the "nth" country will serve as world money. The currency thus chosen to serve as world money, a role Karl Marx (1867/1887, Chapter 3, sec. 3c) characterized as "ultimate universal equivalent," deprives the country of its issue of having the same degrees of freedom other countries have in managing their autonomous policy mix options. That country has to accept running perennial external deficits, becoming a net debtor to the rest of the world, and letting its currency's exchange rates float freely. Such an over-determined system of "n" currencies and "n − 1" policy targets is inherently asymmetric. The only way to overcome such a structural flaw, as already recognized by John Maynard Keynes (1980) in his "Bancor Plan" for an International Clearing Union, is to create a supranational world-money form with a global central bank integrating all the "n" currencies and national central banks.[16]

The "n − 1" problem makes clear that the dollar standard is an intrinsically asymmetric system. We can thus generalize the Triffin Dilemma, beyond its initial application specifically in the Bretton Woods context, as an inherent conflict between domestic policy objectives of the country issuing the vehicle currency and its international responsibilities as provider of world money. Former US Treasury Secretary John Connally

[15] A good example of those arguing that the Triffin Dilemma was specific to Bretton Woods are Bordo and McCauley (2019). See Ghymers (2017) and Snoy (2018), both authors of the Robert Triffin Institute, on use of the term "built-in destabilizer".

[16] This problem of over-determination when using a national currency as world money is also known as the "redundancy" problem after Mundell (1969), or the "n – 1" problem. For more on this see also McKinnon (2010).

expressed this sense of asymmetry quite succinctly at a G-10 meeting in late November 1971, organized to negotiate a new regime of exchange rates in the immediate aftermath of Bretton Woods' collapse three and a half months earlier, when he told his astonished counterparts "The dollar is our currency, but it's your problem." Implied here is also an asymmetry in how the United States prioritizes its role as the "nth" country whereby it responds to the challenge of the aforementioned redundancy problem by prioritizing pursuit of domestic policy objectives and letting other countries adjust to the eventual spillover effects embedded in the dollar standard. But one asymmetry to counteract another asymmetry does not make for symmetry. They may counterbalance for a while into a coherent global growth pattern, but cannot escape an eventual reckoning as sources of instability bound to rock the world economy.

Asymmetries invoked by the Triffin Dilemma, in its updated and generalized version applied to the dollar standard, arise on several levels. There is the tension between centrifugal forces, mediated by the dollar outflows from the center to all corners of the periphery, versus the centripetal forces concentrating international transactions into USD denomination and recycling back to the center. Within that dollar circuit between the United States and the rest of the world US domestic policy conduct will alternately fuel inflationary pressures via excessive liquidity injections or aggravate deflationary forces either because of inadequate liquidity distribution or in the face of liquidity traps, all mediated by fluctuations in the dollar's effective exchange rate as well as movements of strategic interest rates and their spreads. We also have to consider the currently prevailing balance between the public and private spheres of the international monetary system which central banks try to manage as both their government's bank and the banks' bank. The US central bank has to assure a workable distribution of global liquidity within that balance or risk setting off incidences of financial instability which may be serious enough to trigger regional, if not altogether global, downturns as happened right after the collapse of Bretton Woods in 1973–1975, amidst a double-dip recession of the early 1980s breaking the inflationary fever of the global stagflation crisis, and during the Great Financial Crisis of 2007–2008.[17]

[17] Poszar (2011) has highlighted one aspect of the contemporary Triffin Dilemma in terms of worldwide demand for US Treasuries whose use as collateral in shadow-banking arrangements has leveraged otherwise inadequate supplies to meet global liquidity needs.

Stephan Schulmeister (2000) has provided a very thorough analysis of these asymmetries and spillover effects of the dollar standard. His empirically grounded study starts with the proposition that US policy-makers, notably the Federal Reserve, focus most of the time exclusively on domestic policy objectives. But their decisions and actions tend to have uniformly dramatic effects on the rest of the world. Schulmeister then systematically traces, often by means of graphs illustrating convincingly correlated patterns, various transmission channels for identifiable spillover effects such as the relationship between US monetary policy, exchange rates, and commodity prices of globally traded commodities, notably oil (with the latter two inversely related). He also examines the connection between US monetary policy, the transnational structure of interest rates in increasingly inter-connected money and capital markets, and (re-)valuations of assets and liabilities. And, finally, there are consecutive periods of inflationary and deflationary pressures, emanating from shifts in America's policy mix, which the dollar standard's modus operandi accelerates into global liquidity cycles engulfing the planet. Even though mostly focused on the last quarter of the twentieth century, when the dollar standard took root, Schulmeister's (2000) nuanced analysis of the international dollar's transmission channels makes it clear that the world economy is clearly far more than the sum of its parts and instead subjected to a transnationally driven, supra-cyclical growth dynamic within which the national economies are embedded in inherently asymmetric fashion. The institutional framework for this worldwide growth dynamic is the international monetary system, whose structural flaws stemming from its reliance on a key currency make it in the end an inevitable source of instability. We will see in the next couple of chapters how this regime-transforming instability is playing out as we speak.

References

Alon, T., & Swanson, E. (2011, April 25). Operation twist and the effect of large-scale asset purchases. Federal Reserve Bank of San Francisco. *Economic Letters*, 2011–2013. https://www.frbsf.org/economic-research/publications/economic-letter/2011/april/operation-twist-effect-large-scale-asset-purchases/

Bank for International Settlements. (2020). History—the BIS going global (1961–). *BIS History—Overview*. https://www.bis.org/about/history_4global.htm

Bernanke, B. (2005, March 10). The global savings glut and the U.S. current account deficit. Sandridge Lecture, Virginia Association of Economists, Richmond. https://www.federalreserve.gov/boarddocs/speeches/2005/200503102/default.htm

Bernanke, B. (2016). The dollar's international role: An "exorbitant privilege"? *Brookings Blog*. https://www.brookings.edu/blog/ben-bernanke/2016/01/07/the-dollars-international-role-an-exorbitant-privilege-2/

Bibow, J. (1995). Some reflections on Keynes's 'finance motive' for the demand of money. *Cambridge Journal of Economics, 19*(5), 647–666.

BIS. (2019). Debt securities statistics. https://www.bis.org/statistics/secstats.htm

Bordo, M., & McCauley, R. (2019). Triffin: Dilemma or myth? *IMF Economic Review, 67*(4), 824–851. https://doi.org/10.1057/s41308-019-00088-y

Cashin, P., Céspedes, L., & Sahay, R. (2004). Commodity currencies and the real exchange rate. *Journal of Development Economics*, *75*(1), 239–268. https://doi.org/10.1016/j.jdeveco.2003.08.005

Cohen, B. (1998). *The geography of money*. Cornell University Press.

Cohen, B. (2004). *The future of money*. Princeton University Press.

Cohen, B. (2015). *Currency power: Understanding monetary rivalry*. Princeton University Press.

Davidson, P. (1982). *International money and the real world*. Palgrave.

De Conti, B., & Prates, D. (2018). *The international monetary system hierarchy: Current configuration and determinants* (Texto para Discussão No. 335). Instituto de Economia, State University of Campinas. http://www.eco.unicamp.br/index.php/ensino/24-noticias/410-the-international-monetary-system-hierarchy

De Paula, L. F., Fritz, B., & Prates, D. (2017). Keynes at the periphery: Currency hierarchy and challenges for economic policy in emerging economies. *Journal of Post Keynesian Economics, 40*(2), 183–202.

Dow, S. (1999). International liquidity preference and endogenous credit creation. In J. Deprez & J. Harvey (Eds.), *Foundations of international economics: Post Keynesian perspectives* (pp. 153–170). Routledge.

Eichengreen, B. (2010). *Exorbitant privilege: The rise and fall of the dollar and the future of the international monetary system*. Oxford University Press.

Eichengreen, B., Hausmann, R., & Panizza, U. (2002, November 21–22). *Original sin: The pain, the mystery, and the road to redemption*. Paper presented at the conference "Currency and Maturity Matchmaking," Inter-American Development Bank, Washington, DC. http://www.financialpolicy.org/financedev/hausmann2002.pdf

Eichengreen, B., Mehl, A., & Chitu, L. (2017). *Mars or mercury? The geopolitics of international currency choice* (NBER Working Paper No. 24145). https://www.nber.org/papers/w24145

Frenkel, J., & Johnson, H. (1976). *The monetary approach to the balance of payments*. George Allen and Unwin.

Friedman, M. (1956). *Studies in the quantity theory of money*. University of Chicago Press.

Ghymers, C. (2017). *Overcoming the Triffin dilemma today: A plan for a stable international financial architecture*. IRELAC. http://irelac.be/wp-content/uploads/2017/12/Ghymers_RBWC_book_september_2017_VF.pdf

Hume, D. (1752). Of money. In D. Hume (Ed.), *Political discourses* (304 p.). A. Kincaid & A. Donaldson.

IMF. (2020). Annual report on exchange arrangements and exchange restrictions 2019. https://www.imf.org/en/Publications/Annual-Report-on-Exchange-Arrangements-and-Exchange-Restrictions/Issues/2020/08/10/Annual-Report-on-Exchange-Arrangements-and-Exchange-Restrictions-2019-47102

Johnson, S. (2019, April 25). Rise of the renminbi is 'story of the next cycle.' *Financial Times*. https://www.ft.com/content/bfe22922-5ab8-11e9-939a-341f5ada9d40

Keynes, J. M. (1936). *The general theory of employment, interest and money*. Macmillan.

Keynes, J. M. (1937a). Alternative theories of the rate of interest. *Economic Journal*, *47*(186), 241–252. https://doi.org/10.2307/2225525

Keynes, J. M. (1937b). The 'Ex-Ante' theory of interest. *Economic Journal*, *47*(188), 663–669. https://doi.org/10.2307/2225323

Keynes, J. M. (1980). *The collected writings of John Maynard Keynes, vol. XXV, activities 1940–1944 shaping the post-war world—The clearing union*, D. Moggridge (ed.). Cambridge University Press.

Kindleberger, Ch. (1970). *Power and money: The economics of international politics and the politics of international economics*. Basic Books.

Kindleberger, Ch. (1981). *International money: A collection of essays*. Routledge.

Kirshner, J. (1995). *Currency and coercion: The political economy of international monetary power*. Princeton University Press.

Kohlscheen, E., Avalos, F., & Schrimpf, A. (2016). *When the walk is not random: Commodity prices and exchange rates* (BIS Working Papers No. 551). https://www.bis.org/publ/work551.pdf

Krugman, P. (1984). The international role of the dollar: Theory and prospect. In J. Bilson & R. Marston (Eds.), *Exchange rate theory and practice* (pp. 261–278). National Bureau of Economic Research. http://www.nber.org/chapters/c6838

Krugman, P. (1993). *What do we need to know about the international monetary system? Essays in International Finance No. 193*. Princeton University. https://ies.princeton.edu/pdf/E190.pdf

Marx, K. (1867/1887). *Capital* (Vol. 1). Appleton & Co. First published in German as *Das Kapital, Erster Band*.

Marx, K. (1894/1967). *Capital* (Vol. III). International Publishers. First published in German by F. Engels as *Das Kapital: Dritter Band*.

Marx, K. (1910/1951). *Theories of surplus value, parts I, II and III*. Lawrence & Wishart. First published in German by K. Kautsky as *Theorien über den Mehrwert*.

McKinnon, R. (2010). *Rehabilitating the unloved dollar standard* (Working Paper No. 419). Stanford Center for International Development. https://siepr.stanford.edu/?q=system%2Ffiles%2Fshared%2Fpubs%2F419_McKinnon.pdf

Mundell, R. (1960). The monetary dynamics of international adjustment under fixed and flexible exchange rates. *Quarterly Journal of Economics, 74*(2), 227–257.

Mundell, R. (1969). The redundancy problem and the world price level. In R. Mundell & A. Swoboda (Eds.), *Monetary problems of the international economy* (pp. 379–382). University of Chicago Press.

Patinkin, D., & Steiger, O. (1989). In search of the "veil of money" and the "neutrality of money": A note on the origin of terms. *The Scandinavian Journal of Economics, 91*(1), 131–146. https://doi.org/10.2307/3440167

Poszar, Z. (2011). Institutional cash pools and the Triffin dilemma of the U.S. banking system. *Financial Markets Institutions & Instruments*, *11*(190). https://doi.org/10.1111/fmii.12013

Prasad, E. (2014). *The dollar trap: How the U.S. dollar tightened its grip on global finance*. Princeton University Press.

Schulmeister, S. (2000). Globalization without global money: The double role of the dollar as national currency and world currency. *Journal of Post Keynesian Economics*, *22*(3), 365–395. https://martin.falk.wifo.ac.at/fileadmin/homepage_schulmeister/files/GlobalizationWithoutGlobalMoney.pdf

Snoy, B. (2018, September 12). How to wean the global economy off the dollar. *Financial Times*. https://www.ft.com/content/3128fd68-b681-11e8-bbc3-ccd7de085ffe

SWIFT. (2018). RMB internationalization. *RMB Tracker*. https://ctmfile.com/assets/ugc/documents/swift_rmb_tracker_special_edition_january2018(1).pdf

Triffin, R. (1960). *Gold and the dollar crisis: The future of convertibility*. Yale University Press.

CHAPTER 2

Long Waves and Accumulation Regimes

The presence of asymmetries in institutional arrangements governing international monetary systems, such as during Bretton Woods or applying to the dollar standard today, points to the possibility of chronic imbalances undermining the proper functioning of such a system and pressures for changing its operation. If we are to evaluate the durability of the dollar standard beyond just measuring its relatively stable world-market shares per function (as we did in Sect. 1.3.2), we need to have a better sense of the systemic tensions typically at work to transform the international monetary system from one epoch to the next. One way to shed light on that question is to see whether we can identify recurrent historic patterns pertaining to such change, and in this chapter I will argue that there is indeed such a pattern worth exploring.

We have had monetary arrangements guiding the commercial and financial relationship between an imperial center and its periphery ever since Menes, the legendary founder of the Pharaonic dynasty and unifier of Egypt, imposed history's first bimetallic standard more than five millennia ago (around 3000 B.C.). The metallic standards of antiquity's great powers—the shekel of silver in Mesopotamia, the golden *yi* coin of China's unifier Qin, the silver Drachma of Athens, the silver Denarius of Rome—served to crystallize imperial rule, impose taxation, promote commerce, and extend the geographic reach of the administrative power center. At times, sudden changes in the monetary standard

R. Guttmann, *Multi-Polar Capitalism*,
https://doi.org/10.1007/978-3-030-88247-1_2

created havoc followed by profound transformation, as happened when the Ottomans replaced the Byzantine Empire's golden Solidus (or bezant) with their own silver Akce coin after sacking Constantinople, for almost a millennium one of the great centers of the world, in 1453. The long-standing battle between silver-based and gold-based money reached its climax during the nineteenth century, shaping intra-European conflict (e.g. gold-based Britain versus France-led and silver-based Latin Union) as well as domestic American politics (see "Crime of 1873"). Ultimately the protagonists of gold, the harder and more precious of the two metals, won with the establishment of the Britain-led "classic" gold standard in 1879.

There have been two decisive developments affecting the very nature of the international monetary system since then. The first concerned the gradual, but inevitable dematerialization of money which ultimately led to the official termination of gold as world money in the Jamaica Accords of 1976. We now live across the globe in a system of credit-money, that is debt-at-sight, issued in acts of credit extension within the banking system. This type of money, providing for an elastic currency whose supply can respond flexibly to the collective user needs of economic actors, is itself subject to innovation as concerns its forms and circulation. We have a growing array of credit-money and quasi-money forms, and those circulate in increasingly digitalized payments systems spanning the globe. Their accelerating spread and widening span coincide with the growing importance of finance in the economy as these money forms respond to increasingly nuanced liquidity needs.

The other development has been a succession of international monetary systems over the last century. We already mentioned above the Britain-led "classic" gold standard (1879–1914) during which the world economy underwent a first wave of globalization. Following World War I, Britain and the United States tried amidst great difficulties to return the world to a new gold standard which lasted less than a decade before ending in September 1931. Its collapse triggered a period of competitive devaluations and bank failures whiles also necessitating reforms in money and banking which ultimately set the stage for implementation of a new dollar-based, gold-backed Bretton Woods system as World War II drew to a close. That new system worked well into the 1960, supporting a remarkable postwar boom for a quarter of a century, until it disintegrated (in August 1971) at the onset of yet another structural crisis in the form of intensifying stagflation conditions. In a series of policy reforms the

United States managed to overcome the stagflation crisis between 1979 and 1982 while also preserving the world-money status of the US dollar without backing by gold. That new dollar standard set in motion a reconfigured, finance-driven pattern of rapid worldwide growth until the Great Financial Crisis of 2007/2008. Since then we have seen a difficult period of recovery until a global pandemic threw the world economy into a deflationary shock in early 2020 from which we have yet to emerge.

When looking back at this century and a half of international monetary history, we see something of a pattern. We see that institutional arrangements guiding international monetary relations can work for a while to boost growth across the globe before disintegrating into periods of turmoil and crisis. Those tend to get resolved eventually by reforms introducing a new set of "rules of the game."

- The Britain-led "classic" gold standard (1879–1914) was followed by the inter-war period of turmoil, culminating in a global depression (1929–1939) and yet another World War (1939–1945);
- The US-led Bretton Woods system (1945–1971) was followed by the stagflation crisis (1971–1982) whereupon, in the context of a conservative counter-revolution ("Reaganomics"), a new policy regime emerged anchored in a reconfigured dollar standard.
- The dollar standard propelled yet another wave of (finance-led) globalization and rapid growth between 1983 and 2007, only to be followed by major systemic financial crisis whose global unfolding and resolution took years. The dual demand-and-supply shock of the pandemic at the end of this crisis period may ultimately set in motion a new international monetary system as the eventual propellant for recovery.

This pattern warrants a theoretical context, especially since its purported dynamic may well have brought us to the edge of profound change over the coming decade. We can see that periods of (globally) rapid growth are followed by periods of crisis whose resolution necessitates structural reform, including reorganization of international monetary relations. These up- and down-swings, each stretching over several shorter business cycles, resemble so-called "long waves" first identified in the 1920s by Soviet economist Nikolai Kondratiev. In this chapter we shall explore the underlying forces driving those long waves, especially their technological, financial, structural, and institutional dimensions, in order to identify the role and place of the international monetary system in that dynamic.

2.1 Long Waves

A decade before the great British economist John Maynard Keynes (1936) initiated his revolution in economic thinking to help us understand the Great Depression of the 1930s and what best to do about such a threat to stability, a brilliant young Soviet economist named Nikolai Kondratiev (1892–1938) took over the Moscow-based Institute of Conjuncture in 1922 and turned it into a formidable center of economic and statistical research. Integrating a large body of widely dispersed thought on the topic, Kondratiev was the first one to explore and elaborate in systematic fashion the crucial phenomenon of a long-wave pattern of growth driving the evolution of capitalist economies.[1]

2.1.1 Nikolai Kondratiev's Long Waves

Between 1922 and 1928 Kondratiev wrote several books and articles in which he identified and measured relevant empirical variables to trace their long-term fluctuations around trend lines and so identify long waves in their consecutive timelines. The data he used stretched over a century and a half and applied primarily to Britain, France, and the United States. These included commodities prices, food prices, interest rates, wages, foreign trade, and bank deposits. Focusing mostly on wholesale price movements, his data set included only few measures of output (e.g. coal production, pig iron, and lead production). He developed new statistical techniques to model cyclical deviations properly, and his filtering as well as smoothing methods caused quite a bit of debate with his colleagues at the institute which they published for the outside world to judge. Kondratiev also sought to go beyond statistics and embed his cycles in a broader historic and political context. This interdisciplinary

[1] On a trip to Germany, Britain, and the United States in 1924 Kondratiev met John Maynard Keynes, Simon Kuznets, Irving Fisher, and Wesley Mitchell while also visiting the Royal Statistical Society as well as the U.S. Department of Agriculture. These encounters exposed him to an international network of leading economists who would encourage publication of his work in languages other than Russian. Thus, when he set out to write up his work on long waves, he managed to have an international audience right away.

approach added weight to his argument of capitalism's propensity for crisis and renewal, but got him into trouble throughout with communist leaders insisting on the imminent demise of capitalism, causing his dismissal in 1928, arrest in 1930, and eventual execution in 1938. Struggling throughout to come up with an underlying theoretical explanation for this observable long-wave pattern, including a focus on agricultural depressions during downswing phases, Kondratiev ended up emphasizing the life cycle of capital goods and their renewal patterns which generate widespread application of new technologies grouping together to drive boom phases. Downswing phases basically witness the exhaustion of now-aged capital stock amidst excess capacities and declining profitability.[2]

Based on a meticulous analysis of long-run time series of wholesale price movements and other relevant statistical indicators, Kondratiev identified three clearly defined long waves since the Industrial Revolution of the late eighteenth century. The first cycle's upswing phase began in the early 1780s and lasted until the 1810s, notwithstanding the turmoil of the French Revolution and the Napoleonic wars. This was followed by a downswing period stretching from the mid-1810s to 1844–1851 when the next wave's upswing phase set in for a rapid-growth pattern until the early 1870s. The subsequent downswing phase of this second long wave endured for two decades until about 1896 (in Kondratiev's multi-year turning-point specification between 1890 and 1896). From 1896 onwards there was another period of steady and strong expansion in the three countries concerned (Britain, France, United States) whose end he pinpointed to have arrived in the 1914–1920 span dominated by the Great War.

Even though Kondratiev can be justly criticized for not having paid enough attention to trend lines as a result of highlighting cyclical deviations, for not bringing to bear output fluctuations in support of his price-based waves, and for providing inadequate theoretical grounding in explaining the underlying accumulation dynamic driving these long

[2] Among Kondratiev's publications while director of the Conjuncture Institute, several were made rapidly available to a wider audience by being published abroad. See here in particular Kondratiev (1925a, 1925b, 1926/1935). There was a revival of his long-wave theory in the 1970s and 1980s which prompted further translations of his work, notably Kondratiev (1984) and the four-volume collection of all his major writings in Kondratiev (1998).

waves, his work on those cycles was path-breaking. We should note here that Kondratiev characterized his own decade, the 1920s, as unfolding amidst a downswing phase.[3] If we were to apply his empirical approach to subsequent periods, we would arrive at a fourth long wave whose upswing phase started in the mid-1940s and ended in the 1968–1973 period, followed by a stagflation-marked downswing phase stretching into the early 1980s. A fifth wave had its upswing from the mid-1980s until the Great Financial Crisis of 2007/2008. Ever since we have been in a slow-growth state. What happens once we will have put the global pandemic of 2020/2021 behind us remains to be seen.

2.1.2 *The Marxist Argument*

Stalin's Great Purge of 1936–1938, a particularly ruthless dictator killing off his country's intelligentsia to impose uniform thought and absolute social control, saw Kondratiev executed still a young man. Had the Stalinists had a greater appreciation of Karl Marx as economist, they would have understood that Kondratiev's pinpointing of capitalism's capacity for reorganization did not necessarily contradict Marx's insistence on capitalism's finite time horizon. Marx, after all, had predicted revolution to arrive in the most advanced capitalist economies experiencing the most severe crises precisely as a result of their maturity, not in a relatively backward society like Russia.

In all of his major works Karl Marx (1859/1904, 1867/1887, 1894/1967, 1939/1973) emphasized capitalism's cyclical growth pattern, subject to business-cycle fluctuations of recovery, boom, peak, downturn, and trough which together he saw typically taking between seven and eleven years to unfold. Marx viewed such cycles as driven by the system's tendency to overproduction, in contrast to Keynes' emphasis on under-consumption. In either case aggregate demand eventually fails to match aggregate supply, causing excess inventories which trigger price wars, production cutbacks, and unemployment. For Marx the dilemma stemmed from the dual role of the wage as private business cost and largest social source of income constituting demand ("consumption"). Being for the most part determined individually on the micro-level as

[3] Later empirical work by other economists using different variables largely confirmed Kondratiev's periodization of those long waves. See in this context, for example, the works of Van Duijn (1983), Freeman (1987), Goldstein (1988), and Tylecote (1992).

a cost and as such typically kept at a minimum, the totality of wages often ends up insufficient on the macro-level to maintain adequate levels of aggregate demand. The ensuing recessionary adjustment in the face of overproduction requires slashing supplies faster than demand, itself depressed by the feedback loops from spending cutbacks and layoffs.

This cyclical dynamic unfolds around a longer-term secular trend line of steadily declining profitability. While many earlier Classical economists (e.g. David Ricardo, John Stuart Mill) had emphasized a tendency of profit rates to decline for one reason or another, Marx (1894/1967, Chapter 13) elaborated this trend in more compelling fashion than any of his predecessors as "the most important law of political economy" (Marx, 1939/1973, p. 748). To the extent that capitalists opt for increasingly capital-intensive production methods as they compete with each other, they end up having fewer and fewer workers to extract surplus value from relative to the size of capital they deploy in this effort. In other words, the labor-saving bias of technological change applied to increasingly automated production methods deprives profit-seeking enterprises of the very foundation of profit, the workers able to create (surplus) value as "living labor." Marx (1894/1967, Chapter 14) viewed this process only as a tendency, since there were also "counteracting influences" none of which strong enough to reverse this trend for long. Inasmuch as profit rates were meant to decline steadily over the long haul, cyclical downturns would turn into progressively deeper crises.

While Marx made repeated references to capitalism's eventual breakdown, his own analysis of crisis also emphasized its unfolding as a process of re-balancing aimed at correcting the very imbalances which triggered such adjustments in the first place—slashing inventories, eliminating excess capacities through plant closures, wiping out the weakest firms, reducing debt overhangs, lowering prices and interest rates, and so forth. It is this crisis-induced adjustment capacity of capitalism which has prompted Ernest Mandel (1980) to offer a Marxist interpretation of long waves. Much of Mandel's argument concerned a crucial asymmetry in the unfolding of long waves. Upswing phases, such as the postwar boom analyzed by Mandel (1975/1999) in minute detail, have an internal dynamic bound to cause their eventual end in crisis. Apart from the build-up of excess capacities as capitalism's overproduction propensity takes root, Mandel emphasized in this context also the exhaustion of technological rents when initially path-breaking technologies get widely adopted across the economy in the wake of a long boom, an upsurge of workers' militancy amidst full employment near the peak, and the rise of new powers challenging the hegemon to trigger heightened inter-imperialist rivalries. Crisis-ridden downswing phases, however, do not automatically end in a renewed upswing, typically needing exogenous "system shock" factors capable of restoring corporate profitability on a large scale.

Actually, Mandel (1980) made a two-pronged argument with regard to how downswing phases of long waves may end and give way to a new phase of sustained expansion. For one, he emphasized the likely confluence of Marx's (1894/1967) "counteracting influences" of "increasing the intensity of exploitation," "depression of wages below the value of labor-power," "cheapening of elements of constant capital," "relative overpopulation," "foreign trade," and "the increase of stock capital." We can easily imagine how several of these counter-forces get mobilized in much stronger fashion precisely during the course of sustained downturns, notably making workers work harder and/or longer while slashing wages against the backdrop of mass unemployment ("relative overpopulation"). Foreign trade can capture markets abroad to absorb excess capacities building up at home and/or spur foreign investments carrying higher profit rates. Cheaper imports can lower the socially necessary labor time of the basket of necessities representing the average wage or reduce the cost of constant capital via lower prices of commodities. A sustained slow-growth period is also likely to cause significant shifts in how the total surplus value gets distributed between profit, interest, dividends, fees, and taxes, with any of the latter four categories under pressure to protect the former.

Whereas Mandel (1980) saw all of these counter-tendencies gaining strength during crises, he also argued for the need of additional factors outside the normal modus operandi of capitalism to strengthen corporate profitability. Yet many of these supposedly "exogenous" forces were not really disassociated from the accumulation dynamic of capitalism, just open-ended in their outcome and timing. Attacks on the workers' wages and working conditions will surely intensify during periods of high unemployment, but it is not clear when, or even whether, the working class will suffer a decisive political defeat. Crisis-induced shrinking of markets will wipe out weaker firms, but it is not obvious to what extent increased market concentration will allow surviving firms to translate greater market shares into higher profit margins. There may well be a correlation in the long run between the average profit rate and long-term interest rate, but how long is the long run and at what point are financial innovations kicking in to allow producers to live once again with higher leverage? Inter-imperialist rivalries and inter-capitalist competition will surely intensify during downswings, but it remains to be seen how such conflicts may yield sudden access to large new markets. Mandel also stressed the importance of advances in transportation and communication technologies in order to reduce the turnover time of constant capital inputs as well as recent advances in information technologies (i.e. increasingly powerful and cheap microprocessors) to reduce the costs of key constant capital items. But it is not preordained, by any means, whether and when such crucial technological change produces a broad, sustained upswing. In the end, Mandel demonstrates how each long-wave upswing, representing the onset of a new Kondratiev cycle, arose from a combination of macroeconomic, technological, political, and policy factors which at the time seemed entirely unique, but can in retrospect be traced to a pattern of reorganization and transformation restoring the conditions for faster accumulation of capital.

2.1.3 *Joseph Schumpeter's Technological Dimension*

Joseph Schumpeter's (1939) path-breaking work on the different kinds of cyclical fluctuations pinpointed the "Kondratieff waves" as a central phenomenon in capitalist economies and rendered this phenomenon better known to an English-speaking audience. Schumpeter managed to give these long cycles the status they deserved by providing a more convincing theoretical explanation for their recurrent upswing-downswing dynamic and the time lines of these phases. Nowadays globally recognized as an evolutionary economist theorizing the crucially important process of technological change and innovation, Schumpeter made the entrepreneur the central figure of the capitalist growth dynamic. The entrepreneur serves as vector of innovation turning ideas into new products, improved versions of existing products, or more efficient methods of production and thereby rendering capitalism's growth dynamic anything but stationary.[4] Schumpeter explicitly meant to apply his central notions of innovation and entrepreneurship in very broad terms. When he spoke

[4] In what is arguably his most widely quoted concept Schumpeter (1943) characterized the entrepreneur's impact to be one of "creative destruction" as s/he brings forth new sources of growth while rendering prevailing industrial structures and practices obsolete.

of innovation, he referred not only to new products or production methods, but also organizational changes, improved transportation, new energy sources, better materials, or steps to create new markets. And Schumpeter was also careful to embed all these innovative impulses into a macroeconomic context by connecting them to business investment spending needed to realize entrepreneurial initiatives which he saw in turn as depending on the availability of credit at sufficiently low interest rates to finance those innovation-carrying investments.

In Schumpeter's theory of economic development innovation, itself a dynamic yet discontinuous process motivated by entrepreneurs chasing profit, becomes the engine of a boom. When strategic inventions succeed, their adoption gains momentum among a larger number of users while at the same time spurring other innovations in related fields. Take, for example, the crucial role of the car in the postwar boom. Cheaper versions of this most strategic consumer durable, whether the Chevrolet in America, the VW Beetle in Germany, the Citroën CV2 in France, the Fiat 500 in Italy, made it a mass product afforded by most. Its dramatic spread in the 1950s spawned additional innovations in road construction (interstate highways), petroleum products, rubber (tires), insurance, consumer finance, shopping malls, urban sprawl, and so forth to the point of transforming society at large. Schumpeter compared such spread of innovation to a "swarm-like cluster" and viewed such clustering as the key driving force behind economic booms. The acceleration of growth from such innovation clusters creates a secondary wave of new entrepreneurs entering the economy as it expands rapidly and credit is amply available.

The car-based innovation cluster, so crucial to the postwar boom of the 1950s and 1960s, also highlights the strategic importance of energy and transportation in the technological dimension of long-wave upswings. Coal and steamboats drove the Industrial Revolution in the early nineteenth century. Oil and railroads transformed capitalism around the turn of the century. Besides cars, the postwar boom also saw the emergence of natural gas as well as nuclear power as key global energy sources. The upswing of the early twenty-first century has been dominated by the internet, and renewable energy (wind turbines, solar panels, etc.) is bound to drive the transition to a low-carbon economy at the heart of the next upswing. Changes in energy sources—from coal to oil to natural gas to nuclear power to renewables—have served regularly to reinforce the emergence of new powers on the global scene, and that might be true again with China's leadership role in the promotion of solar power. We will see later (in Sect. 4.3.1) that there is a connection between the principal energy source and the choice of vehicle currency as world money at the time—coal and Britain's pound sterling in the late nineteenth century, oil and the US dollar during much of the twentieth century, et cetera—to the point where we can observe an inverse relationship between the price of that globally traded commodity and the vehicle currency's effective exchange rate.

Beyond energy and key products such as the car, we must recognize that long-wave upswings have also been shaped more broadly by cross-sector innovation clusters remaking the industrial matrix of core nations amidst investment booms:

- The mechanization of production at the heart of the Industrial Revolution driving the 1780s–1815 upswing depended a lot on growing use of steam power, spread of machine tools, new chemical and iron processing technologies, and introduction of the factory system as that cluster transformed the textiles, iron, steel, and chemical industries.
- During the second long-wave upswing (1844–1873) industrial processes were transformed by the spread of turbine technology while agriculture benefited enormously from the introduction of harvesting machinery. The strategically placed textile sector, a vector of industrialization everywhere, saw its productivity leap with use of the sewing machine. As steamboats became widespread, rivers and canals turned into important lifelines of commerce while oceanic travel opened up. And the telegraph revolutionized how people communicated with each other, greatly speeding up the spread of information.
- The upswing at the turn of the century (1896–1914) was driven by the rapid growth of steel, electricity, and heavy engineering. That period was, as already mentioned, also marked by the railroad boom, boosted further by the emergence of the electric locomotive and the streetcar. Gas engines and the vacuum pump gave industry great boosts, while the telephone dramatically altered the way we communicated.
- We have already mentioned the car at the heart of the postwar boom (1945–1968). That period of extraordinary growth was in the end driven forward at great speed by the productivity gains arising from

widespread adoption of mass production technology (i.e. assembly line).

- The high-tech nature of the latest upswing phase (1984–2007) centered on advances in information and telecommunications technologies, crystallized in the path-breaking internet.
- We can already see the technological engines of the next long wave emerge, from artificial intelligence and quantum computing to the exigencies of a low-carbon economy.

While Schumpeter viewed investment- and technology-driven booms as self-feeding, he was also aware that such forward momentum could not last forever. What then causes this process to become unsustainable so that it triggers a crisis, yielding a distinct pattern of cyclical fluctuations? Schumpeter stressed an inevitable confluence of destabilizing forces comprising squeezed profitability from boom-induced price hikes in investment goods, declining prices from added supply capacity as new products enter the market, and a credit deflation when entrepreneurs pay back their credit. In Schumpeter (1943), his pessimistic chef d'oeuvre explaining how increased concentration and bureaucracy risk eroding capitalism, crisis also arises from the dislocating effects of "creative destruction" rendering older technologies obsolete and outmoded organizations ineffective. There he argued, very much under the influence of Karl Marx whose analysis of capitalism he dedicated a great chunk of the book to, that crises serve as a sort of "cleaning-out mechanism" devaluing and ultimately destroying superfluous production capacities by means of deflation in the capital-goods sector, plant closures, and bankruptcies.[5]

2.1.4 Hyman Minsky's Financial Dimension

When looking at the stylized facts underpinning the dynamics of long waves, we note the prevalence of major financial crises with global contagion potential at the onset of downswing phases. Take for illustration the Panic of 1873 triggering a worldwide six-year depression, the Crash

[5] These "clearing-out" mechanisms in the wake of crisis were described, for instance, in Marx (1863/1951, Chapter 17), a somewhat unstructured yet fascinating critique of Ricardo illuminating how recurrent crises affect key relationships of the capitalist accumulation process.

of 1929 knocking out the gold standard in an avalanche of bank failures, the collapse of Bretton Woods in 1971 setting off a decade of intensifying stagflation, or the "Subprime Crisis" of 2007/2008 driving the world economy to the edge of the abyss. Whenever major financial crises pushed the world economy onto a path of sustained stagnation, if not depression, financial institutions and their clients continued to face pressures which they had to work out before any lasting recovery could take hold. An important contribution helping us to clarify the role of finance in such cyclical unfolding of capital accumulation is Hyman Minsky (1982, 1986). His so-called "financial instability hypothesis" (Minsky, 1992) argues that the innate business-cycle dynamic gets reinforced by a credit cycle inclined to widen the amplitudes of the former in both directions—on the upside of the boom and on the downside of the recessionary adjustment. Throughout his four decades of writings Minsky returned again and again to the idea of capitalism's endogenously cyclical growth dynamic, framed in the end most convincingly in terms of Michal Kalecki's (1939, 1969) profit-investment feedback loop.[6] However the endogenously cyclical growth dynamic gets ultimately modeled, it depended centrally on investment spending driven by profit expectations of businesses. Such spending is often large-scale and hence debt financed, whether by means of bank loans or issue of corporate bonds, as long as the anticipated rates of return exceed the rate of interest to be paid on such borrowings. Rapid growth and optimistic expectations motivate businesses to take on more debt in the chase for greater profits, and such leveraging sows the seeds for an eventual overextension causing bouts of acute financial instability.

Minsky distinguished three different debtor positions, based on the relationship between current income generated and debt-servicing charges which include recurrent interest payments and repayment of the principal borrowed. In the "hedge finance" position, borrowers have sufficient income to repay all of their debt any time. These borrowers face no default risk. In the "speculative finance" position borrowers have enough income to service their debts but not enough to pay those off, thus incurring some degree of default risk. Finally, when in the so-called "Ponzi finance" position, borrowers' income is no longer sufficient to

[6] Minsky made in this context also recurrent reference to the multiplier-accelerator model of Samuelson (1939) and to the cyclical growth-distribution framework of Goodwin (1967) as alternative business-cycle models in the Keynesian tradition he approved of.

pay existing debt servicing charges so that new debt needs to be taken on to deal with old debt. This is obviously a dangerous position to be in, likely to get worse over time. In such a vulnerable Ponzi-finance position debt-servicing charges grow rapidly while the average maturity of debts shortens to put debtors under steadily intensifying refinancing pressure. Add to this the fact that near the cyclical peak interest rates tend to rise while business profits peak and then may well start to decline, a double squeeze making an already difficult debt-servicing situation that much more challenging. To the extent that debt-driven expansion pushes more debtors into speculative-finance and then Ponzi-finance positions, the financial system becomes more fragile and prone to crisis. At one point a significant borrower succumbs to such financial fragility and goes into default, a disturbing event illustrating the degree of overextension having built up and so likely to set off a strong reaction among lenders cutting back credit just when so many borrowers are in dire need of more funds. We have come to refer to such onset of financial crisis as a "Minsky moment".[7] When the moment arrives, a downturn surely ensues in the wake of spreading credit freeze and spending cutbacks. As the recessionary adjustment runs its course, its duration and depth might both be reduced with the help of fiscal and financial stabilizers put into place by the government providing deficit spending and lender-of-last-resort interventions of the central bank.

While most of his analysis of financial instability applied to shorter-term business cycles (7–11 years), Minsky (1964) early on sought to extend his analytical framework also to long waves. The best way to summarize the logic of his extension is that "stability breeds instability." When going through a boom period lasting a couple of decades or more (as the world did from 1896 to 1914, 1948 to 1969, or 1994 to 2007), business leaders become progressively more optimistic, even euphoric, and so inclined to downplay risks. The same bias of excessive confidence afflicts their lenders and investors willing to provide ample supplies of funds. The occasional recessions, few and far between during such a long-wave upswing, are simply too mild to make a lasting dent in this widespread buoyancy. Short and shallow, such downturns also lack the force to oblige

[7] The term "Minsky moment," first coined by PIMCO's Paul McCulley in 1998 when the Russian bond crisis sank U.S. hedge fund Long Term Capital Management, revived with the onset of the "subprime crisis" in mid-2007, as discussed in Lahalt (2007) or Cassidy (2008).

sufficient "clearing-out" adjustments bringing down debt levels and asset prices. Overextension thus builds up from cycle to cycle during a long-wave upswing, as does the systematic underestimation of risks, until the entire financial system has become fragilized and hence susceptible to a major breakdown, a long-wave phenomenon Minsky referred to as "more severe depressions." Those occur in the wake of a financial panic as trigger event, hit a lot of overextended actors whose margins of safety had eroded during the expansion phase in the wake of growing fragilization, and set off a deflationary spiral of forced asset sales and spending cutbacks greatly depressing consumption and investment demand. During what Minsky (1964, p. 325) termed the "liquidation phases of a deep depression" he saw the combined adjustment processes of reduced debt levels, sharply lower asset prices, and increased liquidity as setting the "financial stage" for resumption of a new long-wave expansion, thus clearly depicting such depression-like crises as clearing-out processes.

But as proved true for most of his work, Minsky (1964) was less interested in studying the dynamic of financial crises than identifying the underlying conditions causing them in the first place. Crucial in this regard is Minsky's notion of "financial structure," the amalgam of financial institutions, instruments, and markets with which an economy mobilizes credit and issues money for the funding of economic activity, and how it evolves during the course of a long-wave expansion. While Minsky was very clear that each long wave and every country had its own unique financial structure so that no bout of financial instability repeated itself in exact fashion, he did try to highlight meaningful characteristics which might be generalized. One key question concerns the role of the money supply and the precise modalities of its interaction with economic activity. Of particular importance here is the money supply's shrinkage during those deflationary spirals, a factor which Minsky acknowledged to have played a decisive role during the Great Depression of the 1930s but which need not be indispensable factor in all severe depressions.[8]

[8] Minsky (1964) tied the important role of a shrinking money supply in "more severe depressions" to large numbers of overextended debtors and their bank lenders incurring large losses. This endogenous process stands in contrast to the argument of Friedman and Schwartz (1963) of an exogenous fall of the money supply caused by the Fed's incompetence or negligence. At the same time, Minsky stressed the role of the central bank in explicitly countering any such endogenously crisis-induced money-supply shrinkage in order to avoid such "more severe depressions," as happened with "quantitative easing" policies of central banks across the world in the course of the 2007–2008 crisis.

Minsky also afforded financial innovations an important role which, besides impacting directly on the financial structure, enable economic actors to live with higher leverage and are often associated with the launch of speculative asset bubbles (e.g. margin credit in the 1920s, junk bonds in the 1980s, mortgage-backed securities during the 2000s). Focusing his later work increasingly on financial structure evolution, Minsky stressed in particular the emergence of all kinds of funds (pension funds, mutual funds, etc.) as a new financial-intermediation layer and majority owners of corporations. He considered this institutional development so profound that he thought it merited being characterized as a whole new type of capitalism, which he termed "money-manager capitalism".[9]

Most importantly, long-wave expansion phases lasting up to two decades gradually transform the financial structure of an economy in the direction of greater fragility so that stability literally breeds instability. Minsky (1964) actually identified at least four long-run financial-fragilization forces. First and foremost is the build-up of debt relative to income, at the heart of the aforementioned "financial-instability hypothesis" he developed later. Second is the rise in prices of strategic assets, such as stocks or real estate, whose relatively inelastic supplies make them attractive objects of speculation and thus vectors of asset bubbles which may trigger major financial crises when they collapse as happened in 1929 or 2007. Third would be the gradual erosion of liquidity in the course of the long-wave expansion period relative to payment commitments and refinancing needs. Finally, Minsky also argued that with maturing expansion safe income-related sources of payments (e.g. salaries) would become gradually less important while intrinsically less-assured "balance-sheet" payments (e.g. interest, dividends) or "portfolio" payments (financed out of asset sales) get more strongly relied on.[10] As these various financial-fragilization vectors gain in importance, their combined impact renders

[9] The notion of "money manager capitalism" was introduced by Minsky (1989) and then further elaborated in Minsky and Whalen (1996). See also Whalen (2002), Wray (2009), as well as Tymoigne and Wray (2014) for more extensive discussions of this Minskian concept denoting a capitalism dominated by highly leveraged institutional investors inclined to pursue speculative motives while at the same time turning into majority owners of corporate America.

[10] Some of these fragilization trends were subsequently further elaborated in a follow-up article published three decades later, as a retrospective reflection of how his 1964 arguments stood up in the face of a new period of sustained financial instability starting in the 1970s (Minsky, 1995).

the financial system as a whole progressively less stable and so more vulnerable to defaults leading to open crisis.

Throughout the nearly four decades of his writings Minsky expressed keen interest in effective counter-cyclical stabilization in the face of such intrinsic financial instability so as to avoid miring capitalist economies in severe depressions of long duration of the kind we had last experienced in the 1930s. Piero Ferri and Hyman Minsky (1992) framed such stabilization in terms of "floors and ceilings" within which to keep the endogenously unstable economy from spiraling out of control. Such containment has to be organized institutionally, as a matter of customs, institutions, or policy interventions designed to thwart the instability inherent in the behavior of profit-seeking agents. Such "thwarting" systems include in large measure also fiscal stabilizers (Minsky's "Big Government" sustaining individual actors' incomes by means of deficit spending) as well as financial stabilizers (Minsky's "Big Bank" serving as lender of last resort and emergency injector of liquidity).

In a fascinating discussion of Minsky's long-wave framework Tom Palley (2011) took up the theme of "thwarting institutions" in more systematic fashion to explain how these institutional constraints may work for a while, but in the end fail to prevent a structural crisis which brings the upswing phase of a Minskian "super-cycle" (i.e. long wave) to a painful end. The key to Palley's argument is that such "thwarting institutions" are bound to erode over time. There are several reasons for such institutional erosion. For one, the expansion's intrinsic tendency to feed growing optimism, which also prompts buoyant investors to downplay, if not altogether ignore, risks, is accompanied by a process of what Palley characterized as "regulatory relaxation." Implied here is the gradual weakening of institutional constraints on excessive behavior, notably regulatory restrictions weighing on financial institutions. There is what Palley referred to as "regulatory relapse" where over time regulators, just as much as the investors they are supposed to regulate, suffer from memory loss and/or reinterpret past events so that they collectively forget the lessons of history. After a couple of decades of rapid growth any sense of crisis will have faded and hence no longer be a matter of behavior-shaping concern. On the contrary, regulators too get imbued with the growing optimism of the time and so may become quite careless. Regulated financial institutions exert pressure on regulators through such channels, as lobbying, revolving-door movements of personnel, or corruption, to weaken regulatory constraints. These relentless efforts contribute to a gradual, possibly accelerating process of regulatory relaxation. To the extent that regulatory constraints are initially binding, they will act as a check on profitability. This creates an incentive to weaken them by means of such regulatory "capture." Finally, sustained booms are typically carried forward by strategic financial innovations. These may not only boost the tendencies toward greater risk-taking and higher leverage driving such booms, but also often involve "regulatory escape" inasmuch as they are aimed at bypassing regulatory restraints. Such circumvention requires ongoing fine-tuning and adjusting of existing regulations. Yet such adjustment is increasingly difficult to come by in the face of intensifying regulatory relapse and/or capture.

The combination of increased risk-taking and regulatory relaxation gradually weakens the "floors and ceilings" which the (now steadily eroding) thwarting institutions have imposed on an otherwise intrinsically fluctuating economy. That propensity for greater instability manifests itself most dramatically in major, possibly systemic, financial crises triggering what Minsky referred to as "more severe depressions." Palley (2011) ultimately presents the "subprime" crisis of 2007–2008 as a fitting case study of how the combination of increased risk-taking and regulatory relaxation eventually caused such fragility conditions across the entire global financial structure that a relatively minor event, a wave of defaults among high-risk "non-traditional" US mortgages, could threaten to bring down the entire system.

2.2 The French "Théorie de la Régulation" (RT)

The various dimensions of long-wave dynamics, whether the long-run tendency of the profit rate to decline and its crisis-mediated countertendencies (Mandel), technological (Schumpeter), or financial (Minsky), were integrated into a holistic approach by the French "théorie de la régulation," starting with the path-breaking study of the US economy by Michel Aglietta (1976/1979). Aglietta's historical analysis of how America's economy evolved from the Civil War (1860–1865) onwards for over a century to the onset of its pernicious stagflation crisis in the 1970s introduced a new conceptual framework with which to identify distinct stages in the development of capitalism on a national scale—a theory of capitalist regulation, as suggested by the title of his masterpiece.

2.2.1 Accumulation Regime

At the core of this approach is the notion of *accumulation regimes*, applied to national economies and framing the long haul of their development in terms of consecutive institutional configurations around which the secular trend lines of those countries' respective growth processes unfold. Closely affiliated with the Marxist tradition of focusing on economic growth in terms of the accumulation of (productive) capital, the Régulationists' notion of "accumulation regime" connects production conditions, technical progress, the (functional as well as personal) distribution of income, and social composition of aggregate demand absorbing the nation's product. Key to this implied connection between production, income distribution, and consumption norms is the currently prevailing inter-sectoral matrix of goods and services industries whose elaborate inter-connections shape the system's reproduction over time.

Accumulation regimes are self-balancing inasmuch as they are capable of reproducing themselves in forward motion, expanding production capacity, incomes, and spending levels over time while regulating complex social relations underpinning economic activity (e.g. between buyers and sellers, workers and their bosses, creditors and debtors) within institutionally imposed compromises. Such expanded reproduction may generate a good deal of frictions and imbalances as it unfolds in time and space. But a well-functioning accumulation regime can contain those, even use them as impetus for productive adjustments. What enables a given accumulation regime to achieve such self-balancing is its *mode of régulation* by which Régulationists, such as Alain Lipietz (1983/1985, 1985/1987), refer to the amalgam of institutions, conventions, and norms guiding the behavior of economic actors and shaping their interactions with each other.

2.2.2 Mode of Régulation

More specifically, Régulation Theory (RT) argues that any prevailing mode of régulation guides whatever accumulation regime might be in place through a hierarchy of *institutional forms*, each of which aimed at stabilizing key social relations underpinning economic activity (Boyer, 1986/1990).

- One such institutional form, typically placed at the center of any accumulation regime, concerns the so-called wage-labor nexus which encompasses a broad range of aspects shaping the capital-labor relation, including direct and indirect determinants of wage income (e.g. fringe benefits, cost-of-living adjustments), the types of means of production and organization of work shaping the technical and social division of labor, practices of recruitment and retention of workers by companies, the workers' way of life.

- Another crucial institutional form concerns money whose socially accepted forms, the modalities of its creation (and convertibility among different forms), circulation in a payments system, and valuation in terms of interest rates and exchange rates as its prices occur within a given monetary regime, itself subject to historic change in the face of recurrent financial instability and innovation. Depending on such a monetary regime's constituent elements, notably monetary policy, financial regulations, lender-of-last-resort interventions of crisis management, and international monetary arrangements, the mobilization of economic activities (exchange, production, credit) as monetary circuits plays out within regime-specific monetary constraints and ties to finance.[11]
- A third institutional form defining how an accumulation regime operates in practice relates to its forms of competition. RT (Boyer, 1986/1990) distinguishes here between a competitive system, which assures a market balance *ex post* by having prices adjust flexibly to demand, and a monopolistic (or oligopolistic) system whose rules of socialization determine a level and structure of social demand largely geared to supply so that companies know they can administer prices and target profit margins *before* production takes place. Some, such as Pascal Petit (1985) or Benjamin Coriat (1991, 1997), have gone beyond this juxtaposition to highlight how technological and organizational determinants of production processes shape corporate behavior in pursuit of market shares and profit margins, thus providing a broader, more nuanced view of competitive strategies tied to the exercise of market power.

[11] I have focused my own contributions to the advancement of Régulation Theory in terms of studying such monetary regimes and their historic evolution, notably in Guttmann (1994, 2016). See also Guttmann (1997, 2002) for shorter summaries of the monetary regime concept. Other Régulationist contributions (in English) helping us clarify the crucial notion of monetary regime are Aglietta (2016/2018) and Théret (1999). The monetary constraint faced by all economic actors in a fully monetized capitalist economy has been superbly analyzed in De Brunhoff (1973/1976).

- Ever since the Keynesian Revolution of the 1930s provided us with a public-policy apparatus of macroeconomic stabilization tools (monetary policy, fiscal policy) to steer an inherently cyclical growth pattern along a less unstable path, the role of the state has come to be acknowledged as crucial to the modus operandi of capitalist economies. Régulationists typically take a close look at the relationship between the state and the economy. Their research highlights the multi-faceted "embeddedness" of the state in the economy beyond its imposition of taxes and provision of social services while analyzing the institutionalized compromises which determine what they characterize as the "relational, integrated, and complex state," notably the postwar "welfare state" proving so crucial to the integration of the working class.[12] A key régulationist concept applying to the institutional form of the state as it evolves from one accumulation regime to another is what Bruno Théret (1999) refers to as the "fiscal and financial regime."
- RT emphasizes the national trajectories of accumulation regimes and in that way sheds useful light on the prevailing varieties of capitalism, such as the neoliberal "free-market" Anglo-Saxon model in the United States and Britain, Germany's social-market economy also referred to as "Rhine Capitalism," France's "dirigisme" model of state capitalism, or China's state-managed "Capitalism with Chinese characteristics." Yet RT also stresses the "international regime" guiding the interactions of nation-states and national economic actors across borders as a whole institutional form on its own.[13] Countries engage with the rest of the world in a variety of cross-border activities which they take account of in a ledger known as the balance of payments. Deficits and/or surpluses in the balance of payments need to be settled between nations, and the modalities

[12] While most of their important contributions are in French, the key Régulationists analyzing the state—Christine André, Robert Delorme, Frédéric Lordon, and Bruno Théret—have written succinct summaries of their major arguments, analytical concepts, and findings on the role of the state in modern capitalist economies in their respective contributions—in English—to the edited volume on Régulation Theory by Boyer and Saillard (1995/2002, pp. 94–100, 115–135).

[13] See in this context Michel Aglietta's chapter on the "International monetary system" (pp. 64–72) as well as Jean-François Vidal's chapter on "International regimes" (pp. 108–114) in Boyer and Saillard (1995/2002).

of such settlements depend on the prevailing international monetary system's choice of acceptable world-money forms, exchange-rate regimes, cross-border payments systems, and adjustment options keeping excessive imbalances in check. Whatever combination these four determinants of any international monetary system come up with, they are—as a "system"—part and parcel of a broader configuration of formal agreements, normative contexts, rules of behavior, and supranational institutions guiding the cooperation and competition between nation-states making up what Régulationists have referred to as the "international regime".

2.2.3 PostWar Fordism

Based on these five institutional forms – wage-labor nexus, money, forms of competition, state, and international regime—Régulationists distinguish between an extensive accumulation regime dominating the nineteenth century (specifically applied to the period 1850–1914) followed by an intensive accumulation regime. The latter tends to be subdivided between its "Taylorist" variant of the inter-war period (1918–1939) and its perfected "Fordist" version driving the postwar boom (1945–1971). This distinction has its micro-level roots in Karl Marx's juxtaposition of absolute surplus value to relative surplus value. The extensive accumulation regime spreads prevailing capitalist production conditions and social relations to new branches and new markets, as occurred during the Industrial Revolution branching out from Britain to the European continent and beyond, without however transforming those conditions technologically so that the efficiency of labor or capital remains more or less unchanged. Intensive accumulation, by contrast, aims to boost labor's productivity through systematic deepening of the capital intensity of production so that the capital stock per worker steadily rises.

While both tendencies apply during any given period, capitalism shifted decisively from the former to the latter in the early part of the twentieth century with the emergence of mass production technology, notably the assembly line first introduced by Ransom Olds in 1901 and later perfected by Henry Ford with the introduction of the conveyor belt in 1911. That period also saw the rapid development of finance, in particular banks and the stock market, while key industrial sectors came to be dominated by large capitalist enterprises. Those developments boosted productivity growth, as did widespread application of Frederick Winslow Taylor's "scientific management" techniques of time and motion studies to optimize work-flow streamlining. But wages were still settled competitively so that aggregate spending levels lagged behind accelerating production capacity. The ensuing overproduction tendency culminated in the Great Depression of 1929–1939. The Taylorist inter-war accumulation regime thus proved unsustainable as productivity gains outpaced real wages while governments still lacked tools to boost otherwise inadequate demand.

Policy reforms first launched during the 1930s (e.g. Roosevelt's New Deal, France's Popular Front) and further extended after World War II among a large number of industrial nations moved us into a new accumulation regime, which RT has characterized as "Fordist".[14] Taken together, these reforms transformed each of the aforementioned institutional forms. Collective-bargaining agreements linked real-wage increases to productivity gains so that both could go up in tandem for rapid wage-led growth. Cost-plus pricing supported targeted profit margins, with prices often administered among otherwise competing firms to let the less-efficient producers survive. Monetary reforms yielded an elastic currency created by banks in acts of credit extension which supported higher levels of debt, further boosted by central bank accommodation of bank reserves and low-interest rates. The creation of a "Welfare State" provided income maintenance support and offered social services as public goods (e.g. education, health), with the ensuing chronic budget deficits partially monetized by the central bank's open-market operations. And the Bretton Woods agreement (July 1944) instituted a new international regime based on the US dollar as world money, fixed exchange rates, and the progressive liberalization of trade. Chronic and large-scale capital exports by the United States to furnish the rest of the world with sufficient dollars in international circulation, coupled with an overvalued US-currency, made it easier for other advanced capitalist economies to catch up after managing to recover rapidly from extensive war damage (e.g. Germany, Japan). The complementarity and co-evolution of these institutionalist forms can be considered "Fordist" inasmuch as they allowed workers to share in the productivity gains, matching mass production technology

[14] In reference to Henry Ford's introduction of the widely affordable Model T car and pace-setting five-dollar-a-day salary for his employees, the notion of "Fordism" denotes the mass production of inexpensive consumer durables coupled with high wages for workers thus enabled to buy all these goods, like Ford's own cars.

with social norms of mass consumption, while at the same time also integrating the working class socially and politically into the capitalist system.

2.2.4 *Types of Crises*

From its very beginning RT was primarily focused on the specifics of the Fordist accumulation regime to explain the postwar boom (Aglietta, 1976/1979) as well as the unprecedented stagflation crisis following this long period of expansion from the early 1970s onward (Boyer & Mistral, 1984; Lipietz, 1983/1985, 1985/1987). Here it is worth pointing to the extensive body of work by Régulationists on crisis as a central phenomenon in the accumulation dynamic of capitalist economies, especially the typology provided by Boyer (1986/1990).[15] There exists, of course, always the possibility of "exogenously triggered crisis" caused by external factors such as natural disaster or war. But the protagonists of RT, just as other heterodox approaches such as the Post-Keynesians or Marxists, are prone to argue that this type of crisis is the exception rather than the norm, in contrast to the standard neo-classical theory's argument that free-market economies can only be derailed from their inherent equilibrium position by external forces of disruption (such as market-thwarting trade unions or government regulation). Heterodox economists are instead more inclined to stress that capitalist accumulation dynamic is intrinsically cyclical, with upswings giving regularly way to downturns which Boyer & Co. have characterized as "endogenous" or "cyclical" crisis in a given country and period. Such cyclical downturns, commonly referred to as recessions, leave intact the prevailing mode of régulation whose operation they arise from.

It has been one of the noteworthy achievements of RT to have stressed the recurrence of crises which are deeper and of a more lasting impact than those typically short and shallow recessions. These occasionally bigger crises are of a more serious nature inasmuch as they paralyze (and/or break down) one or more institutional forms comprising the actual mode of régulation.[16]

[15] See in this context also Mazier et al. (1984/1999) as one of RT's classics on crisis.

[16] It is useful to think of those bigger crises, big enough to change the structure of the economy, as "structural crisis." See Guttmann (2015) for a discussion of this concept's meaning in various heterodox economic theories.

- An example of this kind of "crisis of the mode of régulation" was the collapse of the Bretton Woods system in a series of devastating speculative attacks on the overvalued US dollar starting in 1968, forcing the United States to suspend the dollar's promised convertibility into gold in August 1971 and let the dollar float in March 1973. These kinds of crisis break established patterns and feed tensions and/or conflicts which push for reforms of the broken institutional forms as occurred in our example with the Jamaica Accords of 1976 reorganizing the post-Bretton Woods international monetary system into what we will discuss (in Chapter 3) as the "dollar standard."
- And then there are what Régulationists consider to be the "great" crises. Those emerge from time to time when the breakdown of an institutional form destabilizes other institutional forms so that there is a spread of ruptures in the wake of deepening contradictions disintegrating in the end the entire accumulation regime. The transition from Taylorist to Fordist accumulation regime amidst worldwide depression (in the 1930s) and war (in the early 1940s) was an example of such a "crisis of the accumulation regime," as was the stagflation crisis of the 1970s.
- Finally, very rarely an economy may experience an existential crisis. Such a "crisis of the production mode" puts into question the entire economic system, as happened with the collapse of the Soviet Union during 1989–1991 whose centrally planned economy had simply stopped working despite frantic last-minute efforts to change its accumulation regime in the late 1980s under Mikhail Gorbachev's *glasnost* and *perestroika*. That dual reform program was too little, too late to save its command economy from imploding spectacularly.

What makes RT a long-wave theory is its insistence, put forth already by its very founders (see Aglietta, 1976/1979; Boyer & Mistral, 1984), that accumulation regimes are historically distinct phases in the evolution of capitalist economies which last from one "great" crisis to the next.[17] Their

[17] Setterfield (2011) has also argued that Régulation Theory's key notion of accumulation regime, sandwiched as it is between structural crises denoting its launch and its disintegration, makes it in effect a long-wave theory. While the author stresses the overlaps between Régulation Theory and Post-Keynesian Theory, Kotz (1990) points to a more pertinent comparison with the so-called "Social Structure of Accumulation" approach put

argument implies a crucial role for those so-called "crises of the accumulation regime" as vehicles of transformation altering the wage-labor nexus, the monetary regime, forms of competition, state intervention in the economy, and even the international context of economic relations. The new institutional forms emerging through such crisis-induced structural reforms must be complementary to the extent that they manage to co-exist in mutually reinforcing fashion so that they gradually form a coherent novel accumulation regime in their entirety, capable of launching and sustaining a renewed period of expansion which might last a couple of decades, perhaps even more. In this transition one institutional reform typically comes to dominate the entire configuration shaping the others and so putting its imprint on the emerging mode of régulation associated with the new accumulation regime. This was true for the reorganization of the wage-labor nexus begun under Roosevelt's New Deal becoming the dominant anchor for postwar Fordism, as was also the case for the deregulation of money and banking in the 1970s and early 1980s giving rise to a "financialized" mode of régulation in the finance-led capitalism of the 1990s and 2000s. And as we emerge out of a global pandemic, we may intensify our efforts to address the many ramifications of environmental degradation over the coming decade and thereby lay the groundwork for a more sustainability-oriented mode of régulation in decades to come.[18]

Such regime-transforming crises of the accumulation regime do not happen at a whim. They are the result of a steady build-up of underlying contradictions, tensions, and imbalances within a prevailing accumulation regime whose interactive matrix of institutional forms no longer works sufficiently well together to contain all those pressures. Even when the build-up of such stressors in the regime's structure suddenly breaks into the open, typically through a major financial crisis, we may not see sufficient impetus for regime change for quite some time. All we can see at that point of acute crisis conditions is that the accumulation regime, which had been in place driving a long-wave upswing, is no longer in a position to assure continued expansion. As a matter of fact, when looking at past downswing phases of long waves, whether the turbulent inter-war period of the 1920s and 1930s, the stagflation crisis rocking the world

forth by left-wing U.S. economists grouped together in the Union of Radical Political Economists, notably Gordon et al. (1982) or Bowles et al. (1983).

[18] See Guttmann (2018) for a discussion of the planned push for a zero-carbon transition opening the path leading us to a new accumulation regime.

economy from the late 1960s to the early 1980s, or the most recent slow-growth episode following the Great Financial Crisis of 2007/2008, we can typically identify two significant periods of acute crisis book-ending these periods. Analysts of long waves, whether Schumpeterian, Minskian, or Régulationist, may do well examining the full meaning of such a two-step crisis pattern more closely. The first crisis ends the long wave's upswing phase and sets in motion a downswing phase of slowing growth and a confluence of new or shifting imbalances. The second crisis, at the tail end of the downswing phase, typically intensifies crisis-induced cleaning-out processes while creating conditions of heightened instability ripe for fundamental reform. In Chapter 3 we will take a closer look at past long waves to see how such a pattern of two structural crises in a row has been decisive in shaping the transition from one accumulation regime to another.

Before we do so, we have to stress another point relevant to long-wave dynamic, and that is its relentlessly supranational dimension. The followers of Schumpeter, Minsky, or Aglietta have put more emphasis on a national-economy framework of analysis, even though Régulationists in particular have been consistently aware of the "international regime" as a highly relevant dimension of whatever stage of capitalism they were referring to. But we need to go further than this, and in doing so we will hopefully be able to provide an appropriate long-wave context for the international monetary system which it has lacked so far. My reference above to the "relentlessly supra-national dimension" of long-wave dynamic relates first of all to capitalism's globalization speed-ups during the upswing phases of long waves. These get mediated by having in place an international monetary system facilitating the catching-up process of a selected group of countries to the productivity, technological know-how, financial-maturity, and income levels of the then-dominant leader. Once several of those have caught up with the leader, trouble ensues amidst overproduction conditions and a flare-up of inter-imperialist rivalries. The first structural crisis is thus typically both global in dimension and financial in nature, as it disrupts the modus operandi of the international monetary system now no longer able to assure the same fast-growth dynamic driving the convergence that prevailed during the upswing phase. The second structural crisis has its own supranational dimension, as it scrambles the international hierarchy of power relations to allow new leaders to the fore. These multi-layered dynamics require an extension of our long-wave framework of analysis to the relationship between countries and forces beyond the level of nation-states, thus a closer look at the international dimension of the long-wave analytical framework.

2.3 The International Dimension

Most economic theories, from the standard "open-economy macroeconomic" model including trade and capital flows to the Post-Keynesian model of balance-of-payments-constrained growth known as Thirlwall's Law, conceive of the international dimension primarily from the point of view of a national economy interacting with the rest of the world via its balance of payments and exchange rates.[19] The advantage of RT in this regard is to look at the international economic and political dynamic *sui generis* as a configuration of decisive importance in and of itself. One implication of this emphasis is to have a proper sense of the institutional framework within which the waves of globalization as well as the counter-reactions to those leaps in integration unfold, including the sequencing of different international monetary arrangements from the so-called "classical gold standard" (1879–1914) via Bretton Woods (1945–1971) to the dollar standard (1976–present). In that sense RT has the advantage of explicitly taking account of the full scope of international monetary and economic relations as an "international regime" representing a pillar of whatever accumulation regime prevails.

2.3.1 World-System Theory

Such an internationalist view has also informed a multidisciplinary, historically grounded approach to the study of social change known as "World-System Theory" (WST), elaborated first by Immanuel Wallerstein (1974–1989, 2011a) in a massive four-volume opus tracing the origins of capitalism and the stages of its evolution on a global scale over the last six centuries. This approach, rooted mostly in Marxist theory and combining economics with political science and sociology, takes explicit account of Kondratiev's long waves as a determinant force shaping history as convincingly argued by leading WST theorists Leonid Grinin, Andrey

[19] See Thirlwall (1979) for the original presentation of what then came to be known as "Thirlwall's Law".

Korotayev, and Arno Tausch (2016).[20] Responding to the Great Financial Crisis of 2007/2008, Wallerstein (2010, 2011a) himself has recently sharpened his focus on "structural crisis" as a transformative process reshaping the dynamic of global capitalism, not unlike Régulationists would have emphasized. In many ways it is possible to connect WST to RT as a more extensive clarification of the underlying forces driving the international dimension of the accumulation regime. At the heart of WST's analysis of the prevailing international regime is its lead economy, or lead economies, and the economic as well as political interactions this "core" has with the rest of the world in terms of the evolving international division of labor and inter-state relations. While various Marxist-leaning dependency theories have explored different facets of the core-periphery relationship structure, one of WST's innovations is to have introduced a "semi-periphery" sphere comprising a group of countries in the intermediary range of economic development. Those have each the potential to become one day the core, have already invested significantly in the periphery, and at the same time are still facing a complex set of dependencies in their many interactions with the core—conditions which apply with great relevance to today's so-called "emerging-market economies" such as India or Brazil. China, which until quite recently was still part of that semi-periphery, is now moving quite decisively into "lead economy" status.

At the center of the WST's focus is the lead economy's ability, as the "core' of the world system, to turn radical technological change (usually emerging first during the preceding downswing phase) into new growth industries. Each long wave has a specific "core" grabbing technological leadership to lead its upswing phase by the force of innovation clusters taking root there. As was the case with Britain for much of the nineteenth century or the United States during the second half of the twentieth century and early twenty-first century, "core" powers can sustain their leadership position over two full long waves, not least by counteracting crisis-induced declines with new innovations and policy reforms. William Thompson (2012) has argued convincingly that the

[20] Wallerstein (1992, 2011b) has recurrently put his own WST framework into the long-wave context of Kondratiev, analyzing in some detail how changes in the international division of labor and in inter-state relations transform the core as well as its interactions with the (semi-) periphery to move these cycles through their different up- and downswing phases.

technology-based leadership position of the "core" is reinforced by the emergence of new energy sources under its control. We could see that with Britain and coal during the nineteenth century, just as much as that connection also applied to the United States and oil in the early twentieth century or later with natural gas. The strong lead-economy positions of Japan, France, and even Germany during the postwar boom certainly had something to do with their respective successes in nuclear power. And China's current surge to the core is possibly reinforced by its pursuit of global leadership in renewables, in particular solar power. When new energy sources emerge to the point of dominance, countries having easy access to those and thereby turning themselves to strategic suppliers reinforce their "core" status in the international realm. Their comparative advantage as key energy suppliers can be further reinforced to the extent that they develop profitable growth-industry extensions rooted in those energy sources. Britain managed to master steam engines powered by coal to cement its leadership in the Industrial Revolution of the nineteenth century. And when oil and gas grew into the world's primary energy sources during the first half of the twentieth century, the United States gained also a decisive leadership role in the development of internal combustion engines propelling it towards successful launch of Fordism as the successful post-war accumulation regime. Thompson (2012) extends this connection beyond prime movers to other kinds of strategically placed "engines," such as for example the internet boosting America's technological leadership. In the same vein we can mention here Japan's edge in robotics or foresee China's rise to superpower status with its "Made in China 2025" industrial-policy push into artificial intelligence, electric vehicles, and other high-tech manufacturing industries.

In one of the most influential WST contributions, Giovanni Arrighi (1994) has conditioned the lead economy's "core" status on its ability to turn into a hegemon extending its influence over the rest of the world. The hegemon projects power and leadership through a strategy of global reach. To the extent that upswing phases of long waves are characterized by rapid expansion in the core, much of this growth acceleration comes from benefits related to the exercise of hegemonic power giving it favorable terms of trade through unequal exchange, access to cheap resources abroad, a degree of monopoly power for its exports in foreign markets, and political control. The core's main producers will also be tempted to invest abroad in order to secure larger markets and greater profits. But these foreign investments, while possibly strengthening individual firms, may ultimately end up causing the lead economy to suffer relative decline, if not outright erosion. Recipients of the core's foreign direct investment, especially large-population countries in the semi-periphery, will benefit from the added capital, technology transfer, and managerial know-how and start catching up with the leader. The international dimension of long waves is thus characterized by distinct phases of divergence and convergence between lead economies at the core and faster growing economies located in the semi-periphery or even periphery. The Japanese economist Kaname Akamatsu (1962) captured this dynamic very well by characterizing it as a "flying geese" pattern of economic development according to which the production of manufactured goods moves from more advanced economies to newly industrializing economies and then later onto the next layer of lesser developed economies, perhaps even beyond. So-called "Akamatsu Waves" reframe the core-periphery interaction as a cyclical dynamic of alternate periods of catching-up ("convergence") and growing divergence between the advanced and developing economies, linking WST[21] and Kondratiev's long waves through shifts in the international division of labor based on dynamic comparative advantage.

2.3.2 *The International Monetary System*

These aspects of the international regime—the core's initial establishment of the lead, its growth acceleration from its advantageous interactions with the periphery, the latter's catching-up process in the course of "Akamatsu Waves"—are mediated by the international monetary system in place. Whatever variant of the international monetary system currently prevails, its modus operandi reflects the lead economy's hegemony and the cyclical convergence-divergence dynamic underpinning core-periphery relations.

The lead economy at the core may reinforce its hegemonic position through the world-money role of its national currency. To the extent that its currency comes to serve extensively as international medium of exchange, it ends up also circulating abroad. Even though that

[21] See Tausch (2016) for a detailed analysis of the so-called "Akamatsu Wave". It should be noted that more traditional trade theories, notably the "technology gap" theory of trade by Posner (1961) or the "product life cycle" theory of international trade by Vernon (1966), also see dynamic comparative advantage shifting over time from the lead economy to lesser developed countries which are thereby allowed for a certain period to close the gap with the leader.

currency gets initially created within the domestic banking system, its world-money role necessitates its ongoing transfers to the rest of the world through the lead economy's purchases of goods, services, or assets abroad. Foreign direct investment becomes eventually a major, if not the most important channel for world-money transfers from the core to the semi-periphery and then to the periphery beyond. Exchange rates may reinforce the core's advantages in its trade and investment interactions with the periphery, especially to the extent that a strongly valued key currency renders raw materials, imports of manufactured goods, and foreign assets cheap for the economic actors of the core.

Countries in the semi-periphery or periphery will find that their correspondingly undervalued currencies not only attract foreign investments from the core, but also facilitate export-led growth as their products are cheap in the world market when paid for in the key currency. Exchange-rate adjustments between the world money and other currencies may well shape the catching-up process of newly industrializing economies just as much as they impact on the core's initial competitive edge. And then there are the interactions between exchange-rate differentials and interest-rate spreads which affect the continuous balancing act between the centrifugal (core => periphery) and centripetal (periphery => core) portfolio-investment flows around which the disproportionately faster globalization of finance organizes itself to preserve the core's advantage while allowing the periphery to access global financial markets.

The international monetary system thus provides a crucial institutional framework for the multi-layered interactions between lead economies, the semi-periphery intent on catching up, and the periphery's coping with dependencies in its pursuit of socio-economic development. And just as the broader global regime of core-periphery interactions shaping the international division of labor and inter-state relations gets transformed in the wake of long waves, so too is the international monetary system subject to ongoing parallel change. New variants arise during upswing phases, only to disintegrate under the pressures of structural crisis during long-wave downswings. We have been able to observe this pattern for at least two centuries:

- To start with, the London-centered gold-sterling standard framed the extensive accumulation regime and its competitive mode of régulation during much of the nineteenth century (especially following its reform in the Bank Charter Act of 1844).

- And its extension into what came to be known as the "classical gold standard" (1879–1914) boosted an upswing phase guiding us toward the transition to a monopolistic mode of régulation.
- The absence of a coherent and effective international monetary system during the inter-war period was surely one of the key reasons why the Taylorist accumulation regime proved so chaotic and ended in disaster on a global scale during the 1930s.
- It was no coincidence that the postwar boom of the 1950s and 1960s was greatly helped along by a highly accommodating new international monetary system known as Bretton Woods whose collapse in the early 1970s helped disintegrate the other institutional forms of Fordism in a new structural crisis known as stagflation.
- International monetary reforms replacing Bretton Woods begun with the Jamaica Accords of 1976. Transitional developments, such as the spread of market-determined ("flexible") exchange-rates after 1973 got anchored more solidly in the second half of the 1980s. During 1987 we saw the Louvre Agreement for coordinated exchange-rate management as well as the introduction of the Brady bonds, two nearly simultaneous steps in the direction of a new dollar standard. Its neoliberal policy prescriptions known as the "Washington Consensus" ultimately pushed the entire globe into finance-led capitalism driven forward by the relentless globalization of finance.
- The worldwide growth pattern arising from this push forward, rooted in very large US deficits absorbing the catching-up process of emerging-market economies reliant on export-led growth and their progressive integration into global supply chains, took a huge hit in 2007–2009 when America's housing bubble driving this supranational growth dynamic collapsed.

We are now, a dozen years later, in the midst of yet another post-crisis transition period calling, among other regime-altering structural changes, for international monetary reform away from the damaged dollar standard. This last point, the challenge of reforming the international monetary system as we transition to a new accumulation regime, motivates much of the second half of the book. In the next chapter we shall illustrate the most salient characteristics of two successive long waves fueled by the US dollar's role as world money, Fordism (1945–1982) and finance-led capitalism (1982–2020), to gain a better understanding of the modus operandi of the dollar standard all the way to the beginning of its structural crisis in the Great Recession of 2007–2009 and its troubled aftermath in yet another secular-stagnation downswing phase. In the process of discussing these two long waves as distinct accumulation regimes we shall be able to demonstrate, by looking at the stylized facts of greatest relevance, how meaningful the contributions of Schumpeter, Mandel, Minsky and Wallerstein have been to our understanding of capitalism's long-term evolution and how well Régulation Theory integrates these technological, financial, institutional, and geopolitical dimensions into a coherent theoretical framework. That framework makes it possible for us to project different scenarios going forward once we will have managed to put the global pandemic of 2020/2021 behind us.

References

Aglietta, M. (1976/1979). *A theory of capitalist regulation: The US experience*. Verso Books. First published in French as *Régulation et crises du capitalisme*.

Aglietta, M. (2016/2018). *Money. 5,000 years of debt and power*. Verso. First published in French as *La monnaie, entre dettes et souveraineté*.

Akamatsu, K. (1962). A historical pattern of economic growth in developing countries. *The Developing Economies, 1*(1), 3–25.

Arrighi, G. (1994). *The long twentieth century: Money, power, and the origins of our times*. Verso.

Bowles, S., Gordon, D., & Weisskopf, T. (1983). *Beyond the wasteland: A democratic alternative to economic decline*. Anchor Press/Doubleday.

Boyer, R. (1986/1990). *The regulation school*. Columbia University Press. First published in French as *La théorie de la régulation: un analyse critique*.

Boyer, R., & Mistral, J. (1984). *The present crisis. From an historical interpretation to a prospective outlook*. Cepremap.

Boyer, R., & Saillard, Y. (1995/2002). *Régulation theory: The state of the art*. Routledge. First published in French as *Théorie de la rgulation: l'état de savoirs*.

Cassidy, J. (2008, February 4). The Minsky moment: Subprime mortgage crisis and possible recession. *The New Yorker*. https://www.newyorker.com/magazine/2008/02/04/the-minsky-moment

Coriat, B. (1991). *Technical flexibility and mass production: Flexible specialization and dynamic flexibility*. Pinter, Belhaven.

Coriat, B. (1997). *Globalization, variety, and mass production: The metamorphosis of mass production in the new competitive age*. Cambridge University Press.

De Brunhoff, S. (1973/1976). *Marx on money*. Urizen Books. First published in French as *La Monnaie chez Marx*.

Ferri, P., & Minsky, H. (1992). Market processes and thwarting systems. *Structural Change and Economic Dynamics, 3*(1), 79–91.
Freeman, C. (1987). Technical innovation, diffusion, and long cycles of economic development. In T. Vasko (Ed.), *The long-wave debate* (pp. 295–309). Springer.
Friedman, M., & Schwartz, A. (1963). *A monetary history of the United States 1867–1960*. Princeton University Press.
Goldstein, J. (1988). *Long cycles: Prosperity and war in the modern age*. Yale University Press.
Goodwin, M. (1967). A growth cycle. In C. H. Feinstein (Ed.), *Socialism, capitalism and economic growth* (pp. 54–58). Cambridge University Press.
Gordon, D., Edwards, R., & Reich, M. (1982). *Segmented work, divided workers*. Cambridge University Press.
Grinin, L., Korotayev, A., & Tausch, A. (2016). *Economic cycles, crises and the global periphery*. Springer International. https://doi.org/10.1007/978-3-319-41262-7_2
Guttmann, R. (1994). *How credit-money shapes the economy: The United States in a global system*. M. E. Sharpe.
Guttmann, R. (1997). Defining monetary regimes. In R. Guttmann (Ed.), *Reforming money and finance: Toward a new monetary regime* (pp. 253–258). M. E. Sharpe.
Guttmann, R. (2002). Money and credit in *régulation* theory. In R. Boyer & Y. Saillard (Eds.), *Régulation theory: The state of the art* (pp. 57–63). Routledge.
Guttmann, R. (2015). The heterodox notion of structural crisis. *Review of Keynesian Economics, 3*(2), 194–212. https://doi.org/10.4337/roke.2015.02.04
Guttmann, R. (2016). *Finance-led capitalism: Shadow banking, re-regulation and the future of global markets*. Palgrave Macmillan.
Guttmann, R. (2018). *Eco-capitalism: Carbon money, climate finance and sustainable development*. Palgrave Macmillan.
Kalecki, M. (1939). Essays in the theory of economic fluctuations. In J. Osiatynski (2007, Ed.), *Collected Works of Michael Kalecki, Vol. I; Capitalism, business and full employment* (pp. 235–252). Clarendon Press.
Kalecki, M. (1969). *Theory of economic dynamics*. Augustus B. Kelley.
Keynes, J. M. (1936). *The general theory of employment, interest and money*. Macmillan.
Kondratiev, N. D. (1925a). The conjuncture institute at Moscow. *Quarterly Journal of Economics, 39*(2), 320–324. https://doi.org/10.2307/1884878
Kondratiev, N. D. (1925b). The static and dynamic view of economics. *Quarterly Journal of Economics, 39*(4), 575–583. https://doi.org/10.2307/1883266
Kondratiev, N. (1926/1935). Die langen Wellen der Konjunktur. *Archiv für Sozialwissenschaften und Sozialpolitik, 56*(3), 573–609. Translated (abridged)

in 1935 as The long waves of economic life. *Review of Economics and Statistics*, *17*(6), 105–115.

Kondratiev, N. (1984). *The long wave cycle*. Richardson & Snyder.

Kondratiev, N. (1998). *The works of Nikolai D. Kondratiev* (4 vols). Edited by W. Samuels, N. Makasheva, & V. Barnett. Pickering & Chatto.

Kotz, D. (1990). A comparative analysis of the theory of regulation and the social structure of accumulation theory. *Science & Society*, *54*(1), 5–28.

Lahalt, J. (2007, August 18). In time of tumult, obscure economist gains currency—Mr. Minsky long argued markets were crisis prone; His "moment" has arrived. *Wall Street Journal*, p. A1.

Lipietz, A. (1983/1985). *The enchanted world: Inflation, credit and the global crisis*. Verso. First published in French as *Le monde enchanté: de la valeur à l'envol inflationniste*.

Lipietz, A. (1985/1987). *Mirages and miracles: Crisis in global fordism*. Verso. First published in French as *Mirages et miracles. Problèmes de l'industrialisation dans le Tiers-Monde*.

Mandel, E. (1975/1999). *Late capitalism*. Verso Classics. First published in German as *Der Spätkapitalismus*.

Mandel, E. (1980). *Long waves of capitalist development—A Marxist interpretation*. Cambridge University Press.

Marx, K. (1859/1904). *A contribution to the critique of political economy*. Charles H. Kerr & Co. First published in German as *Zur Kritik der Politischen Ökonomie*.

Marx, K. (1863/1951). *Theories of surplus value*. International Publishers. First published in German as *Theorien über den Mehrwert*.

Marx, K. (1867/1887). *Capital* (Vol. 1). Appleton & Co. First published in German as *Das Kapital, Erster Band*.

Marx, K. (1894/1967). *Capital* (Vol. III). International Publishers. First published in German by F. Engels as *Das Kapital: Dritter Band*.

Marx, K. (1939/1973). *Grundrisse: Foundations of the critique of political economy*. Penguin.

Mazier, J., Baslé, M., & Vidal, J. F. (1984/1999). *When economic crises endure*. M. E. Sharpe. First published in French as *Quand les crises durent*.

Minsky, H. (1964). Longer waves in financial relations: financial factors in the more severe depressions. *American Economic Review*, *54*(3), 324–335.

Minsky, H. (1982). *Can 'it' happen again? Essays on instability and finance*. M. E. Sharpe.

Minsky, H. (1986). *Stabilizing an unstable economy*. Yale University Press.

Minsky, H. (1989, January 1). Money manager capitalism. *Hyman P. Minsky Archive*, Bard College Digital Commons, Levy Economics Institute. https://digitalcommons.bard.edu/cgi/viewcontent.cgi?article=1012&context=hm_archive

Minsky, H. (1992). *The financial instability hypothesis* (Working Paper No. 74). The Jerome Levy Economics Institute. https://www.levyinstitute.org/pubs/wp74.pdf

Minsky, H. (1995). Longer waves in financial relations: Financial factors in the more severe depressions II. *Journal of Economic Issues, 29*(1), 83–96.

Minsky, H., & Whalen, C. (1996). Economic insecurity and the institutional prerequisites for successful capitalism. *Journal of Post Keynesian Economics, 19*(2), 155–170.

Palley, T. (2011). A theory of Minsky super-cycles and financial crises. *Contributions to Political Economy, 30*(1), 31–46. https://doi.org/10.1093/cpe/bzr004

Petit, P. (1985). *Slow growth and the service economy*. Pinter.

Posner, M. V. (1961). International trade and technological change. *Oxford Economic Papers, 13*(3), 323–341.

Samuelson, P. (1939). Interactions between the multiplier analysis and the principle of acceleration. *Review of Economic Statistics, 21*(2), 75–78.

Schumpeter, J. (1939). *Business cycles: A theoretical, historical, and statistical analysis of the capitalist process*. Mc-Graw Hill Books.

Schumpeter, J. (1943). *Capitalism, socialism and democracy*. George Allen & Unwin.

Setterfield, M. (2011). Anticipations of the crisis: On the similarities between post-Keynesian economics and regulation theory. *Revue de la Regulation, 10*. https://journals.openedition.org/regulation/9366

Tausch, A. (2016). Kaname Akamatsu. Biography and long cycles theory. In L. Grinin, T. Devezas, & A. Korotayev (Eds.), *Kondratieff waves: Cycles, crises, and forecasts* (pp. 65–81). Uchitel Publishing (Russia). https://www.sociostudies.org/upload/sociostudies.org/almanac/k_waves_3/065-081.pdf

Théret, B. (1999). The socio-political dimensions of the currency: Implications for the transition to the Euro. In T. Vissol (Ed.), *The Euro: Consequences for the consumer and citizen* (pp. 51–79). Springer.

Thirlwall, A. (1979). The balance of payments constraint as an explanation of international growth rate differences. *Banca Nazionale Del Lavoro Quarterly Review, 32*(128), 45–53.

Thompson, W. (2012). Energy, K-waves, lead economies, and their interpretation/implications. *Journal of Globalization Studies, 3*(2), 59–78.

Tylecote, A. (1992). *The long wave in the world economy*. Routledge.

Tymoigne, E., & Wray, R. (2014). *The rise and fall of money manager capitalism: Minsky's half century from world war two to the great recession*. Routledge.

Van Duijn, J. (1983). *The long wave in economic life*. Allen & Unwin.

Vernon, R. (1966). International investment and international trade in the product cycle. *Quarterly Journal of Economics*, *80*(2), 190–207. https://doi.org/10.2307/1880689

Wallerstein, I. (1974–1989). *The modern world-system* [Volumes I (1974), II (1980), and III (1989)]. Academic Press.

Wallerstein, I. (1992). A brief agenda for the future of long-wave research. In A. Kleinknecht, E. Mandel, & I. Wallerstein (Eds.), *New findings in long-wave research* (pp. 339–342). Palgrave Macmillan.

Wallerstein, I. (2010). Structural crises. *New Left Review, 62*, 133–142.

Wallerstein, I. (2011a). Structural crisis in the world-system: Where do we go from here?. *Monthly Review, 62*(10), 31– 9. https://doi.org/10.14452/MR-062-10-2011-03_2

Wallerstein, I. (2011b). Prologue. In I. Wallerstein (Ed.), *The modern world-system III: The second era of great expansion of the capitalist world-economy, 1730s-1840s* (pp. xiii–xxi). University of California Press.

Whalen, C. (2002). Money manager capitalism: Still here, but not quite as expected. *Journal of Economic Issues, 36*(2), 401–406.

Wray, R. (2009). The rise and fall of money manager capitalism: A Minskian approach. *Cambridge Journal of Economics, 33*(4), 807–828.

CHAPTER 3

A Short History of the Dollar Standard

The long-wave approach provides a good fit to trace the evolution of advanced capitalist economies, whether individually or bound together through the prevailing international regime. Here, in this chapter, we seek to present the stylized facts of a historic pattern that in the end should help us understand where we are at the moment and what we may face moving forward. We are specifically tracing the history of the US dollar as primary form of world money through two long waves, the first encompassing the postwar boom and the stagflation crisis (1945–1982) followed by yet another long wave in the wake of the Reagan Revolution all the way to the global pandemic we are facing now (1982–2021). The consecutive K-waves, after Kondratiev, correspond to two distinct accumulation regimes, which Régulationists have characterized as Fordism and finance-led capitalism, respectively. This short history of the dollar standard will enable us to identify the forces at work in recent years which have been pushing the world economy toward a distinctly multi-polar configuration bound to usher in a new international monetary system and, with it, possibly also a different accumulation regime.

R. Guttmann, *Multi-Polar Capitalism*,
https://doi.org/10.1007/978-3-030-88247-1_3

3.1 The Era of Bretton Woods (1945–1971)

The inter-war period following World War I had seen a weakened lead economy, Britain, vie for dominance with an emerging superpower, the United States. Their fraught coexistence during those turbulent years prevented necessary reforms in the international realm and adequate cooperation between them for effective containment of two other powers, Germany and the Soviet Union, coming under the dictatorship of ruthless leaders with expansionist ambitions and politically extremist agendas. This volatile mix ended in a worldwide depression and yet another war spanning the globe. America's eventual leadership became anchored precisely then, when newly elected President Franklin Delano Roosevelt launched an ambitious reform program at the bottom of the depression to replace the collapsed gold standard with a new monetary regime of nationally administered credit-money (e.g. Glass-Steagall Act of 1933), switch US trade policy from protectionism to trade liberalization, make the income tax system far more progressive, set up a safety net of income maintenance programs (e.g. Social Security Act of 1935), transform labor relations, regulate business, and launch infrastructure programs for job creation. This "New Deal" remade almost every aspect of America's economy—its financial system, public spending, industry, labor, trade. Together Roosevelt's reforms provided an institutional framework for a new accumulation regime, centered on mass production technologies, social norms of mass consumption for a broad middle class, elastic currency, and budget deficits. America's ability to launch such productive and complementary reforms underlined its global leadership position. But first it had to confront another rising power bent on conflict under its autocratic leader, Hitler's Germany. World War II began on September 1, 1939 with Hitler's attack of Poland, and by December 1941 the initially reluctant United States had joined the war to defeat Nazi Germany and its allies, including Japan.

As World War II drew to a close, the United States and its allies began to plan for a new international economic order whose details were successfully negotiated at the Bretton Woods Conference in July 1944. That gathering witnessed a historic confrontation between John Maynard Keynes heading the British delegation and Harry Dexter White representing the United States. Keynes had spent the war years at the UK Treasury preparing for this moment with a series of radical proposals containing a new supranational world currency to be managed by an international clearing union (his "Bancor Plan"), a new organization putting in place multilateral trade-liberalization agreements, and public storage of commodities in buffer stocks managed by yet another international organization to assure adequate supplies of key raw materials at stable prices.[1] Under Keynes' Bancor Plan countries with positive international balances would commit funds into the clearing union which countries with external deficits could draw from as credit, a sort of overdraft facility assuring automatic recycling of surpluses to cover deficits. Such a system would obviously favor deficit countries (like postwar Britain) which the United States, then a chronic surplus country, rejected. Instead the forty-four countries meeting at Bretton Woods adopted the White Plan which established a gold-backed US dollar as new international medium of exchange and set up two new multilateral lending agencies—the International Monetary Fund (IMF) to assist countries facing acute balance-of-payments crises, and the International Bank for Reconstruction and Development (IBRD, nowadays known as the "World Bank," to help fund large-scale infrastructure and development projects.

3.1.1 *Turning the US Dollar into World Money*

At the core of this new postwar order was the US-guaranteed automatic convertibility of dollars and gold at the assured exchange rate of $35 per troy ounce of gold, a promise made credibly at the time when the United States had amassed two-thirds of the world's gold reserves and so rendering the US dollar "as good as" gold. Actually, as it turns out, even better than gold! By picking the same rate of exchange as set a decade earlier in the Gold Reserves Act of 1934, the US government consciously chose to overvalue its currency relative to gold. The year 1934 marked the bottom of the depression-induced deflationary spiral, and prices had been rising steadily since then especially after 1939 when the war caused a spike in inflation. If the Americans had wanted to set a realistic exchange rate reflecting the cumulative decade-long increase in the general price level, they would have valued the dollar at about half the level, say $70/ounce. But they did not! By overvaluing the US dollar, they wanted to encourage its usage as international medium of exchange

[1] Keynes' preparatory work and proposals for Bretton Woods are documented in volumes 25 (Keynes, 1980a) and 26 (Keynes, 1980b) of his *Collected Writings*.

in lieu of (the correspondingly undervalued, hence relatively less attractive) gold. It should be noted here that other currencies, as they became increasingly convertible over the coming decade or so, were either set at more realistic levels or allowed to devalue so that the dollar's intrinsic overvaluation extended to those monies as well.

The key challenge early on, after the new Bretton Woods system had been put into place in 1945, was a serious global shortage of dollars which hampered reconstruction efforts to put the war-damaged economies of Western Europe and Japan back on their feet. How were these economies going to get their dollars needed to pay for imports? Created inside the US banking system, those dollars had to flow out of their country of origin by means of American balance-of-payments deficits. In the face of chronically large US trade surpluses, such external deficits could only come about with even greater net exports of capital. The Americans ultimately mobilized three large channels of capital exports to assure steady supplies of US dollars into international circulation and for reserve purposes:

- By 1947 the U.S. launched large-scale aid and assistance programs to its allies, most importantly the Marshall Plan for Western Europe funding strategic imports, domestic infrastructure programs, and (after 1950) a successful multilateral settlement system known as the European Payments System as the first step in the direction of European integration.
- As the world slipped into the Cold War after 1947, the United States launched military alliances with its allies, notably the North Atlantic Treaty Organization, to encircle the Soviet Union. NATO involved stationing large numbers of American soldiers on forward bases and offering support for the allies' military forces, both channels transferring billions of dollars to Europe. Similar military alliances also pumped dollars into Japan, Australia, New Zealand, and other non-European allies.
- Finally, American firms across many sectors invested heavily abroad as they turned themselves into multinational corporations seeking a global reach. Following successful reconstruction, European and Eastern Asian economies began to boom and so came to represent attractive markets with strong growth potential. Reduction of trade barriers, another central plank of the new postwar economic order overseen by the multilateral General Agreement on Tariffs and Trade

(GATT), added to the attractiveness of foreign direct investment in Europe as it gradually turned into a more open and integrated continental market. Europeans and other nations welcomed such US investments in their economies, not only for their supplies of capital, but also of managerial know-how and technology.

As evident from the first two dollar-export channels, the aid programs and military resources directed toward strategic allies, US leadership within the framework of the Bretton Woods system was profoundly shaped by the ongoing Cold War confrontation with the Soviet Union whose containment within the boundaries of its own "empire" across a divided Europe became the collectively shared priority of the Western Alliance. Similar motivations of deepening ties in the face of a common powerful enemy also drove the progressively more ambitious European integration project which started in 1950 with the aforementioned European Payments Union as well as the European Coal and Steel Community providing for a successful cartel formation across six countries in two key strategic sectors that needed restructuring in the face of crisis. Those same six countries—the three Benelux countries as well as Italy joining West Germany and France at the center—then set up a customs union in 1958 from which followed a common agricultural policy (1962), a fixed exchange-rate mechanism (1979), creation of a common market (1987), and monetary union (1992) all the while expanding its membership from the original six to twenty-eight countries. The Communist threat also motivated Western European nations to develop a fairly progressive mixed-economy "social market" model which integrated the well-organized working classes by means of strong labor representation (unions, collective-bargaining rights) and adequate income maintenance (unemployment benefits, pensions) while at the same time having the state maintain control over key sectors of the economy serving as basic material inputs for either industry (steel, energy, transportation, communications) or the electorate (health care, education).

3.1.2 Fueling the Postwar Boom

Notwithstanding important national differences in its design and application across the industrial world, this integrative mixed-economy model provided the institutional pillar for a rapid-growth pattern combining full employment and price stability. The ensuing "economic miracle" had rapid productivity gains matched by proportional increases in real wages to boost living standards for a large majority of Americans and Europeans on a continuous basis for a quarter of century (1948–1973). A crucial collective-bargaining agreement between US car giant General Motors and the United Automobile Workers in 1948 paved the way for wage increases in line with productivity gains and inflation ("cost-of-living adjustments") while introducing employer-provided pension and health insurance plans for workers. This formula, tying real-wage improvements to productivity while also boosting the "social" wage package of key fringe benefits, became sufficiently widespread to translate into a macroeconomic balance between aggregate supply (fueled by productivity gains) and aggregate demand (rising in line with wage-earners' real purchasing power). Steady improvements in workers' living standards made possible by the GM-UAW formula combined with a baby boom to spread "middle class" social consumption norms which fueled the postwar boom for decades—suburban home ownership, consumer durables filling the house, cars giving people an unprecedented degree of mobility, higher-calorie diets helping (heavily subsidized) domestic agriculture and local restaurants, the spread of education, all embedded in an expanding (energy, housing, communications, and transportation) infrastructure attracting much public investment spending.[2]

The Bretton Woods system allowed Western Europe and Japan after the war to adopt the monetary-reform framework first applied in the 1930s by Roosevelt combining government-issued currency and private bank money ("checking deposits") issued in acts of credit extension. The international dimension of this new postwar monetary regime, set up under Bretton Woods, came to full fruition in 1958 when continuous American capital exports had overcome the initial global shortage of dollars to render other currencies (e.g. British pound sterling, Japanese yen, German mark) fully convertible. The industrial nations could now finally enjoy the full benefits of a well-performing multilateral payments system tying countries and regions together. Some countries, such as France, drove the regulatory framework for their nationally administered regime of credit-money quite a bit further than the US version in terms

[2] There are, of course, many good studies of the postwar boom in the industrialized world. It is important in this context to highlight the leading role of the United States in shaping that "Golden Age" period in capitalism's evolution, as so well explained by Aglietta (1976/1979) or Marglin and Schor (1992).

of having the state direct credit access selectively. Lacking Glass-Steagall's separation of commercial banking and investment banking, leading European and Japanese banks generally occupied strategically more powerful positions at the center of their national economies compared to their American counterparts while keeping domestic stock and bond markets less developed than in the United States (where investment banks were important and institutional investors emerged early).

Be that as it may, the postwar monetary regime's ample credit supplies responding in elastic fashion to the public's loan demand financed all four pillars in support of rapid growth stretching over decades at affordably low-interest rates. Corporate debt supported large-scale investment projects boosting mass production capacity across sectors. Consumer debt, from mortgages via car loans to credit cards, funded the increasingly ambitious social consumption norms of the middle classes. Government debt financed continuous budget deficits which arose not least due to the more generous income maintenance and redistributive subsidy programs of the "Welfare State." And international fund transfers covered external deficits sufficiently to avoid painful austerity measures while war-induced debts were gradually paid off. This well-regulated "debt economy" had a long way to go before accumulated debt would rise to uncomfortably high levels. Budget deficits remained in most countries moderate enough, compared to their spikes during World War II, for the public debt/GDP ratio to fall gently over time. Private-sector debt, starting from a low base after depression and war, could thus rise more easily and longer because of such relative retrenchment of public-sector debt. Overall indebtedness benefited from low-interest rates, whose nominal levels remained for the most part below growth rates, as well as fixed exchange rates. In other words, those two strategic prices of money were managed in a pro-growth and stability-enhancing fashion.[3]

These ingredients of the long postwar boom, present in nearly all industrial nations, were further reinforced by an international policy framework supporting rapid growth. Once again, as was the case with the first wave of globalization around the turn of the century, you had an effective international monetary system whose center supplied the

[3] I have analyzed these private-sector, public-sector, and external sector pillars of the postwar "debt economy," as anchored institutionally in the monetary regime of that period, and their respective contributions to the long boom from the late 1940s to the early 1970s elsewhere in Guttmann (1994).

periphery amply with capital to facilitate a catching-up process—except that now the center was the United States rather than Britain, supplying US dollars in lieu of pound sterling. The dollar's overvaluation extended beyond gold to the European and Japanese currencies, making it easier for those countries to launch export-led growth strategies on the back of their artificially cheap currencies. Another benefit of an overvalued dollar was that it kept (dollar-denominated) commodity prices low, especially oil and natural gas which emerged as the main energy sources on a global scale. High growth rates among industrial nations were further sustained by the rapid expansion of world trade, greatly facilitated by the systematic lowering of tariffs and later also non-tariff barriers to trade under the auspices of GATT in several "rounds" of multilateral negotiations for trade liberalization. The volume of world trade (among non-communist nations) grew annually by six percent per year from 1948 to 1963 and during much of the 1960s by an even faster eight percent per year, a rate of expansion twice as fast as world output.

3.1.3 Postwar Wave of Globalization

That postwar wave of globalization was, however, at once narrower and deeper than the first wave half a century earlier. It was narrower, because it engulfed fewer countries. The first wave of globalization from 1879 to 1914 extended industrialization beyond Britain to the European continent, Northern America, and Japan while also allowing those newly industrialized countries to pursue their imperialist ambitions, just as Britain had done, across the continents through aggressive thrusts of colonization. What happened to China during that period is a good case in point. Now, in the years following World War II, the situation was quite different to the extent that a large number of countries simply took themselves out of the US-led world market opening. For one, you had the Soviet Union as one of the victors of World War II extending its control over much of Eastern Europe and cutting the continent effectively in half through what soon was to become the "Iron Curtain." Other countries would also fall under the spell of Communism, notably China in 1949, Cuba in 1959, and Vietnam (after a long war) in 1975. And then there was a second group of countries mostly in Asia and Africa gaining independence after World War II when colonialism no longer proved a viable option for Britain and its European neighbors. These new post-colonial states, led by former leaders of nationalistic independence movements now imposing one-party rule, adopted an import-substitution strategy of industrialization behind considerable protectionist walls.[4]

But the second wave of globalization, while confined to the fifty or so countries committed to the trade-liberalization principles of GATT, was in some key ways also deeper than the first wave more than half a century ago. Beyond reinforcing inter-industry trade through progressively stronger tariff reductions in six consecutive "rounds" of GATT from 1947 to 1967, the postwar boom also witnessed an explosion in intra-industry trade involving the same good or service (e.g. the French buying Boeing planes and the Americans buying Airbus planes) as well as direct foreign investments by market leaders transforming themselves into multi-national corporations. Such intra-industry trade was motivated by a number of factors, all of whom decisively important for the kind of competition now practiced among large firms:

- One was the relentless hunt for economies of scale ("increasing returns to scale") arising from larger production runs pushing down unit ("average") costs so that firms would end up with either higher profit margins or in a position to underprice their competitors, possibly deploying a combination of both. As automation yielded more capital-intensive production technology, fixed costs associated with the productive capital stock (i.e. depreciation allowances, debt-servicing charges) crowded out variable costs tied to labor (e.g. wages). The resulting dominance of fixed costs made total costs more sluggish than output so that the unit-cost ratio (i.e. total costs/output) declined with expanding production volumes made possible when capturing markets abroad.
- Intra-industry trade also took off in the wake of product differentiation becoming more important as large firms tried to seek brand loyalty and cater to different market segments.
- A third factor fueling intra-industry trade was the product cycle whereby the maturing of once-new products into standardized, mass-produced products would change the resource mix needed for their production (from entrepreneurs to managers, from highly

[4] This import-substitution strategy of industrialization, which found widespread application in the Southern hemisphere after World War II, was first espoused in Latin America from the 1930s on and later theoretically justified for a worldwide audience by influential Argentinian economist Raúl Prebisch (1959).

skilled workers figuring out the new product to semi-skilled assembly workers, from venture capitalists to institutional investors, etc.) and so shift the comparative advantage from innovator to imitators. The overvalued dollar made it comparatively cheaper for US corporations to set up shop abroad than reach those foreign markets through exports from home, and this preference fueled the rise of multinationals seeking to extend their global reach.[5]

3.2 The Stagflation Crisis 1969–1982

The postwar boom ran its course in the late 1960s when the US economy overheated. President Johnson's "War on Poverty" involved a series of new entitlement programs (e.g. Medicare). At the same time there were massive increases in military spending caused by the Vietnam War, which could not be financed by tax increases due to that war's growing unpopularity. This combination of fiscal stimulation pushed aggregate demand beyond the potential-output ceiling to heat up inflation from about 1.3 percent in 1966 to nearly 5 percent three years later. This was a classic case of demand-pull inflation. But then, during the recession of 1969/70 US inflation stayed stubbornly high rather than exhibiting its typical slowdown-induced decline. From then on an accelerating inflation trend coincided with slowing growth and mounting financial instability to produce for more than a decade a new pattern never witnessed before, so-called *stagflation* (combining "stagnation" and "inflation"). This inflation is different in nature, an indication of crisis rather than the result of strong growth of spending.

3.2.1 Cost-Push Inflation

There was an uptick in labor militancy during the late 1960s as workers tried to protect the threatened purchasing power of their wages amidst broader social movements for greater equality and peace. France's general strike of May 1968 and Italy's "Hot Autumn" of 1969 brought home with even greater urgency that the social contract tying real wage growth

[5] New economic phenomena always beget new economic theories, and so it was also the case with intra-industry trade. The so-called "New Trade Theories" stressing economies of scale and product differentiation were launched in the path-breaking article by Paul Krugman (1979). Product-cycle theory has been elaborated by Vernon (1966).

to productivity gains was coming to an end—and with it the postwar boom. Massive labor-market entry of new workers (women, minorities, baby-boomers) slowed productivity growth while rising inflationary pressures amidst full employment fueled worker demands for higher wages. The progressive erosion of the wage-productivity balance planted the seeds for demand-pull inflation at the end of a boom to turn into a different kind of (cost-push) inflation signaling a new type of structural crisis, the aforementioned stagflation. Slow growth, causing stagnant productivity, made for greater unit-cost pressures in response to which firms tried to maintain profit margins by raising output prices proportionately. This reaction seemed to have gained in intensity amidst steadily declining profit rates. Ultimately, firms tried to counter declining profitability by using the inflationary process to create accounting-based "paper" profits when booking their revenues in current dollars whereas costs were carried on corporate balance sheets at their original ("historic cost") level.

The stagflation process also fed an intensely redistributive dynamic as it deepened over the years. Inflation obviously favored those in a strong market position to raise prices disproportionately more than others, just as it hurt those on fixed incomes the most (retirees, minimum-wage-earners, etc.). There was also a temporal dimension to the inflationary process, benefitting those raising their prices earlier ahead of the generalized decline in the value of money and so incentivizing the acceleration of inflation. All these redistribution mechanisms depended on continuous accommodation by the monetary regime, which allowed accelerating lending (and thereby money creation) in response to nominally rising funding needs and credit demand by the public. But such accommodation was by no means a smooth affair. With the Fed capping interest rates (under its Regulation Q dating back to the Glass-Steagall Act of 1933) and failing to adjust those caps upward in the face of rising inflation, "real" interest rates would recurrently end up in negative territory which in turn would prompt creditors to refuse lending at such loss-incurring returns.

America's stagflation crisis thus unfolded in a series of successive credit crunches (e.g. 1966, 1969/70, 1973–1975, 1979/80, 1981/82) whenever accelerating inflation moved beyond interest-rate ceilings to shut down lending.[6] The cyclical dynamic of that crisis masked a deeper structural problem arising from the pro-debtor bias of the monetary regime in place. Not only were creditors restricted by fairly inflexible interest-rate caps how much they could charge on loans while also carrying lots of older fixed-rate loans now earning negative returns. But inflation also benefitted debtors who could repay their loans with devalued dollars. As both stagnation and inflation intensified from cycle to cycle, amidst progressively deeper credit crunches, the different pillars of the postwar monetary regime were torn apart one by one—and that is surely the most important legacy of the stagflation crisis rocking the 1970s.

3.2.2 The End of Bretton Woods

The progressive disintegration of the postwar monetary regime began early and with a bang. On August 15, 1971 the Nixon Administration suspended the convertibility guarantee of $35 per ounce of gold that had underpinned the international monetary system for over a quarter of a century. A confluence of three forces had led to this fateful demise of the postwar Bretton Woods system. Already by 1960 declining US gold reserves had stopped matching growing supplies of dollars circulating or held in reserve abroad, and this *de-facto* inconvertibility of dollars then necessitated a consensus among the industrial nations not to rock the boat by calling in too many dollars for conversion. Such consensus prevailed for a while, but started getting frayed with America's accelerating inflation in the late 1960s which rendered the dollar's overvaluation even more pronounced, especially against the low-inflation German mark and Japanese yen. In March 1968 the United States, in an attempt to preserve fixed exchange rates at set parities, entered into an agreement with six European countries to allow a higher market price for gold while maintaining at the same time the official gold-dollar parity. Such creation of a two-tiered pricing system for gold, a fairly modest adjustment compared to devaluing the dollar outright, might have worked had it not been for the increasingly violent speculative attacks on the overvalued dollar.

Where did those sudden waves of currency speculation come from? Here we need to pinpoint the emergence after 1960 of a new private

[6] Those recurrent credit crunches, which ended up marking the stagflation crisis as a period of intensifying financial instability, were succinctly analyzed by Wojnilower (1980) as well as Wolfson (1986).

banking network connecting the world's leading banks and operating beyond the reach of any central bank—the so-called *Eurocurrency Market* or "Euromarket" (see Sect. 1.1.4). Initially centered in London, this network soon engulfed the entire globe and began accepting deposits or making loans in dollars as well as other internationally accepted key currencies outside their respective country of issue. So-called "Eurodollars" first emerged when the Soviet Union, fearful of having its dollar holdings frozen by an increasingly hostile US government, asked London-based banks in 1959 to accept those reserves. The British government, wanting to assure London's (otherwise declining) status as the world's leading financial center, then allowed banks under its jurisdiction to offer deposits and make loans denominated in US dollars. Two electronic fund-transfer and communications networks, the Clearing House Interbank Payments System (CHIPS) set up in 1970 and the Society for Worldwide International Financial Telecommunications (SWIFT) introduced in 1973, provided the technological payments-system infrastructure to make the Euromarket global and include most banks of the world tied together in what is known as the "correspondent" system.[7]

For much of the 1960s that new global transnational banking network comprised mainly Eurodollars as the banks operating outside the United States absorbed the flood of excess dollars which US balance-of-payments deficits pumped into international circulation. But as the technological infrastructure of this network matured, it became easier for the Eurobanks and their international clientele to move funds from place to place and switch from one currency to another. When the chronic overvaluation of the dollar became de facto untenable amidst America's sudden acceleration of inflation in 1968, the Eurocurrencies market turned into a vehicle for diversifying out of dollars into marks, yen, or other currencies. These sell-offs would recurrently grow into concerted speculative attacks on the dollar whenever news of the day would confirm how much the dollar had become overvalued. The US announcement in June 1971 of its first trade deficit since 1873 was in that context one such speculation-triggering news item, and two months later Bretton Woods was dead!

[7] See also Einzig (1973), McKinnon (1977), and Gibson (1989) for meaningful discussions of the Eurocurrency market as a transformative leap in the development of international finance.

3.2.3 *The Eurocurrency Market Revisited*

We have to grasp the strategic significance of the Eurocurrency markets as a quantum leap in the development of money and banking. Its origins, moving the Soviet Union's dollar-denominated assets beyond America's reach, coincided with the restoration of currency convertibility permitting free exchange of national monies and Bretton Woods' initial dollar shortage turning into its opposite, an excess supply of dollars getting pumped into international circulation in the wake of America's growing balance of payments deficits. These international dollars were now getting absorbed by a transnational network of commercial banks operating beyond the jurisdiction of central banks, hence outside their regulatory reach and official payments system. It did not take long for the Euromarket to absorb other internationally accepted currencies, such as pounds, marks, or yen, and to provide banks with easy access of funds from other banks. Turning rapidly into a potent vehicle of financial globalization while bypassing Bretton Woods' official central-bank-controlled payments system, the Eurocurrency market co-existed as an essentially unregulated "stateless" banking system parallel to tightly regulated domestic banking systems. Since businesses, rich individuals, and all sorts of non-bank financial institutions could move funds in and out of the Eurocurrency markets on short notice, that global banking network undermined in one swoop pretty much all domestic banking regulations by facilitating their effective circumvention. Just as much as the Euromarket had to be incorporated into the international monetary system after the demise of Bretton Woods, its omnipresence also forced the systemic dismantling of domestic regulatory barriers on money and banking. The Euromarket thus turned into the vehicle for a new dollar standard, a process that went through several chapters over a couple of decades before leading us into a new finance-dominated accumulation regime during the 1980s.

Having already turned into a platform of currency speculation during the late 1960s, Eurobanks became the vector of a devastating attack on the overvalued US dollar during the summer of 1971. Nixon's suspension of the dollar-gold link at the heart of Bretton Woods on August 15, 1971 opened the way for a broad realignment of exchange rates that had not been properly adjusted for decades. A half-hearted attempt by the leading industrial nations to redefine a system of fixed (and newly adjusted) exchange rates without any anchor in the aftermath of Bretton

Woods' demise, the so-called Smithsonian Agreement of December 1971, was blown to bits by continued speculative runs on the dollar which the United States finally let float in March 1973. Since then we have had a system of flexible (i.e. market-determined) exchange rates for the US-dollar to which the rest of the world has had to adjust one way or another, a key feature of the emerging dollar standard.

Sharp dollar depreciation helped push the once-low prices of dollar-denominated commodities rapidly higher. This stagflation-feeding trend accelerated greatly when oil prices quadrupled in October 1973, facilitated by an oil-supply embargo triggered by Arab oil-exporting nations (e.g. Saudi Arabia, Kuwait) in the wake of the Yom Kippur war with Israel. Capital controls, made essentially ineffective by the presence of an alternative global capital-flow circuit organized by the leading banks in the Euromarket, began to be dismantled in 1974. In the wake of that oil-price explosion the Euromarket started an elaborate petro-dollar recycling circuit whereby its Eurobanks loaned out the surpluses of the oil-exporting nations (OPEC) to developing countries now having to foot much larger import bills thanks to higher energy prices.

In June 1974 the failure of a small German bank, the Herrstatt Bank, in the wake of losses from currency speculation triggered a foreign-exchange crisis which for the first time led to calls for reining in this highly volatile Eurocurrency market. In the Basel Concordat of 1975 the world's leading central banks agreed to cooperate in the face of a financial crisis spilling beyond national boundaries, reviving thereby a supranational institution known as the Bank for International Settlements as their main coordinating mechanism.[8]

3.2.4 *Saving the US Dollar as World Money*

The Herrstatt crisis froze the Euromarket which in turn set off a deep global recession lasting throughout 1975. The unusually deep and long downturn intensified discussions how to adjust the international monetary system after the fall of Bretton Woods, but also made any collective approach more difficult as national and regional interests took

[8] The Basel Concordat set up the Basel Committee for Banking Supervision within the BIS' governance structure. The BCBS would later become the global Euromarket's primary banking regulator, starting with the Basel Agreement of 1988 all the way to Basel III in 2010.

center stage. The Europeans could not agree how best to meet the threat of a steadily depreciating dollar to their industrial competitiveness. Fearing that an especially pronounced appreciation of its currency would hurt its firms disproportionately and put a lot of strain on Europe's economic-integration ambitions, Germany wanted the nine members of the European Community to have their currencies float together against the dollar by maintaining fixed exchange rates among them. The EC's other large economies—France, Italy, Britain—wanted no part of that, preferring instead to depreciate their currencies in what turned ultimately into futile "competitive devaluations" canceling each other out while putting upward pressure on their domestic interest and inflation rates as their currencies too became objects of speculation-driven sell-offs. The Germans, in the meantime, tied currencies of their smaller neighbors to the mark in a fixed-rate arrangement known as the "snake" (short for "snake in a tunnel" depicting the arrangement's intended objective of limiting exchange-rate movements to small ups-and-downs within a tightly set ± 2.25% band). The Japanese economy, continuing to run large trade surpluses despite a steadily appreciating yen, became the target of intensifying tensions with Europe and the United States which led to the most ambitious GATT-sponsored trade-liberalization negotiations yet—the so-called Tokyo Round (1975–1979)—targeting for the first time also non-tariff barriers such as anti-dumping duties and preferential government procurement practices.

Amidst these divergent trends the Jamaica Accords of 1976 brought intense post-Bretton Woods discussions of international monetary reform to a minimalist conclusion pretty much enshrining the status quo. Gold's role as world money was officially ended. Countries were allowed to choose their exchange-rate regimes, provided those did not hurt others. And the International Monetary Fund saw its intervention capacity somewhat enhanced. Most importantly, the new accord gave license to continue the world-money status of the US currency as such, thus providing an official *de jure* imprimatur for the dollar standard in its second post-Bretton Woods iteration. But the US dollar still had to justify this privilege de facto by regaining international credibility. This required restoring global confidence in America's ability to manage its currency properly amidst a decade-long accumulation of financial instability.

America's unabated intensification of stagflation pressures during the second half of the 1970s triggered a drawn-out speculative attack on the dollar in 1978 which the Carter Administration was not able to stop despite increasingly frantic efforts to alter its policy mix. On the contrary, Carter's zig-zagging policy switches from stimulation to restraint and back created even more nervousness among currency traders. At that point it had become clear that Keynesian counter-cyclical stabilization policy, a postwar mainstay ever since Britain and the United States had passed their respective Employment Act(s) in 1946, was becoming increasingly counter-productive in a stagflation-type crisis. Switching constantly between targeting inflation or fighting unemployment created such uncertainty as to aggravate both. Here, in this policy conundrum, were planted the seeds for the subsequent conservative counter-revolution known as Reaganomics which rocked the world in the early 1980s.

In the meantime, however, the accelerating fall of the dollar over a year and a half led to growing signs that the world was getting ready to go beyond the dollar standard. Three developments coincided to push in this direction:

- OPEC countries had begun to discuss being paid for their oil in a basket of currencies rather than just dollars.
- The European Community managed to extend the mark-led "snake" to a much more far-ranging European Monetary System. The EMS included France and Italy, later on even Britain. It introduced the so-called Exchange Rate Mechanism (ERM) which set fixed exchange rates both bilaterally as well as against a weighted currency basket known as the European Currency Unit (ECU), giving the German mark a good deal of weight in the new system. Any exchange-rate adjustment had to be symmetrical which lessened the burden typically borne by the weaker deficit countries. A new European Monetary Cooperation Fund (EMCF) was empowered to issue actual ECUs for member countries to use as reserves and settle official payment obligations among themselves.[9]
- Finally, the IMF was considering setting up a so-called Substitution Account allowing excess dollars to be swapped against IMF-issued Special Drawing Rights serving as alternative international reserve asset. Such an arrangement would give SDRs much greater importance, compared to the rather marginal presence they have had since

[9] For more information on the EMS and its different components see Cohen (1981), Coffey (1984), and Ferri (1990).

their introduction in 1969, gradually making them a world-money alternative to the US dollars.

It was against this troubling background, punctuated by the dollar's steepening slide pushing US inflation way above ten percent, that newly appointed Federal Reserve Chair Paul Volcker abandoned the Fed's decades-long low-interest policy on October 6, 1979. Three weeks later the Fed's key policy rate had tripled to 21 percent, triggering a deep two-step recession whose second half—in 1981/82—finally broke America's inflationary fever at the expense of unemployment rates approaching 11 percent. Volcker's audacious policy move spurred a much more widespread deregulation of interest rates over the next three years which other countries adopted as well. His historic policy shift also saved the status of the US dollar as world money.

3.3 The Rise of Finance-Led Capitalism

In the midst of this dramatic denouement of the stagflation crisis conservative Republican Ronald Reagan won the election in November 1980, just a bit more than a year after "Iron Lady" Margaret Thatcher had taken the helm in Britain with a similar commitment to radical change. The Thatcher-Reagan reforms were at heart a conservative counter-revolution against Keynesianism, aimed at reducing the role of the state in the economy and restoring the power of "free market" forces as prescribed by the neoliberal "Austrian School" economist Friedrich Hayek, Monetarist Milton Friedman, and supply-side guru Arthur Laffer.[10]

3.3.1 The Reagan Revolution

The policy shift to the right under Reagan (and Thatcher in the UK) meant in practice rolling back cumbersome regulations of key sectors and activities in the economy, privatizing state enterprises, attacking trade unions, cutting social welfare programs, and sharply lowering taxes. Reagan's 1981 tax cuts and 1986 tax reform lowered the top tax rate from 70 to 28 percent, reduced the number of tax brackets while also

[10] Meaningful references of key works by these influential conservative economists are Hayek (1944), Friedman (1962), as well as Canto et al. (1983).

indexing them for inflation, and offered especially attractive tax rates on capital gains to boost investments. At the same time Reagan also launched a huge military spending program, ostensibly to stretch the Soviet Union beyond its limits trying to keep pace in the arms race, which had the effect of stimulating economic activity across the nation. His "Star Wars" program amounted to a (not so) disguised industrial-policy boost for future "growth" industries such as space technology, advanced materials, supercomputing, as well as laser technology and high-energy physics. These measures helped launch a durable low-inflation recovery in the United States, boosted further when the Fed started in November 1982 to nudge previously sky-high "real" interest rates gradually lower—a slow and often halting process that took more than a decade to complete.

Reagan's pro-growth policy mix also boosted the standing of the US dollar, rendered additionally attractive by America's comparatively high "real" interest rates, sharply lower domestic inflation rates having stabilized in the 2–4 percent range, and stock-market boom. From June 1980 to March 1985 large capital inflows into the US dollar caused its real effective exchange rate against a basket of currencies of America's most important trading partners, adjusted for inflation, to rise by 52 percent. This unprecedented currency appreciation caused US exports to come under considerable pressure, turning an initially balanced external position into a large current-account deficit (reaching 3.5 percent of GDP) on top of what had by then also become a massive budget deficit . Such twin deficits were not sustainable. In October 1985 the Reagan Administration concluded the so-called *Plaza Agreement* with its allies Britain, France, Germany and Japan to coordinate an orderly devaluation of the US dollar. After the dollar had fallen by over 40 percent over the next year and a half, the partners, including this time also Canada, decided in the *Louvre Agreement* of February 1987 to stabilize the dollar through coordinated central bank interventions in currency markets and simultaneous interest-rate adjustments. This important experiment in exchange-rate stabilization did not last long, petering out in the aftermath of the stock-market crash of October 1987. But the lessons of its failure may well be worth further reflection if we ever feel compelled to consider keeping exchange rates of several internationally traded currencies within an adjustable band rather than have them float freely against each other (see Sect. 7.4).[11]

3.3.2 *The "Washington Consensus" as the Global Dimension of the Reagan Revolution*

America's exit from the stagflation crisis, in the wake of dramatic interest-rate hikes and the squeeze of a double-digit recession, triggered a global financial crisis in August 1982 when Argentina, Brazil, and Mexico all declared themselves in imminent default on their foreign debt. Volcker's tightening move had dramatically increased these countries' debt-servicing charges (as most of their dollar-denominated Euromarket loans carried variable rates). And the subsequent downturn had pushed their export earnings much lower as a result of falling sales and lower commodity prices. Many other lesser developed countries (LDCs) in Latin America, Africa, Asia, and even Eastern Europe faced the same double whammy. This so-called *LDC Debt Crisis*, engulfing over fifty countries facing debt-servicing problems, posed a major threat to many leading banks active in the Euromarket where those sovereign loans had originated as part of the aforementioned "petro-dollar recycling" (see Sect. 3.2.3). Together Argentina, Brazil, and Mexico had borrowed the equivalent of 225 percent of the capital base of the nine largest American banks, thus putting in one swoop the entire US banking system at risk.

The crisis required a new international lender-of-last-resort mechanism where de-facto defaulting countries accepted structural-adjustment programs imposed by the International Monetary Fund which served as "green light" for new loans, rescheduling of old debt, and eventual debt restructuring. This crisis management bought banks time to take whatever losses slowly while debtor countries experienced dramatic recessions and undertook far-reaching reforms imposed by the IMF. The IMF required developing countries to get their budget deficits under control, widen their tax base while lowering tax rates, privatize state enterprises, invest in infrastructure and social goods (health, education) while cutting subsidies, deregulate industry, allow interest rates to be determined by market forces, adopt competitive exchange rates, strengthen property

[11] The theoretical framework underpinning the Louvre Agreement's attempt at exchange-rate coordination, the idea of so-called "target zones," was introduced first by Williamson (1986).

rights, remove trade barriers, and open their doors for foreign direct investment. These neoliberal prescriptions were summarily referred to as the "Washington Consensus."[12] The crisis was resolved some five years later with the introduction of US backed sovereign bonds (known as "Brady bonds") replacing LDC loans at lower face value as a way to write down unsustainable debts in (fifteen) debtor countries deemed to have succeeded with their reforms.

Those pro-market reforms, while imposed by the center on the periphery in the midst of a systemic financial crisis , addressed a much deeper structural problem hitting scores of developing economies across the planet in the early 1980s—the exhaustion of the post-colonial "import-substitution" model of industrialization and its single-party political superstructure underpinning a highly interventionist and protectionist state. That model could not sustain initially high growth rates as its "national champions" turned into inefficient monopolies, protection of local markets became a source of corruption, crucial public goods (infrastructure, health services, education) withered, and rapid population growth created jobs crisis for the youth. The LDC debt crisis of 1982–1987 thus served as catapult for a different development path of these hitherto closed post-colonial societies, one centered on their progressive integration into the capitalist world economy in return for greater access to capital. The Brady bonds served as springboard for a new global sovereign bond market which tied these developing countries to global finance as they transformed into "emerging markets." A similar transition occurred in centrally planned ("communist") economies following the disintegration of the Soviet Union and collapse of its "empire" starting in November 1989. Within a decade over three billion people previously cut off from the rest of the world were thus all of a sudden thrust into the world economy—a demographic shock which rendered the 1990s a period of far-reaching domestic policy reforms, volatile transition scenarios, social tensions, and recurrent financial instability in the form of currency crises.

[12] The term "Washington Consensus" was first coined by John Williamson in 1989 (see Williamson, 2004) to refer to the simultaneous adoption of neoliberal "free-market" policy preferences in the early 1980s by three crucial Washington-based agencies—the US Treasury, IMF, and World Bank—exerting huge influence on policy-making in the rest of the world.

In this rather chaotic context 1994 proved to be a crucial moment, a year in which key countries facing difficult transition paths finally got their act together. Mexico survived a major currency crisis and civil war to hook its economy much more tightly to those of the United States and Canada under the auspices of the North American Free Trade Agreement (NAFTA). Brazil, the largest economy of Latin America, got its hyper-inflation under control and launched a successful recovery program with the so-called "Plano Real." Having gone through two bouts of violent currency crises in 1992/3, the European Union finally moved decisively toward implementation of its single-market and single-currency projects. Nelson Mandela became president of South Africa and began to push Africa's largest economy out of its apartheid turmoil. Manmohan Singh's ambitious reform program of the early 1990s started taking root in India. Last but not least, China set off its decades-long fast-growth path with a flurry of fiscal, regulatory, and political devolution reforms that it punctuated with a 40 percent devaluation of its currency to render its products irresistibly cheap in world markets.

We should also note here that during the same year (1994) America's central bank struck a preemptive interest-rate hike out of the blue whose widespread reaction of market tumult ultimately set the stage for a low-inflation growth path managed with increasing effectiveness by the Federal Reserve. Greenspan's monetary-policy coup reinforced the Fed's credibility as an inflation fighter. Coupled with an increased emphasis on communication, the US central bank managed from then on to jawbone long-term bond yields over which it did not have direct control, but which it could influence by shaping market expectations of future inflation and growth.[13] As these rates moved (not least in response to Fed statements), they would in turn affect demand for mortgages and home-loan re-financings, construction activity, business investments, and exchange rates—all strategic determinants of macroeconomic performance which would spill over to the rest of the world via ever-growing US current-account deficits.

[13] After 1994 the Federal Reserve began to implement a multi-faceted and increasingly sophisticated strategy of communication consisting of post-meeting statements by its policy-making FOMC, policy action announcements, congressional testimony of its chairman, press conferences, and forward-guidance clarifications of future policy intentions. For more on the evolution of the Fed's communication strategy see Bernanke (2013).

3.3.3 *The Transformation of Finance*

This much enhanced influence of US monetary policy had its roots in a more profound transformation of America's economy into what I have elsewhere (Guttmann, 2008, 2016) characterized as "finance-led capitalism." In that new type of capitalism variable interest rates came to occupy a strategic double role as key determinants of prices for financial assets (stocks, bonds) and of credit demand, both of which had gained much greater importance due to the increasingly financialized nature of capital accumulation. Such *financialization* refers beyond the growing importance of financial assets and liabilities in the balance sheets of non-financial actors also to the primacy of financial motives in their decision-making, the extraordinary expansion of financial institutions and markets, and a growth pattern relying more than ever on easy access to credit as well as on asset bubbles.[14]

The centrality of finance is a byproduct of its thorough deregulation which ultimately went beyond exchange rates (March 1973), capital controls (June 1974), and interest rates (October 1979) to include the progressive abolition during much of the 1980s and 1990s of long-standing regulatory barriers separating the different types of finance—commercial banking, investment banking, insurance, fund management, asset management. Of key importance in that regard were the European Commission's Second Banking Directive of 1989 and the Clinton Administration's Financial Services Modernization (Gramm-Bliley-Leach) Act of 1999 both of which deregulated the financial structure of the European Union and the United States, respectively. The emergence of *universal banks* integrating all the different functions of finance under one roof created a new layer of much larger ("too big to fail") banks whose money creation capacity became more often directed toward the collective self-expansion of increasingly connected financial institutions and markets rather than mostly funding production or consumption activities. Gaining access to short-term borrowings on demand in the rapidly evolving money markets, banks were no longer constrained by their deposit base in terms of how much they could grow. Whereas before they

[14] Key contributions on the "financialization" phenomenon are Stockhammer (2004), Epstein (2005), Krippner (2005), Bellamy Foster (2007), Hein and Van Treeck (2010), Fine (2013), and Lapavitsas (2013). In Guttmann (2016) I provide an overview of what separates and unites these different heterodox approaches on the question of financialization.

had to match their deposit liabilities with liquid assets to meet eventual withdrawals, now they simply set whatever asset growth they wished to target and then fund those commitments in the money markets. That more aggressive posture enabled banks to survive two fundamental structural changes which otherwise could have threatened their commanding position. For one, bank deposits were increasingly crowded out by all kinds of funds—pension funds, mutual funds, hedge funds, private-equity funds, index funds, exchange-traded funds, and so forth—as primary form of saving yielding higher returns. And bank loans gave increasingly way to securities as principal form of credit, a trend not least reinforced by all these different funds buying those tradeable claims. Deregulation made exchange rates and interest rates much more volatile which spurred speculation as well as hedging strategies using new financial derivatives (futures, options, swaps). Computerization led to electronic fund transfers at the heart of the payments system and transformed financial markets into electronic communications networks, a technological revolution speeding up transactions and boosting their volume.

The banks, the largest of which had operated transnationally ever since the emergence of the Eurocurrency market in the 1960s and then turned themselves into multi-functional universal banks, were given a global regulatory framework based on supervised self-regulation. At first, following the resolution of the LDC debt crisis in 1987, there was an international effort to bring the hitherto unregulated Euromarket operations of the world's leading banks under some kind of regulatory constraint for better risk-return calculation. This was supposed to be done under the auspices of the Bank for International Settlements, the Basel-based umbrella of the world's leading central banks, obliging the banks to set aside more capital for riskier loans more likely to cause default losses. The Basel Accord of 1988 imposed on banks a risk-weighted capital-asset ratio of 8 percent, the so-called Cooke Ratio. The risk targeted here was credit risk (i.e. probability of default) on bank loans classified into five broad categories each of which carried different weights (and hence different capital requirements). But banks decided early on that this mechanism was too blunt, inasmuch as its broad categories grouped together a great variety of loans with vastly different risk profiles. Banks decided to sell off their low-risk loans for which the new capital requirement was considered too high, thereby giving an enormous boost to loan securitizations. At the same time they kept their high-risk loans, for which the required capital protection was considered a good deal, and then insured those with credit default swaps. These steps of "regulatory escape" had the perverse effect of encouraging banks to get rid of their best loans and hold on to their riskier loans, thus defeating the initial purpose of Basel I. Follow-up agreements in 1996 and 2004, together referred to as "Basel II," then asked banks to calculate their own capital requirement for every asset on their balance sheet while expanding the risk weighting beyond credit risk (i.e. loans) to market risk (i.e. securities) and operational risk. The transnational banks responded to this regulatory adjustment both by systematically underestimating the riskiness of their asset items and by creating a whole new "shadow" banking system off their balance sheets beyond the reach of the BIS. Either reaction left the banks severely undercapitalized and hence ill-prepared for a major crisis, such as the one they would eventually end up facing in spectacular fashion during 2007/08.

3.3.4 *Three Consecutive Asset Bubbles*

This transformation of finance, driven forward relentlessly by its simultaneous deregulation, computerization, and globalization amidst wave after wave of financial innovation, had to anchor itself institutionally at the center of capitalism to render that system finance-led. And such centering occurred early on, in the 1980s, in the wake of a historic stock-market bubble. The disinflation shock of the 1979–1982 double-dip recession had left most US corporations suddenly deprived of their nominal "paper profit" gains and seriously undervalued in the stock market. In the course of the non-inflationary recovery after 1983 many of those firms faced hostile takeover bids by a group of aggressive investors known as "corporate raiders" (Ivan Boesky, Carl Icahn, T. Boone Pickens, etc.) and/or private-equity funds (e.g. Kohlberg Kravis Roberts) all of whom were funded by issuing so-called "junk" bonds—a crucial financial innovation.[15] In the face of such targeted attacks on key US corporations which rippled through their respective sectors and thus came to engulf much

[15] These "junk" bonds, the invention of financier Michael Milken at investment bank Drexel Burnham, carried high yields, because they were rated below investment grade and thus off-limits for pension funds and mutual funds. Still, Milken managed to create a large market for these bonds so that they became a funding machine for hostile takeover bids and leveraged buy-outs shaking corporate America to the core. Milken's fascinating story, the collapse of Drexel in 1990, and the reorganization of "junk" bonds into "high-yield" bonds are recounted in Abelson et al. (2015) as well as Cohan (2017).

of the American economy, institutional investors (pension funds, insurance companies, mutual funds) often sided with management only under the condition that the latter promised to make rising share prices its overriding priority. This dictate of shareholder value maximization was further reinforced during the "bull" market of the 1980s by the widespread adoption of stock options as the principal form of compensation for top managers, rendered even more attractive by the low (post-Reagan) taxes on capital gains. Once CEOs had made stock prices their overriding concern, they became more inclined to undertake ruthless cost cutting (which prompted massive industrial restructuring in the United States during the 1980s and 1990s), use much of the firm's cash to buy back shares, push expansion through mergers and acquisitions rather than invest in new productive capacity, and prioritize quarterly earnings (on which managerial bonuses depended) over longer-term objectives. Most corporations thus came to be dominated by financial motives crowding out commercial or industrial objectives.

The stock-market bubble on Wall Street ended spectacularly in late October 1987. Its burst was followed by a recession in 1990/91 in the wake of the "thrift" crisis (involving the collapse of over 1,000 savings and loans associations). Greenspan's Fed flooded the economy with liquidity in the early 1990s (until the aforementioned monetary policy reversal in 1994). Out of that emerged another stock-market bubble dominating the second half of the 1990s, the so-called "dot-com" boom responding to the extremely rapid growth of the internet as a potential medium of e-commerce. That bubble was fueled not least by the transformation of the NASDAQ into a stock market for high-tech firms (which rose by 400 percent from 1995 to its peak in March 2000) and by initial public offerings creating huge gains for internet entrepreneurs, venture capitalists as well as investment banks alike even though many of the dot-com firms thus taken public had yet to earn a profit. The recession of 2000/01 following the bursting of that bubble once again prompted massive Fed easing, and this extremely accommodative US monetary policy encouraged a recovery after 2002 which turned into a boom shortly thereafter.

Neither of the two bubbles compared in scale and intensity to the third bubble, that of housing in the 2000s, whose combination of rapidly rising prices for homes across the nation and easy mortgage (re)financings enabled millions of Americans to draw instant cash from their increased real-estate equity. Securitization made possible a dramatic expansion of real-estate lending as banks got rid of their mortgages as soon as they could, thereby greatly accelerating the turnover of their loan commitments. With two-thirds of American households owning homes and banks pushing mortgage products aggressively, the strength of this bubble—both its width and its length—was exceptional. Its macroeconomic impact, fueled by a massive wealth effect affecting millions of Americans in their decisions and behavior, manifested itself in continuously rising excess consumer spending, a shrinking private savings rate actually turning negative after April 2005, growing current-account deficits peaking in 2007 at minus 7.8 percent of GDP in 2007, and a build-up of fixed-cost household debt matched by much more volatile real-estate assets rendering those debtors prone to financial fragility.[16]

America's "bubble" economy connected in mutually feeding fashion with the rest of the world as its rising current-account deficits absorbed a large percentage, almost three-quarters by 2007, of the trade surpluses of industrial nations (e.g. Germany, Japan) and emerging-market economies (e.g. China). After a traumatic global currency crisis of 1997–1999 had cut a huge swath from Thailand to Argentina (via the rest of East Asia, Russia, and Brazil), many EMEs committed to large external surpluses through export-led growth, a build-up of foreign-exchange reserves as protective buffer, and recycling those to the United States. European and Asian banks preferred to put much of their excess dollar-denominated cash into higher yielding mortgage-backed securities rated triple-A rather than US Treasuries or corporate bonds, thereby feeding America's housing bubble and the global recycling circuit sustaining it. So once again we end up having an international monetary system, this time the reconfigured dollar standard, help periphery countries catch up with the center during an upswing phase, here of finance-led capitalism, until that growth pattern exploded in a global financial crisis, the Great Recession of 2007–2009, signaling a turning point in the long wave.

[16] Fed Chair Alan Greenspan himself analyzed the housing bubble, wanting to know how its "wealth effect" of making households richer would impact on their behavior (see Greenspan & Kennedy, 2005). For additional influential empirical studies of the wealth effect see Case et al. (2005) or Carroll and Zhou (2010).

3.4 The Great Recession, a Systemic Crisis

The financial crisis of 2007/08 was a systemic crisis affecting in paralyzing fashion large segments of the financial system on a global scale. Such systemic crises have the (admittedly costly) advantage of revealing hitherto unknown features of the economy because of the tensions and ruptures arising in their course. This was certainly true for the shadow banking system, the locus of the crisis, which not even its practitioners had understood as an integrated system before it came to haunt the world in 2007 and 2008. Shadow banking, an unregulated part of finance escaping supervision and accountability, had grown rapidly over a decade or so to absorb between a quarter and a third of the total financial sector. It has had many local configurations, as in China or India where it thrived in circumvention of heavily regulated domestic banking. Its dollar-denominated variant, however, was a global affair from its very inception in the mid-1990s as it managed to attract a growing portion of the dollars in international circulation getting recycled back into the United States by offering attractive returns compared to lower-yield Treasuries and bank deposits. Those foreign investments fed both America's loan-securitization machine spawning attractively priced, highly rated mortgage-backed securities as well as the money markets providing funds on short notice in support of large asset portfolios. With those two pillars of shadow banking assured steady supplies of funds from all over the world, US banks were able to finance an ever-growing real-estate bubble while at the same time enabling homeowners to cash in on the appreciation of their homes for a huge consumer-spending boom that turned Americans into the buyers of the last resort for the rest of the world. Having thus created a bubble-fed growth pattern spanning the globe, the bursting of that bubble from March 2007 onward was bound to have devastating consequences for the entire world economy.[17]

[17] Among the best accounts of the progressive pillar-by-pillar disintegration of the dollar-based shadow-banking system during 2007/08 are Lewis (2010) or the Financial Crisis Inquiry Commission (2011). See also the opening chapter of Guttmann (2016) for a somewhat different take of how and why the shadow-banking system driving the housing bubble fell apart.

3.4.1 Bursting of America's Real Estate Bubble

America's housing market, which had already shown strong growth in the 1980s and 1990s, got pushed toward a historic boom during the 2000s thanks to the spread of unorthodox mortgages (like the "sub-primes" offered to less creditworthy borrowers), easier re-financings (at larger principals reflecting increased collateral values amidst rapidly rising home prices), and the growing popularity of home-equity loans giving homeowners access to borrowed cash that could be used for any purpose. Banks could move mortgage loans off their books by setting up nominally independent special-purpose vehicles, known as "structured investment vehicles." These SIVs organized an increasingly complex infrastructure of loan securitizations in such a way that a large portion of their securitization products (mortgage-backed securities, collateralized debt obligations, asset-backed commercial paper) could be given fail-safe AAA ratings and hence sold to investors across the globe. As the housing boom turned into a bubble thanks to its access to a huge funding pipeline of hundreds of billions of dollars in international circulation being recycled back into the United States, a gigantic shadow-banking system formed as an opaque network of commercial banks, SIVs, investment banks, hedge funds, and money-market funds connecting loans, asset-backed securities, derivatives, repos and other money-market instruments into a tightly interwoven web of commitments and intermediations.

All asset bubbles eventually come to an end. And when big ones burst, their demise can do a lot of damage rippling through the economy and rocking the financial system. This one was no exception. Eventually speculation-driven housing-price appreciation became unsustainable. Demand for homes and/or mortgage loans saturated. Add to this the Fed's gradual tightening which started to bite after seventeen quarter-point interest hikes in a row had moved the Federal funds rate from 1 percent in June 2004 to 5.25 percent in August 2006 (where it stayed for a year). The moment housing prices started declining in key regions in early 2007, riskier borrowers using sub-primes and other unorthodox mortgages defaulted in large numbers which caused losses big enough to eat up the lower-rated tranches of mortgage-backed securities as well as collateralized debt obligations and trigger confidence-shaking downgrades of their AAA-rated tranches. That in turn set off a fateful chain reaction involving the collapse of the loan securitization machine (with many MBS and CDOs worthless), repeated panic runs targeting asset-backed commercial paper issued by the SIVs which destabilized the money markets (e.g. triggering "haircuts" in the repo market), the defaults of these bank-sponsored intermediaries, big losses for undercapitalized banks from those SIV defaults, a series of spectacular bank failures during 2008, and their expensive bail-outs.[18]

3.4.2 The Collapse of Lehman Brothers

The crisis reached its peak when Lehman Brothers collapsed in mid-September 2008. The Bush Administration has always claimed that it did not have the authority to bail out an investment bank. The reality is that it could have, not least by invoking the Fed's so-called Sect. 13(3) emergency lending powers long enough to have arranged a Lehman takeover by UK bank Barclays which was in the works at the time. More likely, the Bush Administration, long worried of feeding the moral-hazard problem following so many earlier bail-outs, wanted to set an example and thereby re-impose a modicum of market discipline on the banking sector. Ironically, the Lehman bankruptcy and subsequent liquidation did not cause that much of a problem, as even the much-maligned credit default swaps kicked in properly to do their job as prescribed.

What triggered the subsequent super-panic were related losses from Lehman's debt securities by America's oldest (and hence well-known) money-market fund Reserve Primary which forced it to declare a temporary suspension of the so-called "net asset value rule" maintaining the share value of MMFs at $1 per share at all times, a sacrosanct promise designed to reassure the public that whatever amount put into a money-market fund would be preserved dollar for dollar so that MMF shares could be considered as safe as government-insured bank deposits. When Reserve Primary "broke the buck" on September 16, a panic ensued withdrawing $300bn. from the $3.7tr. MMF sector in just three days until the US Treasury stepped in with a so-called Temporary Guaranty Program insuring money-market fund shares. At this point, however, the world economy faced an intense credit crunch which would trigger in short order the worst economic downturn since the Great Depression.

[18] On the panics of the ABCP market see Tett et al. (2007) or Covitz et al. (2013). For more on the repo run, which shrank what the authors characterized as "private shadow money" by $3 trillion during the 2007–2009 crisis, see Gorton and Metrick (2009) and Garcia (2012).

3.4.3 *The Great Recession of 2008/09*

A systemic financial crisis: like the: one hitting the US economy and beyond from mid-2007 to mid-2009 is tantamount to a huge shock. One meaningful way to demonstrate this kind of shock is to trace the sudden and dramatic shifts in the macroeconomic sectoral balances juxtaposing savings S and business investment I in the private sector, government spending G and tax revenues T in the public sector, as well as exports of goods and services X and imports of goods and services M in the external sector, as defined by the equation $X - M = (S - I) + (T - G)$.[19] During the speculative housing bubble preceding the crisis American households had ended up with a gradually increasing negative savings rate, reaching an astounding minus 3.1 percent of GDP at the peak in March 2007 according to the national income and product accounts data collected by the US Bureau of Economic Analysis. This is itself a bubble-related phenomenon, as American homeowners drew cash from their (steadily rising) home equity through widespread refinancing of their mortgages while at the same time also succumbing to a wealth effect in the wake of bubble-driven capital gains, whether realized or not. A few months later the housing bubble burst, refinancing disappeared, and euphoria gave way to panic amidst a deepening credit crunch. Facing rising debt servicing charges while increasingly cut off from new funds and getting deeply worried about their future, households started to hoard cash desperately which by May 2009 had pushed up savings to 6.9 percent of GDP. This huge 10 percent shift reversed America's private-sector balance $(S - I)$ from a 2.5 percent deficit to a positive 7.6 percent over the same two-year period, and that surplus was set to grow further in the aftermath of recession-induced slashing of investment outlays by business.

Such a major reversal in the private-sector balance in just two years will feed rapidly through the other two balances. Normally, inter-sectoral adjustments get transmitted through corresponding price changes (including interest rates and exchange rates) and/or policy responses. Other than those two adjustment mechanisms the sectoral balances react to each other through changes in the growth dynamic. Everything else held constant, a 10 percent shift from private-sector deficit to surplus

[19] This equation derives from putting together Keynes' (1936) aggregate demand function $Y = C + I_g + G + (X - M)$ and national-income function $Y = C + S + T$ as two sides of the same coin.

amounts to a massive cut in aggregate demand triggering near-depression conditions, especially when the shift is so sudden and violent that neither price-induced nor policy-driven adjustments have enough time to unfold as countervailing forces. The sharp downturn of the US economy especially during the fourth quarter of 2008 and first half of 2009 helped lower its current-account deficit (X – M) from minus 5.1 percent to minus 2.5 percent over those nine months. This reversal, of course, hit other countries that had become dependent on large American external deficits for their export-led growth. At the same time we also saw a remarkably rapid adjustment in America's public-sector balance (T – G) from a budget deficit of minus 2.4 percent of GDP in mid-2008 to minus 10 percent a year later. Some of that adjustment, perhaps a third, arose as the automatic fiscal stabilizers kicked in forcefully in response to the sharp recession lowering tax-revenue collections across the board (local property taxes, state sales taxes, federal income taxes, etc.) while at the same time triggering larger outlays in federal income-support programs (e.g. unemployment benefits, food stamps). But the other two-thirds of the dramatic budget deficit increase during the Great Recession came from discretionary policy action, notably passage of the Bush Administration's $700 billion Troubled Asset Relief Program (TARP) in late September 2008 and Obama's $787 billion stimulus package passed in February 2009.[20] The latter helped put the US economy on a path to recovery after nine months of near-depression conditions (from September 2008 to June 2009).

3.5 The Federal Reserve's Crisis Management

While fiscal policy did its job of injecting spending power into the economy to compensate for both private sector and external sector pulling back sharply at the same time, a systemic financial crisis puts the onus of rapid and substantial policy response at first on the central bank. When credit freezes up as happened after the collapse of Lehman Brothers in September 2008, it is as if the economy had suffered the equivalent of a

[20] The TARP funds were initially used for recapitalization of America's fifteen largest financial institutions which amounted to a partial nationalization of the banking system. Later Obama also used TARP funds to bail out General Motors and Chrysler in 2009. His stimulus package was a political balancing act combining tax cuts, aid for hard-pressed state and local governments, and infrastructure spending.

heart attack. There is precious little time before the patient dies, in this case having the credit-starved economy thrown into a debt-deflation spiral of the kind described by Irving Fisher (1933) which pushes economies into depression. The spiral starts with a bubble bursting, setting off a scramble for cash, pull-back of credit, forced asset sales, falling prices, defaults and bankruptcies as the burden of debt is made heavier by deflation. It is then up to the central bank to throw the kitchen sink at the spiral before it has a chance to pull the economy under its grip. This is exactly what the Fed ended up doing, managing to stave off self-feeding debt deflation with a stunning array of interventions.

3.5.1 The Fed's Section 13(3) Emergency Lending

In the wake of Lehman's collapse the Fed slashed the two short-term interest rates under its direct control, the so-called Federal funds rate in the domestic inter-bank market and the discount rate charged when lending itself to banks, from two percent to just above zero percent. Such super-low interest rates did not, however, do much to stimulate economic activity. Just as American households had switched in a very short period of time from debt-fueled excess spending to massive precautionary saving and in the process had begun to hoard cash, so had US banks changed from easy lending to credit rationing. The US economy thus found itself in a liquidity trap which, if left untreated, risked triggering long-term deflation as had beset Japan during the 1990s and 2000s. Facing this trap would ultimately push the Fed, as well as other leading central banks, into uncharted territory.

But before the US central bank could properly address this structural downward shift in credit supply and demand implied by a liquidity trap, it had to manage a raging crisis of financial-market instability and large lenders facing collapse. The cumulatively intensifying nature of the systemic crisis of 2007–2009 translated into huge losses for financial institutions which necessitated many expensive bail-outs.[21] For the first

[21] The Federal Deposit Insurance Corporation, America's insurer in charge of coping with insolvent depository institutions, dealt with 489 bank and thrift failures between 2008 and 2013 after several years of zero or only a handful of failures per year. In two and a half years, from the beginning of 2008 to mid-2010, the FDIC's fund balance fell from \$52bn. to a negative \$21bn. and then stayed in the red for seven quarters (see Federal Deposit Insurance Corporation, 2017).

time ever the Federal Reserve decided to use its Sect. 13(3) emergency lending powers, which it can apply broadly if needed "in unusual and exigent circumstances," to deal with the collapse of large financial institutions, such as investment banks Bear Stearns and Merrill Lynch or leading insurer AIG.

Those same Sect. 13(3) powers found an even more remarkable outlet in a dozen or so innovative liquidity-injection and backstop facilities the Fed set up during 2008 in order to revive strategic parts of the dollar-based credit system that had come undone as the systemic crisis unfolded in such destructive fashion. The $200bn. Term Securities Lending Facility (TSLF), for example, offered primary dealers (i.e. the world's leading twenty banks) safe US Treasuries in exchange for damaged securities (e.g. MBS). The Primary Dealer Credit Facility (PDCF) provided renewable overnight loans to primary dealers in exchange for a wide range of eligible collateral. The Asset-Backed Commercial Paper Money Market Fund Liquidity Facility (AMLF) gave non-recourse loans to banks to buy up the ABCP of money market funds. The $600bn. Money Market Investor Funding Facility (MMIFF) offered credit to money-market investors. The $738bn. Commercial Paper Funding Facility (CPPF) created a lending pipeline in support of commercial paper issuers. And the $200bn. Term Asset-Backed Securities Loan Facility (TALF) tried to revive consumer and small business access to credit.[22]

Those targeted Fed interventions to unblock clogged-up money-market pipelines, while helping to relieve the asphyxiation of funding liquidity which the Lehman bankruptcy had triggered, did not suffice to counteract the debt-deflation spiral facing the US economy in late 2008. In the end, the US government was obliged to offer a blanket guarantee for the banking sector as a whole, authorizing for that purpose a $700bn. Troubled Assets Relief Program (TARP) used to recapitalize and thereby partially nationalize) America's fifteen largest banks. That same month, October 2008, other countries followed suit with sector-wide guarantees of their banks, including Ireland, United Kingdom (a £500bn package!), Germany, France, Denmark, Iceland, Italy, Australia, and New Zealand.

[22] Guttmann (2012) offers a more detailed analysis of these various Sect. 13(3) emergency lending facilities introduced by the Fed during the Great Financial Crisis (GFC) of 2007–2009, stressing their highly customized nature to target specific bottlenecks in the damaged and clogged U.S. credit system.

3.5.2 The Fed's FX Swap Lines

On August 9, 2007 the bursting of America's housing bubble often referred to as the "subprime crisis" became in one swoop a global affair. That day France's largest bank, BNP Paribas, announced that it would halt redemptions from three mortgage-related investment funds because, as its press release put it quite succinctly, "the complete evaporation of liquidity in certain market segments of the U.S. securitization market has made it impossible to value certain assets fairly regardless of their quality or credit rating." By the end of that fateful day the European Central Bank had pumped an emergency €94.8bn. (= $131bn.) into the Eurozone banking system after the inter-bank market froze and so cut off banks' normal access to short-term funding. Actually, BNP Paribas' announcement triggered two devastating panics. One was in the market for asset-backed commercial paper, on which SIVs relied to fund their long-term mortgage-related assets. Its volume of outstanding paper shrank dramatically from $1.223tr. to just $785bn. by year-end as ABCP rollovers and re-financings stopped from one day to the next. And the other panic hit the global inter-bank market where liquidity suddenly became a whole lot less forthcoming. The degree of disruption in this crucially important part of the world's financial system can be measured by the so-called LIBOR-OIS spread which shot up from less than 10 basis points to 50 points on August 9 and then close to 100 points over the next couple of turbulent weeks.[23] The spread ranged from 40 basis points to 110 basis points over the next thirteen months, indicating continued tensions, before exploding to a peak of 360 basis points in the aftermath of Lehman Brothers' collapse in September 2008. And the spread was consistently higher for the US dollar than for the euro, with the latter peaking at just 208 basis points after Lehman. This difference indicated much more stressed conditions for European banks in the dollar segment of the global inter-bank market, the heart of the global dollar standard.

It did not take long for the Federal Reserve to realize that its crisis-management focus had to include dollars in the offshore Eurodollar

[23] The overnight indexed swap (OIS) rate is a measure of average expected overnight borrowing rate typically rolled over automatically. The London interbank offer rate (LIBOR) is the rate charged by a bank for an unsecured loan of up to three months. The spread between the two, representing a "term" premium to be paid for borrowing longer than just overnight, might reflect either diminishing ease of access to liquidity or lender evaluations of rising counterparty risk.

market, notably the need to stabilize the global dollar-denominated interbank market through which banks from all over the world finance their operations tied to their own or their clients' international engagements. On December 12, 2007 the Fed entered for that purpose into currency swap agreements with the European Central Bank and the Swiss National Bank. Each side offers the other its own currency, getting an equivalent amount of the other's currency in return and reversing the transaction at a specified date at the same exchange rate. The ECB, and on a much smaller scale also the SNB, then used these US dollars obtained through those foreign-exchange swaps to pass them onto commercial banks under their jurisdiction and so ease their dollar funding challenges. In the week following the Lehman Brothers collapse, which sent shockwaves through global financial markets and essentially froze the money markets, the Fed dramatically expanded these FX swap lines. For one, it extended currency swap lines to eight more central banks, the Bank of Canada, the Bank of England, the Bank of Japan, the Reserve Bank of Australia, the Reserve Bank of New Zealand, the Danmarks Nationalbank (Denmark), the Norges Bank (Norway), and the Sveriges Riksbank (Sweden). Moreover, it dramatically boosted the total volume of dollars provided from the initial $24bn. cap for the ECB and SNB to a maximum $620bn. for the eight together. On October 13, 2008 the Fed removed the caps on its swap lines with the ECB, the SNB, the Bank of England, and the Bank of Japan which enabled those central banks to offer their banks a much greater variety of bids for variable-rate and fixed-rate tenders ranging from overnight to three months. Finally, on October 28 and 29, 2008 the Fed extended $30bn. swap lines each to five more central banks—the Reserve Bank of New Zealand, the Bank of Korea, the Monetary Authority of Singapore, the Banco Central do Brasil, and the Banco de Mexico.

At the peak, in December 2008, currency swaps outstanding totaled $582bn. which at the time amounted to a quarter of the Fed's balance sheet. These large injections of dollar reserves into the global banking system eased the post-Lehman pressures gradually so that by January 2009 the LIBOR-OIS spread had fallen back to below 100 basis points for both dollars and euros. Throughout 2009 the spread drifted steadily lower while drawing on the central banks' FX swap lines subsided as well, both indications of money-market stabilization. When the LIBOR-OIS spread first emerged following BNP Paribas' announcement early on in the Great Financial Crisis (GFC) of 2007/08, it indicated that from then on, after this global extension of the initially US-centered systemic crisis , on-shore dollars and off-shore dollars in international circulation would no longer trade at par. If allowed to go unchecked, this gap risked bringing the entire dollar standard down in a potentially devastating banking crisis. The Fed thus had to set up an international lender-of-last-resort mechanism from scratch to protect the Eurocurrency market of off-shore dollars, made up of its bilateral FX swap lines. When these had done their job during late 2008 and throughout 2009, they were allowed to expire in February 2010. Two months later, after pleading from the European Central Bank finding itself at the onset of its own systemic euro-zone crisis (see Sect. 4.2.2), they were restored among the six leading central banks (Fed, ECB, BoE, BoJ, SNB, BoC), eventually made available more cheaply in limited amounts at OIS + 50bps (instead of the OIS + 100bps cost during the GFC). In October 2013 the bilateral swap lines were turned into a permanent standing facility of reciprocal FX swap lines among each and all of the six members of this central bank cartel (i.e. C6). When that web of swap lines was (re)-activated in a hurry at the onset of the global pandemic in March 2020 (see Sect. 5.6.2), their cost was lowered to OIS + 25bps and term extended (from 7 to 84 days).[24]

3.5.3 *Quantitative Easing*

In addition to the first-time use of 13(3) emergency lending powers and the introduction of foreign-exchange swap lines, the Fed's crisis management came up with yet another institutional innovation of great strategic importance—that of "quantitative easing," also often referred to as "unconventional" monetary policy. This new policy tool involves massive asset purchases, including possibly even riskier assets, by the central bank over a pre-committed period of time as a further means of stimulation when interest rates under its control are at zero or close to it. Such purchases, which directly expand the balance sheet of the central bank, pump large amounts of liquidity into a damaged banking system still recovering from a systemic financial crisis which typically finds itself in a so-called *liquidity trap* where economic actors prefer to hold very liquid assets, if not altogether cash, while in the same vein banks prefer to sit

[24] For more details on these FX swap lines as a crucial institutional innovation of financial crisis management for the prevailing dollar standard, see Fleming and Klagge (2010), Mehrling (2015), and Kaminska (2020).

on a lot of excess reserves rather than loan those out. Such crisis-induced preference for liquidity, a byproduct of the aforementioned private-sector shift to a savings surplus (see Sect. 3.4.3 above) and indicative of a deflationary environment taking hold, renders conventional monetary policy ineffective just as reaching the zero lower bound has. Apart from signaling to financial markets and economic actors still reeling from the crisis that the central bank is willing to go to great lengths securing post-crisis recovery, such massive asset purchases also aim to push long-term interest rates lower, thereby boost securities prices (bonds, stocks), and hopefully overpower the liquidity trap getting banks to extend more credit.

In late 2008 the Fed adopted a massive dose of so-called "quantitative easing" (QE) which ultimately unfolded in three distinct phases over the next six years to quintuple the size of its balance sheet from $858bn. in August 2007, just at the beginning of the crisis, to $4.5tr. at the peak in late 2015.

- During QE1 the Fed bought $1.25tr. worth of mortgage-backed securities from November 2008 to September 2010 which helped revive this heavily damaged segment of the American bond market at the center of the GFC of 2007–2008 and resume mortgage lending in support of the US housing sector's recovery.
- In QE2 the Fed bought $600bn worth of Treasury bonds over a year (November 2010–November 2011).
- Between September 2011 and June 2012 the Fed conducted an "Operation Twist," a move it had first tried in 1960 (see Sect. 1.6.1), whereby it sold $400bn. of short-term Treasury bills and notes and then used the proceeds to buy the same quantity of long-term Treasury bonds. The purpose of this swap was to drive already fairly low long-term rates even lower.
- In September 2012 the Fed launched QE3 when it committed in open-ended fashion to monthly $40bn. purchases of agency mortgage-backed securities issued by the government-owned lenders Fannie Mae, Freddie Mac (both nationalized in July 2008), and Ginnie Mae in support of their mortgage lending which over the last decade has together provided about 70 percent of all funding of home purchases in the United States. In December 2012 the Fed more than doubled the amount of these monthly purchases to $85bn. On June 19, 2013 Fed Chair Ben Bernanke set off the so-called "taper tantrum," an unexpectedly strong panic reaction in

> bond and stock markets, when he suggested that the time may soon come for some gentle scaling back of quantitative easing. Realizing how addicted investors had become to such continuous stimulation, the Fed ultimately tapered off its purchases more slowly and ended them only at the end of October 2014, three months later than initially planned.

It took until late 2015 before the Fed started to raise the primary interest rate under its control, the so-called Federal funds rate for inter-bank lending, from its near-zero floor it had been sitting at for seven years, a complex operation the US economy was strong enough to absorb without any glitches thanks to an effective communication strategy under new Fed Chair Janet Yellen. Between December 2015 and January 2019 the Fed funds rate rose from 0.2 percent all the way to 2.4 percent before stabilizing at that level for the next six months, notwithstanding vehement criticism by President Trump of those interest-rate hikes all the way to calling Fed chair Jay Powell (whom he appointed) an "enemy." On September 17, 2019 a combination of seasonal factors draining bank reserves (i.e. corporate tax payments due, large settlements of Treasury auctions), occurring against a backdrop of the Fed's gradual tightening moves, spiked the repo rate from its then prevailing "normal condition" range of 1.89–1.95 percent to 10 percent. The turmoil spilled over into the Fed funds market as well, pushing the market rate there temporarily above the 2.25% ceiling of its target range. This shocking indication of the money market's vulnerability to massive demand–supply disequilibria ten years into recovery made the Fed rethink its stance of gradual tightening. The next day it lowered the Fed funds target range to 1.75–2 percent. And three weeks later, on October 11, 2019, Fed Chair Jay Powell announced that the Fed would start yet another asset-purchase program of $40bn. per month in Treasury bills which he did not want to have characterized as QE4 to indicate its more limited purpose of stabilizing money market tensions. The Fed was already in a loosening stance not too far away from the zero lower bound when the pandemic hit in March 2020, thus necessitating its massive reaction to this deflationary shock because of the limited size of its interest-rate cut.

The Fed was not alone in conducting quantitative easing . Other key central banks did so as well. The Bank of England, for example, bought a total of £375bn. (= about $600bn.) of gilts (i.e. UK government bonds) and, to a lesser extent, highly rated corporate bonds between March

2009 and July 2012. The Bank of Japan, faced with deflationary pressures much earlier than anyone else and experimenting with quantitative easing before other central banks (already in 2001), steadily increased its post-GFC bond buying program from ¥40tr. (=$504bn.) per year in August 2011 to ultimately double that level in October 2014. The European Central Bank, facing its own systemic financial crisis from late 2009 to mid-2012 (see Sect. 4.2.2), committed in January 2015 to a €60bn. per month bond-buying program which it increased in March 2016 to €80bn. per month and at the same time widened to include also corporate bonds. Substantial asset purchase programs were also conducted by the Sveriges Riksbank of Sweden and the Swiss National Bank. All these monetary authorities were facing a stubbornly deflationary environment years into recovery, a fact perhaps even more tellingly illustrated by the gradual spread and deepening of negative interest rates everywhere (with the exception of the United States).

In conclusion, in this chapter we have analyzed the last two long waves. Our analysis relied on a chronology of stylized facts, informed by the Régulationists' notion of accumulation regimes whose emergence turns into an engine driving a long boom (as did Fordism during the 1950s and 1960s or finance-led capitalism during the 1990s and 2000s). We were able to locate the combination of structural crisis and policy reforms setting the stage for a long-wave upswing. We could see this pattern play out first with the New Deal amidst Great Depression of the 1930s followed by the Bretton Woods framework giving rise to Fordism. And then we saw it again with a double-dip recession in the early 1980s coinciding with the Reagan Revolution and its subsequent international extension through the Washington Consensus, eventually yielding a new upswing phase driven forward by finance-led capitalism.

The downswing phases of those two long waves came about in the wake of systemic financial crises, that of Fordism with the breakdown of Bretton Woods in the early 1970s and that of finance-led capitalism with the Great Financial Crisis/Great Recession 2007–2009. Those downswing phases are very much characterized by steadily intensifying instability and its global propagation through the prevailing dynamics of the international monetary system, as was clearly evident with stagflation being fed by continuous dollar depreciation over a whole decade. By contrast, the downswing phase we have faced since the GFC 2007/08 has been one of deflationary pressures, kept so far in check by unconventional monetary policy. Now that the world has been hit by a brutal shock of a global pandemic against this backdrop of "controlled deflation," we would do well taking a closer look at the underlying dynamic of deflationary pressures and their propagation by the dollar standard turned on its head.

References

Abelson, M., Kelly, J., & Carey, D. (2015). Renegades of junk: The rise and fall of the Drexel Empire. *Bloomberg*. https://www.bloomberg.com/graphics/2015-drexel-burnham-oral-history/. Accessed 8 March 2017.

Aglietta, M. (1976/1979). *A theory of capitalist regulation: The US experience*. Verso Books. First published in French as *Régulation et crises du capitalisme*.

Bellamy Foster, J. (2007). The financialization of capitalism. *Monthly Review, 58*(11), 1–12. https://doi.org/10.14452/MR-058-11-2007-04_1

Bernanke, B. (2013). Communication and monetary policy. Herbert Stein Memorial Lecture. https://www.federalreserve.gov/newsevents/speech/bernanke20131119a.htm. Accessed 19 Nov.

Canto, V., Joines, D., & Laffer, A. (1983). *Foundations of supply-side economics: Theory and evidence*. Academy Press.

Carroll, C., & Zhou, X. (2010). Measuring wealth effects using U.S. state data. Federal Reserve Bank of San Francisco. *Economic Research*, 1–29. https://www.frbsf.org/economic-research/files/Zhou.pdf. Accessed 25 July 2012.

Case, K., Quigley, J., & Shiller, R. (2005). Comparing wealth effects: The stock market versus the housing market. *Advances in Macroeconomics, 5*(1), 1–34. https://www.nber.org/papers/w8606.

Coffey, P. (1984). *The European Monetary System – Past, present and future*. Springer.

Cohan, W. (2017). Michael Milken invented the modern junk bond, went to prison, and then became one of the most respected people on Wall Street. *Business Insider*. https://www.businessinsider.com/michael-milken-life-story-2017-5?IR=T. Accessed 2 May.

Cohen, B. (1981). The European Monetary System: An Outsider's View. *Essays in International Finance*, no. 142, Princeton University. https://ies.princeton.edu/pdf/E142.pdf. Accessed 20 November 2021.

Covitz, D., Liang, N., & Suarez, G. (2013). The evolution of a financial crisis: Collapse of the asset-backed commercial paper market. *Journal of Finance, 68*(3), 815–848.

Einzig, P. (1973). *The Euro-Dollar system: Practice and theory of international interest rates* (5th ed.). London.

Epstein, G. (2005). *Financialization and the world economy*. E. Elgar.

Federal Deposit Insurance Corporation. (2017). *Crisis and response: A FDIC History, 2008–2013*. FDIC. https://www.fdic.gov/bank/historical/crisis/. Accessed 17 March 2019.

Ferri, P. (1990). *Prospects for the European Monetary System*. Palgrave Macmillan.

Financial Crisis Inquiry Commission (2011). *The financial crisis inquiry report: Final report of the National Commission on the Causes of the Financial and Economic Crises of the United States*. Government Printing Office.

Fine, B. (2013). Financialization from a Marxist Perspective. *International Journal of Political Economy, 42*(4), 47–66. https://doi.org/10.2753/IJP0891-1916420403

Fisher, I. (1933). The debt-deflation theory of great depressions. *Econometrica, 1*(4), 337–357.

Fleming, M., & Klagge, N. (2010). The Federal Reserve's Foreign Exchange Swap Lines. Federal Reserve Bank of New York. *Current Issues in Economics and Finance, 16*(4). https://www.newyorkfed.org/medialibrary/media/research/current_issues/ci16-4.pdf. Accessed April.

Friedman, M. (1962). *Capitalism and freedom*. University of Chicago Press.

Garcia, C. (2012). When safe assets return. FT Alphaville. *Financial Times*. https://ftalphaville.ft.com/2012/04/05/941741/when-safe-assets-return/. Accessed 5 April.

Gibson, H. (1989). *The Eurocurrency markets, domestic financial policy and international instability*. Palgrave Macmillan.

Gorton, G., & Metrick, A. (2009). *Securitized banking and the run on Repo* (NBER Working Paper No. 15223). https://www.nber.org/papers/w15223. Accessed 19 September 2012.

Greenspan, A., & Kennedy, J. (2005). *Estimates of home mortgage originations, repayments, and debt to one-to-four residences* (FEDS Paper No. 2005-41). https://doi.org/10.2139/ssrn.874821

Guttmann. R. (1994). *How credit-money shapes the economy: The United States in a global system*. M. E. Sharpe.

Guttmann, R. (2008). A primer on finance-led capitalism and its crisis. *Revue de la Régulation*, no. 3/4. regulation.revues.org/document5843.html. Accessed December.

Guttmann, R. (2012). Central banking in a systemic crisis: The Federal Reserve's 'credit-easing'. In L.-P. Rochon & S. Olawoye (Eds.), *Monetary policy and central banking: New directions in post-Keynesian Theory* (pp. 130–165). Edgar Elgar.

Guttmann, R. (2016). *Finance-led capitalism: Shadow banking, re-regulation and the future of global markets*. Palgrave Macmillan.

Hayek, F. (1944). *The road to Serfdom*. Routledge.

Hein, E., & Van Treeck, T. (2010). Financialisation and rising shareholder power in Kaleckian/post-Keynesian models of distribution and growth. *Review of*

Political Economy, 22(2), 205–233. https://doi.org/10.1080/09538251003665628

Kaminska, I. (2020). Why FX swap lines are back. *Financial Times*. https://www.ft.com/content/eb1685b1-2ded-4f5f-8723-85cea4ade637. Accessed 17 March.

Keynes, J. M. (1936). *The general theory of employment, interest and money*. Macmillan.

Keynes, J. M. (1980a). *The Collected Writings of John Maynard Keynes, vol. XXV, Activities 1940 – 1944 Shaping the Post War World – The Clearing Union*, D. Moggridge (ed.). Cambridge University Press: Cambridge, UK.

Keynes, J. M. (1980b). In D. Moggridge (Eds.), *Collected Writings of John Maynard Keynes, Volume XXVI, Activities 1941 – 1946, Shaping the Postwar World, Bretton Woods, and Reparations*. Macmillan.

Krippner, G. (2005). The financialization of the American economy. *Socio-Economic Review, 3*(2), 173–208.

Krugman, P. (1979). Increasing returns, monopolistic competition, and international trade. *Journal of International Economics*,*9*(4), 469–479. http://econ.sciences-po.fr/sites/default/files/file/krugman-79.pdf

Lapavitsas, C. (2013). The financialization of capitalism: 'Profiting without producing.' *City*, 792–805. https://doi.org/10.1080/13604813.2013.853865

Lewis, M. (2010). *The big short: Inside the doomsday machine*. W. W. Norton.

Marglin, S., & Schor, J. (1992). *The golden age of capitalism: Reinterpreting the postwar experience*. Oxford University Press.

McKinnon, R. (1977). The Eurocurrency Market. *Essays in International Finance*, no. 125, Princeton University. https://ies.princeton.edu/pdf/E125.pdf. Accessed 20 November 2021.

Mehrling, P. (2015). *Elasticity and discipline in the global swap network* (Working Papers No. 27). Institute for New Economic Thinking. https://www.ineteconomics.org/uploads/papers/WP27-Mehrling.pdf. Accessed 14 January 2017.

Prebisch, R. (1959). Commercial policies in the underdeveloped countries. *American Economic Review, 49*(2), 251–273.

Stockhammer, E. (2004). Financialisation and the slowdown of accumulation. *Cambridge Journal of Economics, 28*(5), 719–741.

Tett, G., Davies, P., & Cohen, N. (2007). Structured investment vehicles' role in crisis. *Financial Times*, August 12.

Vernon, R. (1966). International investment and international trade in the product cycle. *Quarterly Journal of Economics, 80*(2), 190–207. https://doi.org/10.2307/1880689

Williamson, J. (1986). Target zones and the management of the dollar. *Brookings Papers of Economic Activity, 1*(1986), 165–174. https://www.brookings.edu/wp-content/uploads/1986/01/1986a_bpea_williamson.pdf

Williamson, J. (2004). A Short History of the Washington Consensus. Institute for International Economics. https://piie.com/publications/papers/williamson0904-2.pdf

Wojnilower, A. (1980). The central role of credit crunches in recent financial history. *Brookings Papers in Economic Activity*, *2*, 278–339. https://www.brookings.edu/wp-content/uploads/1980/06/1980b_bpea_wojnilower_friedman_modigliani.pdf

Wolfson, M. (1986). *Financial crises: Understanding the postwar U.S. experience*. M. E. Sharpe.

CHAPTER 4

The New Deflation: From Great Recession to Global Pandemic

Ever since the Great Financial Crisis of 2007/08 ended the upswing phase of the latest long wave driven forward by finance-led capitalism, we have seen sluggish growth across most regions of the world. It took quite a while for the recovery from that systemic crisis to gain a solid footing, and even then (after 2015) growth has been tangibly slower in both advanced and emerging-market economies ever since. We have thus arguably been in a downswing phase for more than a decade, and it behooves us to take a closer look at the global dimensions of its dynamic to see new trends emerging and identify the changing context of policy challenges. As is typical for downswing phases of long waves, the prevailing international monetary system—in this case the dollar standard—turns from a pro-growth force facilitating broad-based catching-up processes into an instability-enhancing engine of deepening contradictions and fissures. Even before a global pandemic imposed a second major crisis on the world economy in early 2020, we could see the dollar standard feed currency wars, trade wars, commodity-price collapses, and other de-globalization processes into a new deflation context which bears further analysis of the kind attempted in this chapter.

R. Guttmann, *Multi-Polar Capitalism*,
https://doi.org/10.1007/978-3-030-88247-1_4

4.1 The Great Recession as Structural Crisis

The remarkable crisis of 2007–2009 (see Sect. 3.4) has been alternately referred to as the Great Financial Crisis or Great Recession, evidence of its two-phase nature whereupon a systemic financial crisis starting in a small corner of the American financial system morphed rapidly into globally paralyzing credit freeze to send the world economy into a tailspin not seen since the Great Depression of the 1930s. Be that as it may, the double characterization of *Great* in conjunction with that financial crisis or recession of a dozen years ago implies correctly a major crisis, one whose scope and scale far exceeded normal downturns in the course of business cycles. We are talking here evidently about a structural crisis that we have already discussed in the context of long waves as transformative in nature. You may recall from that discussion (in Sect. 2.2.4) a typology of structural crises whereby Régulationists distinguished between:

- a "crisis of the mode of régulation" rupturing a key institutional form at the center of the accumulation regime driving the preceding long-wave upswing;
- a "crisis of the accumulation regime" transforming the accumulation regime as happened during the Great Depression of the 1930s (from "Taylorism" to "Fordism") or the stagflation crisis of the 1970s and early 1980s (from "Fordism" and its crisis of Keynesianism via the Reagan Revolution to "finance-led capitalism"); and finally
- a "crisis of the production mode" which changes the very nature of the economic system as happened with the collapse of the Soviet Union in 1990/91 or already earlier with the decade-long radical reforms transforming Maoist China into a mixed economy under Deng Xiaoping (1977–1989).

If we look at the Great Recession of 2008/09 per se, we can see that, at a minimum, it was a crisis of the mode of régulation. The crisis emanated from finance-led capitalism's dominant institutional pillar, a largely self-regulated and US-centered financial system spanning the globe in continuously expanding fashion, whose progressive implosion from March 2007 to December 2008 pushed the world economy to the edge of a potentially devastating debt-deflation spiral. In the course of its systemic crisis, global finance as a system had broken apart, saved only from chain bankruptcies by trillions in government aid among most leading economies of the world. In the wake of this once-in-a-lifetime Great Financial Crisis (GFC), as it came to be called, policy-makers decided early on, still in 2009, to launch a global effort at re-regulation of finance. This coordinated initiative has led to a better protected and less aggressive financial system.

4.1.1 The Re-regulation of Finance

When the Great Recession hit in 2008, heads of states of the world's leading nations, the Group of Twenty (G-20), comprising together nearly three-quarters of the world's total output set up a series of twice-yearly get-togethers to coordinate their crisis response.[1] Early on in this process, during the April 2009 meeting in London and then at the September 2009 summit in Pittsburgh, the G-20 leaders committed themselves to the building blocks of an ambitious re-regulation effort to reshape the structure and inner workings of the world's financial system.

A key focus was to make banks more resilient, especially those deemed systemically important because of their size or interconnectedness for which the G-20 empowered banking regulators to put in place a new categorization system ranging from global systemically important banks (G-SIBs) to domestic systemically important financial institutions (banks, insurance companies) and systemically important financial-market utilities (SIFMUs) such as clearinghouses and cash settlement processors. Toward this objective the Bank for International Settlements, whose Basel Committee on Banking Supervision (BCBS) had already emerged as a global banking regulator with the passage of the Basel Accord of 1988, concluded in 2010 a new agreement generally referred to as "Basel III" to

[1] The G-20 members include (in alphabetical order) Argentina, Australia, Brazil, Canada, China, France, Germany, India, Indonesia, Italy, Japan, Mexico, Russia, Saudi Arabia, South Africa, South Korea, Turkey, United Kingdom, and the United States. Also included are the two governing bodies of the European Union, the European Commission as well as the European Council, and a host of international organizations. These are regional groupings, notably the Association of Southeast Asian Nations (ASEAN) and the New Partnership for Africa's Development (NEPAD), or multi-lateral organizations representing pillars of the global governance structure, such as the Financial Stability Board, the International Monetary Fund, the Organization for Economic Co-operation and Development (OECD), the United Nations, the World Bank, and the World Trade Organization (WTO). Summit hosts rotate. Whoever is in charge can invite (typically) a few additional countries to join that particular get-together.

reinforce regulation, supervision, and risk management practices of internationally active banks.[2] It did so by targeting bank capital, liquidity, and leverage with provisions to be phased in gradually over a decade (2010–2019).

- Basel III imposed a much higher level of bank capitalization as (equity) cushion, often two to three times as high as before the GFC so that banks could henceforth absorb much larger losses before facing insolvency. This new and far more stringent regulatory regime for bank capital introduced different layers, including a countercyclical buffer to draw from during hard times and build up during good times, as well as a supplementary buffer for the "too-big-to-fail" G-SIBs and D-SIBs. At the same time the new rules also greatly restricted what could be counted as capital, confining it to core Tier 1 capital, in recognition that broader and more ephemeral Tier 2 and 3 categories of bank "capital" had proven shaky the moment banks came under stress.
- Basel III also obliged banks to provide for much larger levels of liquidity as protection against the other crisis-related stressor, namely a run on a troubled bank whose ensuing shortage of cash subjects it to paralyzing illiquidity. Banks pursuing rapid-growth targets have moved beyond their deposit base to draw on short-term "borrowed liabilities" (e.g. repos, inter-bank loans, commercial paper) for funding of larger long-term asset portfolios, requiring repeated refinancing in the money markets to keep carrying their loans or bonds. Those banks are more exposed to liquidity squeezes when interest rates rise and, even more so, when refinancing becomes more difficult during periods of financial instability. Basel III required banks to have sufficient amounts of eligible liquid assets (cash, short-term Treasury bills, etc.) on hand to withstand a month-long period of net cash outflows indicating money-market stress or a bank run (the so-called "liquidity coverage ratio"). In addition, banks were also expected to match their liquid asset structure with an appropriate composition of short-term funding sources, the so-called "net stable funding ratio."

[2] For a summary of relevant Basel III documents laying out its regulatory framework piece by piece see Bank for International Settlements (2019).

- Finally, Basel III introduced a so-called "leverage cap" expressed as the ratio of capital over assets and to be kept above a minimum of 3 percent. Unlike the risk-weighted capital-asset ratios defining the bank capital buffers, this supplementary regulation included all bank assets irrespective of their supposed riskiness and extended to shadow-banking assets normally not included in a bank's balance sheet. In essence, the cap defined a bank's overall size as a function of its top-quality capital and so made sure that aggressive banks in search of rapid growth would not end up severely undercapitalized, as had happened in the run-up to the GFC of 2007/08.[3]
- In 2023 the BIS is going to limit how much banks can lower the capital they set aside for risk-weighted assets when using their own internal risk-assessment models, as compared to the regulators' standardized models authorized for use. This tightening of risk management seeks to prevent systematic underestimation of risk which many banks had been guilty of under Basel II before the crisis. The practical implication of this "Basel IV" agreement will be to require more bank capital and push banks toward greater use of widely accepted risk assessment methods.[4]

The Basel III and IV agreements thus put in place a new global regulatory regime for banks, including the transnational banking activity in the offshore Euromarkets which had started out initially in the 1960s as an entirely unregulated parallel banking network (see Sects. 1.1.4 and 3.2.3). But the re-regulation of finance did not stop there. The two G-20 meetings of 2009 laid out the priorities for a much broader effort at re-regulating finance and provided a roadmap for national legislative efforts in that regard. The Obama Administration passed for that purpose the Wall Street Reform and Consumer Protection Act of 2010, also known as the Dodd–Frank Act. Britain followed suit with the Financial Services (Banking Reform) Act of 2013. And the European Union undertook a two-pronged strategy to strengthen its regulatory apparatus for its financial system on a supra-national (i.e. European) level. First, it introduced

[3] See Masters (2012) for the broader implications of Basel III's leverage cap.

[4] For different, European versus American, perspectives on Basel IV's new approach to risk management see McKinsey (2017) and Baer (2018).

in September 2010 a new regulatory infrastructure in the form of the so-called European System of Financial Supervision (ESFS) which included a European Banking Authority, a European Securities Markets Authority, a European Insurance and Occupational Pensions Authority, and a European Systemic Risk Board (see also Sect. 6.3.1). Then the European Commission introduced a series of separate directives which, when put together, achieved the same broad overhaul of financial system regulation as aforementioned American and British legislation in accordance with the principles laid out by the G-20 in 2009. These directives included the Alternative Investment Fund Management Directive of 2011 (for hedge funds, private-equity funds, real-estate funds), European Market Infrastructure Regulation of 2012 (for over-the-counter markets), Capital Requirements Directive IV of 2013 (putting in place the provisions of Basel III), Solvency Directive II of 2014 (for insurance companies), UCITS Directive of 2014 (for mutual funds), Bank Recovery and Resolution Directive of 2014, as well as the Markets in Financial Instruments Directive II of 2017 (for financial markets).[5]

These laws incorporated several new regulatory principles which the world's leaders had agreed to in their G-20 meetings in 2009. Having just gone through the terrifying Great Financial Crisis of 2007/08, regulators wanted to have new tools at their disposal for preventing or containing systemic financial crises which, if left unchecked, might take the whole system down. Regulators would, as already indicated above, identify "too-big-to-fail" or "too-interconnected-to-fail" banks and non-bank financial institutions which, once classified as "systemically important financial institutions" (SIFIs) be they G-SIBs, R-SIBs, D-SIBs, SIFMUs, et cetera, would be subjected to more stringent capitalization requirements, more information disclosure, tighter supervision, and regular stress tests evaluating their resilience in the face of various crisis scenarios. Regulators also tried to address systemic risk by setting up new regulatory umbrella structures bringing together central banks, financial-market regulators, and finance ministries (e.g. US Treasury) to identify buildup of potentially destabilizing forces in the financial system and assess their severity on the basis of new systemic-risk measures. These bodies, such as the US Financial Stability Oversight Council (FSOC) and the European Systemic

[5] To keep up to date with the complex, ever-changing landscape of the European Union's rule-setting efforts pertaining to banking and finance, I recommend European Commission (2021).

Risk Board, have broad and vaguely defined powers to conduct macro-prudential regulation involving the imposition of controls, restraints, or limits aimed at counteracting the identified source of brewing trouble.

Committed to avoid the tremendously expensive and wildly unpopular bank bailouts of the GFC 2007/08, governments have sought to put in place an alternative approach to managing bank failures known as "resolution." Americans and Europeans have taken different approaches here. The United States is more inclined to liquidate at least heavily damaged parts of any bank in accordance with a prescribed "living will" pre-approved by regulators whereas the EU is more committed to restructuring failing banks through recapitalization and debt restructuring. Toward this objective the European Union set up the so-called Single Resolution Mechanism in 2014 as a bank-financed fund supporting the resolution of failing institutions and introduced at that point also a new type of bonds called "Contingent Convertibles" (CoCos) which turn into equity under pre-determined conditions for the recapitalization of banks. This is a work in progress that has yet to prove the test of time during another major banking crisis (see Sect. 6.3.1).[6]

Beyond banks, the re-regulation effort has also focused on strengthening financial markets. Much of that push has been rooted in assuring greater transparency by demanding more information disclosure from key market players, such as mutual funds or hedge funds, and regulating public-interest priorities of brokers and advisors. Credit-rating agencies, whose business model has relied problematically on getting paid by those whose securities they rate, should be reformed to get funded publicly, to have a rotation so as to prevent excessively cozy relations between them and their corporate clients, and to promote competition among a greater number of (even possibly government-run) CRAs. This project has yet to get going. The biggest effort in the market-strengthening area of re-regulation, however, has been the regulators' insistence on reinforcing over-the-counter (OTC) markets which the crisis of 2007/08 had revealed to be intrinsically quite fragile and thus prone to disintegrate under pressure. The focus here has been on transforming OTC "markets" into organized public exchanges or, where not possible, at least interjecting third parties into OTC transactions as clearinghouses and trade

[6] CoCos have been incorporated into Basel III's new bank capitalization regime as a separate "Additional Tier 1" buffer. For more on those potentially crucial new hybrid instruments see Avdjiev et al. (2013) as well as Gledhill (2020).

depositories whose very presence should add resilience to what in essence resembled insider networks more than markets. Regulators will eventually also want to meet the challenges of electronic markets and high-frequency trading with a new regulatory framework fit for those technologically complex developments in financial-market structures.

The GFC of 2007/08 became a systemic crisis because of the progressive disintegration of a dollar-based shadow-banking system which leading American banks had set up off-balance sheet from the mid-1990s onward in circumvention of the risk-weighted capital requirements imposed by the original Basel I and II agreements.[7] This system had financed the American housing bubble by repackaging US mortgages into highly-rated mortgage-backed securities sold to investors all over the world as part of the dollar standard's surplus recycling circuit. When that bubble finally burst, the shadow-banking system financing its rise fell apart with it. No surprise then that regulators worldwide wanted to shore up different structures and institutions of that system and so secure them against future shocks. The securitization of loans was given a makeover, with banks incentivized to be more prudent in how they handle this practice. Special-purpose entities, which had served banks as convenient vehicles to move activities off their balance sheets while maintaining control and access to income from those, were reformed. Money markets, so crucial to the larger banks' funding liquidity, were reinforced, not least by restructuring repurchasing agreements (i.e. secured short-term loans between financial institutions) and money-market funds both of which had played an outsized role in the GFC.

Interestingly enough, regulators in the United States and EU also vividly debated structure regulations aimed at isolating commercial banking, the taking of deposits and making of loans, from a bank's other activities such as investment banking, asset management, or insurance. The deregulation of finance during the 1980s had given rise to the multipurpose universal bank, a kind of financial supermarket aiming to combine economies of scale with economies of scope and network economies, at the heart of finance-led capitalism. These multi-product financial giants had used the money-creating capacity of their commercial banking core to fund other, riskier activities—from investment banking to shadow banking

[7] I have traced the evolution of this dollar-based shadow-banking system from its inception to its spectacular disintegration amidst the bursting of America's housing bubble a dozen years later in Guttmann (2016, 2017).

and a global reach in all corners of the world—and so turn themselves into "too-big-to-fail" giants. They blew themselves up like balloons until they actually blew up. Post-crisis discussions of structure regulation centered on how best to impose an arms-length distance between commercial banking and other financial-services activities as separately capitalized subsidiaries under the umbrella of banking holding companies or other ring-fencing arrangements. In the end, actual structural reform ended up far less ambitious than initial plans. Dodd–Frank's rather modest Volcker Rule banned proprietary trading by banks on their own accounts and pushed for limits on banks' control over hedge funds. After much discussion around the so-called Liikanen Rule separating certain risky trading activities from the banks' deposit-taking business if the former endangered the latter, the EU withdrew legislative proposals to that effect in 2018 without resolution of the issue. In Britain, however, the 2013 banking reform included the so-called Vickers Rule ring-fencing retail "utility" banking from investment banking and other riskier financing activities.[8]

Even without adequately scaled structure regulations, the overall re-regulation of banks has had a major impact in terms of containing their previously unfettered chase for profits at the expense of safety. They are now much safer and less aggressive institutions, and this change in posture has altered the modus operandi of our system away from finance-led capitalism. Make no mistake, finance is still large-scale and of strategic importance. But it has become less dominant. It no longer dominates the growth pattern as it used to by repeatedly launching US-centered asset bubbles driving the world economy (see Sect. 3.3.4). As a matter of fact, the world's leading banks all went through major internal restructuring after the GFC away from the universal-banking model by refocusing on their core capacities and scaling back, or getting altogether out of, more marginal activities. Their international reorientation has often involved retrenching from certain regions. They are both smaller and deeper than they were before the crisis, with individual banks choosing very different reorganization strategies so that there are now a plethora of somewhat more specialized banking strategies and structures. Some of the vacuum thus created has been filled by other non-bank financial institutions, such as hedge funds getting more involved in corporate lending or finance companies pushing consumer lending.

[8] For discussions comparing the Volcker, Vickers and Liikanen Rules see Viñals and Pazarbasioglu (2013) and Van Putten (2015).

4.1.2 Liquidity Traps and Savings Gluts

The changing nature of bank behavior, confirming that the combination of GFC 2007/08 and Great Recession 2008/09 amounted together to at least a crisis of "the mode of régulation" weakening finance-led capitalism, can also be seen by how much banks have increased the excess reserves they keep over and above their central bank's reserve requirements. Normally banks keep excess reserves to a minimum since they prefer to loan them out for income creation. Whereas US banks held excess reserves totaling just $1.876 billion in August 2008, those had risen to $2.677 trillion (sic!) by September 2014. After that peak, they gradually fell by half to $1.305 trillion in September 2019 before exploding to $3.217 trillion in May 2020 amidst the deflationary shock of a pandemic. Over the same time period, EU-based banks saw their excess reserves increase manifold from just €677 million in August 2008 to €1.528 trillion (sic!) in September 2019 and a pandemic-induced leap to €2.884 trillion in January 2021.[9] While excess reserves have surely been greatly boosted by their respective central banks' "quantitative easing" programs (see Sect. 3.5.3) injecting massive amounts of liquidity into the American and European banking systems respectively, it is nonetheless remarkable that banks have held on to so large a portion of additional (excess) bank reserves thereby created for such a long period of time. Whatever the precise constellation of demand-and-supply forces underpinning those unprecedented levels of excess reserves (e.g. introduction of a positive interest rate on bank reserves in December 2008 by the Fed, weak loan demand), banks have seemingly become that much more cautious since the systemic crisis of 2008/09, exhibiting a preference for cash akin to some sort of post-traumatic stress disorder.

This cautious bank behavior harks back to the "liquidity trap" phenomenon evoked by John Maynard Keynes (1936, Chapter 15) in his aptly named chapter "The Psychological and Business Incentives to Liquidity":

[9] Data on banks' excess reserves are collected by the St. Louis Fed's FRED Economic Data (fred.stlouisfed.org/series/EXCSRESNS) and the European Central Bank's Statistical Data Warehouse (sdw.ecb.europe.eu) Quick View. See also the detailed analysis by Craig and Koepke (2015) on causes for the massive increase in excess reserves accumulating since the crisis within the U.S. banking system.

> There is the possibility, for the reasons discussed above, that, after the rate of interest has fallen to a certain level, liquidity preference may become virtually absolute in the sense that almost everyone prefers cash to holding a debt which yields so low a rate of interest. In this event the monetary authority would have lost effective control over the rate of interest. But whilst this limiting case might become practically important in future, I know of no example of it hitherto. Indeed, owing to the unwillingness of most monetary authorities to deal boldly in debts of long term, there has not been much opportunity for a test. Moreover, if such a situation were to arise, it would mean that the public authority itself could borrow through the banking system on an unlimited scale at a nominal rate of interest. (p. 103)

There are many ways to interpret this famous passage from Keynes' *General Theory*. Let us remember, to start with, that one of Keynes' key departures from standard theory was having looked at money not as a good, but as an asset in contradistinction to bonds, the "other" financial asset, to highlight the money asset's unique quality of embodying liquidity. This point of departure then opened up a reconsideration of demand for money beyond merely the motive of transactions to highlight speculative and precautionary motives. The question then is which of these supplementary money-demand motives predominates the liquidity trap, as both may apply. It is possible, for example, to argue his liquidity trap from the point of the view of the speculative motive for money demand. Once interest rates have fallen to what he referred to as a "nominal" (i.e. very small) level, the public will want to hold onto cash for fear of holding bonds bound to decline in value when interest rates rise, as they may well be expected to do soon once having fallen to such low levels. But it is also reasonable, perhaps even more so when in the midst of a depression as at the time of Keynes' writing, to argue that a worried public prefers to hold onto cash as a precaution, especially when the low-interest rates on bonds have rendered the opportunity cost of cash quite minimal. Keynes claims not yet to have witnessed such a situation, even while in the midst of a depression. But he also makes clear that this has to do with central banks confining their open-market operations to short-term Treasury bills and hence not doing their bit to drive down long-term interest rates on bonds sufficiently low for the liquidity trap to kick in.

Today, of course, we are in that "future" Keynes was referring to when central banks trade securities across their entire term structure, from bills and notes to long-term bonds. Perhaps even more telling is that Keynes' original juxtaposition of money and bonds has been upended by the public treating widely traded, hence hyper-liquid high-quality government securities, not just bills but even bonds, as a close substitute to cash so that the liquidity trap extends to them as well. This brings us to a dramatic modern example of the liquidity trap, namely Japan's "Lost Decade" from 1991 to 2001 following the spectacular collapse of an asset (stock-market, land-price) bubble and initially hesitant policy responses. During that decade, and actually continuing more or less in the same fashion for another two decades all the way to today, Japan's growth slowed to a crawl, deflation took root in seemingly inescapable fashion, interest rates fell to zero and beyond into negative territory, and monetary policy was rendered ineffective. Nobel Prize winner Paul Krugman (1998) used Japan's example to update Keynes' notion of liquidity trap which he defined as:

> ..that awkward condition in which monetary policy loses its grip because the nominal interest rate is essentially zero, in which the quantity of money becomes irrelevant because money and bonds are essentially perfect substitutes. (p. 137)

Krugman makes it clear throughout that, while Japan's liquidity trap is in many ways unique, the conditions triggering it and then locking it into place may recur elsewhere. We have seen in recent years enough references to "Japanification" to appreciate how prescient Krugman's warnings of liquidity traps occurring elsewhere have turned out to be. An essential feature of Krugman's reappraisal of the liquidity trap is to bring financial intermediaries into the picture, of which massive accumulation of excess reserves in the banking system is a hallmark indicator. And he also makes the salient point that at heart the liquidity trap boils down to a credibility problem for central banks having to convince a skeptical public that they are willing to undertake radically expansionary "unconventional" monetary policies, massive quantitative easing to wit, sufficiently long to create inflation as a way out of the morass. Both of these points have proven quite valid for the US and EU economies in the post-crisis environment.

Ever since 2008 we have seen both the United States and the European Union struggling not to fall into a durable liquidity trap of the kind experienced by Japan.[10]

Why do economic actors acquire what Keynes characterized as a "virtually absolute liquidity preference" in the aftermath of an asset bubble bursting into a major incidence of financial crisis? At first, the rush into cash (or nowadays also fail-safe, hyper-liquid government bonds) is a matter of survival, just like oxygen. Debtors need to secure cash for continued debt servicing, to absorb losses from collapsing asset values, to withstand disruption of income generation, to survive getting cut off from credit. All these motives drive Irving Fisher's (1933) "debt-deflation spiral." There is also a mass-psychological switch from greed driving the bubble to fear when that bubble burst, a fear that may last a long time and needs to be managed by building up a reliable cushion of liquidity as precaution. The accumulation of excess reserves in the banking system is an indication of such a cash hoard. From a macro-economic point of view that same prevalence of "virtually absolute liquidity preference" expresses itself as a lasting surplus in the private sector's financial balance between savings and investment ($S > I$), in other words as a "savings glut" where desired saving exceeds desired investment.[11]

We already mentioned (in Sect. 3.4.3) the colossal ten-percent shift in America's private-sector financial balance from deficit to surplus during the crisis of 2007–2009. What we have to add here is how persistent that surplus has been ever since. The Fed's FRED data shows the US private-sector balance to have kept within a certain narrow range of minus 2 percent to plus 3 percent between 1994 and 2007, dipping into deficit territory at the height of consecutive asset bubbles (between 1997 and 2000, then again between 2004 and early 2007). It shot up from minus 1 percent all the way to plus 9 percent during the 2007–2009 crisis, a frighteningly large shift and as such indication of how terrifyingly intense a

[10] For more on Japan's decades-long liquidity trap and how economists should reframe theoretical arguments about that phenomenon in light of what the Japanese have gone through for over a quarter of a century, see Akram (2016).

[11] Ben Bernanke (2005) already talked of a "global savings glut" at the peak of the U.S. housing bubble, two years before it burst. He was referring here to the excessive build-up of current-account surpluses by China and other Asian economies, a phenomenon whose origins we can trace back to yet another major financial crisis, the 1997 Asian financial crisis.

systemic financial crisis we faced then. During the first four years of consequently slow recovery that surplus barely fell (to a still historically very high 5 percent by 2015). By the end of 2019, just before the pandemic hit, America's private-sector surplus was still sitting at 4.4 percent of GDP. The European Union's EUROSTAT national accounts data show a very similar pattern, especially for the stressed eurozone economies of Greece, Ireland, Italy, Portugal, and Spain after 2011 when their hitherto typically negative (i.e. deficit) balances between saving and investment turn positive. Since then the ($S > I$) surplus has been rising steadily to an average of nearly 5 percent of GDP in those five economies most heavily affected by the eurozone crisis of 2010–2012 (see Sect. 4.2.2).

We have had two inter-related attempts at contextualizing such stubborn private-sector surpluses arising in the wake of systemic financial crises. Both are worth noting. Early on in the lackluster recovery Richard Koo (2011) identified the Great Financial Crisis of 2007/08 and its complicated aftermath as a *balance-sheet recession* that involves lasting cutbacks in spending by consumers and businesses as they try to pay down debts after having suffered sharp declines in asset prices. Such "deleveraging" necessitates a massive shift to a private-sector surplus of the kind we have noted for the US economy in the wake of the Great Recession (see Sect. 3.4.3). Lawrence Summers (2020) has referred to this new slow-growth pattern as *secular stagnation*, the result of inadequate levels of private investment failing to absorb significantly higher levels of private savings and as a consequence yielding persistently insufficient levels of aggregate demand. Both Koo and Summers, referring to the large private-sector surplus arising with a bang in the wake of a massive financial crisis, hark back to Irving Fisher's (1933) debt-deflation spiral of which the balance sheet recession is a more moderate version resulting in secular stagnation rather than outright economic depression.[12]

[12] Gordon (2016) has given us yet another explanation of the current slow-growth pattern of the past decade, tracing it to a significant deceleration in productivity growth which has occurred despite what appears to have been relatively rapid, albeit mostly incremental technological change.

4.2 Currency Wars

In the face of liquidity traps, central banks have undertaken massive asset-purchase programs generally referred to as "quantitative easing" (see Sect. 3.5.3). Such "unconventional" monetary policy is not only designed to push down interest rates across the entire term structure but also to lower the value of the domestic currency in exchange with other monies. This happens both on the demand and supply side. With interest rates lower, the currency is less attractive to invest in. Foreign investors will be dissuaded while domestic investors prefer to deploy their capital abroad. And to the extent that the central bank's massive asset purchases blow up bank reserves, a portion of these liquidity additions will seep into the foreign exchange markets as additional supplies of the currency. After the Fed had launched QE1 in November 2008 with a by-then unprecedented \$1.25 trillion monetary-base expansion, the trade-weighted index of the US dollar against a basket of currencies of America's most important trading partners fell from 102.4 to 91 a year later (100 = January 2006) and in the wake of the Fed's \$600 bn. QE2 all the way down to 85.7 by late July 2011. This depreciation helped boost the battered US economy by making imports more expensive and exports cheaper.

But that benefit came at the direct expense of other national economies suffering added squeezes from the appreciation of their respective currencies rendering their imports cheaper and exports more expensive. In some instances, such currency appreciation would be reinforced as investors across the globe redeployed funds out of dollars into higher-yielding currencies, such as Brazil's Real, whose central bank, the Banco Central do Brasil, tended to have a policy of comparatively high policy rates due to that country's bout of hyperinflation during the 1980s and early 1990s. It is precisely in that context that in September 2010 Brazil's finance minister Guido Mantega characterized the Fed's push to lower interest rates and exchange rates at the expense of thereby squeezing other countries as an "international currency war."

4.2.1 A Distinct Pattern

It is worth noting here a distinct pattern of post-crisis "competitive devaluations" which shape the way the downswing phase of the long wave in place ultimately unfolds. When the long wave shifts from upswing to downswing, it does so typically amidst a major financial crisis as a turning point. That crisis, usually one with international reach, breaks the upswing's growth pattern and leaves excess capacities as well as debt-servicing squeezes in its wake. There may at this point be a flirtation among competing powers to secure their market share in shrinking markets by protecting their domestic producers. Indeed, during the long wave of the interwar period, the stock-market crash of October 1929 was followed by the United States putting in place a prohibitive across-the-board tariff in the Smoot-Hawley Tariff Act of 1930 and so launching a very damaging trade war. When four decades later the next long wave turned from upswing to downswing amidst the collapse of the Bretton Woods system in August 1971, Nixon's suspension of the dollar-gold convertibility also had him impose a ten-percent across-the-board tariff, as part of his New Economic Policy (NEP) which included also wage and price controls. Such commercial warfare did not feature in the latest long-wave turning point, thanks to a commitment by G-20 members to refrain from protectionism in the London Summit of 2009.

What did, however, happen in the wake of the Great Financial Crisis of 2007/08 was yet another manifestation of monetary protectionism, the other dimension of a pattern that typically emerges after crisis-induced turning points in long waves. Systemic financial crises impose a downswing phase in their wake not least by destabilizing the prevailing international monetary system enough for the issuer of the world money to devalue the vehicle currency under its control and thereby set off competitive devaluations among competing powers jockeying for position which in the end leave all countries involved worse off. It is precisely this monetary instability that is the dominant, albeit less well understood, engine of crisis propagation across the world and as such always ends up relentlessly marking downswing phases of long waves.

We find that pattern already in the 1930s when at first Britain, the issuer of what then was still considered to be the world's leading vehicle currency, was forced off the gold-exchange standard in September 1931. That crisis arose amidst speculative attacks on its impossibly overvalued currency, the pound sterling, which Churchill had somewhat recklessly anchored at the prewar parity of $4.86 when returning the country to a gold standard in 1925. The pound immediately devalued by 25 percent once no longer tied to gold. But then Roosevelt devalued the dollar by 40 percent in the Gold Reserves Act of 1934, and this action greatly intensified competitive devaluations which came to be referred to as "beggar-thy-neighbor" policies aimed at improving one's own economy at the expense of others. Britain, France, and the United States engaged in a currency war during the mid-1930s until their conclusion of a cease-fire in the Tripartite Agreement of September 1936 meant to stabilize their respective currencies in the international exchange markets and also joined by Belgium, Netherlands, and Switzerland.[13]

As regards the postwar period, the US dollar had been overvalued from the very inception of Bretton Woods in 1945 when it was fixed at the same prewar parity of $35/ounce put in place by the Roosevelt Administration a decade earlier at the nadir of the depression, in 1934. And once again such systemic overvaluation of the vehicle currency at the center of prevailing international monetary arrangements could not last, exploding the system in August 1971 in the wake of massive speculative attacks pushing for corrective currency-price adjustments. Exchange rates were appropriately reset four months later, in the Smithsonian Agreement of December 1971 concluded among the Group of Ten members (United States, Britain, Germany, Japan, France, Italy, Canada, Netherlands, Belgium, and Sweden), when the gold-dollar parity was changed to $38/ounce amounting to a 7.9 percent devaluation of the US currency. Other G-10 members accepted significant revaluations of their respective currencies against the dollar, notably a 13.6 percent hike of the D-Mark and a 16.9 percent rise for the Yen. These currency-price corrections proved inadequate for the onset of a US-centered inflationary acceleration spreading across the globe by fusing soon into a self-feeding process of Federal Reserve accommodation, US dollar flows into the offshore Eurodollar markets, and relentlessly upward pressures on commodity prices. That pump drove persistent speculation against the US dollar until March 1973, when it was allowed to float, and then turned into a carousel of "competitive devaluations" pushing down the British pound, the Italian lira, and the French franc to a point of currency crises for all three in 1976 whereupon pressure returned against the US dollar depreciating nearly 20 percent over the next couple of years. This turmoil in currency markets during the first six years of market-determined flexible exchange rates was key to the global propagation of stagflation conditions, a unique combination characterizing that particular downswing phase (see Sect. 3.2.4).

[13] See Nurkse (1944) as the classic work discussing the turmoil of floating exchange rates after the demise of the gold standard in 1931 disintegrating into a "currency war."

For the third time in a row, a downswing phase of a long wave started with significant exchange-rate turmoil as leading powers manipulated currency prices for competitive advantage in the wake of the Great Financial Crisis of 2007/08. This time the trigger at the center of the system came into play when the issuer of world money adopted unconventional monetary policy, so-called "quantitative easing," which then unleashed a large and sudden depreciation against other leading currencies squeezing those countries issuing them. As those countries reeled from the hit suffered amidst suffocating currency appreciation, they then adopted quantitative easing on their own to drive their currencies sharply lower. Their response hurt yet another group of countries, and those in turn adopted measures amounting to currency devaluation, and so forth. Such propagation of competitive-devaluation strategies saw the United States squeeze Europe's single-currency zone in 2009. The eurozone's own systemic financial crisis between late 2009 and mid-2012 prompted its central bank, the European Central Bank (ECB), to launch its own quantitative easing which in turn put pressure on China and, by extension, to commodity producers seeing their export earnings collapse. That decade-long pattern, detailed here, has turned the dollar standard on its head when the issuer of world money becomes the perpetrator of centrifugal forces feeding a gradually spreading global downturn.

4.2.2 The Eurozone Crisis 2009–2012

Even though Guido Mantega's characterization applied to the United States hurting the emerging-market economies like Brazil, it was the nineteen-member eurozone which got badly squeezed first at the onset of the Fed's quantitative easing in late 2008 and early 2009. At that point it was not only the United States, but also Britain, Switzerland, and Japan, all of whom launched aggressive QE programs lowering their currencies. From early November 2008 to late October 2009, the euro's effective exchange rate against its major trading partners rose from 102.4 to 114 (1999 = 100) just after the Eurozone's banks had been hit by America's subprime crisis and its member countries' current account balances had been hurt by the global recession. America's subprime crisis of 2007/08 thus spread to the other side of the Atlantic not just because of massive losses imposed on European banks or the collapse of US households' excess demand for European goods, but also because of the Fed's quantitative easing pushing the US dollar lower. The ensuring appreciation of the euro (by about 10 percent) during a crucial period in 2009 was literally "the straw that broke the camel's back."

The swift and sudden rise of the euro put even more pressure on those countries within the euro area, such as Greece, Portugal, or Spain, which had already seen the international competitiveness of their industries erode in the preceding decade. In addition, it accentuated the demand shock from the sharp reversal of America's excess spending on foreign goods and services during the Great Financial Crisis and subsequent recession between August 2007 and June 2009, making Eurozone goods and services more expensive in the US market. The higher euro may also have reinforced denomination mismatches on the balance sheets and in the cross-border income flows of European banks from dollar-denominated assets on their books, thereby adding to the losses already suffered from the unfolding financial crisis in the United States. These three transmission channels of crisis contagion coming from the United States hit the different Eurozone economies from a variety of angles and with uneven force, depending on where those were in their financial-cycle dynamic at the time and how well (or ill) balanced the interactions between their respective external, private, and public sectors were set up when the triple shock arose. We are talking here about an asymmetric shock *par excellence*.

Be that it as it may, already during late 2008 and early 2009 many European economies suffered the impact of the Great Financial Crisis in terms of worsening external imbalances ($M > X$) and shifts in private-sector balances to surpluses ($S > I_g$), much in line with what we witnessed during the same period in the United States (see Sect. 3.4.3).[14] Both of these crisis-induced shifts raised public sector deficits ($G > T$) as compensatory counterweight. Rising budget deficits raised concerns among institutional investors as well as EU policy-makers. One key policy rule dominating the Eurozone concerns the so-called Stability and Growth Pact (SGP), introduced in 1997, which limits permissible budget deficits to 3 percent of GDP. Enforced on a yearly basis rather than over the full economic cycle, the SGP was not set up at the time to distinguish properly between structural deficits (set by policy) and cyclical deficits (subject to business-cycle fluctuations). The latter would automatically get bigger with slowing economic activity, as automatic fiscal stabilizers kick in to

[14] See the excellent discussion of the different phases of the Eurozone crisis in Hein (2012).

lower tax revenues and push up such income-maintenance spending as unemployment benefits or anti-poverty programs. In the decade leading up to this moment of crisis the European Commission had proven unable to enforce the SPG rule against both Germany and France, the two largest EU economies, running excessive budget deficits, further undermining the credibility of the pact's applicability.

Against this background of brewing trouble, on 18 October 2009, Greece's newly elected Socialist prime minister George Papandreou made an announcement that stunned the world and marked the opening shot of the Eurozone crisis of 2009–2012. He announced a new estimate of 12.7 percent of GDP for the 2009 budget deficit of Greece which was twice as high as the previous figure. Intending to damage his political rival Constantine Karamanlis with the implication of the latter's administration having fudged the budget numbers before the election, Papandreou's announcement set off instead a crisis of confidence which over the next six months involved multiple downgrades of Greece's credit ratings, fraught negotiations with the European Commission, austerity plans provoking outrage among his left-wing electorate, and Greece's request for a rescue package—the first of ultimately three rescues between 2010 and 2015.

Greece was surely an outlier. But its tragic six-month slide into bankruptcy was just the beginning of a much broader panic "flight" out of sovereign bonds of countries in the periphery of the Eurozone suddenly deemed suspect. This run was a classic case of "shift contagion," whereby you get significantly increased correlations in financial-market behavior after a shock. Between the start of the Eurozone in 1999 and the breaking point in October 2009, the long-term yields of government bonds from the different Eurozone countries had converged toward the level of the German 10-year *Bund* bonds, with barely any spread between them. In other words, for a whole decade following the inception of a single-currency zone across Europe investors had assumed that government bonds of all its member countries were pretty much as good as Germany's, the group's leader. After downplaying default risks and country risks so persistently for so long, investors over-reacted in the opposite direction toward exaggeration once they suddenly had to acknowledge the presence of such risks.

Starting with Papandreou's fateful press conference on 18 October 2009, government bond yields for a number of countries exploded in secondary markets in the wake of massive sell-offs. Any yield above 7 percent threatened the financial viability of governments due to the compounding of debt-servicing charges. Greece's 10-year yield peaked at 29.79 percent (February 2012), Lithuania's at 14.5 percent (November 2009), Portugal's at 13.85 percent (January 2012), Latvia's at 13.76 percent (January 2010), Ireland's at 12.45 percent (July 2011), Italy's at 7.06 percent (November 2011), Cyprus' at 7 percent (October 2011), Slovenia's at 6.9 percent (December 2011), Spain's at 6.79 percent (July 2012). Germany's 10-year Bund yield stayed between 1.83 percent and 3.43 percent during the entire 32-month period of crisis.[15]

The other dimension of the Eurozone crisis concerned massive bank bailouts by national governments which began already during 2008 in the context of losses from the US financial crisis, notably on holdings of suddenly worthless mortgage-related securities, and continued through the Eurozone crisis all the way to October 2012. The EU members authorized a total of €5 trillion in aid to banks, distributed as €3.6 tr. in loan guarantees, €800 bn. in recapitalization, €400 bn. in asset relief interventions, and €200 bn. in liquidity measures. Only a fraction of these funds, a total of €1.6 trillion, was actually spent of which €1.1 tr. were allocated for the loan guarantees, about €300 bn. for recapitalization and €100 bn. each for the asset relief interventions and for the liquidity measures. While Britain, whose capital London is the center of international banking, and Germany, whose recycling of large chronic trade surpluses made its banks heavily vested abroad, both spent between €270 bn. and €300 bn. to rescue their banking sectors, Ireland had to commit an astounding €350 bn. to save its largest four banks after those had gone on an international spending binge blowing them up in size comparable to the largest British banks. France, Spain, the Netherlands, and Denmark each had to spend about €100 bn. on their respective banks after many of those had overextended abroad or on domestic asset bubbles that burst.[16]

Even though these bank bailout costs stemmed from different institutional sources, some off-budget, and ended up being accounted for in a variety of ways, they did push up budget deficits of countries concerned at a time of great stress in government bond markets. As the crisis unfolded with relentless intensity during 2010 and 2011, a negative feedback

[15] The data on 10-year government bond yields come from European Central Bank (2020).

[16] See Thomson Reuters (2016) as source for these bailout cost details.

loop ("doom loop") emerged between banks and governments which, if allowed to run its course unimpeded, carried the great potential for utter disaster. On the one hand, you had a lot of undercapitalized banks already teetering on the verge of failure whose typically large holdings of their country's government bonds suffered continuous and significant losses in value in the wake of sky-rocketing market yields. And on the other hand, you had governments already facing rapidly rising budget deficits and a crisis of investor confidence that would have to commit themselves to spend even more on failing banks. Devaluing government bonds were pulling down banks, and in turn, bank failures were aggravating the squeeze on governments.

As this deadly spiral took hold, it became clear that the existing institutional setup of the Eurozone lacked crisis management tools to break that dynamic. Maastricht Treaty's "no bailout" clause meant that there was no mechanism for intra-EU bailouts. Moreover, the same clause also precluded the European Central Bank from targeting specific country debt in its open-market purchases to help bring their sky-high yields down.[17] And without a Eurozone-wide deposit insurance scheme, bank failures were still the responsibility of national deposit insurance funds, many of which proved inadequately funded in the face of a systemic crisis so that the cost burdens of bank bailouts transferred quite rapidly to national governments and their stressed budgets. Ireland, for instance, faced a budget deficit of 32.5 percent of GDP after having had the government itself bail out the four largest Irish banks.

When Greece was obliged early on in the European sovereign-debt crisis to ask for help, it ended up negotiating a €110 bn. rescue package with the International Monetary Fund, the European Commission, and the European Central Bank in return for promising painful fiscal austerity measures and structural reforms. That agreement of May 2010 involved separate bilateral commitments by the Eurozone countries which, in light of the Eurozone's long-standing "no bailout" commitment already anchored in the founding Maastricht Treaty of 1992, proved politically difficult to pass in several countries. In response, the Eurozone decided

[17] As Moore (2016) explains well, the European Central Bank (ECB) buys and sells portfolios of government bonds of Eurozone member states according to a strict formula known as the "capital key" which corresponds to that country's share in the capitalization of the ECB. For instance, Germany's capital key is 18 percent, which determines the percentage of the ECB's open-market operations involving German bonds known as Bund.

to create a new lender-of-the-last-resort mechanism from scratch to deal with its sovereign-debt crisis more effectively, bypassing in effect that prohibition against intra-EU bailouts. In June 2010 Eurozone members created for that purpose a tripartite mechanism which was authorized to mobilize a total of €750 bn. in financial assistance to member countries in economic difficulty. The European Financial Stability Facility (EFSF), set up as a special-purpose vehicle to isolate member countries from financial risk and financing itself by issuing member-guaranteed AAA-rated bonds for up to €440 bn., could make loans to eurozone countries facing financial troubles, recapitalize banks, or buy sovereign debt. The European Financial Stabilization Mechanism (EFSM) provided €60 bn. in funds raised by the European Commission, collateralized by the EC budget, which could be loaned out to eurozone members as part of broader rescue packages. The International Monetary Fund (IMF) set aside €250 bn. of its own funds to help the eurozone cope with its sovereign-debt crisis. Subsequently, the tripartite EFSF-EFSM-IMF lender-of-last-resort mechanism provided €85 bn. in aid to Ireland in November 2010, €78 bn. in aid to Portugal in May 2011, and a second rescue package totaling €164 bn. in aid for Greece in March 2012.

Both the EFSF and EFSM were conceived as only temporary stop-gap mechanisms which needed to be replaced with a more permanent structure within three years. In September 2012 the eurozone member states ratified by inter-governmental treaty the so-called European Stability Mechanism and endowed the ESM with a maximum lending capacity of €500 bn. The ESM Treaty provides for a well-defined intervention procedure which involves evaluation, assistance defined in a memorandum of understanding outlining the specific fiscal consolidation and/or structural reform commitments of the recipient country, and the country to be assisted having ratified the new 2012 European Fiscal Compact (see Sect. 6.3.1).[18] The ESM offers five different types of assistance programs, including support lending within a macro-economic adjustment program for countries shut out of the sovereign bond markets, bank recapitalization, precautionary financial assistance in the form of credit lines to draw from, a primary market support facility helping countries return to

[18] The European Fiscal Compact, a reform passed in January 2012 to tighten the wobbly Stability and Growth Pact, centralized European Commission control over national budget making and streamlined excessive-deficit procedures for better enforcement of budget-deficit and public-debt limits, as well explained by Dullien (2012).

the sovereign bond market for the issue of new bonds, and secondary market support facilities aimed at stabilizing government bond yields under pressure. The ESM financed nearly half of Spain's €100 bn. bank recapitalization program launched in December 2012. In April 2013, the ESM offered Cyprus €9 bn. (with an additional €1 bn. from the IMF) of which €4.1 bn. were allocated for the refinancing and amortization of debt liabilities, €3.4 bn. to cover fiscal deficits, and €2.5 bn. for bank recapitalization.

During the acute phase of the Eurozone crisis from early 2010 to mid-2012, when Greece, Ireland, Portugal, Spain, and Cyprus all required bailouts, the European Central Bank (ECB) injected lots of liquidity into the banking system from the onset. In December 2011, the ECB upped its ante significantly when it introduced three-year loans at 1 per cent known as "Long-Term Refinancing Operations" (LTRO) against a wide range of bank collateral, a massive new lender-of-last-resort mechanism that the ECB has perfected since then to keep hundreds of badly damaged Eurozone banks going until such time that they can be successfully reorganized. And in August 2012, the ECB announced a targeted bond-purchase program known as "Outright Monetary Transactions" (OMT) as an insurance program against crisis-induced spikes in bond yields which came with a sterilization mechanism and so, in contrast to quantitative easing, would not add liquidity to the banking system. Only announcing this initiative sufficed to calm bond market nerves, as it has yet to be used once.

Even though the combination of LTRO and OMT helped move the Eurozone out of an acute crisis, locked-in fiscal austerity across the European Union made for a slow recovery in most European economies many of which were further kept below their potential by weak banks reluctant to lend. The Eurozone's chronic-deficit countries in the periphery, notably Greece, Cyprus, Ireland, Portugal, Spain, and Italy, had to undergo a painful deflationary adjustment known as "internal devaluation" which put much of their citizens through an economic depression. With so many of its member countries in the grip of stagnation and high unemployment, the post-crisis recovery of the Eurozone proved too slow to overcome the crisis-induced liquidity trap making banks hesitant to lend and the private sector loath to borrow. This difficult adjustment period rooted in austerity and deleveraging was rendered even more painful by the euro's post-crisis reversal from decline to sharp rise during 2013/14. Whereas the euro's effective exchange rate had fallen by 17.5

percent during the Eurozone crisis between October 2009 and July 2012 (from 114 to 94.5), it rose by 10.2 percent over the next two years (from 94.5 in July 2012 to 104.1 in March 2014). In January 2015 the European Central Bank announced its own massive quantitative easing which eventually, over the next four years, amounted to €2.6 trillion worth of purchases of government bonds, corporate bonds, asset-backed securities, and covered bonds. Besides lowering interest rates and boosting stock markets, this huge QE program immediately made the euro cheaper as intended, lowering it by 9.6 percent against the currencies of its partners over just four months (from 98.5 in January 2015 to 88.5 in April 2015).

4.2.3 *China's Currency Challenge*

Such a sharp currency-price reversal sent shockwaves through the rest of the world. In the face of a dearer dollar, US economic growth slowed during much of 2015. But the spillover from the euro's QE-driven depreciation (and concomitant US dollar appreciation) extended beyond the United States also to emerging-market economies. We are looking here in particular at what happened in China which during that period also faced a strong QE-driven depreciation of the Japanese yen in the wake of a three-pronged stimulation and reform program known as "Abenomics" in reference to Prime Minister Shinzo Abe's unprecedented efforts after December 2012 to pull his country out of its long-suffering deflation. On August 11, 2015, China saw a sudden devaluation of its typically tightly controlled currency, the Renminbi (also referred to as Yuan), which ended up having major repercussions for its domestic economy, Xi Jinping's reform program, and the People's Bank of China's management of exchange rates. This moment of crisis, as it turned out, marked the beginning of a new chapter in China's long history of experimenting with its exchange-rate regime.

Following its inflation-stabilizing currency reform of 1994, which pegged the renminbi (RMB) at a very competitive 8.28 RMB per dollar for the next decade, China's economy took off amidst rapid export growth and inflows of foreign direct investment. China's real GDP growth rate averaged a spectacular 10 percent p.a. while inflation remained well-behaved below 5 percent (after a peak of nearly 25 percent in 1994) until the Great Financial Crisis of 2007/08. Facing growing complaints from trading partners and intensifying domestic-policy pressures in connection with its long-standing currency manipulation, China's policy-makers finally decided in July 2005 to relax the peg. After revaluing the renminbi by 2.1 percent to 8.1 RMB per dollar, China's "redback" was then allowed to move gradually in a crawling peg within a narrow band against a reference basket of currencies.[19] Over the next three years, the RMB appreciated gradually but steadily by 20.8 percent to 6.83 RMB per dollar.

During the Great Financial Crisis of 2007/08, China redoubled its efforts to shield its economy from that shock, just as it had done in the context of the East Asian currency crisis of 1997/98. One measure was to re-peg its currency at 6.83 RMB per dollar in July 2008, an arrangement it maintained for nearly two years until June 2010. At the same time, China's policy-makers embarked on a huge fiscal stimulus package of 4 trillion yuan (= $586 billion), co-financed by the national, provincial, and local governments, which was, for the most part, a public-works program in infrastructure (housing, rural development, post-disaster reconstruction, industry) and also contained some social welfare spending for health and education. This large injection of public spending succeeded in reversing a momentary slowdown in growth to about 6 percent in 2008 back up to 10 percent real growth in 2010, an acceleration which the rest of the world welcomed as providing a helpful boost to a battered world economy and its still-fragile recovery.

While powering through the Great Recession so that it amounted to barely a blip at home, China's largesse soon began to weigh heavily on the structural foundations of its economic growth. Its huge fiscal stimulus package compensated for the large decline in its trade surplus from 9.3 percent in 2008 to just 2.1 percent in 2014. In its wake, China's already high investment share (which had been 34 percent of GDP in 2000 and 41 percent in 2007) rose all the way to 48 percent in 2010, before drifting slowly lower to about 45 percent in 2015. Most of that spending injection focused on building unneeded dwellings and excess industrial capacity, so that much of this increased investment ended up being by and large

[19] In announcing the new exchange-rate regime, the PCoB never specified in detail the composition of the "reference basket" of currencies known as the China Foreign Exchange Trade System (CFETS), only that it would comprise "currencies of countries to which China has a prominent exposure in terms of foreign trade, external debt, and foreign direct investment." This rather imprecise definition invited much discussion as to possible alternative baskets, a point well analyzed by Spiegel (2005). The rate-setting formula for the daily adjustments was to allow the RMB to fluctuate within a ±0.3 percent band from the "central parity" rate corresponding to the closing rate of the preceding day.

quite wasteful. A good proxy measure of the efficiency of investment, the incremental capital output ratio (measured as the gross fixed capital formation share in GDP divided by real GDP growth), rose from 3.5 in 2008 (which conformed with the long-run average level throughout the reform period) to about 5.7 which indicates "far less bang for the buck." In that context, it was also troubling that the credit-fueled investment boom raised China's private (non-financial) sector debt-to-GDP ratio from 111.9 percent in the fourth quarter of 2008 to a dangerously high 201.9 percent in the first quarter of 2016, among the highest ratios in the world. Especially problematic in this context is the debt accumulated by China's state-owned enterprises. These make up about a third of total GDP but account for more than half of all bank loans and 90 percent of corporate bond issues.[20]

The combination of overinvestment and excessive leverage eventually began to weigh on China's hitherto super-fast growth path. Whereas real GDP expanded by an impressive 10.6 percent in 2010, it slowed to 9.6 percent in 2011, 7.9 percent in 2012, 7.8 percent in 2013, 7.4 percent in 2014, and just 7.0 percent in 2015. Having settled within a fairly narrow 6.10–6.20 RMB per USD range during 2014 and into 2015 while the dollar appreciated strongly (by 16 percent on a trade-weighted basis), the RMB was clearly overvalued against such key currencies as EUR, JPY, or KRW (South Korea's Won) and, given China's falling trade surplus, probably the USD as well. During the second half of 2014, the RMB came under sustained selling pressure thanks to accelerating capital outflows. Those sped up even further during the first half of 2015, doubling from about $100 billion per quarter to $200 billion per quarter. There were several factors driving this capital-flow reversal. A key one was the unwinding of carry trades in response to China's monetary policy easing pushing interest rates lower and feeding expectations of impending currency devaluation which spurred repayment of loans from non-residents and repatriation of deposits from non-residents, two of the principal carry-trade channels. In addition, there was also an acceleration in the acquisition of foreign assets by residents, both recorded as well as unrecorded (i.e. bypassing of restrictions through loopholes such as

[20] The data on China's debt-to-GDP ratios, total and private non-financial, are from the Federal Reserve Bank of St. Louis FRED data (see https://fred.stlouisfed.org/series/QCNPAM770A). The data pertaining to China's investment and its eroding efficiency come from Wolf (2018).

over-invoicing of exports, cash transactions, or flows recorded/included as "errors or omissions"). In the face of these net outflows putting pressure on the RMB's crawling peg, the PBoC ended up having to buy up its currency (and sell reserves). For the first time in many years, China's foreign exchange reserves fell from a June 2014 peak of \$3.99 trillion to \$3.557 trillion in August 2015. These PBoC interventions to support its currency had the less-than-welcome side effect of draining reserves out of the banking system at a time when growth was already slowing down a lot.

As if there was not already enough trouble brewing, Chinese stock valuations suddenly caved. After a spectacular stock-market boom driven by ample margin credit and a risk-taking culture among a dominant group of young (and inexperienced) retail investors prone to speculative excess, both the Shanghai and the Shenzhen stock markets turned sharply lower in mid-June 2015. Margin calls forcing sell-offs into already sharply declining markets turned this market correction rapidly into a full-blown crash, pushing leading market indices, such as the CSI 300 or the Shanghai Composite Index, a third lower in less than a month. This stock-market collapse came about despite several unusually intrusive government interventions aiming to stabilize the turmoil, a failure which only served to erode already shaky confidence in the Chinese economy further and convinced policy-makers that they had to act more decisively.[21]

At the same time, the PBoC very much wanted the International Monetary Fund (IMF) to include the RMB in the basket of currencies making up the IMF's Special Drawing Rights (SDRs) which at the time was composed of the USD, the EUR, the GBP, and the JPY. Such international recognition of the RMB's new global reserve-currency status depended not least on further steps to loosen its peg in favor of a more market-oriented approach to currency pricing. After widening the daily band of permissible fluctuations from the central RMB/USD parity rate from ±0.5 percent to ±1 percent in April 2012, that band was doubled to ±2 percent in March 2014 which would allow for substantial cumulative changes in the exchange rate if so desired. As financial instability intensified steadily during the first half of 2015, from renminbi sell-offs to stock-market crash, China's leaders felt compelled to tackle the thorny

[21] For a summary of the unusual market-stabilization efforts by China's stock-market regulator and their relatively limited or counter-productive impact see Lee (2015).

question of currency valuation finally in a more decisive fashion in the hope of thereby at once calming nervous investors and appeasing the IMF. On August 11, 2015, the PBoC announced a new exchange-rate regime in the direction of a more genuinely "managed float," reinforcing that move with a 1.9 percent devaluation of the RMB (see People's Bank of China, 2015).

Wanting to give market forces more say in setting the exchange rate, the PBoC decided to have the RMB's central parity rate set each day in alignment with the spot rate established at the closing of the previous day in the by-then global offshore market for renminbi which Chinese authorities had systematically set up step by step between 2009 and 2015. By mid-2015 the daily turnover of offshore renminbi transactions had reached $120 billion/day, half of which traded among authorized banks in Hong Kong and the rest in renminbi clearing hubs operating in other financial centers of the world (London, Singapore, etc.). The so-called CNH spot rate (CNH for Hong Kong-centered renminbi offshore trading) established in this network of trading centers for the most part closely tracked the government-managed renminbi exchange rate due to unrestricted arbitrage flows between them by Chinese firms. But now, with the sudden move from crawling peg to managed float, the signaling causality would be reversed from the CNH spot rate to what henceforth would come to be named the onshore CNY parity rate (replacing RMB). The terse two-sentence PBoC announcement left many crucial details unclear.

The immediate impact of this policy change was to have two additional days of further devaluation by another 1.8 percent, as the CNH spot rates fell steeply amidst renminbi sell-offs. This surprise announcement of China's first currency devaluation in over two decades was a bombshell, interpreted worldwide as an admission of worries among China's leadership about the economic slowdown. Expectations of further currency devaluation intermingled with widespread confusion about the precise modalities of the new exchange-rate policy. Stock markets, commodity prices, and emerging-market currencies all tanked while bond prices rallied as deflationary sentiments intensified in the immediate aftermath of this botched devaluation attempt. Capital outflows out of China greatly accelerated over the next three months, from a monthly pre-crisis average of $65 billion to post-crisis average of about $100 billion per month, which put further pressure on the currency and equity shares. Subsequently, the PBoC intervened heavily to stabilize the CNY, extending its interventions even to the offshore CNH, whereupon it spent another $350 billion until the end of the year to prop up the renminbi.[22]

4.3 Commodities and Currencies

As the deflationary impact of the US-centered crisis of 2007–2009 moved across the Atlantic to trigger the eurozone crisis 2009–2012 and then put China under pressure from 2014 on to its currency crisis of August 2015, global commodity prices started tumbling in the summer of 2014. This crash created significant problems for many commodity-exporting nations that had enjoyed favorable terms of trade and strong income gains from a decade and a half of booming commodity markets. Their troubles marked the extension of secular stagnation and its deflationary bias to the rest of the planet.

4.3.1 The Commodity Super Cycle

Going back to the long-wave framework and Nikolai Kondratiev's analysis of long-term price trends (see Sect. 2.1.1), we can see that commodities fit that pattern neatly as objects of concentrated global demand whose relatively inelastic (because land-bound) supplies make for amplified price movements. Subject to a long-wave pattern, commodity prices have been characterized to move in a so-called "super cycle."[23] While individual commodity groups—foodstuffs, metals, livestock, oil—all have their own distinct price cycles characterized each by considerable volatility, they tend to sync up into an aggregate macro trend of longer-term up- and down-swings. The upswing phase of such a super cycle is driven by strong demand from population growth and rapid industrialization in key regions entering the world economy (e.g. the United States in the late nineteenth and early twentieth century, Europe and Japan in the postwar period, China and other emerging-market economies during the

[22] For more information on global market turmoil in the immediate aftermath of China's surprise devaluation see Desjardins (2015) and Stewart (2015). Donnan (2016) discusses China's accelerating capital flight and counter-measures for its containment.

[23] Among meaningful discussions of the global commodity super cycle, especially as a long-wave phenomenon, see Erten and Ocampo (2012) and LePan (2019).

1990s and 2000s). Sustained commodity-price increases over a decade or longer will boost the otherwise rather inelastic supplies of commodities by inducing higher-cost producers, now rendered profitable, to enter the market. But just when commodity supplies finally increase, demand starts slacking off or even declining as we enter the downswing secular-stagnation phase of a long wave. And thus we end up with long-term commodity-price deflation.

Even though the price movements of various commodities ultimately tend to fuse into a macro trend, there are some commodities that are more important than others. As a matter of fact, each of the four global commodity super cycles over the last century and a half has been dominated by just a couple of commodities. One such strategic commodity, of course, is gold not least because of its long history as a globally accepted money form. Even today, nearly half a century after its dematerialization, gold still serves as a store of value and hedge against inflation. A second commodity of crucial importance is the one representing the principal source of energy prevailing at the moment for which there is hence guaranteed large demand on a global scale. In the era of the Industrial Revolution, notably during the second half of the nineteenth century, this was coal. Since the end of World War II, we have lived in a world economy shaped by oil, and more recently also gas, as a dominant source of energy. We should note here that the key energy source seems tied to whatever currency serves as world money at the time. The dominance of coal during the nineteenth century was tied to the world-money role of the British pound sterling all the way to the coalminers' strike of 1926 following Britain's resumption of a gold-exchange standard a year earlier. And the emergence of oil as a principal energy source after World War II coincided with the US dollar becoming world money. This connection gets us to the bigger question of how commodities and currencies relate to each other.

4.3.2 An Inverse Price Relation

Globally traded commodities are invoiced and paid for in US dollars, a crucial support pillar of that currency's world-money status. Commodity prices and the USD's effective exchange rate are thus intimately related, typically moving in inverse relation to each other. A stronger dollar, for example, means that non-US buyers of commodities have to put up more of their currency for any given dollar-based price, making commodities thus more expensive in the local currency and leaving less space for those to rise in dollar terms. On the contrary, dollar prices of commodities are more likely to go down when the dollar appreciates, both because of depressed demand from sources having to pay more for them in depreciated local currencies and also in compensation for that de-facto price hike (in local currency).

A more indirect cause of that inverse relation relates to the underlying monetary and financial conditions driving the world money's exchange-rate evolution which also affect global demand conditions in general and for commodities in particular. A looser Fed policy, especially one of quantitative easing, will drive down the dollar against other currencies and also pump more dollars into international circulation which in turn boosts demand for globally traded commodities. The reverse holds true when the Fed tightens which feeds through the global banking system as a restraint on credit and financial-market conditions pushing commodity prices lower.

And then there is ever-growing speculation for which both currencies and commodities serve as attractive objects of attention, due to their inherently volatile prices. Ever since the appearance of financial derivatives around 1980 we have seen the proliferation of instruments of speculation (and hedging, as a sort of defensive speculation for loss prevention) such as options and futures. This is almost as true for commodities, whose trading has been transformed by financialization in recent decades, as it has been for currencies. Once speculators have come to appreciate the inherently inverse relation between the two, between the dollar's exchange rates and commodity prices, they will play both at the same time and thereby just amplify that inverse relationship.

We can see in Table 4.1 how closely intertwined these two price movements, measured here as the USD's nominal effective exchange rate (NEER) against the currencies of America's major trading partners and the IMF's All Commodity Price Index (ACPI), have been for the entire duration of the super cycle.[24] This includes the temporary crisis-induced

[24] For the US-dollar's exchange-rate index we used the figures provided by the Bank for International Settlements, Broad Effective Exchange Rate for United States, retrieved from FRED, Federal Reserve Bank of St. Louis; https://fred.stlouisfed.org/series/NBUSBIS. For the IMF's All Commodity Price Index we used the monthly price index tabulated by Index Mundi, retrieved from https://www.indexmundi.com/commodities/?commodity=commodity-price-index&months=300.

Table 4.1 Inverse relation between USD-NEER and ACPI

Time period	*%-change NEER (USD)*	*%-change APCI*
Feb. 2002–July 2008 (NEER) Dec. 2001–July 2008 (ACPI)	−26.97	+318.99
July 2008–March 2009	+17.86	−49.88
March 2009–July 2011 (NEER) March 2009–April 2011(ACPI)	−15.76	+91.60
July 2011–July 2014 (NEER) April 2011–July 2014 (ACPI)	+7.73	−14.76
July 2014–Jan. 2016 (NEER) July 2014–Feb. 2016 (ACPI)	+21.73	−47.46

Source Bank for International Settlements (NEER), International Monetary Fund (ACPI)

trend reversal at the height of the Great Recession in 2009/10 as well as the impact of the Eurozone crisis from 2011 to 2014. It was precisely at that point that the cycle finally broke in the direction of commodity-price deflation. The USD experienced a 20 percent appreciation over the next year and a half, with its NEER moving from 100.19 in July 2014 all the way to a January 2016 peak of 121.96, while commodity prices collapsed during the same period from 166.32 (July 2014) to a February 2016 bottom of just 87.39. The dollar's exchange rate and global commodity prices have thus indeed proven to be strongly correlated in an inverse relation.

4.3.3 Commodity Currencies and Carry Trade

The commodity super cycle also affected currencies of commodity exporters as it drew them irresistibly into the global financial system (see Sect. 1.3.1) When the Fed lowered its policy rates to zero and launched its first round of quantitative easing, it also set off dramatically increased USD-funded carry trades from March 2009 on into various commodity currencies, such as the AUD or the BRL. This new carry-trade arrangement is precisely one of the principal reasons prompting the "international currency war" comment by Brazil's finance minister Guido Mantega in September 2010, as it forced the BRL sharply higher by 25 percent against the USD since the beginning of 2009.

Such large currency-price movements are incidentally very much a byproduct of the carry trade as its volume gets boosted further by the prospect of additional capital gains and speculation-inducing expectations both of which arise from the funding currency's depreciation against the asset currency. Such overshoot inevitably sets the stage for a crisis, and that moment arrived in mid-2014 when the commodity boom collapsed in the wake of a sharply appreciating US dollar and decelerating Chinese economy starting to weigh heavily on commodity markets. The subsequent unwinding of USD-fueled carry trades out of commodity currencies only served to make their crash worse, confirming the pro-cyclical nature of the global financial cycle that had emerged after 2001.[25]

4.4 A Dangerous Turn in US Trade Policy

In the midst of the GFC, in November 2008, the G-20 countries made a "No Protectionism" pledge at their meeting in Washington so as not to repeat the mistakes of the Great Depression when the United States had started a disastrous trade war with passage of the Smoot–Hawley Tariff Act of 1930. What we got instead in the aftermath of the 2008–2009 crisis was monetary protectionism, mediated through successive waves of quantitative easing and currency devaluation, which eventually also hit China and commodity exporters. Once this sequence had run its course, by 2016, the world economy was still mired in global excess capacities plaguing key sectors (e.g. cars, steel, oil) and relatively slow growth worldwide (i.e. "secular stagnation"). At that point consensus to refrain from trade wars also started to erode. Part of that erosion was political, crystallized around the rapid strengthening of right-wing populist movements sweeping across many countries on the wings of post-crisis

[25] See Humpage and Herrell (2010) for a more detailed analysis of the USD-funded carry trade taking off during 2009. It is worth pointing here also to the important work on the "global financial cycle" as a vector of pro-cyclical destabilization by Rey (2015) or Miranda-Agrippino and Rey (2020).

anger. A key target of widespread disaffection was globalization and, by extension, also "free" trade. The other reason was institutional, as the postwar order in favor of "free" trade was coming to a close. In 2015 the Obama Administration officially abandoned the so-called Doha Round, launched in November 2001 to conclude a broad tariff-reduction deal between advanced capitalist economies and developing economies while also providing international code-of-conduct rules for a host of other trade-related issues (e.g. restraints on multinational firms, competition policy, government contracts, customs procedures). This failure, the first after eight successful global trade agreements in a row, marked the end of the multilateral approach to trade liberalization put in place in 1947.[26]

Two monumental developments unfolded during 2016 which very much exemplified the shifting winds amidst rising populist anger against globalization, relatively open borders, immigration, and trade—the surprising June 23 victory of the "Leave" campaign in Britain's European Union Membership Referendum and Donald J. Trump's even more stunning November 8 victory in the US presidential election. In a six-month window, the two consecutive superpowers committed to free trade (in Britain's case since the Congress of Vienna in 1815, in America's case since Roosevelt's New Deal, specifically the passage of the Reciprocal Trade Agreements Act of 1934) had opted for isolationism.

4.4.1 Trump and America's Trade Deficits

It is fair to say that Trump's electoral success derived from his ability to mobilize a large voter base who, among several convictions, strongly approved of his incessant complaints about "unfair" trade deals having decimated America's industrial heartland. After decades of de-industrialization and massive job losses in manufacturing, the majority of which due to automation, there are millions of Americans having suffered unemployment and/or lasting income losses from having to accept lower-earning jobs in service sectors. Their anger is more easily directed at trade, especially when concretized in terms of supposedly abusive practices by other countries (e.g. China, Mexico), rather than technology. Trump took full advantage of that latent reservoir of rage in a masterfully demagogic campaign propelling him to victory. It is

[26] See Bouet and Laborde (2010) or Elliott (2015) for the long-term implications of Doha's collapse.

noteworthy, but not surprising, that Trump defeated Clinton in the once-thriving, now-depressed industrial heartland of America—Pennsylvania, Ohio, Michigan, Wisconsin—which used to be solidly in the Democrats' camp.

At the center of Trump's case against long-standing US trade policy has been an obsession with America's large trade deficits as proof of other countries "taking advantage of us" and acting "unfairly." But those trade deficits have little to do with getting cheated by others. Looking at the equation $X - M = (S - I) + (T - G)$ (see Sect. 3.4.3), America's trade deficits are related to corresponding imbalances in the private sector (low savings causing $S - I < 0$) and the public sector (where we run large budget deficits so that $T - G < 0$ as well). In other words, our chronic trade deficits are embedded in the very structure of the consumption-driven, low-tax US economy. Moreover, to the extent that the US economy grows consistently faster than other advanced capitalist nations such as Germany or Japan, it draws in disproportionately larger amounts of imports. Our chronic trade deficits with China have more to do with the latter's strategic place at the center of global supply chains whereby American multinationals ship parts and components to China for assembly and then reimport them back at a higher value added as finished consumer or capital goods (e.g. Apple's iPhone). Finally, chronic US trade deficits, which became a key factor shaping the growth dynamic of the world economy in the mid-1980s, are part and parcel of the dollar standard, inasmuch as they mobilize the net outflows needed to transfer dollars created within America's domestic banking system to the rest of the world where they serve as an international medium of exchange or reserve asset. The dollar standard requires continuous US balance-of-payments deficits. In the absence of being a net exporter of capital such external deficits have to come about via the current account, meaning in the case of the United States its merchandise trade balance. But the other side of the coin also holds to the extent that the rest of the world automatically finances US trade deficits by absorbing dollars thereby ejected into international circulation when paying each other or keeping those as reserves. In that sense, US trade deficits are not only a necessary ingredient of the current international monetary system, but also far less problematic than Trump imagines them to be.

Still, none of these arguments about America's trade deficits mattered any longer in the era of Trump. Instead he has been obsessing for years over America's chronically large trade deficits as a cause of job losses and source of economic pain, blaming other countries' unfair trading practices and/or "stupid" deals made by earlier American presidents for this imbalance. That stance captured mounting frustrations of American blue-collar workers with the country's de-industrialization process while also putting the light on Trump's supposed prowess as a deal-maker. In the same vein, Trump has long opposed America's long-standing leadership in global governance as "too costly," contrasting it with his "America First" vision of unfettered nationalism. This "go-it-alone" sentiment too fell on eager ears, appealing to a long tradition of isolationism found on both the populist Right and the populist Left in American politics.

4.4.2 *Trump's Opposition to Regional Trade Deals*

Just three days after being sworn into office, Trump took the United States out of the Trans-Pacific Partnership (TPP) which Obama had concluded negotiating in February 2016 with eleven countries bordering the Pacific Rim on both sides (e.g. Japan, Philippines, Malaysia in Asia; Canada, Mexico, Peru, and Chile in the Americas). Its provisions set new standards for environmental protection, labor, intellectual property rights (especially for pharmaceuticals), good governance, human rights, regulatory cooperation, and transparency in investor-state dispute settlements—all objectives for which there exists a bipartisan consensus among the American body politic to push other countries for more stringent standards. The agreement had the added advantage of re-anchoring America's presence in East Asia in its battle for regional influence with China for whom the TTP set a variety of normative standards if it ever wanted to join this new configuration taking root in its backyard. Following Trump's decision to quit the TTP, the remaining eleven countries negotiated a trimmed-down alternative known as the Comprehensive and Progressive Trans-Pacific Partnership (CPTPP) which lacked several provisions the United States had insisted on. And in November 2020, China concluded a deal for a free-trade area known as the Regional Comprehensive Economic Partnership (RCEP) with the ten members of the Association of Southeast Asian Nations (ASEAN), including Thailand, Malaysia, Singapore, Philippines, Indonesia, Myanmar, Vietnam, Cambodia, Laos, and Brunei, as well as Japan, South Korea, Australia, and New Zealand. In one swoop the most dynamic region of the world economy has thus ended up de-coupling from the United States and re-anchoring itself with the regional power center China, a strategic switch of great importance.

Apart from the TPP, Obama had also pushed for a comprehensive agreement on several twenty-first-century trade issues with Europe to set new standards in the absence of a global agreement like Doha. Coming close to a conclusion before faltering on the contentious question of investor-state dispute-settlement provisions, the so-called Transatlantic Trade and Investment Partnership (TTIP) would have included ambitious and path-breaking agreements on e-commerce, cross-border investments, competition policy, public procurement, and intellectual property while at the same time also proposing sector-specific agreements beyond the confines of existing sectoral WTO rules (e.g. financial services). A pro-trade successor to Obama could have, or should have, tried to conclude a deal with the European Union. Not so Trump! His enthusiastic backing of Britain's Brexit and incessant criticisms of the NATO military alliance, while showing himself strangely partial toward Russia's Putin, were all meant to strain relations with our long-standing European allies. As regards trade, Trump launched a series of attacks on the European Union, with substantial US tariffs over a wide range of often iconic products (e.g. French champagne, Italian parmesan cheese) triggered by a long-standing dispute over airplane subsidies pitting Boeing against Airbus and also in response to digital taxes imposed on American tech giants by France and other EU countries.

Following his decision to withdraw from the TTP, Trump also decided to end the North America Free Trade Agreement (NAFTA), a trilateral trade bloc with America's neighbors Canada and Mexico set up in 1994. This step has to be seen in the context of Trump's relentless attacks on Mexico in support of his push for a "beautiful border wall" which so delighted his voter base. In response to enormous pressure from the business community and America's neighbors not to abandon regional integration, he finally renegotiated a replacement, known as the United States-Mexico-Canada Agreement (USMCA), in November 2018. Compared to NAFTA, the USMCA boosted car production within the region (with possibly more accruing to the United States), gave American farmers more access to the Canadian market, and reduced uncertainty in digital trade. At the same time, it added uncertainty by including a sixteen-year sunset clause, preceded by a tripartite review after six years. Following many months of deadlock, the US Congress passed the new agreement finally in December 2019 after Democrats obtained amendments to strengthen labor standards, environmental protection, and dispute-settlement provisions.[27]

4.4.3 *Trump's Trade Wars*

Branding himself as the consummate deal-maker to his adoring base, Trump's strategy was to negotiate bilateral deals where he thought the United States would get more concessions from its smaller counterparties than in regional or multilateral agreements. Negotiations had to be conducted under pressure, and for that reason Trump threatened, and often imposed, painfully high and/or targeted tariffs. He started this tactic with a bang only a couple of months into his presidency when he threatened across-the-board tariffs on steel imports (25 percent) and aluminum (10 percent) which he finally put into effect a year later, in March 2018. Evoking the national-security clause (i.e. Section 232 of the Trade Expansion Act of 1962) as justification made it abundantly clear to other governments that the Trump Administration would use any available protectionist weapon, whether truly justifiable or not, in support of a more combative unilateral approach to trade. In the meantime he got bilateral negotiations going with South Korea and Japan, both ending in treaties.

Trump's most consequential trade-policy move, however, was surely his increasingly high-stakes trade conflict with China, during which a series of tit-for-tat tariff extensions over a two-year period came to cover pretty much the entire half-trillion range of products traded between the two giants. It did not take long for both sides to realize that having significantly disrupted trade between the world's two largest economies was going to inflict a lot of pain on either, more than their leaders were perhaps willing to bear. China's leadership was already struggling with a slowing economy in need of structural rebalancing. Starting with the imposition of new US restrictions on telecom equipment giant Huawei in May 2019, there was a real threat for the conflict to expand in scope to foreign investments and access to technology, a prospect quite worrisome for China's high-tech leaders. Concerning the costs of conflict on the United States, its trade war with China hurt in particular American farmers, a crucial constituency of political support for Trump. He

[27] For additional details on how USMCA differs from NAFTA see Beattie and Politi (2018).

felt obliged to offer disgruntled farmers a supplementary $28 billion aid package on top of the usual farm subsidies so as not to undermine his own re-election prospects. American corporate leaders were also less than enthusiastic about hitting China with severe trade restrictions, worrying about disruptions to their global value chains and access to the largest, fastest-growing market in the world.

Seeking to step back from the abyss of all-out trade war, the two sides agreed in December 2018 to arrange for a narrowly focused truce before engaging in more ambitious negotiations over a wide range of issues many of which go to the heart of how China's state-dominated economic system operates. In December 2019 both sides, under political pressure at home, concluded the so-called "Phase One" mini-deal whereby the United States reduced or canceled some of its tariffs in exchange for Chinese promises of larger purchases of US farm products, better protections for intellectual property and forced technology transfers, greater market access for US financial-services companies, and new rules for currency transparency. It remains to be seen whether a more comprehensive deal tackling outstanding issues, notably China's extensive use of industrial subsidies, can be negotiated subsequently by the Biden Administration.

Such trade wars used to be contained by the World Trade Organization (WTO), set up in 1995 to replace the General Agreement on Tariffs and Trade (GATT) whose exclusive reliance on voluntary compliance had gradually rendered it increasingly ineffective. By contrast, the WTO had been endowed with strong dispute-settlement powers which enabled it to intervene quite actively in trade disputes. Trump effectively sidelined this mechanism in December 2019 when his administration refused to allow the replacement of retiring judges in the DSM's Appellate Body so that the number of still active AB judges fell below the required minimum threshold of three. This attack on the WTO has to be seen in the broader context of the Trump Administration systematically undermining multilateral institutions which up to that point had given the world community a crucial institutional framework of global governance and conflict management. In short order, Trump withdrew the United States from the Paris Climate Agreement in June 2017, from the United Nations Educational, Scientific and Cultural Organization (UNESCO) in October 2017, from Obama's painstakingly negotiated nuclear deal with Iran in May 2018, from the United Nations Human Rights Council

(UNHRC) in June 2018, and in the middle of a global pandemic from the World Health Organization in June 2020.[28]

4.4.4 *Financial Warfare*

Trump also aggressively used the US dollar's world-money position to pursue financial warfare against adversaries and force allies into compliance. We have already seen (in Sects. 3.3.3 and 3.4.3) that at the center of the world economy, as currently constituted, there is a dollar-based financial system on which most countries' interactions with the rest of the world depend. The moment anyone outside the United States transacts in US dollars anywhere in the world, the US government claims extraterritorial jurisdiction over such transactions which gives it extraordinary reach and power to use America's financial superpower hegemony as a weapon.

That weapon began to be used more actively after the 9/11 attacks in 2001 when America's "war on terror" included pursuing international networks of funding so-called "terrorist organizations" which extended to the US oversight over the global inter-banking SWIFT network. When its Justice Department imposed an enormous $8.9 bn. fine on BNP Paribas in 2014 for violating US sanctions on Cuba, Iran and Sudan, the United States signaled its willingness to pursue "secondary" sanctions penalizing third parties doing business with a sanctioned country, person, or entity. Trump has used a lot more sanctions against entities than any of his predecessors, notably against Russian firms (e.g. Ruslan), Chinese firms (e.g. Huawei, ZTE, SMIC), Iran, Venezuela, Turkey. He has also repeatedly threatened imposition of "secondary" sanctions, especially against EU firms and governments trying to preserve the Iran nuclear deal which the United States left in May 2018 in favor of reimposing a brutal sanction regime on its long-standing enemy.

Trump's aggressive "weaponization" of the dollar's international status has prompted other countries to consider for the first time seriously how to make themselves less dependent on the US currency and consider

[28] Both Rachman (2018) and Pascal (2019) discuss well the strategic implications of Trump's "America First" sledgehammer approach to the multilateralism of the post-war order which the United States was instrumental in creating and then greatly benefited from.

alternative international monetary arrangements.[29] Putin, ever since his annexation of Ukraine's Crimea in 2014 subject to stringent US sanctions, has launched a Russian equivalent to the SWIFT financial transfer system known as SPFS. China's PBoC set up its China Inter-Bank Payments System (CIPS) in 2015. There are discussions to connect these two, just as Putin and Xi have already increased the use of their own currencies to avoid dollars in their bilateral transactions, while also extending these payment-system alternatives to other countries such as India, Turkey, and Iran. In 2019 the EU set up a special-purpose vehicle known as INSTEX (for Instrument in Support of Trade Exchanges) for transactions with Iran as part of EU members' efforts (Germany, France, Britain) to salvage the nuclear deal. INSTEX was supposed to escape the US reach by conducting its transactions not in US dollars and outside of the SWIFT network.

4.5 Additional De-globalization Trends

Even before Trump brought to bear his disruptive measures in 2017, globalization—so powerful an engine of growth during the heydays of finance-led capitalism in the 1990s and 2000s—had shown worrying signs of stress and reversal.

4.5.1 Slowdown of Trade

Take trade, for example! During the heydays of globalization's latest wave, in the 1990s and first half of the 2000s, global trade grew at an annual rate of nearly 8 percent, twice as fast on average as gross domestic product. Since the crisis of 2007–2008 trade has grown a lot more slowly, by a mere 2.6 percent in 2018 and actually declining during the first half of 2019 (for the first time since the crisis a decade ago). The world-trade-to-GDP ratio, which rose from 38.8 percent in 1990 to 60.7 percent in 2008, has consequently drifted lower over the past decade to around 57 percent. This slowdown in trade has structural causes beyond the spread of trade barriers. Rapid advances in automation have reduced the comparative advantage of cheap-labor manufacturing. The sharp decline

[29] Discussions of Trump's "weaponization" of America's financial hegemony causing other countries to consider alternatives to the dollar standard can be found in Fleming (2019), Frenkel (2019), and *The Economist* (2020).

in transportation costs during the 1990s and 2000s has come to a halt. Trade in services, after rising swiftly with the global spread of the internet, has in recent years reached a plateau at 6–7 percent of world GDP. Most importantly, trade in intermediate products tied to global value chains (GVC) has never recovered its explosive pre-crisis pace and has lingered instead.[30]

4.5.2 *Squeezing Global Value Chains*

One of the more dynamic features of the most recent globalization wave of the 1990s and 2000s was the swift and thorough reorganization of production through outsourcing and off-shoring. This resulted in complex consumer goods, such as cars, computers, or smartphones, being produced in integrated multi-firm global value chains comprising several countries. An Apple iPhone, for example, maybe designed at headquarters in Cupertino (California), but then use components from Taiwan, the Philippines, and China while also including conflict metals from war-ravaged regions in sub-Saharan Africa and rare-earth elements mostly produced in China. Apple's supply chains stretch over forty-three countries.

Such GVCs involve a huge amount of intra-company trade in parts and components, meaning intermediate goods, getting shuffled from country to country and thus often exported more than once. Intermediate imports rose over two decades from a very low base to 19 percent of world GDP in 2008, but that share has since then declined to 17 percent. Another measure for the size of GVC-related trade in intermediate goods is the ratio of gross exports to GDP. Gross exports capture components getting re-exported as parts of a product, even repeatedly so, whereas GDP is a value-added measure of final goods and services. As reported by Hyun Song Shin (2019) on the basis of BIS calculations (whose research department he heads), that ratio expressed in constant prices moved from a base index of 100 in 2000 to 116 in 2008 before collapsing during the global financial crisis to 97 in 2009. While it then recovered swiftly to 110 by early 2011, that level was still significantly below the pre-crisis peak. More

[30] The trade ratios discussed in this paragraph stem from World Bank (2019) calculations based on its national accounts data and those from the Organization of Economic Co-operation and Development (OECD). Alternatively, one can establish those same trends about world trade also by looking closely at World Trade Organization (2018).

significantly, the ratio has since then steadily drifted lower to about 103 right now, indicating a significant retrenchment in the use of GVCs as they get scaled back, shortened, or altogether reversed by re-shoring.[31]

Shin identified several reasons for this trend. China, emerging during the preceding boom as the central node in the worldwide organization of GVCs, has greatly enhanced its ability to produce many of the strategic parts on its own (e.g. microchips). The mobilization of GVCs requires participating firms to have large amounts of working capital because of the massive inventories carried and large accounts receivables on the books, and banks all over the globe have become both less willing and able to provide the funding needed in support of that working capital. Over 80 percent of bank lending in support of GVC working capital is denominated in dollars, making such trade finance more expensive for non-US firms during periods when the dollar is strong.

4.5.3 Pullback of Cross-Border Investments

The eroding capacity of GVCs has coincided with a pullback by multinationals. Foreign direct investment, whereby firms expand their production capacity abroad, has fallen significantly from its peak of 5.3 percent of world GDP in 2007 to just a puny 1.3 percent in 2018. Restrained by tightening of domestic capital controls and more hostile reception in both the United States and European Union, FDI by Chinese firms into those two regions fell by a spectacular 73 percent in 2018, a major factor behind the overall 20 percent decline in worldwide FDI during that year reported by UNCTAD (2019). Its "Investment Trends Monitor" reported in January 2021 that in 2020, the year of the global pandemic, global FDI flows fell by 42 percent from $1.5 trillion to just $859 billion, more than 30 percent below the trough after the GFC in 2009.[32]

Some of that unusually large fall can also be attributed to Trump's tax-cut legislation which encouraged US firms to repatriate funds kept abroad, about $650 bn. in 2018 alone, to benefit from a tax amnesty.

[31] Shin's argument about the post-crisis trend reversal concerning GVC has also been meaningfully explored in Tett (2019).

[32] See UNCTAD (2021). It is also noteworthy in this context that 2020 was the first year ever during which FDI inflows into China exceeded those into the United States while Europe had a negative net outflow of –$4 billion.

But a more profound reason for this pullback may just be lower profitability amidst global excess capacities that have built up since the crisis of 2007–2008 imposed permanently lower levels of worldwide aggregate demand. This can be discerned by the drop in the rate of return on all multinational investment from an average of 10 percent at the 2005–2007 peak to just 6 percent in 2017. The share of global profits of all listed firms accruing to multinational corporations has shrunk from 33 percent in 2008 to 31 percent a decade later. In addition, more aggressively protectionist competition policies in the United States, European Union, China, even India, have begun to bear on one key element of FDI, cross-border takeovers, whose volume has recently slipped.[33] The growing geopolitical risk afflicting key sectors (high tech, e-commerce, cars) and emanating from a growing number of countries implementing discriminatory policies in violation of the national-treatment clause will oblige MNCs to raise their cost of capital as the "hurdle rate" for foreign investments.

The post-crisis retrenchment of foreign direct investment has been part of a broader decline in cross-border capital flows. Those surged during the 2000s from about $2.5 tr. in 2002 to $12.3 tr. in 2007, but then fell back to levels last seen in the late 1990s. Even during 2016, they amounted only to $4.3 tr., a 65 percent decline from the peak. Whereas cross-border capital flows averaged 11.5 percent of global GDP in the 2000s, that number fell to an average 7.1 percent in the 2010–2016 period. According to annual data provided by the BIS (see Aldasoro & Ehlers, 2019; Lund & Härle, 2017), the contraction was particularly pronounced in inter-bank lending. Nowhere has this retreat been greater than among Europe's large banks many of which have been obliged to undo some of their excessively risky pre-crisis expansion pursuits as part of their post-crisis restructuring (e.g. Austrian banks in Eastern Europe, British banks feeding Spain's real-estate bubble, Italian banks' ill-fated push into Turkey). All this implies a very different financial globalization dynamic than before the crisis, a process that has surely slowed down while at the

[33] In August 2018 the U.S. Congress passed the Foreign Investment Risk Review Modernization Act to strengthen the Committee on Foreign Investment in the United States (CFIUS) in its ability to vet foreign investments. China, in turn, has taken tougher anti-trust actions against foreign high-tech firms. The French have also interfered more actively against foreign mergers and acquisitions in recent years. India too has restricted the operations of U.S. e-commerce firms.

same time perhaps put on more solid footing as banks eschew the most risky and unstable practices which got them into so much trouble a decade ago.

4.5.4 Regionalization

Within the gradual de-globalization reversal observed over the last decade, itself indication that we are finding ourselves in a downswing phase of a long wave, there are signs of greater regionalization around three blocs through which power centers—the United States, China, Germany—build and extend their sphere of influence. This is especially true for the re-routing of GVCs.

- Trump's replacement of NAFTA by the USMCA (US-Mexico-Canada Agreement) focused principally on reinforcing the GVCs of automakers spanning those three countries, besides also pushing for stricter labor and environmental provisions, intellectual property-right protections, and digital trade rules. Trump's signature tax legislation, the Tax Cuts and Jobs Act of 2017 encouraged US multinationals to repatriate some of their $3 trillion in cash hoarded abroad and to re-shore production activities.
- As wages rise rapidly even in inland China away from the booming coastal zones, its large firms are pushing labor-intensive operations more aggressively to neighboring countries (e.g. Vietnam) where labor is cheaper. China's November 2020 free-trade deal with fifteen neighboring countries, the aptly named Regional Comprehensive Economic Partnership (RCEP), explicitly incentivizes supply chains across the region. Add to this President Xi's Belt and Road Initiative (BRI), a gigantic infrastructure project launched in 2013 meant to connect China and scores of other countries along several sea and land tracks all the way to London or Madrid. This gigantic infrastructure project involves the construction of a complex network of ports, railroads, highways, energy pipelines, border crossings, and special economic zones across Central Asia, South Asia, the Middle East, Russia, and Europe.
- Germany has created tight GVC linkages beyond the Eurozone (Austria, Slovakia) with its EU neighbors in Central Europe (Poland, Hungary, Czech Republic), as illustrated convincingly by Ambroziak Lukasz (2018). The EU is preparing a legislative proposal for Spring

2021 requiring European firms to carry out mandatory supply chain due diligence that would eliminate suppliers and countries violating human rights or environmental protection regulations. One practical effect of this new supply chain law would be to incentivize re-locating GVC nodes within the EU and its allies found in compliance.

We also have empirical proof of supply chains becoming more regionally focused. OECD data (see *The Economist*, 2019, Chart 2) shows that the share of cross-border supply chain foreign inputs from within their own region has risen steadily since 2011 in North America, Asia, and Europe. This regionalization reinforces a trend away from the US-dominated globalization wave (1990–2007) and toward a more complex multi-polar configuration in which three distinct regional blocs, each with its own unique policy approach, compete for space and influence.

In conclusion, we have seen in this chapter how the downswing phase of the latest long wave, which we have been finding ourselves in since the GFC of 2007/08, engulfed us in a gradually deepening deflationary context. The worldwide transmission of this new deflation has involved sequences of quantitative easing and competitive devaluations hitting one region after another, commodity-price collapses, trade conflicts, and reversals of capital flows. These de-globalization trends have intensified centrifugal forces toward greater regionalization around three distinct blocs in North America, Europe, and Asia. All this even before a pandemic hit us in March 2020 with a worldwide lockdown, the most disruptive shock to economic activity in our lifetime, the subject of our next chapter.

References

Akram, T. (2016). *Japan's liquidity trap* (Levy Institute Working Paper, No. 862). http://www.levyinstitute.org/pubs/wp_862.pdf

Aldasoro, I., & Ehlers, T. (2019, June). Concentration in cross-border banking. *BIS Quarterly Review*. https://www.bis.org/publ/qtrpdf/r_qt1906b.htm

Avdjiev, S., Kartasheva, A., & Bogdanova, B. (2013, September). CoCos: A primer. *BIS Quarterly Review*. https://www.bis.org/publ/qtrpdf/r_qt1309f.htm

Baer, G. (2018, March 1). Basel IV requires serious U.S. review. *Banking Perspectives*. The Clearing House. https://www.bankingperspectives.com/basel-iv-requires-serious-u-s-review/

Bank for International Settlements. (2019). *Basel III: International regulatory framework for banks*. Basel. https://www.bis.org/bcbs/basel3.htm

Beattie, A., & Politi, J. (2018, October 1). How is Donald Trump's USMCA trade deal different from Nafta? *Financial Times*. https://www.ft.com/content/92e9ce0a-c55f-11e8-bc21-54264d1c4647

Bernanke, B. (2005, March 10). *The global savings glut and the U.S. current account deficit*. Sandridge Lecture, Virginia Association of Economists, Richmond (Virginia). https://www.federalreserve.gov/boarddocs/speeches/2005/200503102/default.htm

Bouet, A., & Laborde, D. (2010). Assessing the potential cost of a failed Doha Round. *World Trade Review, 9*(2), 319–351. https://doi.org/10.1017/S1474745609990267

Craig, B., & Koepke, M. (2015, February). Excess reserves: Oceans of cash. *Economic Commentary*. Federal Reserve Bank of Cleveland. https://www.clevelandfed.org/newsroom-and-events/publications/economic-commentary/2015-economic-commentaries/ec-201502-excess-reserves-oceans-of-cash.aspx

Desjardins, J. (2015, August 14). China's Yuan devaluation: The aftermath [Chart]. *Visual Capitalist*. https://www.visualcapitalist.com/chinas-yuan-devaluation-the-aftermath-chart/

Donnan, S. (2016, January 20). Capital flight from China worse than thought. *Financial Times*. https://www.ft.com/content/ae4dee44-bf34-11e5-9fdb-87b8d15baec2

Dullien, S. (2012, May 1). *Reinventing Europe: Explaining the fiscal compact*. European Council on Foreign Relations. https://ecfr.eu/article/commentary_reinventing_europe_explaining_the_fiscal_compact/

Elliott, L. (2015, November 29). Does Doha trade talks' failure suggest second age of globalization is over? *The Guardian*. https://www.theguardian.com/business/2015/nov/29/doha-trade-talks-failure-end-second-age-of-globalisation-wto

Erten, B., & Ocampo, J. A. (2012). *Super-cycles of commodity prices since the mid-nineteenth century* (DESA Working Paper, No. 110). UN Department of Economic and Social Affairs. https://www.un.org/esa/desa/papers/2012/wp110_2012.pdf

European Central Bank. (2020). *Statistical data warehouse: Long-term interest rate statistics*. https://sdw.ecb.europa.eu/browse.do?node=bbn4864

European Commission. (2019). *Single resolution mechanism*. Brussels. https://ec.europa.eu/info/business-economy-euro/banking-and-finance/banking-union/single-resolution-mechanism_en

European Commission. (2021). *Monitoring of banking and finance directives*. Brussels. https://ec.europa.eu/info/business-economy-euro/banking-and-finance/enforcement-and-infringements-banking-and-finance-law/monitoring-banking-and-finance-directives_en

Fisher, I. (1933). The debt-deflation theory of great depressions. *Econometrica, 1*(4), 337–357.

Fleming, S. (2019). Currency warrior: Why Trump is weaponising the dollar. *Financial Times*, July 1. https://www.ft.com/content/5694b0dc-91e7-11e9-aea1-2b1d33ac3271

Frenkel, J. (2019, October 23). How a weaponized dollar could backfire. *Project Syndicate*. https://www.project-syndicate.org/commentary/donald-trump-weaponized-dollar-could-backfire-by-jeffrey-frankel-2019-10?barrier=accesspaylog

Gledhill, A. (2020, August 12). Contingent convertibles. *Washington Post*. https://www.washingtonpost.com/business/contingent-convertibles/2020/08/12/dc4fdc7c-dc7f-11ea-b4f1-25b762cdbbf4_story.html

Gordon, R. (2016). *The rise and fall of American growth: The U.S. standard of living since the civil war*. Princeton University Press.

Guttmann, R. (2016). *Finance-led capitalism: Shadow banking, re-regulation and the future of global markets*. Palgrave Macmillan.

Guttmann, R. (2017). The transformation of banking. In A. Nesvetailova (Ed.), *Shadow banking: Scope, origins and theories* (pp. 25–39). Routledge.

Hein, E. (2012). *The crisis of finance-dominated capitalism in the Euro area, deficiencies in the economic policy architecture, and deflationary stagnation policies* (Levy Economics Institute Working Paper, No. 734). http://www.levyinstitute.org/pubs/wp_734.pdf

Humpage, O., & Herrell, C. (2010, January 5). *The dollar carry trade*. Federal Reserve Bank of Cleveland Economic Trends. https://www.clevelandfed.org/en/newsroom-and-events/publications/economic-trends/economic-trends-archives/2010-economic-trends/et-20100105-the-dollar-carry-trade.aspx

Keynes, J. M. (1936). *The general theory of employment, interest and money*. Macmillan.

Koo, R. (2011). The world in balance sheet recession: Causes, cure, and politics. *Real-World Economic Review*, no. 58. http://www.paecon.net/PAEReview/issue58/Koo58.pdf

Krugman, P. (1998). It's Baaack: Japan's Slump and the return of the liquidity trap. *Brookings Papers on Economic Activity*, no. 2, 137–187. https://www.brookings.edu/wp-content/uploads/1998/06/1998b_bpea_krugman_dominquez_rogoff.pdf

Lee, T. (2015, July 11). China is destroying its stock market in order to save it. *Vox*. https://www.vox.com/2015/7/11/8933341/china-is-destroying-its-stock-market-in-order-to-save-it

LePan, N. (2019, August 2). What is a commodity super cycle? *Visual Capitalist*. https://www.visualcapitalist.com/what-is-a-commodity-super-cycle/

Lukasz, A. (2018). The CEECs in global value chains. *Acta Oeconomica, 68*(1). https://doi.org/10.1556/032.2018.68.1.1

Lund, S., & Härle, P. (2017). Global finance resets. *Finance and Development, 54*(4). https://www.imf.org/external/pubs/ft/fandd/2017/12/lund.htm

Masters, B. (2012, February 13). Leverage cap has the power to reshape banking. *Financial Times*. https://www.ft.com/content/50ee214c-563d-11e1-a328-00144feabdc0

McKinsey. (2017, April). *Basel "IV": What's next for banks?* Global Risk Practice. https://www.mckinsey.com/~/media/mckinsey/business%20functions/risk/our%20insights/basel%20iv%20whats%20next%20for%20european%20banks/basel-iv-whats-next-for-banks.ashx

Miranda-Agrippino, S., & Rey, H. (2020). U.S. monetary policy and the global financial cycle. *Review of Economic Studies, 87*(6), 2754–2776. https://doi.org/10.1093/restud/rdaa019

Moore, E. (2016, September 7). The ECB, bond buying and the capital key: A Q & A. *Financial Times*. https://www.ft.com/content/606724b0-74c5-11e6-b60a-de4532d5ea35

Nurkse, R. (1944). *International currency experience: Lessons of the interwar period*. League of Nations.

Pascal, A. (2019, September 23). Against Washington's 'great power' obsession. *The Atlantic*. https://www.theatlantic.com/politics/archive/2019/09/multilateralism-nearly-dead-s-terrible-news/598615/

People's Bank of China. (2015). *The PBC announcement on improving quotation of the central parity of RMB against US dollar*. http://www.pbc.gov.cn/english/130721/2941603/index.html

Rachman, G. (2018, May 11). The new world order: Donald Trump goes it alone. *Financial Times*. https://www.ft.com/content/4db98f9e-54fa-11e8-b24e-cad6aa67e23e

Rey, H. (2015). *Dilemma not trilemma: The global financial cycle and monetary policy independence* (NBER Working Paper, No. 21162). National Bureau of Economic Research. https://www.nber.org/papers/w21162

Shin, H. S. (2019, May 14). What is behind the recent slowdown? *BIS Publication*. https://www.bis.org/speeches/sp190514.pdf

Spiegel, M. (2005). *A look at China's new exchange rate regime* (FRBSF Economic Letter, 2005–23). Federal Reserve Bank of San Francisco. https://www.frbsf.org/economic-research/publications/economic-letter/2005/september/a-look-at-china-new-exchange-rate-regime/

Stewart, H. (2015, August 20). Eight reasons why China's currency crisis matters to us all. *The Guardian*. https://www.theguardian.com/world/2015/aug/16/china-currency-crisis-yuan-devaluation-why-it-matters

Summers, L. (2020). Accepting the reality of secular stagnation. *Finance and Development, 57*(1), 17–20. https://www.imf.org/external/pubs/ft/fandd/2020/03/pdf/larry-summers-on-secular-stagnation.pdf

Tett, G. (2019, July 18). Global trade was slowing down before the tariff war started. *Financial Times*. https://www.ft.com/content/f44093f0-a934-11e9-b6ee-3cdf3174eb89

The Economist. (2019, January 26). Slowbalisation. https://www.economist.com/printedition/2019-01-26

The Economist. (2020, January 18). Dethroning the dollar: America's aggressive use of sanctions endangers the dollar's reign. https://www.economist.com/briefing/2020/01/18/americas-aggressive-use-of-sanctions-endangers-the-dollars-reign

Thomson Reuters. (2016, March 5). European bank bailouts by numbers. *Blog*. https://blogs.thomsonreuters.com/answerson/wp-content/uploads/sites/3/2016/05/euro-bank-bailout.jpg

UNCTAD. (2019). *World investment report 2019*. United Nations Conference on Trade and Development. https://unctad.org/en/pages/PublicationWebflyer.aspx?publicationid=2460

UNCTAD. (2021, January). *Investment trends monitor*, Issue 38. https://unctad.org/system/files/official-document/diaeiainf2021d1_en.pdf

Van Putten, C. (2015). Changing the structure of banking: Volcker, Vickers and Liikanen. *Moral Cents, 4*(2), 25–38. Seven Pillars Institute. https://sevenpillarsinstitute.org/wp-content/uploads/2017/11/Changing-the-structure-of-banking-EDITED-5.pdf

Viñals, J., & Pazarbasioglu, C. (2013, May 14). Banking on reform: Can Volcker, Vickers and Liikanen resolve the too-important-to-fail conundrum? *IMFBlog*. https://blogs.imf.org/2013/05/14/banking-on-reform-can-volcker-vickers-and-liikanen-resolve-the-too-important-to-fail-conundrum/

Wolf, M. (2018, July 25). China's debt threat: Time to rein in the lending boom. *Financial Times*. https://www.ft.com/content/0c7ecae2-8cfb-11e8-bb8f-a6a2f7bca546?emailId=5b5b3d10ee83630004f71916&segmentId=c393f5a6-b640-bff3-cc14-234d058790ed

World Bank. (2019). *World Bank open data*. International Bank for Reconstruction and Development. https://data.worldbank.org/indicator/NE.TRD.GNFS.ZS

World Trade Organization. (2018). *World trade statistical review 2018*. WTO. www.wto.org/wtsr18

CHAPTER 5

The Great Interruption

The recovery from the Great Recession of 2008/09 was slow and uneven, as is typical for the aftermath of systemic financial crises on a global scale. Post-crisis rebalancing processes have had all the markings characteristic of downswing phases of long waves—deflationary pressures from having to work through debt overhangs and in the face of excess capacities, massive precautionary saving amounting in effect to a liquidity trap, much un- and underemployment whether hidden or openly so. Were it not for the extraordinarily intense central bank injections of liquidity, practiced across the globe, the crisis would have been worse and borne deeper wounds. But these frantic and repeated efforts at "quantitative easing" and "emergency lending" also came at a cost. They set off consecutive rounds of competitive devaluations, a form of monetary protectionism, which transferred financial instability, nourished trade conflicts, and reinforced de-globalization trends from one region to another. By 2016, barely a decade into this downswing phase, the two long-standing pillars of the neoliberal world order—Britain and the United States—had succumbed to isolationist impulses of resurgent right-wing nationalism. Such political polarization to is part and parcel of the long wave's downswing dynamic. And then, just as the double drama of Brexit and Trump was reaching new heights, the world economy suffered a shock not seen in a century, a worldwide lockdown in the face of a deadly pandemic best described as

R. Guttmann, *Multi-Polar Capitalism*,
https://doi.org/10.1007/978-3-030-88247-1_5

the *Great Interruption.*[1] In downswing phases of long waves, it is often the second crisis that ushers in the transformative forces for the next stage in capitalism's development. This time is no different.

5.1 "A Perfect Storm"

The world was surely distracted with more mundane matters when a new coronavirus, labelled SARS-CoV-2, appeared in late 2019 in Wuhan (China) and then, superbly adapted for human-to-human transmission, launched its planetary march of exponential spread in January 2020. We should have been better prepared for the possibility of a global pandemic even though the last such occurrence of comparable danger happened more than a century ago—the "Spanish Flu" of 1918/19. Signs of an impending pandemic have abounded in recent years, with five near misses over the last couple of decades—the Severe Acute Respiratory Syndrome (SARS) virus in 2002, the 2004 avian flu, the 2009 swine flu, the Middle East Respiratory Syndrome (MERS) virus in 2012, and Ebola from 2014 to 2016.

Such a heightened threat of pandemics is not a coincidence. Rather we must recognize it as consequence of stressors our modern capitalist economies have put on the environment altering the relationship between humans and animals—the accelerating destruction of our planet's biodiversity, erosion of wildlife habitats, animal commerce, increased meat consumption, and changing patterns of movement by certain animals key to the production of new viruses and their zoonotic transmission, notably bats. The sad truth is that, even beyond the new coronavirus, the world will remain susceptible to recurrent pandemics as global threat which makes today's experience an important trial run for future episodes.

Even more so than its immediate predecessors SARS and MERS, the novel coronavirus is a formidable foe, combining very efficient transmission, a complex range of symptoms, high morbidity, and significant mortality into what America's leading expert on highly infectious diseases, Dr. Anthony Fauci, has aptly characterized as a "perfect storm."[2] SARS-CoV-2 is highly transmissible by inter-personal contact, as an airborne

[1] I have published a more elaborate, but similarly structured and argued version of this chapter in Guttmann (2021). We owe the term "Great Interruption" to Wolf (2020).

[2] See the *Financial Times* interview with Dr. Anthony Fauci summarized in Kuchler (2020) during which he characterized the coronavirus as the "perfect storm."

aerosol, or even when touching surfaces that may contain concentrations of the virus for significant amounts of time. It spreads often unbeknownst to carriers who may be asymptomatic and thus unaware they carry the virus. Up to 40 percent of infected humans are asymptomatic. Or they may spread the virus while still pre-symptomatic, as it typically takes five to ten days for symptoms to show. If unchecked, one person will on average infect three others, for a basic reproduction number R0 ("R naught") ≥ 3 assuring an exponential rate of transmission: $1 \rightarrow 3 \rightarrow 9 \rightarrow 27 \rightarrow 81 \rightarrow 243 \rightarrow 729 \rightarrow 2187$, and so forth. That pace that can turn a single viral spread event, say at an indoor party, into a local "hot spot" paralyzing a town and surrounding areas in a matter of weeks.

Covid-19 is the official name designated by the World Health Organization (WHO) for the disease symptoms associated with infection by the SARS-CoV-2 virus. These include most commonly high fever, cough, lack of appetite, shortness of breath, fatigue, loss of smell or taste, and muscle or joint pains. As the virus replicates rapidly inside the human body and triggers the immune system response, Covid-19 often attacks the lungs but can also endanger other organs, trigger blood clots, or push the immune system into possibly deadly overdrive ("cytokine storm"). We are still getting to know the wide array of often life-threatening complications that may arise from Covid-19, including pneumonia, septic shock, liver damage, or heart failure. In about 20 percent of the confirmed Covid-19 cases, the virus causes enough havoc attacking the lungs to trigger such respiratory distress that they need intensive care in hospitals, notably the support of ventilators. About 10–15 percent of those patients struggling with their breathing may end up so deprived of oxygen that organs fail and the patient dies. People over 65 years and/or suffering from pre-existing comorbidities, such as chronic lung disease, hypertension, obesity, or diabetes, are at far greater risk of falling seriously ill or even dying from Covid-19 while young people by and large face manageable symptoms.[3] Several months into the pandemic we became aware of possibly long-term effects of Covid-19 among many otherwise recovered patients, from "brain fog" to heart damage. Like other viruses in the past, this new

[3] As described in fascinating detail by Kormann (2020) and Mukherjee (2020), the novel coronavirus has a particularly virulent growth and inflammation capacity among some people it invades. See Mandavilli (2020) on the "cytokine storm" phenomenon as a leading cause of COVID-related deaths and its seemingly arbitrary distribution among younger and middle-aged people of all walks of life.

coronavirus has found more efficient ways to transmit between people and spread within human bodies by mutating into more dangerous variants, notably the Delta variant.

5.2 Locking Down the World

5.2.1 Missing the Chance for Initial Containment

It is not yet clear how the new coronavirus found its way into human-to-human transmission sometime during the second half of 2019, whether in a so-called "wet" market of live animals in Wuhan (China), or escaping from a research lab at the Wuhan Institute of Virology, or originating somewhere else in this large central Chinese city of eleven million inhabitants. More obvious, however, is the failure of Chinese authorities to react swiftly and so contain the virus. When doctors at Wuhan Central Hospital warned in December 2019 on social media of a new SARS-like virus attacking a growing number of patients with mysterious respiratory problems, they were detained as "rumormongers." On December 31 China warned the WHO of a new virus while at that point still downplaying its risks to humans. Worried about disrupting preparations for the all-important week-long Chinese New Year festivities in late January 2020 with a potentially false alert, local authorities had an incentive to downplay the threat. Wuhan's mayor Zhou Xianwang even authorized the traditional Lunar New Year banquet on January 18 where 40,000 families gathered and shared their home-baked food—a "superspreader" event if there ever was one.

Operating in a rigidly hierarchical political system, where they often take the blame for administrative errors or policy mistakes to shield the reputation of the national leadership, local and provincial officials in China have a vested interest in controlling the narrative with regard to any reputational threat which leads them often enough to conceal crucial information and/or cover up mistakes. At the same time, China's law on infectious diseases allows provincial governments to declare an epidemic only after central government approval which depends on getting reliable information in timely fashion about developing facts on the ground. This contradiction had already been a problem when the H51N virus known as "bird flu" first made its appearance in 1997 and then again with SARS in late 2002 and 2003. If anything, the gap between provincial authorities and the central government in Beijing has only gotten worse with the unprecedented amassing of power in the hands of China's current leader Xi Jinping since 2013. During a crucial two-week period, from January 2 to January 16, local authorities downplayed the transmission threat of the virus while five million inhabitants traveled in and out of Wuhan. Xi and other leaders in the Politburo were not heard from. Yet already during those fateful weeks of inaction social media was full of reports and discussions of rising local infection rates, indications of public concern first triggered by the warnings of Wuhan-based doctors one of whom, Dr. Li Wenliang, died on February 7 amidst a rare wave of public anger on the internet following news of his death.[4]

At some point, the central government recognized that it could no longer continue its initial pretense of calm, given the local community spread of the virus in Wuhan and the imminent danger of widespread traveling by hundreds of millions of Chinese returning home to celebrate the Lunar New Year with their families. On January 20, ten days after researchers from Shanghai's prestigious Fudan University had sequenced the coronavirus gene to give the world's scientific community first valuable insights into the epidemic, China's leading epidemiologist Zhong Nanshan announced on state television that the virus was indeed spreading from human to human. Two days later Wuhan was quarantined, followed by massive travel restrictions locking much of China's population in place beyond New Year festivities. Once the country's leadership had finally committed to addressing the epidemic, its competent central command structure and the collectivist mindset of its citizens combined effectively to set up an infrastructure for containment and mitigation in a hurry, introducing testing procedures, developing contact-tracing capacity, building makeshift hospitals (in just ten days), mobilizing health-care personnel, and managing the largest lockdown (of over sixty million people) ever tried.

5.2.2 *The World Shuts Down*

It was at that point, while observing those stunning initiatives of China's leadership, that the world took note of the deadly threat this new virus might pose and the kind of radical measures needed to keep it in check.

[4] Useful information about China's initial cover-up of the coronavirus and its deadly potential can be found in Kynge et al. (2020) as well as Mitchell (2020).

In February 2020 the virus hit a cruise ship in Tokyo Bay, infected thousands of members of a fringe sect in Daegu (South Korea), raced through the otherwise rather isolated country of Iran all the way to the top echelons of its government, and then hit the rich region of Lombardy in Italy with unprecedented force to a point where the overwhelmed provincial healthcare system obliged a quarantine of the entire province on March 7. Images of overcrowded hospitals in Bergamo (Italy), whose barely protected doctors were forced to decide in the face of serious equipment shortages whom to save and whom to let go, shocked the world. On March 9 Italy's prime minister Giuseppe Conti shut down the whole country, and on March 11 the WHO declared SARS-CoV-2 a global pandemic.

At that point governments all over the world, haunted by the images of despair from the hospitals of Italy's richest region, had to figure out how best to deal with a highly contagious and deadly virus for which there was no known effective treatment nor immunity. Most governments decided that they had no choice but to follow Italy's example and lockdown their entire country. Public safety, a key governmental responsibility in any society, demanded the spread of the virus be brought under control while buying some time to beef up the treatment capacity of the domestic healthcare system so that it could face a possibly overwhelming wave of seriously ill Covid-patients without collapsing under their weight. In short order, during March, one country after another faced the prospect of shutting down by imposing stay-home orders and business closures. By early April 2020 more than half of the world's population, 3.9 billion people to be precise, had been asked to stay at home, thereby putting the economies of over a hundred countries into a voluntary coma. These lockdowns were accompanied by frantic efforts to put in place an infrastructure for testing, tracing and isolating people suspected of Covid infection and furnish local hospitals with additional beds, intensive care units, ventilators, personal protective equipment, and staff.

5.3 A Test of Governance and Leadership

It is obvious that this pandemic-induced plunge posed a huge challenge to any country's government, both in terms of its administrative competence and foresight. A lockdown has to be enforced effectively. The dangers of the pandemic have to be communicated clearly to a public that may be alternately skeptical, confused, or panicky. Credible scientists, usually the country's leading infectious-disease specialists best able to explain the medical and public health challenges caused by the virus, have to be allowed to address the public and frame policy. People have to be convinced to change behavior consistently, whether social distancing, wearing masks, washing hands, or self-quarantining for up to two weeks when having been possibly exposed or already feeling sick. Massive investments have to be undertaken to build a testing-and-tracing infrastructure from scratch and boost the public health system's Covid-fighting capacity. All of this must be done in a hurry, as the speed of action matters decisively in terms of keeping the pandemic in check and thus more manageable.

5.3.1 *Highly Varied Responses*

When looking back at how governments met this unprecedented set of challenges during March and April 2020, we can see enormous differences in performance. Some, like Vietnam, Taiwan, Singapore, or South Korea, did well not least because of their prior experience at beating back SARS in the mid-2000s. South Korea also brought an effective high-tech approach to bear, being a global leader in the digital economy which turned out to be a useful comparative advantage for other technologically advanced countries as well, like Japan or Germany. Some poorer countries excelled, because of their effective labor-intense healthcare networks which have done well containing the virus. We can think here in particular of Cuba thanks to its highest doctor-to-patient ratio in the world or of Ethiopia with its nationwide infrastructure of community health centers. Cooperation between national, provincial, and local layers of government has also proven of decisive importance, irrespective of formal governance structures and constitutional arrangements in place. In the end, however, the most important performance indicator turned out to be who was leading the country at the time. Effective leaders brought several strengths to the challenge whether by acting swiftly, communicating well, having a consistent message, putting a lot of effort into intra-governmental coordination, giving credible medical scientists a lot of space, intervening actively in boosting the capacity of their nation's healthcare system, stressing transparency, expressing a lot of empathy, or appealing to unity—across political, regional, and inter-generational divisions.

The importance of leadership found another, much more troubling manifestation as concerns autocracies. We have already briefly mentioned the fateful delays caused by the inherent inefficacies of China's top-down and overly centralized governance structure under Xi's authoritarian leadership style which helped suppress and distort pertinent information about an apparent outbreak of a new viral epidemic flowing from the bottom, Wuhan's hospitals, upwards. Various populists, whether on the nationalist Right (e.g. Hungary's Victor Orban, Poland's Andrzej Duda, Russia's Vladimir Putin, Turkey's Recep Tayyip Erdogan, India's Narendra Modi, the Philippines' Rodrigo Duterte, Brazil's Jair Bolsonaro, and America's Donald Trump), or on the Left (e.g. Nicaragua's Daniel Ortega, Venezuela's Nicolas Maduro, Mexico's Andrés Manuel López Obrador), have by and large mismanaged their response to the virus while at the same time exploiting the pandemic to enhance their dictatorial powers. These largely demagogic leaders have all downplayed the virus and so let it get dangerously implanted among their respective populations. Obsessed with their personal power and distrustful of their own government institutions, they have hesitated to let technocratic administrators and civil servants take charge of mitigation. Matching the scientific nihilism and conspiratorial inclinations of their fanatical followers, they prefer to frame the pandemic as a plot instead of letting science set the agenda. These leaders have also attacked doctors and the media in an effort to control the narrative about the virus. While some autocrats, like Modi, Erdogan, or Duterte, have imposed draconian measures in their management of the epidemic threat, others (e.g. Lopez Obrador, Bolsonaro) have preferred to take a rather relaxed attitude and pursue other priorities instead. In that latter group, we need to focus especially on Donald Trump whose narrow-minded obsession with his re-election prospects and propensity for disinformation led him to mismanage the coronavirus in spectacular fashion, creating disastrous conditions in the United States.

5.3.2 *Trump's Mismanagement of the Pandemic*

Already in 2018 Trump, always keen on reversing anything initiated by Obama, had shut down the pandemic-preparedness infrastructure his predecessor had set up in 2015 after having had to face the swine flu, Ebola, and the Zika virus during his two terms in office. This fateful step left the US government dangerously unprepared when the coronavirus came ashore in the United States in early 2020. Throughout the months of January and February Trump was repeatedly warned of the virus and its potential dangers. This topic was taken up more than a dozen times in the President's Daily Brief on national-security threats which he had a habit of not paying much attention to. Even though forewarned, Trump did not see it fit to go beyond his January 31 announcement of a travel ban from China whose loopholes still allowed 40,000 travelers to come in from there after that restriction was imposed. Instead, he continuously downplayed the threat of the virus. During much of February US public health officials had met recurrently to discuss how best to convince Trump to take the impending epidemic more seriously in order to contain it. But their plan of action came undone on February 25 when Nancy Messonnier, the director of the National Center for Immunization and Respiratory Diseases, issued a warning of the potentially severe disruptions to daily life caused by the virus to which Trump responded in a fit of fury. As late as February 28, in one of his famously raucous rallies with supporters, Trump referred to the virus as "the Democrats' new hoax" aimed at depriving him of another term in the White House.[5]

Trump saw the pandemic as an unwelcome disruption threatening his re-election prospects. By downplaying its dangers Trump sought to minimize its potential impact on America's economic performance upon which he had based his argument for why he deserved another term. But this decidedly neglectful attitude caused his administration to delay action until mid-March, losing weeks during which community spread of the virus, already getting entrenched on the West Coast (brought in by travelers from China) and even more so in New York (brought in by travelers from Europe) during the third week of February, could take sufficient root for eventual exponential spread in many places. It took weeks, until mid-March 2020, before the Trump Administration finally imposed social-distancing guidelines which effectively triggered a lockdown in a majority of states.

As the pandemic first ravaged both coasts of the United States, where the Democrats dominate, Trump decided early on to shift most of the crisis-management responsibilities to the states and their governors, in

[5] Trump's failure to focus in timely fashion and with the attention required on the emerging threat of the pandemic during January and February 2020 has been well documented by Graham (2020), Lipton et al. (2020), and Woodward (2020).

the hope of thereby hurting the political standing of his opponents. Yet the states were rapidly overwhelmed by a lack of financial resources, personnel, and essential equipment needed to fight the pandemic while having to compete with each other for scarce resources, like ventilators. In the face of widespread shortages, from testing kits to protective personal equipment for hospital personnel, Trump could have used his considerable powers under the Defense Production Act to mobilize the private sector for emergency supplies needed to fight the pandemic. The only time he used the DPA was to force meat-packing plants open when many of them were overwhelmed by massive outbursts of Covid infections among their workers. Instead Trump set up his own shadowy, yet largely ineffectual network comprising private equity funds, venture capitalists, and entrepreneurs, run by his son-in-law Jared Kushner, to procure and distribute emergency medical equipment to the states.[6] Easily the most fateful shortage concerned test kits, further compounded by continuous bottlenecks in processing test results, which made it impossible to track the virus effectively.

When Trump finally created a coordination mechanism bringing together the heads of several federal agencies and department secretaries, the so-called White House Coronavirus Task Force, he appointed to its head Vice President Mike Pence, a born-again evangelical with a long record of hostility to science-based evidence (e.g. climate change) or public health advice (e.g. on smoking, sexual preference). The task force soon became the backdrop to daily briefings by President Trump during which he consistently downplayed the dangers of the virus, attacked the media and Democratic state governors, played up presumed successes of his administration, and wondered aloud about all kinds of unproven "miracle" treatments. What also became quite clear on several occasions in those sessions with the press was Trump's hostility to the advice of America's leading public health officials, notably the nation's foremost infectious disease expert Dr. Anthony Fauci with whom he sparred repeatedly, and his inclination to politicize the lockdowns, wearing of masks, and tests as "plots" by Democrats to make him "look bad."

The politicization of the pandemic has had many negative consequences. The highly reputed Centers for Disease Control and Prevention

[6] For more details on the shadowy private-sector procurement network run by Jared Kushner see Baker et al. (2020) and McCarthy (2020).

(CDC) was not allowed to discuss its scientific findings or issue guidance about public behavior without bias, an imposition of censorship which destroyed staff morale and the institution's once-stellar reputation. Public health measures, notably the wearing of masks, became gestures of political allegiance and as such unenforceable. Disinformation about the pandemic crowded out objective evidence and reasoned discussion. Republican governors felt compelled by relentless pressure from Trump to open up their states too early and thus contributed to wave after wave of community spread. All this caused hundreds of thousands of avoidable deaths and in the end worse economic damage than had the pandemic been managed effectively from the very beginning.

Trump did one good thing before losing the November 2020 election deservedly because of his mismanagement of the pandemic, and that was the launch of Operation Warp Speed in May 2020. This operation was a well-funded $10 bn. effort of public–private cooperation to accelerate the development, manufacturing, and distribution of a Covid-19 vaccine, involving eight pharmaceutical and biomedical companies. OWS was part of a global vaccine-development effort, notable for its successful worldwide cooperation among researchers and unprecedented speed of effective product development. Today we have the means to leave the pandemic behind us, thanks to a handful of effective vaccines, if and when we will have assured their worldwide distribution to the point of inoculating the majority of the world's population.

5.4 The Balancing Acts of Virus Economics

When the SARS-CoV-2 virus forced more than half of the world to shut down within a couple of months of its launch, it simply took over the societies it hit. Pandemic-stricken countries have all faced the same interdependent sequence of balancing acts which are difficult to manage even under favorable circumstances of speedy and competent leadership. We can think of these inter-woven balancing acts, which will arise inevitably while trying to manage the pandemic, as ***virus economics***.[7]

[7] I heard the expression "virus economics" for the first time on March 12, 2020 while listening to an interview with Austan Goolsbee (2020), Obama's former economic advisor, on the public radio news program *All Things Considered*.

5.4.1 *Initial Containment Response*

The first balancing act concerns the initial response. Everything else follows from how that first moment is managed. In the case of the SARS-CoV-2 virus, many governments focused early on border controls and travel restrictions. Such measures, while making sense in an age of mass traveling across borders, ignore how much the virus has already taken hold locally and often provide a wrong sense of security. It is crucially important to track right away whether, where, and how much the virus is already spreading. The sooner the government takes determined action to slow the spread of the virus, the better! Ideally, governments are sufficiently prepared for the eventuality of pandemics in terms of needed supplies and planning so that they can evaluate the threat right away, identify carriers, trace their recent contacts, and isolate infected people. The goal here is to fight an epidemic before it gets embedded so widely that its spread becomes exponential whereupon the policy response switches from containment to mitigation.[8] All this requires substantial up-front investments in a public health infrastructure comprising accurate testing, time-consuming contact tracing (rendered nowadays much more technologically sophisticated through apps and smart phones), and effective isolation to take infected individuals out of circulation.

While quite disruptive when the epidemic is still in its infancy, such early mobilization pays off in terms of suffering a lot fewer casualties from the virus over the long haul, putting less stress on the health-care system, and inflicting far smaller damage to the economy. Countries messing up how they respond at first to the virus end up paying a much higher price over the duration of the pandemic. A key lesson here is to be well prepared for any new epidemic and respond right away with a good plan of action. Some countries, notably Taiwan, Singapore, South Korea, Vietnam, and New Zealand, managed to deploy early containment strategies successfully and were thus spared the worst of the pandemic by preventing exponential community spread from taking hold there. Even later infection waves, driven by more contagious mutations of the virus (e.g. Delta, Lambda), have to a significant degree depended on how well the government's public health response capacity had been mobilized and reinforced early on.

[8] Baird (2020a) explains well the difference between containing a pandemic and having to mitigate it once its community spread has gone beyond being able to link newly infected people to known cases. Mitigation requires a very different level of organization and public health resources than containment.

5.4.2 *Mitigation and Public Health*

If and when the virus escapes early containment efforts, then governments have to slow the rate of new infections by imposing broader mitigation measures many of which involve shutting down places where lots of people tend to meet indoors and asking people to minimize close contact with others. Mitigation also requires changing social norms and behavior for prevention—wearing masks, keeping the requisite physical distance from others, washing hands, cleaning surfaces, staying home when feeling ill, and getting tested. There is a need for making cheap, reliable, and rapid tests available on a massive scale, coupled with effective contact-tracing mechanisms and provisions for enforceable self-quarantining by those testing positive.

Given the speed with which the new coronavirus can and will spread unimpeded, it did not take long for governments to shut down their whole country in a desperate effort to "flatten the epidemiological curve." Such unprecedented lockdowns in over one hundred countries by early April 2020 were meant to get control over the spread of the virus while at the same time buying time to bring a nation's often underfunded and/or unprepared public health system up to needed capacity. Governments have had to make sure that the nation's healthcare system would be equipped to cope with the surge of seriously ill Covid-19 patients while still taking care of people with other health problems requiring medical attention. The principal focus here is on hospitals, equipping them in a hurry with more beds, intensive care units, medical machinery such as ventilators and respirators, personal protective equipment (gowns, gloves, masks, etc.), and additional staff. Often enough public health officials have had to build makeshift hospitals in a matter of just days to meet demand. During the pandemic hospitals have proven fragile inasmuch as doctors and nurses work there under enormous stress, often fall ill with Covid-19 themselves due to continuous exposure, face machines breaking down from over-use, and have to cope with shortages. Balancing the effort to "flatten the curve" of virus spread and the push to reinforce the public health system is literally a matter of life and death, as such at the heart of "virus economics."

5.4.3 Macro-Economic Stabilization

Shutting down a society in order to get the virus under control amounts to a huge shock to economic activity. As people stay home and businesses close, they all lose large amounts of their income while still having to pay bills coming due. This dire situation poses an existential threat for many which governments have had to address right away by offering massive amounts of assistance. Lost wage income can be compensated for with direct payments to families, employment subsidies, payment relief, or unemployment benefits whereas businesses can be helped cover their losses through grants or cheap loans. Some vulnerable industries, such as airlines or the tourist sector, risk getting wiped out altogether by the pandemic, forcing governments to provide bailout funds for domestic firms considered important enough to salvage. Additional government expenditures will be required for boosting the public health system, sustaining the food supply chain, and supporting other essential services whose revenues might have taken a huge hit when the economy was put into hibernation (e.g. public transport, postal services, education). At the same time, governments face large tax collection shortfalls due to declining incomes and collapsing economic activity. Within just a few months into the pandemic governments all over the world faced a doubling or tripling of budget deficits, adding significantly to already elevated public debt levels. Governments of all stripes, even those normally committed to fiscal austerity, have realized that they must commit to a much higher level of deficit-spending in the face of this emergency.

That commitment will inevitably move government spending injections beyond immediate income substitution assistance and support for public services under pressure. Even when such immediate assistance is forthcoming, the shock to the economy from a country-wide lockdown is so large that it is bound to set off a negative multiplier effect of spending reductions feeding further income losses which in turn spur more expenditure cuts, and so forth. The danger of such a chain reaction is that it gains traction like an avalanche and so turns into a so-called "debt-deflation" spiral involving forced asset sales, massive cash hoarding, credit freeze, debt defaults, and falling prices.[9] We could see plenty of evidence

[9] We owe the concept of "debt-deflation spiral" to Fisher (1933) who laid bare its inner dynamic as a nine-step process driving an economy into depression. Deflation makes

during the spring of 2020 of the intense deflationary shock we experienced when half of the world shut down all at once, as illustrated by the 40 percent fall in oil prices during March alone, the 34 percent decline of the S & P 500's stock-market index between February 19 and March 23, or the yield of 10-year US Treasuries tumbling from an already low 1.92 percent at the beginning of the year all the way to just 0.58 percent on April 21. The prospect of a debt-deflation spiral triggered by such an intense deflationary shock in the wake of all these lockdowns, representing massive downward shifts of both aggregate demand and aggregate supply at the same time, could drive the world economy into a depression. Governments can avoid such a disastrous outcome by not allowing their economies to fall into such a spiral through additional spending beyond the first round of income substitution assistance which in the aggregate must be large enough to counter-balance rapidly shrinking private sector spending. We have seen many efforts in that regard, such as Joe Biden's \$1.9 tr. American Rescue Plan or the European Union's €750 bn. Next Generation EU recovery program (discussed in greater detail in Sects. 6.1.1 and 6.3.2, respectively).

5.4.4 *A Terrifying Moment in the US Treasuries Market*

There has also been a financial dimension to this huge pandemic-induced deflationary shock which needed an effective policy response, this one involving interventions by the central bank. At the onset of the pandemic financial markets came under enormous stress as they seized up amidst exploding disruptions and suddenly heightened uncertainty. Much of this chaos was driven by a "flight to safety," which initially followed the standard pattern of investors rushing out of higher-risk securities, notably stocks, in favor of risk-free government securities. Very rapidly the yield on ten-year US Treasury bonds fell from about 1.18 percent at the beginning of March to a record-low 0.4 percent on March 9.

any given sum of debt more burdensome as the value of money goes up, while the added debt burden forces more distress selling pushing prices further down. Minsky (1982) brought collapsing asset markets into the picture while Bernanke (1983) added the disruptive impact of widespread bankruptcies on credit intermediation, thus giving us both a broader and more contemporary understanding of the debt deflation process. I would also recommend Von Peter (2005) for a summary of how best to analyze and model the debt-deflation spiral.

Then, however, something strange happened, as investors started dumping even Treasuries in favor of outright cash whereupon the price declines from such sell-offs pushed the ten-year T-bond yield rapidly higher to 1.25 percent on March 18. In retrospect, the unexpected trend reversal was an indication of massive forced selling by hedge funds which had borrowed heavily in pursuit of so-called "relative value" strategies seeking to profit from small yield differences between cash Treasuries and Treasury futures and suddenly saw their solvency threatened in the face of a downward market plunge triggering margin calls. Their sell-off was so massive that overwhelmed dealers ended up widening their bid-ask spreads by a factor of 13, an extremely worrisome indication of market turbulence and dysfunctionality in what had up to then been taken for granted as the world's deepest, most liquid financial market.[10]

Such sudden disruption at the center of global finance prompted an immediate response by the Federal Reserve. On March 23, the Fed announced that it would henceforth commit itself to unlimited purchases of Treasuries as well as mortgage-backed securities, an unprecedented step that served to restore calm in the panic-stricken market for US Treasuries. Even though this radical move by the Fed did the job of restoring orderly market conditions, the crisis should serve as a warning signal that what had been up to then considered a fail-safe pillar of the dollar standard was in effect structurally more vulnerable than anybody had imagined. The rapid growth of the US Treasuries' outstanding stock on a global scale since the GFC of 2007/08, notwithstanding their partial absorption by the Fed's recurrent "quantitative easing" programs, has exceeded the ability of the world's leading banks serving as primary dealers to cope with these supplies. Their ability to do so has been constrained by Basel III restrictions on (much higher) bank capital buffers and liquidity cushions so that the resulting vacuum has been filled by shadow-banking players, notably asset managers and hedge funds, unable to assure adequate market liquidity during periods of heightened market stress.

[10] For more detailed analyses of the March 2020 break-down of orderly market conditions in the US Treasuries market see Tett (2020a), Schrimpf et al. (2020), as well as Plender (2021).

5.4.5 *Central Banks as Market Makers of Last Resort*

The freaky chaos in the US Treasuries market during the third week of March 2020 and the Fed's strong response were just the beginning in a series of noteworthy central bank crisis-management initiatives. Major central banks, including the Federal Reserve, the European Central Bank, the Bank of England, the Bank of Japan, and the People's Bank of China, all ended up taking further unprecedented steps at the onset of the global pandemic in March 2020 whose scope far exceeded even the "unorthodox" monetary-policy and financial-stabilization measures in the aftermath of the systemic financial crisis of 2008/09.

Introducing a new policy known as "yield curve control" central banks set short-term interest rates under their control at or near zero and then pushed long-term interest rates to very low levels through huge purchases of government bonds which have had the added advantage of helping to cover exploding budget deficits. Such additional spikes in central bank purchases of government securities, removing them from the marketplace at a time when there was also exceptionally strong demand for safe bonds from various risk-averse investors, produced a sharp acceleration of a unique trend that had taken hold across much of the world during the second half of the 2010s, that of government bond yields sliding into negative territory. This historically unprecedented phenomenon, itself striking illustration of what we have termed the "new deflation" (see Chapter 4), is caused by very strong demand for bonds pushing up their price in the secondary market way beyond their face value so that bondholders acquiring such expensive bonds would lose money if they waited until maturity even with the (admittedly very low) coupon payments included. Such sub-zero debt, much of it found in Europe and Japan, rose from just below \$8 trillion in late March 2020 to a new record of \$17.05 trillion in November 2020 which at that point comprised about a quarter of the total worldwide stock of highly rated government and corporate bonds.[11]

Stabilization efforts by central banks broke new ground in two additional areas. Going beyond their traditional interventions as lenders of last resort to becoming in effect market-makers of last resort, central banks also launched large-scale purchase programs for other securities, notably

[11] See Stubbington (2020), tracking data on negative yielding bonds all over the world from Bloomberg Barclays Global Aggregate Negative Yielding Debt Index.

corporate bonds and money-market instruments such as commercial paper, in support of sustaining these financial markets. In addition, central banks have also conducted more direct monetary financing, beyond buying newly issued government securities or allowing overdraft facilities for the government's accounts, by setting up lending facilities that can be tapped by non-bank financial institutions and even non-financial corporations in case commercial banks refused to lend enough during a credit crunch.

Over the longer haul, cash-starved economic actors have had to take on a lot more debt during the pandemic on top of often already high levels of indebtedness, setting the stage for possibly widespread debt defaults and bad-credit losses among financial institutions thereby rendered themselves more fragile. While banks all over the world entered the pandemic in pretty good shape as regards their capitalization levels (for loss absorption) and their liquidity cushions (for meeting of withdrawal requests) thanks to re-regulation efforts dating back to 2010, the stressors of financial instability from asset deflation and loan defaults might weaken them over time.

5.4.6 *Operating in a Pandemic*

In the end, the pandemic has obliged governments to flatten two curves simultaneously, the epidemiological one aimed at slowing down community spread of the virus and the economic one keeping the decline of economic activity, with its income losses, bankruptcies, and mass unemployment, in check. The first ultimately necessitated lockdowns putting the economy into a voluntary coma whereas the second required massive macro-economic stabilization efforts to prevent the collapse of the economy while shut down. The two curve-flattening efforts are thus interrelated. Their interdependence works both ways. Coping with the pandemic threw the economy into a tailspin which had to be counteracted by both fiscal and monetary stimulation on an unprecedented scale. The longer the lockdown, the greater the likelihood of lasting damage to the economy in terms of defaults, bankruptcies, closures, and job losses. The collective pain from lockdowns in terms of income losses and business disruptions also nourished public pressure to relax restrictions. Governments thus faced soon intense pressure to reopen their domestic economies as soon as possible while the virus was still active. But when they reopened the economy too early and/or too rapidly before having gained adequate control over the virus, they would find the pace of infection accelerate again to a point where it disrupted the revival of economic activity. Such disruption not only arose from renewed pandemic-fighting restrictions on activity, but also because of the damage caused to public confidence by a resurgent virus.

Local and national leaders have struggled all over the world on how best to balance the omnipresence of a deadly virus with the imperatives of daily economic activity. That balancing act has proven quite challenging everywhere. The pandemic operates in waves, with rapidly accelerating community spread overwhelming public health capacity and obliging activity restrictions until infections decelerate enough to relax those restrictions, only for a new cycle to begin. Regions, which got hit hard in the first or second waves, share a collective trauma that has made their local populations weary of the virus and thus disciplined about collectively elaborated precautions. Areas doing well at the beginning, on the other hand, often ended up getting hit much harder during subsequent waves. With very few countries spared from the full brunt of the virus, most societies have had to figure out how to live with a pandemic while still pursuing a living. Coexisting with a highly contagious virus required having in place an effective virus-tracking infrastructure involving widespread testing, rapid contact tracing, and isolation of those possibly infected. Hot spots, where the virus is seen to spread again, need to be quarantined in a hurry. At the same time, people still have had to follow guidelines for wearing masks, practicing social distancing, washing hands regularly, and avoiding large indoor crowds. Societies, whose leaders downplayed the virus for their own political reasons (Trump's America, Bolsonaro's Brazil, Lopez Obrador's Mexico, etc.), found such precautionary behavior difficult to implement or sustain. Pandemic fatigue also has made it difficult to maintain restrictions on behavior and activity over a sufficiently long time horizon.

At the same time, businesses and other entities across the economy (e.g. schools) have had to implement major organizational changes in terms of how they operate on a day-to-day basis. Having to limit their capacity to accommodate safety needs, such as assuring sufficient space for social distancing, has kept their revenue potential below pre-pandemic levels. Everybody has had to learn how to survive in the "new normal" for the duration of the pandemic. The gap between levels of production considered average before the pandemic hit and what has proven possible now while living with the virus still a constant threat is also a macroeconomic challenge for policy-makers which depends in good measure on how well the course of the pandemic is managed throughout. Keeping the economy running while living with the virus has confronted us all with a societal coordination effort for which we have no precedence. The effort engages each level of government, tests the readiness of the public health system, challenges businesses to reorganize, and requires behavioral adjustments of everyone as an ongoing process, all while trying to maintain a minimum level of economic activity.

5.5 Trend Accelerations, Shifts, and Ruptures

Mastering the tension between virus spread, a country's healthcare capacity, and continuous disruption of economic activity as a series of intertwined balancing acts have made the pandemic a transformative event. A uniquely disruptive force, planetary in scope, and evoking multifaceted adjustments, the novel coronavirus amounts to a major stress test of every society's key institutions and actors, cultural norms, political cohesion, and socio-economic structures. It provides thus a special "window" into a country's soul. Underneath its drama of threatening mass death, the pandemic accelerates trends that were already in place before its arrival, provokes possibly irreversible shifts in the constellation of societal forces, and breaks linkages that have held societies together. We will try to identify the most important of these accelerators, shift factors, and ruptures in this section.

5.5.1 Health Care

One obvious victim of the pandemic is health care, especially where the virus has taken a heavy toll. To the extent that many countries had underfunded their healthcare system before the crisis hit, they inevitably came to regret their neglectfulness when rapid increases in the number of Covid-19 patients needing care during any one of the pandemic's transmission waves stretched hospitals to the limit and in some cases even beyond. Shortages of strategic supplies would arise soon enough, making effective treatment more difficult. Having to cope with shortages when providing healthcare makes an already stressful job that much more daunting. Shortages of live-saving machines, such as ventilators, will kill seriously ill patients who did not have to die. Shortages of personal protective equipment make medical staff even more susceptible to getting infected. As doctors and nurses become sick, hospitals face labor shortages as well. All this saps morale while having to continue the hard work of caring for the sick arriving in waves day in, day out, no matter what the level of exhaustion and how many of these frontline caregivers have been sidelined by illness. To make an already difficult situation even more challenging, Covid-19 has already shown itself to be a formidable foe in terms of the variety and complexity of its pathological symptoms and disease progression.[12]

The onslaught of Covid-stricken patients filling hospitals in short order forced other medical procedures, even fairly urgent ones, to be delayed. Many illnesses failed to get diagnosed as people ended up scaling back their doctor visits. Mental health, in particular, has taken a dive during the pandemic, amidst an explosion of addiction and domestic violence. Luckily, many national healthcare systems have dramatically enhanced their online content, pushing usefully into so-called "telehealth" which allows distribution of health-related services and information using computers and smartphones. Once the pandemic will have been put behind us, officials will probably want to assess how the domestic public health system has held up during that extraordinary challenge and what lessons can be learned to improve healthcare access and delivery in that country.

Such assessment will reveal painful truths in many countries. America's private healthcare system, for example, revealed shortcomings that are unique to any such profit-motivated care. When tens of millions of Americans lost their jobs during the Spring 2020 lockdowns, they also lost their typically employer-provided health insurance. And Trump's relentless efforts to weaken the Affordable Care Act, Obama's landmark healthcare insurance reform, made it more difficult to absorb that massive spike in the uninsured even though Obamacare, as the reform was often referred to in public discourse, proved also its resilience at the same time. Profit-oriented US hospitals had kept medical equipment inventories

[12] The SARS-CoV-2 coronavirus can attack human cells at multiple points, with the throat and lungs its main targets. Once inside a human body, it makes use of a diverse arsenal of molecules. And it can trigger all kinds of inflammatory responses, has a much stronger impact on certain blood types, can cause organ failures for different reasons, and may have a variety of long-term effects we still have not yet fully identified. The challenges posited by Covid's complexity have been captured well by Baird (2020b) and by Cyranoski (2020).

and staffing to a minimum, thus exposing themselves to immediate and disruptive shortages from the very beginning of the pandemic. When the pandemic forced delays of doctor visits and medical procedures for reasons other than Covid-related symptoms, both doctors and hospitals suffered steep income losses. US hospital chains compete against each other which made needed local or regional coordination among them much harder, if not impossible, to come by. This proved a significant impediment to effective handling of the pandemic which public healthcare systems in other countries managed significantly better. Where government-administered healthcare systems suffered the most was a combination of supply shortages and aged equipment resulting from persistent underfunding. Even top-notch universal health care, as is available in France or Germany, came under lots of stress during the pandemic, with valuable lessons about shortcomings and limitations to be learned even there.

5.5.2 *The Digital Economy*

The pandemic has dramatically accelerated a shift to the digital economy, the online organization of economic activity, and social interaction. This has been universally true wherever the internet has already had a growing presence before the pandemic. Lockdowns intensified e-commerce, with people forced to stay home for weeks ordering more goods and services online that they then had delivered to their abode. This habit-forming trend is unlikely to be reversed after the end of the pandemic and poses an existential threat to brick-and-mortar retail stores. Wherever possible, firms have sought to get as much work as possible organized from home during the pandemic. Such remote work has been rendered much more feasible by the phenomenal spread of video-conferencing applications and software, such as Zoom or Microsoft Teams. This new world of work has many advantages and disadvantages, making it hard to predict how much it will continue beyond the duration of the pandemic as a lasting phenomenon.[13] However much of it lasts post-Covid will make a significant difference to the commercial viability of business travel, commuter transportation, upscale clothing, downtown restaurants serving lunch, office space, and a variety of other work-related auxiliaries (e.g. office supplies, cabs). The coronavirus imposed also a massive shift to

[13] On the many, often contradictory implications of remote work, compared to the traditional office work environment, see Neeley (2020) or Newport (2020).

online learning. Education, whose systemic unevenness reproduces long-standing structural inequalities in society, now has also digital inequality to contend with. With people having a lot more time to spare during the lockdown albeit, in physical isolation, the average person's use of social media exploded during the pandemic from already high pre-Covid levels. And this shift has made Twitter, Facebook, TikTok, and other social-media platforms far more influential in terms of how people get their information about the world, engage in relations and activities, and form groups. Spending so much more time online while in quarantine has also made people more exposed to cybercrime which has seen a massive spike during the course of the pandemic.

These socio-economic dimensions of moving a growing proportion of what matters in our lives online has given our tech giants dominating the internet a huge boost, with Google, Apple, Amazon, Facebook, and Microsoft all reaping large increases in profits during the pandemic while the rest of the economy has suffered varying degrees of disruption. Governments must grapple with how best to address the immense power of these tech giants which have gained such far-reaching influence on the lives of billions of consumers across the globe. This is not just a question of competition policy and anti-trust regulation as each of these tech giants has its corporate eye set on higher pursuits turning them into market-dominating conglomerates across many new high-tech areas. There is also the question of how best to deal with data and privacy protections. It is worthwhile noting here that the United States, the European Union, and China have developed fundamentally different approaches in their data policies and as concerns their regulation of the tech giants dominating the internet. Let us briefly summarize the key differences among those three approaches, one of several contemporary policy areas where we can see increasingly nuanced variants of capitalism emerge in competition with each other.

Even though political transgressions have recently brought Facebook, Twitter, Amazon, and to a lesser extent also the other US-based tech giants to the forefront of public attention, even subject of intense debate in US Congress, American policy-makers have up to now preferred a light-touch approach to reining in the enormous market power and socio-political influence of these internet giants. Data and privacy protection are a matter of corporate self-regulation, and this hands-off doctrine has been key to the American tech giant's successful business models rooted in giving value to Big Data as source of profit. There is, however, a better than even chance that the Biden Administration will seek to revisit the increasingly contentious issue of how to regulate hate speech and disinformation propagated on social media while also restoring open-internet "net neutrality" revoked by Trump. Biden's appointments to key positions dealing with competition policy indicate possibly even more ambitious anti-trust initiatives to come.

The European Union, while lacking its own homegrown tech giants and in that way lagging behind the other two power centers, has applied a more aggressive competition policy toward the US tech giants, involving a number of spectacular anti-trust lawsuits. The EU also has developed a stronger data regulation and privacy protection approach in favor of protecting its citizens from invasive overreach, as crystallized in its much-vaunted General Data Protection Regulation (GDPR) of 2016 whose extraterritorial jurisdiction has obliged non-EU companies to comply with its regulatory details and so turned the GDPR into a global baseline standard. In early 2021 the new EU Commission proposed a two-legged regulatory framework for the internet which, besides applying equally across the entire EU's internal market, it hopes to turn into a global standard for the digital economy. Its Digital Services Act aims to foster innovation with regard to online intermediary services, provide an accountability and transparency framework for online platforms, and protect consumers online. Its Digital Markets Act regulates online platforms known as "gatekeepers" which act as key intermediaries in the digital economy. And then there are Europe's pioneering efforts to tax the digital space. Several EU members have already imposed digital services taxes, and the EU itself has agreed to impose a system-wide digital levy as a new revenue source by 2023. Targeting mostly America's high-tech giants. Europe's attempts to tax digital activity spurred the scorn of Trump who threatened retaliation. The Biden Administration has instead pushed for a global corporate-tax reform deal under the auspices of the Organisation of Economic Co-operation and Development (OECD) which, besides imposing minimum tax rates for business across the globe to counter base erosion and profit shifting, also provides for taxation of digital activity.[14]

[14] For more information on the European Commission's two-pronged (Digital Services Act and Digital Markets Act) strategy to regulate online platforms and intermediaries see European Commission (2020). Europe's digital services taxes are discussed in Asen

China has successfully cordoned off its local internet, as part of its authoritarian approach to exercising political control over its citizens, and in the process given rise to its own dominant tech giants such as Alibaba, Tencent, Baidu, or JD.com. Until recently the Chinese government gave those strategic firms a lot of room to build their own multi-product business models through various product-bundling techniques and acquisition sprees to the point where each of them came to control very large consumer networks. The relative importance of these homegrown internet conglomerates may even exceed that of its US counterparts, given how advanced and widespread daily use of the internet has become among the Chinese. But these tech giants are obliged to cooperate closely with Chinese authorities as a prerequisite for their commercial pursuits, thereby enabling those authorities to have turned modern China into a sophisticated "surveillance state." And in late 2020 Chinese authorities quite suddenly started applying significantly tougher anti-trust policy standards to the monopolistic tactics of China's four internet giants, targeting in particular Alibaba's founder Jack Ma after canceling his much-anticipated spin-off of leading financial-services subsidiary Ant Financial at the last minute. This new policy regime is about further tightening state control over the internet. While the system of digital control over people's lives can have significant benefits as when China managed to mitigate an epidemic effectively by means of smartphone apps and online platforms, it is above all a highly efficient mechanism for the repression of dissent and imposition of conformity.[15]

Big Data and the internet are thus one of those strategically important policy areas where we can see fundamentally different approaches taken by the world's three large power centers, an indication that we have here varieties of capitalism evolving which are pushing us toward a tri-polar configuration of the world economy—a key theme developed further in this book. The policy differences between the United States, European Union, and China on Big Data and the internet are likely to become only more impactful over time, as the digital economy grows in

(2021). The OECD's push for a global corporate-tax reform agreement is detailed in Organisation for Economic Co-operation and Development (2020b).

[15] The rapid perfection of China's "surveillance state" under Xi Jinping has been highlighted in often disquieting detail by Mitchell and Diamond (2018) as well as Andersen (2020). For more on China's sudden turn to tougher anti-trust standards for its internet giants in late 2020, see McMorrow and Riordan (2020).

strategic importance. This trend is not least a function of continued rapid technological progress as concerns the internet's infrastructure, including computing power (with quantum computing on the horizon), servers, cloud computing, widening of broadband, miniaturization of computer components (with the help of nanotechnology), blockchains reorganizing how networks operate, and artificial intelligence (AI). The ongoing roll-out of the fifth-generation technology standard for cellular networks, known as 5G, will dramatically enhance the functionality of cell phones whose strategic importance we have been able to witness during the pandemic with the use in many countries of mobile contract-tracing apps. Both AI and 5G will help foster the development of the "Internet of Things" (IoT) creating a much more connected world of interactive devices generating and transferring a lot more data than ever before. One dimension of AI involves machine learning whereby computer algorithms improve their performance automatically through experience. All these improvements in computing power and connectivity of "smart" machines set the stage for a breathtaking wave of automation extending to industrial processes and manufacturing, referred to as the fourth industrial revolution (or "Industry 4.0"), which may render obsolete many jobs or make them quite different than they are today. To the extent that the pandemic has forced many businesses to operate at significantly lower capacity levels for possibly several years, many of them may be tempted to accelerate the adoption of labor-saving automation technologies, notwithstanding considerable start-up costs and a more rigid cost structure due to a larger share of operating costs being fixed.[16]

5.5.3 *Growing Inequality*

Labor-saving automation eliminates many jobs henceforth better done by machines while also creating new, often rather knowledge-intense (and hence well-paid) jobs. To the extent that the pandemic ends up accelerating such automation, it adds yet another channel of structural change toward greater inequality and so reinforces a destabilizing trend that has gained considerable strength over the last quarter of a century. In nearly all of the industrial nations, grouped together in the OECD, we have been

[16] The fourth industrial revolution was coined and analyzed as such by Schwab (2017). Its wide-ranging impact on the world of work, jobs, and widening skill gaps is discussed in detail by Baldwin (2019) and Susskind (2020).

able to witness a steadily growing income gap between, say, the richest 10 percent and the remaining 90 percent of that country's population. This worrisome trend, crystallized around a gradually falling wage share (as percentage of total national income) and shrinking middle class, has had several causes—technological change yielding a growing skills premium in favor of better-educated workers, trade and globalization causing de-industrialization in the advanced "post-industrial" capitalist economies, and policies reflecting political and ideological shifts in favor of tax cuts for the rich, business deregulation, and boosting of financial incomes. The pandemic has both highlighted these distributional inequalities as well as further accentuated them.

We see the inequality brutally revealed in the statistics of the pandemic, in terms of who is more or less likely to become infected, fall seriously ill, or die from Covid-19. In most countries the poorer you are, the greater the likelihood of ending up infected, becoming very sick, and getting killed by the virus. The poor have a greater probability of catching the virus because they are more likely to work outside the home during the pandemic, use public transport commuting to work, and live in crowded settings. They also tend to have less access to good health care and typically lack sick-leave benefits so that they end up going to work even when feeling sick, both reasons for why they get hit harder by Covid-19 when it strikes them. Finally, they stand a greater chance of carrying the underlying pre-existing conditions—hypertension, diabetes, obesity, serious heart conditions, chronic lung disease—associated with significantly higher death rates from Covid-19 as comorbidities. In countries with demographically diverse populations and a history of institutionalized discrimination against targeted minorities, those marginalized groups, often enough making up a large share of the poor, have fared far worse during the pandemic not only in terms of exposure to risk, serious illness, and fatalities, but also when it comes to negative economic consequences such as unemployment and income losses.

When societies locked down, their labor force split into three distinct tiers. It is therefore fair to argue that the lockdowns have only served to reinforce the segmentation of any country's labor market, an important factor behind the recent trend toward greater income inequality now rendered even more pronounced by the pandemic widening the gaps between different groups.

- A privileged group of professionals shifted into working online from home. These so-called "knowledge workers" (e.g. physicians, academics, engineers, architects, lawyers, financial advisors and analysts, bankers) have by and large managed to keep their full pay even if they continue to work remotely.
- A second group of workers, typically larger than the first, provides all kinds of necessary goods (e.g. food) and services (e.g. police, mail delivery) which have to be supplied for any society to survive. These so-called "essential" workers, from hospital staff to delivery people to grocery workers to public transport personnel and beyond, have had to go to work every day, whatever the risk of exposure to the coronavirus, so that the rest of us could continue to function while confined at home.
- The remainder of the labor force simply stopped working or ended up working far less than they used to, with significant loss of income extending to most of the self-employed and sole proprietors running small businesses. There are a lot of (mostly young) free-lancers, part-timers, gig-economy workers, casual non-contract workers, and independent contractors in this highly vulnerable group, including huge numbers of migrant workers in emerging-market economies for whom the lockdown reinforced the physical separation of employment opportunities and home base in disastrous fashion.

Such inequality-enhancing tiering of the labor force in the wake of the coronavirus pandemic has cut through ethnicity as well as generations in very powerful ways. In the United States, for instance, African-Americans or Latinos/as have been two to three times more likely to die from Covid-19 as majority white Americans. At the same time, it is the young who have suffered the most from the un- and underemployment caused by lockdowns, setting the stage for an intensification of inter-generational conflicts as the aging baby-boomer generation continues to use its political power to protect its relatively secure income, generous access to pensions and health care, and disproportionate accumulation of wealth.

In this regard, it has made a strong difference in how robust a government's prevailing social safety net has proven to be. In Europe, for instance, employment protections are typically quite strong as are unemployment benefits. In early 2020 the EU also expanded so-called short-time work schemes which allowed firms negatively affected by the pandemic to reduce temporarily the number of hours worked while providing their employees with income support from the state for hours not worked. This policy kept the basic employment structure of the EU economics intact while on lockdown. By contrast, the US economy suffered over twenty million jobs lost during its lockdown at the beginning of the pandemic, completely overwhelming its underfunded and administratively stressed system of (state-administered) unemployment benefits. That is why the US government had to come up right away with a huge emergency relief package, the $2.2 trillion Coronavirus Aid, Relief and Economic Security (CARES) Act of March 2020 which, among other things, provided directly $2000 per capita payments to most Americans, expanded unemployment insurance, and launched a funding program for millions of small businesses known as the Paycheck Protection Program.

There are other forces related to the pandemic bound to make already bad inequality even worse. The lockdowns have proven devastating to sole proprietorships, the smallest of business units, many of whom lacked the right banking relationships to get government aid in due time. Since they typically also lack emergency funds, a large percentage will not survive this crisis. In general, small businesses, typically the backbone of any national economy, have fared far worse than the larger corporations which, besides being able to withstand a drying up of revenues thanks to cash reserves, are more likely to get government aid, have privileged access to bank credit, and can tap financial markets. As the smaller and weaker firms get crushed by the coronavirus crisis, many sectors will find themselves with even higher degrees of market concentration than we had already arrived at before the crisis hit. But there is also the question of which sectors within the economy will face long-term decline triggered by the pandemic, such as retail stores or commercial real estate, or the hospitality sector, and how their shrinking plays out.

Inequality has been further exacerbated by gains for investors earning capital income. Wide-ranging crisis-fighting measures of central banks have supported large-scale reversals of initially terrifying stock-market declines, even rebounds. Indices, such as the Dow Jones or NASDAQ, have moved into record territory thanks to huge liquidity injections and record-low interest rates even though the virus is still causing havoc and recovery is still fragile at best everywhere. Bonds too have seen their market prices rise amidst falling interest rates. Strong capital gains in both stock and bond markets have given the wealthy investor class a welcome income boost and a positive wealth effect at a time when working people have suffered income losses from falling wages, cutbacks in hours worked, and un- or underemployment.

5.6 The International Crisis Context

We saw already in Chapter 4 (especially Sect. 4.5) that the downswing phase following the Great Recession nourished various de-globalization trends which amounted to trend reversals with regard to trade, foreign direct investment activity, portfolio investment flows, or global supply chains. The world economy was thus already under a good deal of stress when Covid-19 hit in early 2020.

5.6.1 A Massive Shock to Cross-Border Activity

By triggering widespread lockdowns the pandemic further damaged the world economy through several channels of transmission. In short order, governments closed borders, stopped most air travel, slowed port traffic to a crawl, and suspended cross-border tourism. These effects made the logistics of trade more difficult, on top of seeing its volume shrink dramatically when lockdowns caused a massive and sudden downward shift in aggregate demand across the planet. According to data provided by the World Trade Organization (WTO) in August 2020, the volume of world merchandise trade shrank by 14 percent during the second quarter of 2020, after already declining 2.6 percent in the first quarter of 2020 thanks to a precipitous fall in March. That decline is the steepest in recorded history, a bit more than twice the overall volume shrinkage in world trade suffered during the global financial crisis of 2008/09. The extent of the decline has been regionally differentiated in direct proportion to the duration and extent of local lockdowns, far worse in Europe (minus 20.4 percent) and the United States (minus 16.8 percent) than in China (minus 6.5 percent).

The new stage in the internationalization of production, rooted in the organization of global value chains (GVCs) by market leaders offshoring activities to affiliates and subsidiaries in lower-cost countries, works well under normal conditions to minimize costs. But their cost-efficient practices of single sourcing and just-in-time inventory management make GVCs also very vulnerable to disruptions, especially in transportation by air or sea. The pandemic has in that regard turned out to be a phenomenally disruptive event, in essence breaking most supply chains apart. This nightmarish experience has prompted many business leaders to begin rethinking their GVCs by looking for alternate sourcing, shortening their chains, re-shoring some of their activities, and switching from "just-in-time" to "just-in-case" inventory management for greater margins of safety.[17] The debate over reorganizing GVCs in the wake of the pandemic has become intermingled with the question of China's relationship with the West. China's crucial role in GVCs was demonstrated right at the very beginning of the pandemic, when Hubei province, a manufacturing hub producing key components for pharmaceuticals, electronics, and cars, ended up cordoned off from the rest of the world. Its factory closures spurred ripples of disruption further downstream in thousands of global production networks rather rapidly. Given the mounting tensions between China and the United States, fueled even more by the pandemic, the reorganization of GVCs may end up being greatly impacted by eventual American attempts to "de-couple" its economy from that of China's.

The destabilization of financial markets in the wake of lockdowns extended beyond domestic stock and bond markets also to the international realm, where the "flight to safety" phenomenon prompted a huge reversal of capital flows. The pandemic triggered a massive reversal of the $14 trillion "carry trade", fueled by a crisis-induced combination of home bias (encouraging repatriation of funds), risk aversion, and deleveraging pressure. About $103 billion were drawn out of emerging-market economies (EMEs) between mid-January and mid-May 2020, an amount five times larger than during a comparable period at the height of the Great Financial Crisis of 2008/09. These massive capital-flow reversals, confirmed by monthly balance-of-payments data measuring non-resident portfolio flows from such countries as Brazil, Mexico, South Africa, Turkey, Russia, Malaysia, Philippines, or Korea, coincided with sharply lower interest rates in those emerging-market economies and also contributed to declines of between 10 and 25 percent of their currencies. Add to this a drastic decline of longer-term foreign direct investment (FDI) flows, estimated to have fallen by 40 percent during the first few months of pandemic.[18]

[17] For more on the pandemic's impact on disrupting global value chains and prompting attempts to reorganize them for greater resilience see the Organisation for Economic Co-operation and Development (2020a). A recent report by consulting firm McKinsey (2020) explores possible scenarios for the coming reorganization of global value chains.

[18] See the Institute of International Finance's (IIF, iif.com) *Capital Flows Tracker* and UNCTAD's *Global Investment Trends Monitor* of May 2020 for data on those pandemic-induced capital-flow reversals in the wake of the worldwide lockdowns.

5.6.2 A Stress Test for the Dollar Standard

The pandemic's multi-layered disruption of the world economy translated rapidly into a very serious shortage of dollars for many advanced economies, emerging-market economies, and even low-income developing countries (LIDCs). To begin with, the USD's dominant world-money status endows it with a safe-haven function which triggers massive "flights to safety" into dollars among non-US investors whenever they face heightened uncertainty amidst major disruptions of normalcy. We could see such precautionary shifts in global USD demand already at the peak of the Great Financial Crisis (GFC) in the last quarter of 2008. When its global safe-haven role reappeared in March 2020, the flight into dollars pushed the US currency up nearly 10 percent in just three weeks against other key currencies. Over the last decade non-American borrowers, whether Japanese insurance firms, European corporations, EME governments such as Brazil, or Russian oligarchs, have almost doubled their USD-denominated liabilities to nearly $60 trillion according to the Bank for International Settlements' *Debt Securities Statistics*. Such non-US borrowers, exposed to a currency mismatch on their balance sheets between USD-denominated liabilities and assets in local currencies, will find it much harder to service their debts in the face of such a rapid appreciation of the USD.

There were other reasons why international demand for US dollars shot up at the onset of the pandemic, mostly related to lockdown-induced disruptions in cash inflows normally used to cover trade credit, working capital of GVC subsidiaries, or bank-issued letters of credit all of which represent dollar commitments for most non-US businesses engaged in international transactions. At the same time leading banks outside the United States, already having lowered their dollar reserves because of tougher liquidity and leverage regulations put in place during the 2010s, were neither willing nor able to meet such a sudden increase in global dollar funding needs in the face of what they perceived to be suddenly much greater counterparty risks. During the first half of March 2020 we could thus see the cross-currency basis three-month swap spreads, a measure of global funding costs when borrowing dollars through (typically three-month) currency swaps, shoot up in a matter of weeks from the typical minus 10-to-20 basis points all the way to minus 85 basis points for EUR-USD swaps, minus 144 basis points for JPY-USD swaps, and a whopping minus 287 basis points for KRW-USD swaps. Such hikes in the dollar premium indicated a rapidly evolving shortage of the US currency relative to spiking global demand.[19]

In the face of this sudden and massive worldwide dollar shortage America's central bank, the Federal Reserve, did not waste much time before acting decisively as international lender of last resort safeguarding the global dollar standard, as it had already done during the GFC of 2008/09.

- On March 15 the Fed expanded its existing currency-swap lines with five other leading central banks—the European Central Bank, the Bank of England, the Bank of Japan, Swiss National Bank, and the Bank of Canada—whereby it lends these institutions dollars at the prevailing spot rate in exchange for their local currencies for a certain period of time at the conclusion of which the transaction is reversed (which means foreign central banks returning their loaned dollars). Since the reversal occurs at exactly the original spot rate, the swapping of the currencies between the Fed and the other central banks does not affect the exchange rate. When the Fed reopened these decade-old currency-swap arrangements in mid-March 2020 to face pandemic-induced turmoil, it made them both cheaper, charging only 25 basis points above the risk-free overnight rate known as the OIS rate (for overnight index swap), as well as last longer (up to three months, compared to the established norm of just a week). The other central banks would then take those Fed-supplied dollars and transfer them, typically at a higher but still low-interest rate, to banks under their jurisdiction. Those would now have a lot more dollars at hand for their clients, thus making the dollar shortage subside.
- Four days later, on March 19, the Fed extended currency-swap lines to nine other central banks some of whom from emerging-market economies where the global dollar shortage had proven disproportionally worse. Specifically, it offered $60 bn. swap lines each to the central banks of Australia, Brazil, Mexico, Singapore, South Korea, and Sweden as well as $30 bn. swap lines each to the central banks of Denmark, New Zealand, and Norway.

[19] These numbers on the cross-currency swap spread hikes, as well as other indicators of the global USD squeeze, are well presented in the excellent study of BIS staffers Avdjiev et al. (2020). See also Du (2020) on the banks' declining dollar supply capacity.

- Less than two weeks later, on March 31, the Fed introduced a new program to supply needed dollars to a potentially much larger group of countries beyond the fourteen central banks already covered by its swap line arrangements. Its so-called Foreign and International Monetary Authorities (FIMA) Repo Facility allowed central banks or other monetary authorities to exchange their holdings of US Treasuries temporarily for an equivalent sum of US dollars which they could then provide to institutions under their jurisdiction. The repo facility was intended as a backstop, with a fairly high rate set at 0.25 percent above the primary credit rate.

The Fed's three steps to ease dangerous strains in the global dollar funding market met the intended objective very effectively. In the six weeks that followed ten of the fourteen central banks grabbed a total of $449 bn. from those swap lines, of which the Bank of Japan obtained $224 bn. and the European Central Bank took $143 bn. These funds had right away a significantly calming effect on the stressed offshore USD market. Whereas euro- and yen-based borrowers had to pay an additional 200 basis points and 250 basis points respectively when borrowing dollars at the height of the crisis in mid-March 2020, that spread would fall consistently all the way to just 30 bp and 50 bp by the end of April. At that point, the use of the swap lines started to decline steadily to about $100 bn. by mid-August, a further indication of having calmed the offshore dollar funding market.[20]

5.6.3 *Poorer Countries Get Hit Harder*

The pandemic has been especially tough on the seventy-five or so low-income developing countries (LIDCs), hitting them even before many of those poor nations faced their own invasion of the virus. The contraction of global trade has affected LIDCs in asymmetric fashion due to their dependence on inelastic imports of necessities and vulnerable export markets. Many LIDCs rely on exporting commodities, whose world-market prices declined between 5 and 15 percent within a month of the mid-March wave of lockdowns which further depressed LIDC's export

[20] See Federal Reserve Board (2020) as well as Tett (2020b) for more details on these three international-lender-of-last-resort interventions of the Fed supplying dollars to other central banks in dire need during the Covid crash.

earnings. Half of all LIDCs depend on remittances, monies sent home by migrants working abroad, to the point where those inflows exceed 5 percent of GDP. Such remittances fell sharply, by an estimated 20 percent on an annualized basis, when the rich countries shut down. Sharply reduced remittances will also be directly felt by the extended families needing those funds for survival. LIDCs relying heavily on tourism (e.g. Costa Rica, Jamaica, Tunisia, Thailand) were especially exposed to the near-complete halt to global travel.[21]

Squeezed by so many external shocks, LIDCs also have had to face the pandemic right away as a profound domestic challenge. It is much more difficult for LIDC governments to impose open-ended lockdowns on their intrinsically vulnerable populations large percentages of which subsist in the informal economy and may even lack proper documentation to be tracked. Those people have to work no matter what, or they and their families starve. Most LIDCs, having undergone rapid urbanization in recent decades, also have ended up with densely populated cities whose very cramped living, working, and transportation conditions make social distancing impossible. When the pandemic finally moved full force into the Southern hemisphere after several months of delay, more transmissible variants of the virus wreaked havoc in the overcrowded urban centers of Brazil, Mexico, South Africa, India, and elsewhere. Systematically underfunded public health systems, even relatively good ones as in the case of Brazil, were no match for the aggressive virus mutations.[22]

While the combination of vaccine roll-out, large accumulations of household savings, very expansionary fiscal and monetary policies, and pent-up demand provides a recipe for strong recovery once the rich countries will have brought the pandemic under control, poorer countries have far less rosy prospects going forward. Revised IMF estimates foresee a better than expected recovery of the world economy, allowing GDP per capita in the rich countries by the end of 2022 to be barely lower (by only 1–2 percent) than it would have been without the Great Interruption of 2020/21. Poorer countries, by contrast, can expect a GDP per

[21] The commodity-price deflation at the onset of the pandemic is illustrated well by data presented in the World Bank's *Commodity Markets Outlook* (April 2020). The World Bank's *Migration and Development Brief*, on the other hand, pinpoints the collapse of remittances.

[22] For an interesting summary of the many challenges the coronavirus has posed to the LIDCs I recommend Gurara et al. (2020).

capita shortfall of 6.5 percent by the end of 2022, with up to 130 million people pushed into extreme poverty by the pandemic. With their debt-to-GDP ratios raised on average by 10 percent during 2020 in the wake of the pandemic, LIDCs as well as many EMEs are exposed to a double whammy of rising debt-servicing charges and eroding capacity to generate the income needed for those, pushing them steadily closer to the edge of default. Many large EMEs with the greatest dollar needs, such as Turkey, Argentina, Nigeria, or Indonesia, as well as all LIDCs are excluded from the Fed's swap lines and lack the reserves kept in US Treasuries to access the Fed's new FIMA Repo facility. This makes all those vulnerable countries entirely dependent on help from the International Monetary Fund (IMF) and/or active measures of debt relief. Failure to provide adequate assistance in a timely fashion risks setting off a global debt crisis over the next year or two.

Some first debt-relief measures have been put in place. At the onset of the pandemic, the rich G-20 countries launched the Debt Service Suspension Initiative (DSSI) which froze bilateral government loan repayments for seventy-six low-income countries, half of which owed to China in the wake of its Belt and Road Initiative. That measure, initially set until the end of 2020, was further extended through 2021. It would be helpful if this initiative also applied to private creditors. More broadly, the hundred or so poorer and middle-income debtor nations facing acute debt-servicing pressures need a new mechanism for debt relief. The IMF is contemplating pushing both public and private creditors to accept more extensive use of so-called "collective action clauses" for debt restructurings which could be imposed on all bondholders once 75 percent of them have agreed to such a deal. Such clauses could be extended beyond bonds to syndicated loans. Debt contracts could also include clauses that automatically trigger debt-servicing pauses and even reduced payouts when debtor countries suffer disruptions of no fault of their own, as in the case of natural disasters or economic shocks such as a global pandemic. It would be useful to have new protocols increasing the transparency about countries' borrowings to reduce uncertainty and also as a first step toward a more formalized and cohesive approach to the restructuring of debts.[23]

[23] Such a more formalized global approach to debtor countries' debt restructuring would avoid messy, lengthy, often inconclusive negotiations as happened to Argentina after 2001 when so-called "vulture funds" bought up enough of that country's defaulted debt to block any agreement until and unless they were handsomely paid off.

In the meantime, much of the crisis management has been shouldered by the IMF. During the first year of the pandemic, from March 2020 to April 2021, the Fund provided $110 billion in emergency funds to help eighty-one countries facing balance-of-payments difficulties. While much of that money comes from the IMF's general funding resources, it has also worked hard to add new lending facilities or expand existing ones to meet this unique global crisis. In April 2020, for example, the IMF set up a so-called Short-term Liquidity Line (SLL) as a liquidity backstop for otherwise well-managed countries facing capital-account pressures in the wake of external shocks. The IMF has also substantially enhanced its Poverty Reduction and Growth Trust (PRGT) from contributions of richer members for concessionary lending to its poorest members, seeking $18 bn. in new funds. And in April 2021 the IMF decided to launch an unprecedented new $650 bn. issue of Special Drawing Rights (SDRs) which dwarfs any issue up to now, including the last one in 2009 in the wake of the Great Financial Crisis amounting to $250 billion. This new issue of SDRs, approved by the Biden Administration (in contrast to Trump's earlier veto) and distributed to all 190 members of the IMF according to a formula based proportionately on size, will go predominantly to the richer members and only dedicate about a third to the middle-income EMEs and poorer LIDCs. However, negotiations are under way to find new ways whereby the richer members can redistribute their excess SDRs on a much larger scale to the poorer members in need of SDRs beyond their own small allotment. Such an agreement would introduce a new chapter in the use of SDRs as a financial-assistance tool beyond its limited reserve-asset status it has had so far.[24]

5.6.4 *The Global Vaccination Challenge*

One of the striking features of the global pandemic has been the concerted worldwide effort to develop effective vaccines against the coronavirus and its spectacular success in developing several versions within a year (where normal vaccine development takes typically ten to fifteen years). Of course, earlier incidences of highly transmissible coronaviruses, notably the Severe Acute Respiratory Syndrome (SARS) in 2002/03

[24] For more details on the planned $650 bn. allocation of SDRs see Obstfeld and Truman (2021). More general information about how SDRs work is best accessed from a Fact Sheet provided by the International Monetary Fund (2021).

and the Middle East Respiratory Syndrome (MERS) in 2012, had motivated vaccine scientists to focus their research efforts on spike proteins over the last couple of decades and so given them a head start in the race for a vaccine against SARS-Cov-2. That race started as soon as the Chinese published its genetic sequence in mid-January 2020, whereupon scientists used their earlier research on coronaviruses to identify suitable antigens very rapidly. Hundreds of vaccine-development projects were launched within weeks, testimony to the urgency of having to fight a deadly pandemic spreading across the globe. Pharmaceutical companies saw the huge profit potential of a workable vaccine, and the leaders of powerful nations did not take long to grasp the usefulness of vaccines as tools of diplomacy and source of reputational gain.

In May 2020 the Trump administration launched a $10 bn. inter-agency effort known as Operation Warp Speed (OWS) which streamlined vaccine-development procedures so that they could be dramatically accelerated within a much-shortened timeline, invested heavily in vaccine manufacturing capacity and offered participating firms advance purchase contracts which basically underwrote their product development risks. The nine firms drawn into the OWS scheme were working on three different vaccine platform technologies, including the path-breaking messenger RNA technology mastered by Pfizer (in partnership with Germany's BioNTech) and Moderna yielding vaccines with 95 percent efficacy by year's end. Both obtained Emergency Use Authorization (EUA) by the US Food and Drug Administration (FDA) in December 2020 for widespread use. While Trump could count the OWS as one of his greatest policy successes, his administration failed to secure sufficient supplies early on and then refused to implement a nationally coordinated strategy for a mass vaccination infrastructure. Both of these tasks fell to the Biden Administration which immediately went to work at full speed, managing to get 220 million jabs into the arms of Americans within the first hundred days of Biden's presidency—a phenomenal success which turned the United States from the world's worst virus hotspot during the final months of 2020 into the vaccination effort leader six months later (besides the United Kingdom and Israel). However, having turned the pandemic into a highly politicized issue dividing Democrats and Republicans has left many Americans hesitant, if not altogether resistant, to getting vaccinated which bodes ill for achieving the much-evoked herd immunity needed for the pandemic to end.

Operation Warp Speed, with its exclusive focus on the United States, was an early example of a worrisome trend toward "vaccine nationalism" prioritizing vaccine access for the domestic population over anyone else.[25] We have seen such nationalistic proclivities to the detriment of international cooperation needed to address what is in essence a global policy challenge already earlier with regard to the Syrian refugee crisis of 2015 and also concerning climate change. While Trump, who even went as far as taking the United States out of the World Health Organization in the middle of a global pandemic just to divert attention from his own failings, was only the most vocal and explicit proponent of this trend, there were many other leaders preferring to vaccinate everyone at home before supplying jabs to high-risk populations across the globe. In recent months this calculus has become dramatically more consequential with the accelerating trend of SARS-CoV-2 mutating into far more transmissible and potentially more deadly variants such as the beta variant originating in South Africa or the delta variant first found in India. Such variants have exacerbated the pandemic where they have taken root, most tragically so in Brazil and India whose leaders downplayed the virus until such lack of precaution led to public health catastrophe. To the extent that the virus is allowed to accelerate its spread, it is also more likely to mutate into even more dangerous variants. The world is now in a race between vaccines and variants. And this race makes it ever more imperative to vaccinate a large percentage of the world's adult population, say 80 percent, as soon as possible. That challenge is no longer just a moral imperative in the face of the world's glaring inequalities of access but has become a public health necessity since no one is safe from the rapidly mutating virus until all are protected.

Toward that objective the WHO set up a global vaccine coordination effort in April 2020 known as COVAX, co-managed with the Global Vaccine Alliance (Gavi), the Coalition of Epidemic Preparedness Innovations (CEPI), and UNICEF, to which 172 high-, middle-, and low-income countries have signed up to share global procurement

[25] The vexing problem of "vaccine nationalism" has already begun to be recognized as a major threat to the very effectiveness of defeating the coronavirus globally, as discussed in greater detail by Bollyky and Brown (2020), Kupferschmidt (2020), or Weintraub et al. (2020).

and equitable distribution of authorized vaccines across the globe.[26] The COVAX facility is the key mechanism to assure vaccine access to the poorest people in low-income countries. Its goal is to vaccinate 20 percent of the world's population, with priority given to the most vulnerable populations in the poorer countries, by securing procurement and distribution of two billion jabs during 2021 from a portfolio of WHO-authorized vaccines such as Britain's AstraZeneca, America's Moderna and Novavax, China's Sinopharm, and Serum Institute of India's Covishield. Even though vaccine manufacturers have agreed to charge only the comparatively low "at-cost" prices for supplies to the COVAX facility, the effort lacks funding and is about $30 bn. short of what it would need to operate adequately at full potential. The facility also competes with rich countries' national procurement efforts which offer vaccine manufacturers higher prices and often involve supply contracts on a scale in excess of domestic needs as governments are intent on double- or even triple-sourcing vaccine supplies at home in case of disruptions.

Even though the United States is not part of COVAX, the US Congress authorized $4 bn. for Gavi the Vaccine Alliance in December 2020 to boost the COVAX effort. Moreover, the Biden Administration has also adopted a far more helpful attitude than its go-it-alone predecessor. The moment Trump left the White House on January 20, the United States rejoined the WHO. In March 2021 the Biden Administration authorized 60 million AstraZeneca vaccines it had stored to be sent to India and elsewhere. At their June 2021 summit in Cornwall (England) the G-7 members committed one billion vaccines to COVAX within a year, half of which were supplied by the United States. Moreover, the Biden Administration surprised everybody in May 2021 when it faced down its country's powerful pharma lobby and backed a move to end the pharmaceutical companies' rights to enforce their intellectual property on Covid vaccines. Specifically, this break with long-standing US policy involves a waiver of the World Trade Organization's Trade-Related Intellectual Property System (TRIPS) which a 2001 agreement at the Doha Ministerial Conference provided for public health concerns so that poorer countries could have improved access to affordable medicines. The

[26] COVAX is the vaccine pillar of the Access to Covid-19 Tools (ACT) Accelerator which was set up by the WHO, the European Commission, France as well as the Bill & Melinda Gates Foundation in April 2020 to develop and deliver tests, treatments and vaccines which the world needs to fight the Covid-19 pandemic.

practical effects of this decision, meant to accelerate global production of cheap generic Covid vaccines, may be limited given the opposition of the European Union to such TRIPS waivers and the need for massive US follow-up support to expanding the scale and scope of the complex global vaccine supply chains. But the message is nonetheless meaningful inasmuch as it shows a growing US commitment to help address the global policy challenges of a worldwide vaccination campaign without which the pandemic cannot be effectively overcome.

Even though worldwide vaccine distribution has a long way to go while the pandemic rages on more dangerously than ever in places lacking access to jabs, that aspect of the Covid crisis has already produced remarkable change. We see here once again the power of scientific discovery, especially when rendered as a collaborative effort. And we have in Operation Warp Speed an example of private–public cooperation where government acts in the best sense of what leading innovation economist Mariana Mazzucato (2013) has so aptly characterized as the "entrepreneurial state." The COVAX initiative, part of a broader global procurement and distribution effort concerning tests, treatments, and vaccines to deal with a global pandemic (see footnote 26), shows the world community's ability to act together when faced with an acute crisis demanding urgent action. And Biden's move on suspending intellectual property right protections for the politically powerful pharmaceutical companies, especially when they had just come up with a path-breaking new mRNA vaccine technology, indicates a willingness to adopt a different public policy stance, breaking with America's traditional pro-business posture which so dominated the neo-liberal era of finance-led capitalism. Taken together, we have here indications of how a systemic crisis at the tail end of a long wave's downswing phase once again sets the stage for reforms toward a new accumulation regime shaping the next long wave.

References

Andersen, R. (2020, September). The Panopticon is already here. *The Atlantic*. https://www.theatlantic.com/magazine/archive/2020/09/china-ai-surveillance/614197/

Asen, E. (2021, March 25). What European OECD countries are doing about digital services taxes. *Tax Foundation*. https://taxfoundation.org/digital-tax-europe-2020/

Avdjiev, S., Eren, E., & McGuire, P. (2020). Dollar funding costs during the Covid-19 crisis from the lens of the FX swap market. *BIS Bulletin*, no. 1. https://www.bis.org/publ/bisbull01.pdf

Baird, R. (2020a, March 11). What it means to contain and mitigate the coronavirus. *The New Yorker*. https://www.newyorker.com/news/news-desk/what-it-means-to-contain-and-mitigate-the-coronavirus

Baird, R. (2020b, April 5). How doctors on the frontlines are confronting the uncertainties of Covid-19. *The New Yorker*. https://www.newyorker.com/science/medical-dispatch/how-doctors-on-the-front-lines-are-confronting-the-uncertainties-of-covid-19

Baker, P., Haberman, M., Kanno-Youngs, Z., & Weiland, N. (2020, April 2). Kushner puts himself in middle of White House's chaotic coronavirus response. *New York Times*. https://www.nytimes.com/2020/04/02/us/politics/jared-kushner-coronavirus-trump.html

Baldwin, R. (2019). *The globotics upheaval: Globalization, robotics and the future of work*. Oxford University Press.

Bernanke, B. (1983). Nonmonetary effects of the financial crisis in the propagation of the great depression. *American Economic Review, 73*(3), 257–276. https://www.jstor.org/stable/1808111?seq=1

Bollyky, T., & Brown, C. (2020, September/October). The tragedy of vaccine nationalism: Only cooperation can end the pandemic. *Foreign Affairs*. https://www.foreignaffairs.com/articles/united-states/2020-07-27/vaccine-nationalism-pandemic

Cyranoski, D. (2020, May 4). Profile of a killer: The complex biology powering the coronavirus pandemic. *Nature*. https://www.nature.com/articles/d41586-020-01315-7

Du, W. (2020, August 6). Why banks' declining reserves matter for the dollar. *Financial Times*. https://www.ft.com/content/aebbcb39-1591-436f-8dfc-2961077f7d35

European Commission. (2020). *The digital services act package: Shaping Europe's digital future*. Brussels. https://ec.europa.eu/digital-single-market/en/digital-services-act-package

Federal Reserve Board. (2020, May). *Financial stability report*. https://www.federalreserve.gov/publications/files/financial-stability-report-20200515.pdf

Fisher, I. (1933). The debt-deflation theory of great depressions. *Econometrica, 1*(4), 337–357.

Goolsbee, A. (2020, March 12). Former presidential economist examines coronavirus disruption. *All Things Considered*. National Public Radio (WNYC).

Graham, D. (2020, April 29). Why Trump was deaf to all the warnings he received. *The Atlantic*. https://www.theatlantic.com/ideas/archive/2020/04/how-many-warnings-did-trump-ignore/610846/

Gurara, D., Fabrizio, S., & Wiegand, J. (2020, August 27). COVID-19: Without help, low-income developing countries risk a lost decade. *IMF Blog*. https://blogs.imf.org/2020/08/27/covid-19-without-help-low-income-developing-countries-risk-a-lost-decade/
Guttmann, R. (2021). Virus economics: An American tragedy. *Revue de la Régulation, 29*. https://journals.openedition.org/regulation/17322
International Monetary Fund. (2021, February 18). Special drawing rights. *Factsheet*. https://www.imf.org/en/About/Factsheets/Sheets/2016/08/01/14/51/Special-Drawing-Right-SDR
Kormann, C. (2020, March 27). From bats to human lungs, the evolution of a coronavirus. *The New Yorker*. https://www.newyorker.com/science/elements/from-bats-to-human-lungs-the-evolution-of-a-coronavirus
Kuchler, H. (2020, July 10). Anthony Fauci: 'We are living in the perfect storm.' *Financial Times*. https://www.ft.com/content/57834c2c-a078-4736-9173-8fb32cfbbf4e
Kupferschmidt, K. (2020, July 28). 'Vaccine nationalism' threatens global plan to distribute COVID-19 shots fairly. *Science*. https://www.sciencemag.org/news/2020/07/vaccine-nationalism-threatens-global-plan-distribute-covid-19-shots-fairly
Kynge, J., Yu, S., & Hancock, T. (2020, February 6). Coronavirus: The cost of China's public health cover-up. *Financial Times*. https://www.ft.com/content/fa83463a-4737-11ea-aeb3-955839e06441
Lipton, E., Sanger, D. E., Haberman, M., Shear, M. D., Mazzetti, M., & Barnes, J. E. (2020, April 11). He could have seen what was coming: Behind Trump's failure on the virus. *New York Times*. https://www.nytimes.com/2020/04/11/us/politics/coronavirus-trump-response.html
Mandarvilli, A. (2020, April 1). The coronavirus patients betrayed by their own immune systems. *New York Times*. https://www.nytimes.com/2020/04/01/health/coronavirus-cytokine-storm-immune-system.html
Mazzucato, M. (2013). *The entrepreneurial state: Debunking public vs. private sector myths*. London.
McCarthy, T. (2020, April 5). Jared Kushner and his shadow corona unit: What is Trump's son-in-law up to? *The Guardian*. https://www.theguardian.com/world/2020/apr/05/jared-kushner-coronavirus-aid-trump-governors
McKinsey. (2020, August 6). *Risk, resilience, and rebalancing in global value chains*. McKinsey Global Institute Report. https://www.mckinsey.com/business-functions/operations/our-insights/risk-resilience-and-rebalancing-in-global-value-chains
McMorrow, R., & Riordan, P. (2020, November 16). How China's big tech companies upset Beijing. *Financial Times*. https://www.ft.com/content/72317ec5-5a5c-44ab-8b8b-a752f9792168?emailId=5fb3ba2ce00fb10004f21c44&segmentId=2785c52b-1c00-edaa-29be-7452cf90b5a2

Minsky, H. (1982). Debt deflation processes in today's institutional environment. *Banca Nazionale del Lavoro Quarterly Review, 35*(143), 375–395. https://digitalcommons.bard.edu/cgi/viewcontent.cgi?article=1228&context=hm_archive

Mitchell, A., & Diamond, L. (2018, February 2). China's surveillance state should scare everyone. *The Atlantic*. https://www.theatlantic.com/international/archive/2018/02/china-surveillance/552203/

Mitchell, T. (2020, May 21). What Xi knew: Pressure builds on China's leader. *Financial Times*. https://www.ft.com/content/3a294233-6983-428c-b74b-3cc58c713eb8

Mukherjee, S. (2020, March 26). How does the coronavirus behave inside a patient? *The New Yorker*. https://www.newyorker.com/magazine/2020/04/06/how-does-the-coronavirus-behave-inside-a-patient

Neeley, T. (2020, March 16). 15 questions about remote work, answered. *Harvard Business Review*. https://hbr.org/2020/03/15-questions-about-remote-work-answered

Newport, C. (2020, May 26). Why remote work is so hard—And how it can be fixed. *The New Yorker*. https://www.newyorker.com/culture/annals-of-inquiry/can-remote-work-be-fixed

Obstfeld, M., & Truman, E. (2021, March 25). The new SDR allocation will benefit all countries. *Realtime Economic Issues Watch*. Peterson Institute of International Economics. https://www.piie.com/blogs/realtime-economic-issues-watch/new-sdr-allocation-will-benefit-all-countries

Organisation for Economic Co-operation and Development. (2020a, June 3). COVID-19 and global value chains: Policy options to build more resilient production networks. *OECD Policy Responses to Coronavirus (COVID-19)*. http://www.oecd.org/coronavirus/policy-responses/covid-19-and-global-value-chains-policy-options-to-build-more-resilient-production-networks-04934ef4/

Organisation for Economic Co-operation and Development. (2020b, December 10). International community renews commitment to address tax challenges from digitalization of the economy. *Topics—Tax*. Paris. https://www.oecd.org/tax/beps/international-community-renews-commitment-to-address-tax-challenges-from-digitalisation-of-the-economy.htm

Plender, J. (2021, May 25). The demise of the dollar? Reserve currencies in the era of 'going big.' *Financial Times*. https://www.ft.com/content/408d4065-f66d-4368-9095-c6a8743b0d01?segmentId=386fa267-d908-f060-4771-6cfd90556599

Schrimpf, A., Shin, H. S., & Sushko, V. (2020). Leverage and margin spirals in fixed income markets during the Covid-19 crisis. *BIS Bulletin*, no. 2. https://www.bis.org/publ/bisbull02.htm

Schwab, K. (2017). *The fourth industrial revolution*. Crown Business.

Stubbington, T. (2020, November 6). Negative-yielding debt total hits record $17.05tr. *Financial Times*. https://www.ft.com/content/378acc52-b1a5-4d58-8a87-8ea052b2c610

Susskind, D. (2020). *A world without work: Technology, automation and how we should respond*. Henry Holt & Co.

Tett, G. (2020a, March 19). Toilet rolls and Treasury bonds tell the same panicked story. *Financial Times*. https://www.ft.com/content/c70c7ffa-69ca-11ea-a3c9-1fe6fedcca75

Tett, G. (2020b, May 21). Federal Reserve's swap intervention will preserve dollar's reach. *Financial Times*. https://www.ft.com/content/df9e34aa-9b5c-11ea-adb1-529f96d8a00b

Von Peter, G. (2005). *Debt-deflation: Concepts and a stylised model* (BIS Working Papers, no. 176). https://www.bis.org/publ/work176.pdf

Weintraub, R., Bitton, A., & Rosenberg, A. (2020, May 22). The danger of vaccine nationalism. *Harvard Business Review*. https://hbr.org/2020/05/the-danger-of-vaccine-nationalism

Wolf, M. (2020, June 30). The great interruption continues. *Financial Times*. https://www.ft.com/content/69f59534-7f50-4abf-808d-ca8d1ec99097

Woodward, B. (2020). *Rage*. Simon & Schuster.

CHAPTER 6

Transition and Triad

A year into the global pandemic successful vaccination campaigns, first in Israel followed by the United Kingdom and the United States, have shown that the virus can be contained effectively once 75 percent or more of the adult population has been fully vaccinated. Even though global access to the vaccines has so far left much to be desired, amidst a still inadequate effort at worldwide cooperation and coordination, the end of the pandemic is in sight. As more and more places are reopening, economic activity can resume. Despite considerable damage to jobs and businesses, economies have proven remarkably resilient in their ability to bounce back. Recoveries have by and large been quite strong, better for the most part than predicted earlier when the pandemic still raged. Such encouraging signs of revival are certainly the result of extraordinary levels of both fiscal and monetary stimulation providing a strong impetus for pent-up demand and reorganized supply capacity to interact productively. We thus have a chance to shake off the global deflation context to which much of the world economy had been subjected since the Great Financial Crisis of 2007/08. The pandemic will also have left us with new political openings, crucial policy shifts, and profound structural change.

All this points to the potential for the launch of yet another long wave and the emergence of a new accumulation regime driving the latter's upswing phase. It is still too early to know whether this is indeed possible. Will the post-pandemic recovery be sufficiently strong

R. Guttmann, *Multi-Polar Capitalism*,
https://doi.org/10.1007/978-3-030-88247-1_6

and globally balanced to allow much more highly leveraged businesses and governments to work down their debts gradually or will those high debt levels, a relic of the Covid crisis, trigger yet another major financial crisis in which case the start of the next long wave is obviously delayed? Will Covid's impact on society encourage needed policy change to the point of replacing the neoliberal policy framework of finance-led capitalism with an alternative regime or have the political divisions deepened so much in the wake of the pandemic that perennial conflict crowds out a reform-minded consensus? Is the urgency of climate change already sufficiently strong to motivate a global push toward a zero-carbon economy at the heart of the new accumulation regime or do we still have to wait longer for that transformative impetus? And what about the international regime? New accumulation regimes have typically coincided with the rise of new hegemons transforming the international hierarchy of power relations, with concomitant changes in the international monetary system. We can thus speak of a *Pax Britannica* during the nineteenth century (1815–1914) amidst a "classic" gold standard or a *Pax Americana* shaping the second half of the twentieth century from Bretton Woods (1945–1971) to the current dollar standard. Right now, however, the international regime is in flux, with competing power centers fighting for dominance, each representing also a distinct variant of capitalism.

In this chapter we will focus on the post-pandemic dynamic reshaping the United States, China, and the European Union to analyze how their respective internal recovery dynamics play out in a battle between reform and stasis. We will also want to identify which centrifugal forces in place drive them apart, and what prospect for cooperation would allow them to coordinate and converge toward the piecemeal construction of a new accumulation regime.

6.1 Post-Pandemic America

The pandemic, badly mishandled by Trump, took a turn for the better the moment a new administration arrived in January 2021 and focused attention on how best to roll out a massive vaccination campaign in a hurry. Within the first hundred days of the Biden Administration 220 million vaccines were administered, more than twice his initial goal of 100 million jabs. As a result, the coronavirus spread slowed down considerably just when more infectious variants of the virus were outpacing more limited vaccine supplies in many other parts of the world. Biden also rapidly laid out an ambitious policy agenda, starting with the passage of the American Rescue Plan providing a large fiscal stimulus to assure a strong post-Covid recovery.

6.1.1 *The American Rescue Plan*

The new administration spent its first weeks in office pushing through its wide-ranging $1.9 trillion American Rescue Plan Act of 2021 (ARPA) with the help of a complex parliamentary maneuver known as "budget reconciliation" to overcome unified Republican opposition.[1] A major portion of ARPA consisted of pandemic relief measures that built on the earlier $2.2 trillion CARES Act of 2020, including extending expanded unemployment benefits (with a $300 weekly supplement), $1400 direct payments to individuals, targeted grants to small businesses (including specifically earmarked financial support for restaurants, bars, music halls, concert venues, as well as non-profit organizations), and help for colleges and universities.

There was a $350 billion injection of aid for state and local governments whose budgets had been decimated by the pandemic, help that came not a moment too soon after Trump had ruled out any such assistance throughout 2020 so that he could better blame Democratic governors and mayors for the nation's flawed response to the pandemic. Other crucial assistance pipelines in ARPA were the $230 billion committed to rebuild America's exhausted public health system, $130 billion for K-12 schools to reopen, and $170 billion to fight Covid (including $73 billion for an ambitious nationwide vaccine program). Assistance worth $55 billion for subways, commuter rails, airlines, airports, and the Amtrak rail service was meant to compensate for losses from pandemic-induced collapse in ridership. Farmers were helped with a $10.4 billion injection, of which $4 billion were earmarked for socially disadvantaged (mostly African-American) farmers. Woefully under-resourced amidst a frightening intensification of attacks, US agencies in charge of cybersecurity were given an injection of $1.85 billion to strengthen their defenses. ARPA also bailed out 185 insolvent multi-employer pension

[1] Kogan and Reich (2021) discuss the history of the use of budget reconciliation to pass budget-related bills with a single majority in the Senate where the so-called filibuster rule can block other legislative proposals unless there are sixty votes in favor (rather than just fifty).

funds covering 10.7 million workers, most of those industry-wide or union-sponsored defined benefit plans whose promised pay-out levels had become unsustainable, with a $86 billion rescue package.

More striking perhaps than all these income transfers and investments was the fact that ARPA significantly expanded the social safety net for low-income Americans. The Act included a boost to food stamps to help millions of food-insecure households, provided emergency paid leave for over 100 million Americans so that they do not have to go to work when feeling sick, expanded the earned income tax credit serving as a wage subsidy for the working poor stuck in low-paying jobs, made it easier for Americans to access affordable health insurance through Obamacare, and offered rental assistance as well as other housing support to prevent evictions or foreclosures. Most radically, ARPA offered poor and middle-class households a refundable child tax credit (of $3600 per child under six years and $3000 per child under seventeen years) which can be paid in monthly intervals like a subsidy for child rearing. The measure, which is only valid for one year (2021) and still would need to be made permanent at some point soon, carries the potential of reducing America's widespread child poverty by over a half.[2]

This huge spending program came only a couple of months after the end-of-year $900 billion Covid stimulus package which offered $600/person stimulus checks while also continuing jobless aid (of $300/week) as well as the Paycheck Protection Program funding small businesses just days before they would have expired. Whereas the CARES Act provided a fiscal buffer against the initial lockdown shock during the spring of 2020, these two later packages kicked in just when the pandemic peaked. Entirely deficit-financed at a time of extraordinarily low long-term yields, their combined $2.8 trillion spending injection will have pumped in short order the equivalent of about 13 percent of GDP into an US economy at the cusp of post-pandemic recovery—an extraordinary level of fiscal stimulus. In contrast to the Great Recession of 2008/09 when initial fiscal stimulus packages (notably Bush's $152 billion Economic Stimulus Act in February 2008 and Obama's $787 billion American Recovery

[2] As well explained by Greenstein (2021), the ARPA's child tax credit had such a powerful impact on reducing child poverty because of its full refundability irrespective of the family's income and exposure to income tax payments. This feature allows the CTC to be fully accessed by 27 million families who previously could not benefit from that tax break or only partially.

and Reinvestment Act of February 2009) were soon followed by gradual tightening moves which arguably slowed the recovery, Biden insists now on preferring to err on the side of too much rather than repeat the past mistake of too little. He seems to have learned valuable lessons from his previous stint in the White House, as Obama's Vice President.

6.1.2 *The Fed's New Policy Framework*

There has also been a new monetary policy regime worth noting. The extraordinary level of fiscal stimulus put in place at the beginning of 2021 has coincided with similarly unprecedented levels of "quantitative easing" on the monetary policy side which should help absorb huge supplies of newly issued Treasuries financing the enormous budget deficit estimated at $2.3 trillion in fiscal year 2021 (following an even larger crisis-induced $3.3 trillion deficit in 2020). The Fed's balance sheet has nearly doubled during the pandemic over the last eighteen months from about $4 trillion (in January 2020) to $7.9 trillion (in June 2021), three quarters of which came from a three-trillion intervention leap during the lockdown months of Spring 2020. Since then the US central bank has been buying about $120 billion worth of US Treasuries and mortgage-backed securities every month. This level of monthly asset purchases dwarfs earlier pre-pandemic "quantitative easing" programs, itself a noteworthy development in central bank efforts to push back against the New Deflation.

But there is also a broader policy context within which such acceleration of asset purchases has been unfolding, a significant break from past practice. In late August 2020 Fed Chair Jay Powell made an important policy announcement. Henceforth the Fed would no longer pursue its 2 percent inflation target. Instead it would use a new, more flexible "average inflation targeting" formula which implied allowing inflation to run temporarily and moderately above the 2-percent target to make up for past shortfalls.[3] Since the Fed has undershot its two-percent target recurrently during the 2010s, ultimately by a cumulative 5.6 percent, it has considerable leeway letting inflation exceed that target going forward before clamping down. Fed officials have reinforced this bias toward laxity with recent announcements emphasizing the need to let the labor market

[3] See the statement of Powell (2020) explaining and justifying the new, more relaxed monetary policy framework of "flexible average inflation targeting" over the entire cycle.

heal further after having lost 22 million jobs in the wake of the lockdown. Even though job creation has bounced back considerably since the end of the nationwide lockdown in mid-2020, a year later we are now still 5 million jobs short of the pre-pandemic peak. In other words, the Fed is no longer inclined to tighten policy proactively to nip inflation in the bud as had been its policy stance since October 1979. How long it can keep interest rates near zero will surely depend on the behavior of inflation, including inflationary expectations, during the recovery beyond early signs of renewed price pressures.[4]

The Fed's new policy stance is likely to be tested shortly. The revival of economic activity during the first half of 2021 amidst a receding virus and accelerating vaccination drive has coincided with inflation rates rising to between 3 and 4.5 percent, hitting even 5.4 percent in June 2021. A lot of the price increases making up this trend reversal relate to the uneven nature of recovery after such a deflationary shock and are hence of temporary duration. Prices have risen most in those categories where they steeply declined during the lockdown, namely food, energy, commodities, and housing, which creates significant year-to-year distortions when prices can bounce back amidst spreading recovery. There are also shortages raising prices due to ongoing disruptions in supply chains that should work themselves out sooner rather than later. Even more meaningful have been recovery-related labor market developments. Many businesses offering low-wage jobs (e.g. restaurants, retail, tourism) have had a hard time recruiting workers as they are returning to normal activity levels, prompting them to offer signing bonuses, better benefits, and even higher salaries while lowering qualification requirements. It seems for the first time in decades there has been a shift in bargaining power in favor of workers who are not rushing back to work and looking for better jobs, sustained by generous unemployment benefits. Much of that will fade when more workers reenter the labor market, including young mothers waiting for schools to reopen fully, and there will also be better matching between available jobs and job-seekers as the recovery spreads. Still, we are clearly no longer in the kind of deflationary environment we had

[4] As inflation has recently shown signs of revival amidst recovery and aggressive stimulation policies, influential economists such as former Treasury Secretary Summers (2021) have become worried about the Fed's relaxation vis-à-vis inflation. See also Giles (2021) for more details on the emerging debate over inflation and monetary policy.

gotten used to since 2009. A patient Fed will take a "wait and see" attitude, especially as regards wage pressures, but may in the process end up with a slowed reaction function that lets inflationary pressures and expectations take root. If such slowness forces an over-reaction in the opposite direction to extinguish the fires of inflation, any such abrupt policy tightening may well trigger a major bout of financial instability, even extending to the global realm, which could pose very tricky problems for many by now excessively leveraged debtors and their overextended lenders.

6.1.3 Biden's "Build Back Better" Agenda

Known for decades as the consummate centrist, Biden has instead surprised by offering an ambitious policy agenda dubbed "Build Back Better." Beyond the American Rescue Plan, his potentially transformative agenda has crystallized around two additional large spending packages aimed at setting much new policy which the Biden Administration announced in short order before the conclusion of its first hundred days in office. The $2 trillion American Jobs Plan centers on infrastructure, redefined broadly, whereas the $1.8 trillion American Families Plan targets investments in human capital and new social-policy initiatives benefiting lower-income and middle-class households.[5] While ARPA amounts to pure deficit spending, Biden's economic advisors want the AJP and AFP paid for by significant tax hikes on corporations and the wealthy.

The AJP would invest large sums in rebuilding America's run-down physical infrastructure of roads, bridges, ports, airports, and transit systems, an undertaking that had been discussed in bipartisan fashion for years but never acted upon. Decades of neglect have allowed America's infrastructure to deteriorate to a point where it is now ranked only thirteenth in the world. In many places its sorry state has begun to hamper the economy's competitiveness. There is thus indeed a great deal of urgency associated with launching a massive decade-long program to rebuild the country's crumbling physical infrastructure. The energy part of the AJP contains an important climate-mitigation dimension,

[5] For details on the many path-breaking provisions contained in the $2 trillion American Jobs Plan and their respective justifications it is best to go to the original source itself, as put forth in The White House (2021a). Similarly, a good summary and explanation of the main provisions of the American Families Plan and their justifications can be found in The White House (2021b).

promoting carbon-free electricity production, improving the nation's outdated electricity grid, and subsidizing the construction of half a million battery-charging stations for electric vehicles across the country.

Remarkably, Biden has defined infrastructure more broadly than is customary to include a new "at home" category which would commit nearly half a trillion dollars to modernize the nation's increasingly fragile water systems, expand broadband in marginalized urban and rural communities whose access to the internet is still often inadequate, retrofit buildings and repair public housing, as well as upgrade public schools, childcare facilities, and community colleges. In addition, there would also be a large investment in the country's care economy to address a multi-faceted structural crisis in home- or community-based care for the elderly and people with disabilities which predates the pandemic. The $400 billion proposals would greatly expand the supply of affordable high-quality care centers to overcome a national shortage while also improving the pay and working conditions of caregivers, who are predominantly women of color and/or recent immigrants. Finally, the AJP also invests another half a trillion dollars to revitalize America's industrial base by modernizing the nation's research and development infrastructure, strengthening manufacturing supply chains for critical goods, preparing for future pandemics, promoting clean-energy technologies, supporting community-led redevelopment projects, creating a network of small business incubators and innovation hubs, and investing more in worker training, apprenticeships, and community college partnerships.

The third plank of Biden's "Build Back Better" agenda, the $1.8 trillion American Families Plan (AFP), extends key tax credits benefiting lower- and middle-class families (e.g. Child Tax Credit, Earned Income Tax Credit, expanded health insurance tax credits), caps low- and middle-income family expenses for child care to seven percent of household income, and provides comprehensive paid family and medical leave to care for a new child, a seriously ill family member, or to recover from one's own illness. In addition, the AFP contains a crucially important investment in expanded access to education. It adds four more years of free public education beyond the thirteen-year learning cycle currently in place, two of those early on offering universal high-quality pre-school to 3- and 4-year-olds and the other two added on after high school graduation for community college. Greater access to university education will be supported with a large expansion of grants (Pell Grants). Schools serving disadvantaged communities, such as historically black colleges and universities, will get funds for evidence-based strategies boosting the completion and retention rates of minority students. Finally, the AFP makes a significant investment in teacher training and retention.

Conscious of the fiscal stimulus already juicing the economy's recovery and not wanting it to overheat, Biden has insisted that both AJP and AFP must pay for themselves. For covering the AJP package he has proposed a Made in America Tax Plan which would collect $2 trillion in new tax revenues over the next fifteen years from partially reversing Trump's rather unpopular Tax Cuts and Jobs Act of 2017. The plan would raise the corporate tax rate from its current level of 21 percent to 28 percent, end tax loopholes encouraging offshoring jobs, reduce incentives for profit shifting abroad, and phase out tax-incentive subsidies for fossil-fuel companies. To pay for the AFP's expenses, Biden proposes to reverse the second part of Trump's tax cuts by focusing on wealthy Americans. He wants to raise the top marginal tax bracket to 39.6 percent (from 37 percent), eliminate the existing preferential tax treatment for capital gains and dividends, and end key tax breaks for specific niches of the super-rich (e.g. hedge fund investors, real-estate developers, wealth inheritance). Biden also proposes to rebuild the tax collection capacity of the US government by reversing a long series of Republican budget cuts of the Internal Revenue Service which has seen its tax audits of wealthy Americans and businesses drop by 80 percent between 2011 and 2018. He plans to put $80 billion into the IRS for that purpose.

One could argue that Biden's plans are products of the moment, a needed response to an unprecedented economic, social, and public health crisis. And, of course, that is true to the extent that this crisis requires quite an active policy response both in terms of boosting aggregate demand and facing specific challenges such as building from scratch an infrastructure for vaccination of possibly the entire population. The pandemic has also brought to the fore structural weaknesses needing to be addressed—the fragility of America's public health system, segmentation of the labor market, the vulnerability of so many households and businesses to any disruption of income, the degree of inequality, its racialized and gender-based dimensions, the crucial importance of certain professions which society has not valued enough (e.g. nurses, caregivers, teachers, public transport workers). Because the pandemic has shed such clear light on each and any of these issues, there is now a certain urgency to address them. This gives a new administration a golden opportunity for ambitious policy proposals. Even though Biden's "Build Back

Better" plans have certainly responded to that unique moment, they are at the same time more than that. They present a longer-term vision for a different balance between the private sector and public sector, a transformation of the "mix" in our mixed economy.

6.1.4 *"Bidenomics" as Paradigm Shift*

The catchy "Build Back Better" slogan implies a government committed to orchestrate a post-Covid recovery that goes beyond the *status quo ante*. This very notion is itself a departure from the prevailing orthodoxy. Macro-economists wedded to so-called dynamic stochastic general equilibrium (DSGE) models, presuming a market economy inherently tending toward a steady-state balanced growth path, limit government's role to removing rigidities and gently using fiscal and monetary policy to nudge an aberrant economy back to its potential growth, full-employment level so that it can resume its steady-state path going forward. In reality, however, there exist multiple equilibria which yield a variety of possible paths forward, and government can do a lot to steer the economy toward this or that growth path. The call for a more active government role in shaping the economy's growth dynamic seems especially timely in the wake of the Covid crisis, a simultaneous demand- and supply shock without historic precedence which is leaving economies all over the world with a lot of economic scarring effects and lasting hysteresis. In the face of so much damage and uncertainty it makes sense for governments to use all of their powers—spending programs, incentives, signals, regulations, and social mobilization capacity—for ambitious initiatives aimed at faster potential growth, especially after having gone through fifteen years of stagnation before the pandemic hit the world in early 2020.[6]

"Bidenomics," by which we mean the president's three-pronged "Build Back Better" agenda resetting the role of government in America's mixed economy, is a blueprint for a radically different policy agenda, to be pursued if and when the Democrats have the votes. As such it constitutes a decisive break with the neoliberal orthodoxy of "free" markets, low taxes, small government, and deregulated business pursuing shareholder

[6] Thoughtful analyses of Bidenomics' intellectual foundations, which have made precisely this point of having the government actively steer the post-pandemic economy onto a higher growth path, include Greene (2021), Krugman (2021), and Sandbu (2021a).

value maximization along a finance-driven ("financialized") growth path which has dominated US policy over the last forty years. In that regard Biden's three plans directly address several of America's accumulated ills.

- Bidenomics is above all growth policy. It aims to accelerate annual productivity growth beyond its anemic 1.1 percent average during the 2007–2017 decade by investing massively in the country's physical and social infrastructure, human capital, modernization of physical capital (e.g. buildings, semiconductors), and technological capacity. Each investment channel—as, for instance, when improving human capital by endowing the labor force with more education and training—contributes on its own to increased productivity growth. But there is possibly a cumulatively much larger boost to productivity growth, especially in its broadest configuration as total factor productivity, when various ambitious investment programs aimed at different resource quality improvements occur simultaneously and so can feed off each other positively.
- America's small government variant of capitalism has consistently de-emphasized the provision of public goods whose socially beneficial nature justifies their universal accessibility irrespective of income and beyond the profit motive. We are talking here about affordable housing, good education, effective health care, helping those unable to take care of themselves alone (the "care economy"), public transportation, access to the internet, and public safety. In a highly profit-driven economy such as has been the case in neoliberal America, with the government chronically underfunded and its regulatory capacity diminished, these quintessential provisions ended up for the most part insufficiently public and excessively privatized. Americans face often unaffordable housing, a high premium on education that is good, very expensive health care, insufficient caregiving, minimalist public transit, a large digital divide, and unreliable safety. Bidenomics tries to correct these biases and repair the damage done to the nation's key public goods by mobilizing large-scale investments for their restoration after decades of underfunding.
- Bidenomics also addresses America's growing inequality, aiming to reverse four decades of redistributive policies favoring the rich earning capital income and weakening the social safety net of the poor while structural changes driven by trade and technology have squeezed much of the American middle class. Among all

the advanced capitalist economies the United States is the most unequal.[7] Biden's plans would expand the social safety net for low-income wage-earners (e.g. Child Tax Credit, Earned Income Tax Credit), give workers stronger union representation and collective bargaining rights, and restore some progressivity to the income tax system. A more equitable growth dynamic might help support faster productivity growth and calm the fervors of political polarization. Biden's focus on greater equality includes a targeted effort at helping minorities and their communities overcome the many nefarious consequences of deeply rooted systemic racism, part of a broader reckoning with America's troubled history of race relations in the wake of the massive "Black Lives Matter" protests during the summer of 2020 following the murder of George Floyd.

- And then there is climate change, an existential threat to human well-being as well as economic activity. Up to now America has been a laggard on this issue, and Biden wants to change that. He has taken the United States back into the Paris Accord of 2015, reversing Trump's controversial abandonment of this global framework, and then followed up this step in April 2021 with an ambitious commitment to reduce emissions by half from 2005 levels before 2030. Biden's plans make a concerted effort in this direction, taking key steps to launch finally the necessary transition to a zero-carbon economy. These include pushing carbon-free electricity, building a smart electricity grid, incentivizing the switch to electric vehicles, changing the country's energy mix, phasing out subsidies to fossil-fuel companies, ramping up research and development in low-carbon technologies, reforming agriculture, and helping communities become more resilient to climate change. While emphasizing good-paying "green" jobs and technological leadership, Biden has so far avoided the politically fraught question of putting a sufficiently high price on carbon.

[7] We can measure income inequality statistically by the Gini Coefficient, with values between 0 (perfect equality) and 1 (perfect inequality). Most advanced capitalist economies have had Gini coefficients within a fairly narrow range of 0.25–0.35 since World War II. America's post-tax Gini index started rising consistently after 1970 from its postwar low of 0.35 to a comparatively high 0.48 in 2020. See Horowitz et al. (2020) for a discussion of Americans' changing attitudes toward that trend, now favoring increasingly policies in favor of greater equality.

Time is running out to meet the Paris Accord's principal objective of keeping the cumulative temperature increase to less than 2° Celsius. Hence the whole world is gearing up for a necessary transition to a zero-carbon economy which is tantamount to an industrial revolution embedded in a new socio-economic framework of incentives, regulations, and organizational structures rendering economic activity more conscious of its environmental impact. We can think of this zero-carbon transition, with all the changes it entails on a global scale for the structure of our economy, for the behavior of economic actors, for government policy, even for finance, as a new accumulation regime which I have characterized elsewhere as *Eco-Capitalism*, shorthand for "ecologically oriented capitalism."[8]

6.1.5 America's "Flawed" Democracy in Crisis

Much of Biden's policy agenda may not get passed during his first term and remain instead just a blueprint for future action. That applies not only to the AJP or AFP, but also to his plans for reforming immigration, gun control, criminal justice and policing, voting rights, or health care. Democrats have a razor-thin majority in the US Congress. In the Senate the two parties are evenly divided fifty-fifty, with Vice President Kamala Harris having the tie-breaking vote. The so-called "filibuster," a parliamentary procedure in the Senate, allows the minority party to require a sixty-vote majority for any legislation to pass other than budgetary matters or judiciary appointments. Republicans are invoking this barrier automatically for all legislative proposals of the Democrats in the hope that this strategy of pure obstruction will allow them to take back the Senate in 2022. Some conservative Democrats in the Senate, notably Joe Manchin of West Virginia and Kyrsten Sinema of Arizona, oppose any modification of the filibuster which could break this deadlock. Those same senators also want to use budget reconciliation for passage of either AJP or AFP only as a last resort, preferring instead scaled back bipartisan agreements. Going it alone through reconciliation will force Democrats to come up with a plan accepted by all of them. They managed to preserve most of the original American Rescue Plan when it passed in Congress. But can

[8] See in this context Guttmann (2018) where I discuss extensively the constituent institutional forms and sustainability-oriented mode of regulation of Eco-Capitalism as new accumulation regime.

they show such unity once again when it comes to infrastructure? Or to support families?

While public attention is focused on the drama unfolding in the evenly balanced Senate, the more pernicious threat to the Democrats' policy agenda is actually playing out in the House of Representatives where they currently hold only a tiny five-seat majority. The 2020 census, undertaken in the midst of a pandemic and subject to several targeted efforts by the Trump Administration to undercount certain groups prone to vote for the Democratic Party, will reapportion five House seats from heavily Democratic states (i.e. California, New York) to Republican-majority states (e.g. Texas, Florida) where legislatures can redraw new boundaries of House districts so as to maximize their own party's electoral advantage. Such "gerrymandering" is enough to wipe out the current Democratic majority in the House by 2022.

In addition, Republican governors and legislators have spent much of 2021 passing prohibitive voter restriction laws targeting Democratic voters concentrated in the urban centers of Florida, Georgia, Texas, Arizona, and elsewhere to assure Republican victories in future elections. These anti-democratic laws have at times gone so far as to move impartial or bipartisan election certification procedures into the hands of partisan officials to open the door for election results to be overruled. At this point it does not seem that Democrats have enough votes in Congress to counter this assault with their own proposals to protect elections, and the 6-to-3 conservative majority in the Supreme Court is very likely to uphold many of the Republicans' voter restrictions. This concerted GOP attack on long-standing election procedures has been justified by claims of massive voter fraud during the 2020 election, for which there is no evidence whatsoever. But most Trump supporters at the core of the Republicans' voter base fervently hold on to the so-called "Big Lie" which took root after Trump lost the election. Refusing to concede defeat and insisting instead that the election was stolen, Trump pushed all the buttons to overturn the results, filing lawsuits, insisting on recounts, putting pressure on election officials to change vote totals, and ultimately inciting a violent mob on January 6, 2021 to invade the US Capitol with the aim of preventing the Congressional certification of Biden's election victory. Unable or unwilling to break with Trump because of his continued hold over so many millions of voters, Republican governors and legislators have instead used the "Big Lie" to secure a significant edge against the Democrats in future elections.[9]

The Economist Intelligent Unit (2020) considers the United States as a "flawed" democracy, ranking it 25th in the world on the five performance criteria making up its Democracy Index. Among the key "flaws" are America's Electoral College, which allows Republican candidates to become president with millions of votes less than the Democratic candidate (as happened in 2000 and 2016), as well as the representational biases prevailing when you have two Senators for each state irrespective of size, which means that in the evenly divided chamber right now the fifty Democrats represent 41.5 million more people than the fifty Republicans. You also have privately financed elections, which give undue influence to powerful lobbies and rich individuals using campaign financing to exert influence over lawmakers and buy their votes. Since 2017 this already flawed institutional architecture of political democracy has obviously further degenerated in the course of Trump's presidency and his capture of the Republican party. For the first time in its history, the GOP failed to offer an updated policy platform for the 2020 elections and instead committed the party to the "America First" agenda of Trump who in turn never bothered to articulate his second-term priorities. While very likely to take over Congress in 2022, the Republicans are no longer capable of defining a policy agenda addressing the issues facing America. When one party in a two-party system stops paying attention to policy but blocks everything the other party wants to do, then you have a serious problem. This blockage may take several electoral cycles to resolve.

[9] Irrespective of his performance as president, Trump has certainly appealed to a very large segment of voters many of whom normally do not vote had it not been for him on the ticket. After all, he managed to get ten million more votes in 2020 than in 2016. His base, often elderly, predominantly white, culturally nativist and isolationist, distrustful of all elites, and angry at the direction they see the United States taking as a multi-ethnic democracy, comprises close to a third of the voting-age population and constitutes a large majority of Republican voters. As illustrated by the phenomenal spread of the QAnon sect and its bizarre conspiracies, one telling example among many others, Trump's followers tend to downplay factual evidence over made-up stories confirming their biases. No surprise then that they nearly all believe in the "Big Lie."

6.1.6 *A New "New Deal?"*

In the meantime, Biden is practicing politics as the art of the possible, having actively pursued bipartisan negotiations on infrastructure and police reform. In June 2021 Senate Democrats announced a bipartisan infrastructure deal with five Republican senators, which would mobilize $1.3 trillion in spending on roads, bridges, ports, airports, electricity grids, public transport, rails, water supplies, and broadband access, of which half (about $600 billion) represented new money financed by tougher tax collection enforcement and various fairly small-scale fees and taxes. The other half would involve rearranging already allocated funds not yet spent (from CARES and the other late-2020 relief package). It remains to be seen whether this package will get the support of five or six additional Republican senators needed to break the 60-seat barrier of the filibuster and so pass into legislation.

Biden has at the same time pursued a second track, that of budget reconciliation needing only the fifty seats of Democrats in the Senate, with Vice President Kamala Harris adding her vote as Senate President in case of a 50–50 tie, to pass a second $3.5 trillion social-and-climate infrastructure package without Republican votes. This plan combines the social safety net provisions proposed in Biden's American Families Plan (see Sect. 6.1.3), including an expansion of the Medicare program to cover dental, visual, and hearing aid expenses of senior citizens, with the elements of the American Jobs Plan not included in the bipartisan infrastructure deal with the Republicans (see Sect. 6.1.3), notably the sustainability-oriented investments for climate change mitigation in renewables, clean power, smart grids, retrofits of building, rails, and electric vehicles. That much larger plan would be financed by significant tax increases on corporations, incorporating the provisions of a new concluded global corporate tax deal (discussed further below in Sect. 7.2), and on the wealthy. Here Biden has to negotiate the mutually acceptable middle ground in the "Building Back Better" policy agenda of the Democrats between its left wing and its moderate center. In the Senate, for example, such consensus building must bring the Progressives' leader Bernie Sanders (D-VT), now chairing the crucial Senate Budget Committee, on the same plate of compromise as Joe Manchin (D-WV), the lone Democrat hold-out in the "reddest" of pro-Trump states and hugely influential pushing his more conservative priorities as the party's decisive fiftieth vote to pass such legislation.

With a bit of luck and a lot of patient negotiation, Biden thus has a chance to pass a new "New Deal" reorienting US spending and tax priorities toward a more broadly defined "policy for a middle class" platform of public goods, equity, sustainability, justice, education, and citizenship. Keep in mind that Biden is trying to pass this ambitious agenda with a razor-thin majority of possibly only short-lived duration in the face of a slow-motion constitutional crisis of the two-party state possibly disintegrating into a spiral of partisan strife turning violent. Whether Biden's "Build Back Better" agenda prevails to see its day or the country descends into chaos is on a knife's edge and will play out one way or another over the next few years. Much depends here on Biden's qualities as a leader speaking to the whole country for a vision of America beyond partisan strife. A good deal of this vision needs to draw from a more pro-active reappraisal of America's position and role in the emerging multi-polar world which rearranges Trump's nationalistic arguments into a different mix of having to compete both in the marketplace as well as a societal model with other power centers. Those represent a different variant of capitalism—notably Europe as the "social market" variant and China as enigmatic state-directed capitalism finding its own balance in the public–private mix of its unique "mixed-economy" model.

Biden's survival strategy hinges on passing his three social-spending packages of the "Build Back Better" agenda and convince Americans of all stripes that these American Rescue, Jobs, and Families Plans carry programs of great benefit for a majority of Americans irrespective of party preference. He has tried to gain popular support for his agenda by highlighting job creation, higher salaries, a better safety net, restoring union power, progressive redistribution of income, and tackling the excessive concentration of both economic and political power. These issues, it is hoped, should also appeal to Trump's voter base. Worth noting in this regard is the extent to which Biden has built key policy arguments on his predecessor's "America First" discourse and emphasis on competition with China. Starting with ARPA, "Buy American" provisions in government contracts have been strengthened. Fully aware that three decades of globalization benefited above all multi-national corporations, the wealthy, and China's middle classes while helping to hollow out the manufacturing base of the US economy, the Biden Administration has promised to pursue a "foreign policy for the middle class." One consequence of this reset has been a new emphasis on a "worker-centric trade policy" which would push for better global compliance with international labor standards and worker protections.

Biden's focus on China as competitive threat has recently led to three remarkable initiatives, all in early June 2021. The first was a bipartisan 68–32 vote in the US Senate for the US Innovation and Competition Act, the country's largest industrial policy initiative in decades providing $250 billion for investments in semiconductors, artificial intelligence, and quantum computing to match China's efforts in those areas. Then came an executive order banning US investments in dozens of China's leading companies supplying its military-industrial complex and surveillance apparatus, including aircraft manufacturer AVIC, communication firm Huawei, and semiconductor firm SMIC. Finally, there was an agreement at the G-7 summit to counter China's Belt and Road Initiative with a "Build Back Better for the World" (B3W) plan for the construction of infrastructure in lower- and middle-income countries.[10]

6.2 The Rise of China as Challenger

America's intensifying focus on de-coupling from China in order to isolate that country as a competitive threat has had a big impact on China's leaders as they face a crucial moment in resetting their country's path forward. After decades of super-fast growth turning its economy into the world's manufacturing powerhouse, coupled with massive infrastructure investments re-making the country from scratch, China now has the second-largest economy in the world and is prone to overtake the US economy in size within the next few years. It has achieved this remarkable feat with a unique combination of political control, still a single-party state apparatus rooted in the doctrine of communism, and a mixed economy in which a thriving private sector, fueled by a wide pool of intensely competitive entrepreneurs and workers, co-exists with state-owned enterprises dominating strategic sectors and drawing funds in open-ended fashion

[10] Biden's "Foreign Policy for the Middle Class" is analyzed well by Traub (2021). Biden's "worker-centric trade policy" has been laid out recently by US Trade Representative Katherine Tai (see Office of the United States Trade Representative, 2021). On the bipartisan US Innovation and Competition Act see Nuttall (2021). Finally, The White House (2021c) summarizes the main features of the G-7 initiative "Build Back Better for the World" (B3W) agreed to at their Cornwall Summit in June 2021.

from state-run banks. China's large population provides both for a potentially huge consumer market and a relatively cheap labor force willing to work hard for long hours. This double advantage has attracted lots of foreign direct investment by American, European, Japanese, and Korean firms providing their Chinese partners with managerial know-how and valuable technology transfers.

China's remarkable growth performance over the last four decades, combining a rapidly expanding labor force with an extraordinary rate of capital accumulation, depended on two drivers. One was a very high investment share, typically in the 35–45 percent range, which both national and local governments often boosted with ambitious infrastructure investment programs to create the foundations of a hyper-modern industrial economy and accommodate fast-paced urbanization. And the other was export-led, thanks to its growing dominance in many manufacturing sectors, strategic role in global supply chains, and persistently undervalued currency. After the GFC of 2007/08, however, either growth engine began to sputter. As we have already noted earlier (in Sect. 4.2.3), China's huge fiscal stimulus package to power its economy through this global crisis left it with much lower returns on its investment activity and dangerously high debt burdens. And the global slowdown in the 2010s depressed export growth, a slowdown made progressively worse after 2016 amidst intensifying trade tensions with the United States under Trump. With China's GDP growth slowing steadily during the 2010s, its leaders have come to understand the need for an alternative growth model based on raising the level of consumer spending from its unusually low 50–55 percent range of the last decade and accelerating the country's technological innovation capacity.

6.2.1 *China's "Dual Circulation" Strategy*

During 2020, while China was busy containing both the spread of the pandemic and its trade war with the United States, President Xi Jinping put forth his so-called "dual circulation" strategy, according to which China would put greater emphasis on fostering domestic markets while repositioning itself in foreign markets as the foundations for a new growth dynamic. This strategy of greater self-reliance was elaborated in more detail in March 2021 when the Chinese Communist Party (CCP) adopted its 14th Five-Year Plan guiding the 2021–2025 period.[11] At the core of the plan would be a concerted effort to rely more on internal engines of growth, not least to become less vulnerable to US efforts at isolating its economy from the rest of the world. Those would base themselves on boosting domestic consumption, accelerating homegrown technological advances, and reasserting central control over such technological development, if not the economy at large. China's reorientation toward a more internally grounded growth dynamic would then open up new avenues for productive engagement with the rest of the world, attracting capital and encouraging foreign pick-up of its homegrown technologies as a leader in new "growth" sectors redefining the world economy (e.g. see Huawei's first-comer advantage in the 5G technology).

Boosting domestic consumer spending is a complex task. Above all, it would require lowering the exceptionally high household savings rate which typically absorbs more than a third of disposable income. Chinese families began saving a lot more following economic reforms in the late 1970s which left them with much greater income uncertainty once many jobs were no longer government-paid. They also have to provide more for their own retirement which used to be free. China's relatively underdeveloped financial system still makes it difficult to borrow for medical, education, even housing expenses. Owning a home, a dream for many, is expensive and requires down payments of at least 30 percent. China's long-standing one-child policy (now being finally relaxed) and growing income inequality amidst shrinking social insurance programs provide added incentives to save more. Many of these structural factors can be addressed by policy, such as expanding the social safety net, retirement protection, or access to consumer loans.[12]

The central government has recently also tried to expand the size of the middle class by relaxing the hitherto tightly controlled household registration permit known as *houkou* for China's 236 million migrants. Obtaining thereby residency status in the key cities of the country gives migrants access to social benefits such as subsidized health care or pensions which improves their purchasing power and makes them more willing to spend. Ironically, the once-coveted city *houkou* has turned out less attractive than

[11] The CCP's "dual circulation" strategy is well discussed in China Finance 40 Forum (2020), Crabtree (2020), and Sandbu (2021b).

[12] A good analysis of various factors driving up China's savings rate to exceptionally high levels is provided by Zhang et al. (2018).

anticipated, and more than half of the eligible migrants have so far refused to exchange their rural *houkou* for urban residency status. Agricultural reforms have boosted the value of farmland and homesteads tied to those rural *houkou* which many migrants would lose if opting for a city *houkou* instead. And urban centers still prioritize local children, above all those of families owning homes, for access to their best schools. Such discrimination, an important factor given how obsessed parents are with schooling for their only child, leaves cash-strapped migrants deprived of the greatest city *houkou* benefit.[13]

China had already moved from a low-cost manufacturer up the value-added ladder to strive for leadership in several high-tech sectors in 2015 when it announced its "Made in China 2025" plan (MIC 2025) targeting ten sectors for self-sufficiency: advanced information technology; agricultural equipment; aerospace and aeronautical equipment; automated machine tools and robotics; energy saving and new energy vehicles; medicine and medical devices; modern rail transport equipment; new materials; ocean engineering equipment and high-tech shipping; power equipment. A heavily state-directed economy, the CCP-controlled government has a lot of industrial-policy tools at its disposal to boost the country's productive capacity in those targeted high-tech sectors. State-owned banks can offer preferential treatment to Chinese firms in terms of low-interest loans and issues of bonds or stocks. There are sector-specific funds, tax breaks, government procurement, and other forms of subsidies which are distributed based on firms' ability to meet a variety of performance targets. Intellectual property rights have been strengthened to reward innovation while open-source collaboration is permitted for various projects to encourage dissemination of knowledge. Massive public investments in research universities and government labs provide institutional support for basic and applied research, both areas in which China has made rapid advances and which are crucial to commercially exploitable product development. In a matter of just a few years of concerted effort under the auspices of MIC 2025 China has become a global leader in 5G cellular networks, mobile payments systems, artificial intelligence, renewable energy, electric vehicles, and super-fast trains.

Initially viewed as a means to improve its position as a higher-value-added anchor in global supply chains, China's push into high-tech

[13] Yu (2020) offers useful information on the lagging *houkou* reform.

industries is framed today in more protectionist terms of becoming more self-reliant in a less friendly world. Such desire to turn inward was reinforced during 2020 when the Covid crisis caused massive disruptions in China's supply chains (e.g. for medical equipment) and US sanctions cut off Huawei's access to semiconductors which the telecom giant was unable to resource domestically. Those lessons of vulnerability bore heavily on the Politburo and the State Council, China's two leading policy-making bodies, when they launched the "dual circulation" strategy. One important aspect of the new strategy is to re-double efforts at increasing domestic production capacity in strategic items, such as semiconductors or batteries. Another concerns attracting more foreign capital, know-how, and technology transfers. Concrete policy efforts in this direction have been the EU-China Comprehensive Agreement on Investment of 2020 and China's new Foreign Investment Law of 2020.[14] Yet another supply-side dimension of "dual circulation" concerns the government's approach to the internet. This is not just a question of exercising a high degree of state control over online activity, much of it is used for close tracking of citizens with help from strategically placed companies required to be a direct part of the "surveillance state." In 2020 China's leaders abandoned their long-standing hands-off approach to the country's homegrown internet giants Alibaba, Baidu, JD.com, and Tencent in favor of a more active competition policy prescribing in great detail how those firms had to change behavior when it came to the bundling of services, entry barriers, price discrimination, takeovers, and other monopolistic practices.[15]

One might view the recent regulatory tightening vis-à-vis the internet giants as part of a more pernicious trend toward greater political interference in the affairs of private businesses, an easy connection to make

[14] China used to regulate foreign direct investment inflows heavily in terms of closed sectors, joint-venture requirements, mandatory technology transfers, and profit repatriation. Its new FIL 2020 deregulated this activity considerably (see US-China Business Council, 2019), one of the reasons for a huge 40 percent spike in FDI inflows during 2020 when China managed to pass the United States as the largest recipient of such activity.

[15] For relevant references on China's surveillance state and recently changed antitrust approach to its internet giants see Footnote 15 of Chapter 5. See also McMorrow and Riordan (2020) on reasons behind this rather remarkable change in the Chinese leadership's approach to the country's leading high-tech firms and what that may mean for government-industry relations going forward.

considering building tensions between President Xi and Alibaba's founder Jack Ma or the government's last-minute cancelation of the highly anticipated record $37 billion initial public offering of Ant, Alibaba's financial-services subsidiary. Under Xi, China has certainly taken a turn toward autocratic rule, with greater top-down control over an otherwise rather decentralized state and fragmented bureaucracy as well as stronger reliance on state-owned enterprises. This leaves open the question how Xi plans to deal with the private sector which contributes 60 percent to the nation's GDP, provides for 80 percent of urban employment, and makes up 90 percent of all exports. Xi's anti-corruption campaign has cracked down on connections between business owners and local government officials for favorable treatment. And he also has at times put the brakes on China's huge shadow-banking system which, given the state banks' bias in favor of state-owned enterprises getting typically over 80 percent of all bank loans, provides most of the private sector's external funding support. Notwithstanding Xi's recurrent affirmations about the crucial importance of the private sector deserving the government's full support, signs abound that he wants party committees to play a more active role in personnel choices and other important decisions of private companies than had been the case up to now. It remains to be seen to what extent such exercise of political control over corporate management and entrepreneurs will stifle their initiative, thereby hurting the growth potential of China's economy at a crucial time.

The new "dual circulation" strategy redefines China's geo-economic space and geopolitical role in the world away from being an integral part of the globalization dynamic, as was the case during the period of its export-led growth explosion between 1992 and 2014 when its coastal regions became the world's leading manufacturing platform. Instead, China will want to use the development of its large domestic markets and indigenous technological development to strengthen its international position. For example, China's National Standardization Management Commission sets ambitious technological standards at home to facilitate global leadership in various transformative technologies about to emerge, such as those tied to 5G (e.g. Internet of Things, "smart" cities) or to artificial intelligence (e.g. driverless vehicles, facial recognition), and then render those the most widely adopted norms in the global realm. Standards based on patented technologies incentivize foreigners to adopt Chinese versions of cutting-edge technology which in turn yields lots of fee income. This is clearly a crucial area where China uses state funds and political influence to challenge long-standing dominance by Western technical experts.[16]

6.2.2 China's Belt and Road Initiative

With its long-standing reliance on infrastructure spending, China's public sector is replete with construction, engineering, and power companies. Those faced potentially significant excess capacities once China's huge post-GFC stimulus package began to wind down. One way to deal with their overproduction challenge was to intensify their overseas business which had already become more important during the preceding decade thanks to significant development projects in Africa and Latin America. In 2013, China's newly selected leader Xi Jinping wanted to make his mark right away by launching what he has characterized as the "project of the century," a $1.4 trillion global infrastructure program connecting China to the rest of Asia, Europe, and Africa through several road, train, and maritime corridors. Harking back to the trans-continental network of trade routes emerging two millennia ago during the Han Dynasty as the Silk Road, this gigantic twenty-first-century construction program of multi-national inter-connectivity has come to be known as the Belt and Road Initiative (BRI). It engulfs seventy-eight countries, including large-scale projects in Africa and even Latin America. Its 1800 infrastructure development projects include ports, roads, railways, airports, telecommunication networks, and power plants. During the BRI's first four years (2013–2017) the China Development Bank and the Export Import Bank of China, the two Chinese policy banks responsible for the bulk of overseas lending, made together more loans than all of the World Bank's lending combined. The BRI's breathtaking scale bespoke of Xi's ambitions to turn China into an economic super-power firmly embedded in a region spanning three continents and tightly connected to its peoples.

While inspiring much awe and admiration, the BRI has also proven controversial since its very inception. Projects are by and large quite expensive, especially when considering that they are for the most part located in poor countries. Many are also of dubious commercial value, with positive returns not assured even over long investment horizons.

[16] Telling examples of this concerted push by China to gain global dominance in setting technical standards for various cutting-edge technologies can be found in Rühlig (2020) and Pop et al. (2021).

Much concern has been voiced over the negative environmental impact of BRI projects in terms of adding to greenhouse gas emissions, habitat disruption, deforestation, and industrial pollution. With Chinese contractors preferring to bring in their own subcontractors and laborers, project contributions to local economic development are limited. The biggest criticism, however, has been directed at the BRI as a "debt trap" for the recipient countries a large number of which are poor and vulnerable.[17] It did not take long for several of those countries, such as Pakistan, Sri Lanka, Laos, Cambodia, or Montenegro, to feel severely squeezed by the double whammy of spiking trade deficits, made that much worse by having to import expensive capital goods needed for their BRI projects, and heavier debt burdens from large-scale borrowing to fund those projects. The debt trap criticisms became more virulent when Chinese firms took over ownership control of financially troubled projects, as happened with the strategic ports of Hambantota in Sri Lanka and Piraeus in Greece.

Ultimately Chinese leaders had been naïve to think that they could simply transfer their infrastructure investment machinery to much poorer, financially vulnerable, and often less well managed regions abroad and make it work there. They realized soon enough, already during 2018, that the BRI project had been ill-conceived and was unsustainable in its scale. Their policy banks, the CDB and the EIBC, found themselves progressively more overextended, as a steadily growing number of the BRI projects they had funded became mired in delays and cost overruns. They then retreated drastically, cutting their lending in support of BRI projects from a combined $75 billion in 2016 to just $4 billion in 2019. At that point over a third of the BRI projects had become "troubled," many of which in need of debt relief. Disruptions from the pandemic only worsened costs, prospects, and debt servicing problems of many BRI projects during 2020. China has already had to grant eighteen countries debt relief in the form of renegotiating loan schedules and postponing interest payments, and there is surely more to come.[18]

[17] J. Kynge (2018) reports that in 2018 the BRI countries averaged 5.2 in 2018 on the OECD's Country Risk Classification scale (where a rating of 7 represents highest country risk), compared to a 3.5 average for emerging-market economies, and had a median credit rating of Ba2 on Moody's scale which represents a "junk" level of default risk.

[18] Good analyses of the BRI's scope and problems it encountered can be found in Dollar (2020) or in Chatzky and McBride (2020). China's rethinking of its BRI project

China's retrenchment from overseas lending coincides with its reorientation toward domestic growth pillars under its new "dual circulation" strategy. But President Xi has vested too much of his reputation into the BRI to let it simply peter out. His government will have to arrange for large-scale debt restructuring while subjecting BRI projects to stricter debt sustainability analysis and environmental assessments before committing to their continuation. A significant portion of continued lending to BRI recipients might be shifted to the Asian Infrastructure Investment Bank (AIIB) or the New Development Bank, both of which China carries a good deal of weight in notwithstanding their more traditional commercial orientation. And the International Monetary Fund's planned $650 billion issues of Special Drawing Rights may go a long way in offering debt relief, even debt restructuring, to some of the BRI's biggest client states, such as Pakistan, which would let China off the hook considerably.

6.2.3 Debt and Currency

A less widely discussed reason for China's retrenchment has to do with the state-owned enterprises at the heart of the BRI project. Those SOEs, comprising China's leading construction, engineering, power, transportation equipment, and communication firms all of which are administered by the world's largest economic entity, the State-Owned Assets Supervision and Administration Commission of the State Council (SASAC), carry already very large debt burdens.[19] Under direct control of the central government via SASAC, these industrial giants are overseen by party officials and have government backing, leaving them less worried about taking on a lot of debt. In addition, they are funded primarily by the major state-owned banks—Industrial and Commercial Bank of China, China Construction Bank, Bank of China, Agricultural Bank of China, Bank of Communications—all of whom are among the world's largest banks

is discussed by Kynge and Wheatley (2020). Boston University's Global Development Policy Center has a "Global China Initiative" (see https://www.bu.edu/gdp/research/gci/) which keeps excellent track of China's overseas engagements of which the BRI forms a very large part.

[19] A study organized by the *Financial Times*, cited in Kynge (2018), reports that the top Chinese SOEs involved in building, operating and investing in BRI projects have an average total debt to EBIDTA (i.e. earnings before interest, tax, depreciation, and amortization) ratio of 9.2, indicating extreme levels of indebtedness. This compares with a much lower multiple of 2.4 time for the top ten non-Chinese contractors.

when measured by assets. While tightly supervised by the China Banking Insurance Regulatory Commission, the so-called "Big Four/Five" still operate more with a "funding first" mentality typically prevailing among banks in state-run command economies than the "risk/return trade-off" calculus of profit-driven banks pervading capitalist economies as they try to comply with the national planning priorities of their ultimate boss, the State Council. High debt levels among China's SOEs are therefore subject to a different dynamic than the one typically playing out when Minsky's "financial instability hypothesis" descends upon excessively leveraged Ponzi finance units (see Sect. 2.1.4). How different in the end remains to be seen and depends finally on the state-owned banks' resilience in the face of headwinds.

The fact that both state-owned enterprises and banks also pursue national-policy objectives under direct command from the administrative center of the government, the State Council, should not let us get too blinded by our instinctively American reaction of discounting such collectivist arrangements as "inefficient" or "totalitarian." The Chinese, for whom millennia of rich history as empire have produced a sophisticated social contract between a competent government administration looking out for the benefit of the community and loyal citizenship willing to sacrifice if needed for the collective good, have a highly competitive apparatus in place to foster a large class of skilled functionaries at all levels so that great importance can be afforded to competence and meritocracy. The nexus of state-owned enterprises at the heart of the country's industrial matrix and the "Big Four/Five" banks providing affordable funds where appropriate gives the government a powerful lever to direct and shape the economy's growth pattern.

Being also a highly regionalized society, China's provinces are shaped by their own respective localized public-sector engine, combining local government officials, province- or city-based banks, and more locally controlled public enterprises playing an important role in regional economic development. It is more likely that on that provincial level high debt levels are more problematic, as fiscally overstretched and highly leveraged provinces or municipalities carry responsibility for their thinly capitalized local financial institutions who in turn are supposed to help them spurring regional growth with their funding support. It is much more likely that financial-instability problems will emerge on that provincial level, in that "iron embrace" of local administration and finance. In recent years local governments have intensified their search for alternative funding support channels in China's rapidly evolving and strategically placed "shadow-banking" system which has grown over the last decade to a \$13 trillion behemoth (40 percent of the domestic financial system) comprising both banks as well as non-bank lenders (such as finance companies). Its rapid expansion has filled a vacuum for various borrowers crowded out of the official banking system where credit-allocation and interest-rate regulations are tight, notably private enterprises and local governments both of which have also rapidly expanded issues of corporate or municipal bonds in recent years. That \$15 trillion bond market is not as transparent as it should be while also lacking in liquidity as most retail investors still hold bonds until they mature.[20]

Behind these three gigantic pillars of China's financial system—the commercial banks, shadow banking, and domestic bond markets—is a huge homegrown pool of personal savings which has up to now provided ample and solid counterweight to the high levels of indebtedness found across many administrative units, public-sector firms, and municipalities. Household savings rates of ≥35 percent of disposable income (compared to about 8 percent in the United States and circa 14 percent in France) match up against an overall debt-to-GDP ratio of about 270 percent, both far higher than what we are used to live with in Europe or the Americas. Thrifty households have a choice of directing their savings into the traditional deposit channel of official commercial banking, into the shadow-banking system via wealth management products or trust certificates, or investing either directly or via funds in bonds or stocks. Shadow banking offers better yields than regulated bank-deposit ceilings can. But yields in securities markets are also attractive. Unlike all other central banks, the PBoC has resisted quantitative easing and avoided the zero-bound during the pandemic, ending up with key short-term interest rates in positive territory and highly attractive by global (still widely zero lower

[20] See Chen et al. (2020) for recent developments in China's system of local government finance toward greater reliance on shadow-bank funding and bond issues. Good summaries of shadow-banking trends in China and elsewhere are provided by the FSB's annual "Global Monitoring Report on Non-Bank Financial Intermediation" (see Financial Stability Board, 2020). Various institutional shortcomings of China's vast, yet relatively less developed bond market are discussed succinctly by Flood (2020). For regular updates on overall debt trends and composition see the "China Banking News" site of the National Institution for Finance and Development (https://www.chinabankingnews.com/tag/national-institution-for-finance-and-development/).

bound) standards. Right now (June 2021) China's 3-month Treasury bill rate is at 2 percent, Shanghai inter-bank market's SHIBOR in the 2.5–3 percent range.

Under the "dual circulation" reset of 2020 foreign investors are encouraged to invest more heavily in China's securities markets. The government has recently removed shareholding limits on foreign ownership of securities, insurance, and fund management firms. And it also is encouraging foreign investors to set up wealth management firms, currency brokerages, and pension management firms. As soon as these deregulation moves came into effect, foreign investors obliged right away in spectacular fashion with a 37 percent volume increase thanks to China's attractively high yields and relatively early recovery from the pandemic in 2020. Over the longer haul, steady and large foreign capital inflows into China's still-developing financial-services sector will spur innovation, service quality, product choice, and competition there. This in turn will help steady the hitherto rather topsy-turvy process of internationalizing the renminbi, a hotly debated policy objective inside China's highest policy echelons. A much increased volume of capital inflows in the wake of those recent market-opening moves will reduce the artificially complex arbitrage dynamic between the (hitherto regulated) onshore and (more market-determined) offshore platforms of renminbi-denominated financial instruments and fund transfers while also pushing further the ongoing transition from a "crawling peg" exchange-rate regime to a more flexible "managed float" (see Sect. 4.2.3). Both are arguably crucial steps in helping to strengthen the renminbi's internationalization.

6.2.4 *From RMB to CNY*

The 2007/08 crisis made China's leaders acutely aware of their economy's exposure to the pitfalls of the dollar and reinforced their support for international monetary reform. One underlying motivation was to strengthen the international presence of China's own currency, the renminbi. Until then the RMB had been tightly regulated, thus a strictly domestic currency. PBoC Governor Zhou Xiaochuan's (2009) call for international monetary reform marked the start of a concerted effort to lower China's dependence on the USD and make the RMB more present in China's dealings with the rest of the world.

- Between 2009 and 2016, for instance, the PBoC concluded bilateral currency swaps with a maximum authorized value totaling RMB 3333 billion (equaling about half a trillion dollars) with 35 other central banks so that those could access RMB on demand at low-interest rates in support of trade settlement or liquidity needs in their banking system.
- After China opened up its current account in 2009, a growing share of its trade came to be settled in RMB, reaching a quarter of the total in 2013.
- While still maintaining tight control over capital in- and outflows, the central bank's powerful State Administration of Foreign Exchange (SAFE) set up a network of offshore RMB centers for bank deposits, fund transfers, and currency trading. By 2015 that offshore network had reached RMB 1.8 trillion in deposits (2015), most of which were located nearby in Hong Kong, Taipei, and Singapore but also gradually broadening to Tokyo, London, Paris, and Luxembourg.
- Issue of so-called "Dim Sum" bonds, RMB-denominated bonds issued in Hong Kong, reached RMB 300 billion in 2014. We have also witnessed the recent launch of "Panda bonds," which are RMB-denominated bonds issued by non-Chinese borrowers that are sold in China.
- In cooperation with the China Securities Regulatory Commission (SCRC), SAFE has progressively relaxed restrictions on foreign investors wishing to invest in the Shanghai or Shenzhen stock markets as well as the huge over-the-counter bond market to the point, as we already mentioned (near the end of 6.2.3), of recently removing such constraints altogether.

This systematic push to internationalize the renminbi after 2009 bore fruit quite rapidly, raising the global presence of the "redback" from pretty much non-existent to a range of 2–4 percent by the middle of the decade.[21] For example, the triannual BIS survey (2016) reported the RMB's share in global foreign exchange trading to have doubled

[21] Among the many informative sources discussing the internationalization of the Renminbi I want to mention in particular Eichengreen and Kawai (2014), Brummer (2015), Prasad (2017) and the reports listed in the "China Economic Watch" site of the Petersen Institute for International Economics (piie.com) such as Miner (2016).

from 2 percent in 2013 to 4 percent only three years later, growing from $120 billion per day to $202 billion per day. The RMB's share of cross-border payments (SWIFT) peaked at 2.79 percent in August 2015. Another indication of the renminbi's transformation into an internationally traded, if not altogether fully convertible currency has been its renaming into yuan whose acronym is CNY. Whereas renminbi and yuan relate to each other just as sterling and pound in terms of referring to the currency and its units, there is also a more symbolic significance in the former's renaming. Renminbi, the "people's currency," is inexorably linked to Mao's communist China and also known as "redback," whose red-colored notes carry his image. Its origins date back to 1949 when the People's Republic of China was set up by Mao. Yuan, the Chinese word for dollar with symbol ¥, goes back historically to the Middle Ages when Chinese merchants traded with Europeans acquiring in the process silver coins they referred to as "Yuan." It is therefore a symbolically appropriate name for a currency regaining its international standing.

In the wake of these initially effective RMB-internationalization efforts, China's leaders soon enough decided that they wanted the IMF to endow the CNY with official reserve-currency status. Such a step necessitated reform toward a more flexible exchange-rate regime from peg to crawling peg (in June 2010) and then from crawling peg to managed float (in August 2015). The sudden move to a managed float in August 2015 misfired initially, as we already discussed in Sect. 4.2.3, triggering massive capital flight, financial-market crashes, and costly central bank interventions in support of the yuan. Toward the end of 2015 and early 2016 the PBoC took several steps to tighten capital controls which eventually stabilized the yuan's exchange rate against the central bank's key currency basket index known as China Foreign Exchange Trade System (CFETS) used as anchor for the new managed float. These restrictions helped reverse the trend toward the yuan's greater internationalization, already suffering a global confidence hit in the aftermath of the botched yuan devaluation of August 2015, with the CNY's international market shares falling by about a half back to a 1.5–2.5 percent range by the end of 2018.[22]

[22] For data on the reversal of the CNY's internationalization process following its botched devaluation in August 2015 and subsequent re-imposition of capital controls see Johnson (2019) and McDowell (2019).

In the face of all this turmoil the IMF still decided in November 2015 to include the CNY into its reconfigured SDR basket, with the third-largest weight of 10.92 percent. That decision surely reflected official recognition of China's dominance in international trade as the world's largest exporter. But it also presumed that the yuan was "freely tradeable" which, ironically perhaps, it was becoming less so with tightening of capital controls. In the long run, the IMF's attribution of reserve-currency status to the CNY will surely help it secure a growing role in the international monetary system. We have seen this already happen in recent years. The ultimately successful transition to a managed float has kept the yuan within a fairly stable and narrow trading range of 6.3–7 yuan per dollar over the last five years, itself an attractive feature for an international currency. China has basically phased out capital and exchange controls for foreign investors in both directions, maintaining them only for domestic households while even loosening them again gradually for Chinese firms. With the CNY becoming a key currency in the SDR basket, China's yuan-denominated bond and stock markets have been included in Bloomberg's or MSCI's global benchmark indices which boosts foreign investor appetite for Chinese securities. There has been a record influx of foreign funds into China's bond and stock markets during 2020 and 2021. This confluence of positive trends has allowed the yuan to resume its trend toward growing internationalization. A handy way to see this trend play out is through Standard Chartered's Renminbi Globalization Index which has tracked the yuan's internationalization process since its launch in 2011. The RGI peaked in September 2015 at 2563, then fell all the way to 1832 in December 2017, only to have risen since then back to 2224 by November 2020.[23]

It is also worth noting that China has in recent years taken active steps to lessen its dependence on US dollars. This policy priority of "de-dollarization" has become more urgent since exposure to the Trump Administration's launching of tariffs and high-tech sanctions, producing a sense of vulnerability which Biden's rather combative stance toward Xi's

[23] The Standard Chartered Renminbi Globalization Index reflects monthly volume changes concerning CNH deposits and certificates of deposit in key offshore centers (Hong Kong, Singapore, London), CNY-denominated trade settlement and other international payments, as well as dim sum bonds. For more on the SCRGI and its recent upward trend indicating the resumption of the yuan's internationalization see Szalay and Lockett (2020).

China is not going to dissipate anytime soon. For example, over the last few years China has reinforced a kind of financial alliance with Putin's Russia, itself subject to severe financial sanctions from the West, with both countries inclined to use each other's currencies. As a result, Russia has strongly diversified its reserves and trade settlement denominations from dollars to yuan. The world's largest oil importer, China is also pushing its suppliers, starting with Russia and Angola, to pay for its oil imports in yuan rather than dollars. SAFE, the central bank's foreign exchange management subsidiary, has progressively lowered the dollar's weight in its CFETS basket index used for its managed-float exchange-rate regime. The BRI project provides many avenues for greater use of the CNY along the new trade routes thereby created, as will China's focused approach on entering into dozens of regional and bilateral trade agreements. The imminent introduction of a digital currency, a central bank project that has advanced more in China than anywhere else in the world, will further reduce the country's dependence on the USD while at the same time providing a new electronic fund-transfer platform for the cross-border utilization of CNY.[24]

It is therefore not surprising to see that there has been a growing body of empirical studies in recent years analyzing the complex dynamics of an emerging "yuan bloc." These studies analyze a geo-economic phenomenon very much at the beginning of its life cycle. While bringing different methodologies to bear, size estimations run from a 10–15 percent range of world-money shares for the yuan across the matrix of international money functions by 2028 (BIS) to a 26 percent share of anchor currency influence for the yuan, depending on the configuration of the yuan bloc (IMF). We can imagine the geographic shape of such an emerging yuan bloc to include much of Eastern, Central, and South-East Asia, to comprise the members of the Shanghai Cooperation Organization (SCO) including Russia, Pakistan, India, and Iran, and/or correspond to the BRICS formation of large emerging-market economies including also Brazil and South Africa. Either way, across all these possible

[24] On China's "de-dollarization" steps, especially those in conjunction with Russia, see Simes (2020). Its efforts to pay for its massive oil imports in yuan are discussed in Ferreira Marques (2020). Adrian and Mancini-Griffoli (2019) study the wider implications of the rise of digital money, including central bank digital currencies. Based on their study for the IMF, Ahmed (2021) views the PBoC's pilot project for a digital yuan (denoted e-CNY) as a potentially ground-breaking step in the CNY's ongoing internationalization process.

configurations of its "zone(s) of influence," China is rapidly emerging as a geopolitical and economic power, trying to bring its financial muscle to bear as well. There is also a long-term dimension to this trend. Its rapidly aging population, a demographic challenge with many implications, will surely lower China's super-high personal savings rate, which in turn will move its current account from chronic surpluses to perennial deficits. This reversal will not only add to regular CNY outflows boosting the yuan's internationalization, but also nourish the desire of China's leaders to benefit from the global seigniorage advantages that come from paying for foreign debts in one's own currency.[25]

6.3 Making the Eurozone Work

A third regional currency bloc has been emerging around the Eurozone which extends beyond the heart of Europe to its peripheral areas (Scandinavia, Central and Eastern Europe, "Maghreb" region in Northern Africa) as well as former colonies sprinkled across other continents in the Southern hemisphere. The euro is a young currency, dating back to the beginning of the century (1999–2002). Its construction was hurried and dominated by mostly political considerations, thus badly designed and implemented, for which its members ended up paying a huge price when they faced a violent systemic crisis between October 2009 and July 2012 which almost broke the zone apart (see Sect. 4.2.2). Since then Eurozone members have pushed several reforms of the currency bloc's architecture, a difficult process in a highly diverse set of nation-states. The pandemic has given this process new impetus, but also highlighted difficult challenges ahead.

6.3.1 *Post-Crisis Reforms and Recovery*

The crisis of the Eurozone proved to be a watershed event inasmuch as it forced Europe's leaders to confront the institutional shortcomings of the single-currency arrangements and embark on a series of corrective steps. We have already discussed immediate crisis-management initiatives (in Sect. 4.2.2), from the European Stability Mechanism (ESM) as a new

[25] Among the empirical studies of the emerging yuan bloc and its different geographic reach as well as various size estimates I want to mention in particular Kawai and Pontines (2016), Tovar and Mohd Nor (2018) as well as Cheung et al. (2019).

lender-of-last-resort mechanism to the extensive "unorthodox monetary policy" measures of the European Central Bank (ECB). While extraordinarily difficult for many countries in the zone, especially those subjected to painful adjustments in the wake of bail-out assistance (i.e. Greece, Portugal, Spain, Ireland, Cyprus), the crisis was eventually overcome sufficiently to launch an initially slow and rather tenuous recovery from 2012 onward. That recovery, supported by better macro-economic (public-sector and current-account) balances of the zone's periphery countries thanks to their adjustment efforts and the ECB's massive liquidity injections, lasted more or less until the pandemic hit the continent in March 2020. This recovery, while far from spectacular, created sufficient space for some more long-lasting structural reforms the 2009–2012 crisis had revealed as necessary.

The first major policy reform was the 2012 European Fiscal Compact we had mentioned briefly in Chapter 4 (including its Footnote 18). Having widely interpreted the crisis as a sovereign-bond crisis fueled by excessive public sector deficits amidst poor administration of the Stability and Growth Pact's (SGP) prescription of budget deficit and public debt limits, EU leaders agreed to strengthen enforcement of those limits through a set of new procedures, the so-called fiscal compact, enshrined in the "Treaty on Stability, Coordination and Governance in the Economic and Monetary Union" (TSCG). Its provisions included a mandatory balanced-budget rule adding to the overall 3 percent-deficit limit a structural-deficit limit of either 0.5 or 1 percent of GDP, a pathway to meet those targets (including an automatic correction mechanism if voluntary convergence measures fail to hit those targets), a clause for permissible temporary deviations in the face of exceptional circumstances beyond the control of the country concerned (e.g. the Covid-19 pandemic), a debt brake requiring sustained lowering of any public debt-to-GDP ratio in excess of 60 percent along a prescribed adjustment path, and strengthening the "excessive deficit procedure" so that it now kicks in more assuredly. At the heart of the new fiscal compact are increased monitoring and sanction powers of the European Commission (EC) over the fiscal policy process of member states. Whatever you may want to say about the appropriateness of this reform, it clearly limited discretionary spending powers of nation-states making up the union and thereby precluded national governments from using larger budget deficits for faster growth. As a result pressure increased for more spending on the federal level, notwithstanding the fact that EU budgets were still tiny (barely exceeding 1 percent of GDP) and set over seven-year budget cycles.

In November 2014 the European Commission (EC), under its newly selected leader Jean-Claude Juncker, responded with a so-called "EU Infrastructure Investment Plan" which committed up to €315 billion over a three-year period (from 2015 to 2018) to upgrade transport links, power grid connections, broadband networks, school, and hospital buildings, as well as climate-related action (including agriculture, forestry, and what the EC refers to as the "bioeconomy"). In the absence of any EU-level "Eurobonds" being issued to give the EU, notably the EC, any deficit spending capacity on the federal level, the plan depended on a complex funding structure. At its core was a newly set up €21 billion European Fund for Strategic Investments (EFSI), jointly financed by the EC and the European Investment Bank (EIB), which would co-finance selected projects with contributions from institutional investors in the private sector, primarily sovereign wealth funds, pension funds, and insurers. Given a long history of wasteful EU-supported infrastructure projects, EFSI put in place a better targeted project selection procedure. The plan was extended by another two years, to 2020, and beefed up to €500 billion in total spending, with the EIB ultimately mobilizing €65 billion of its own funds that it financed by issuing bonds in international capital markets.[26]

A second reform track targeted Europe's financial structure and banking sector. One of the more horrifying aspects of the Eurozone crisis had been its so-called "doom loop" threatening to pull banks and their national governments into a negative spiral (see Sect. 4.2.2). As the crisis dynamic unfolding during 2010 and 2011 drove long-term government bond yields of vulnerable countries in the Eurozone relentlessly upward to cause sharp declines in bond prices, local banks already weakened by the GFC 2007–2008 suffered significant losses from typically large holdings of their government's bonds. These losses among banks raised the frightening prospect that fiscally stressed governments would have to bail them out, thus making budget deficits possibly that much worse, a prospect that only added market pressure on their bond yields. Because of this mutually reinforcing negative feedback loop pulling both government bonds and

[26] A summary of relevant details pertaining to EFSI and its EU Infrastructure Investment Plan can be found in European Council (2020). The EIB's eib.org website provides a list of EFSI projects financed by the plan.

banks down, the ECB's new head Mario Draghi had to make his famously panic-breaking "whatever it takes" commitment in July 2012 and back up this promise with potentially large firepower by launching his "Outright Monetary Transactions" (OTM) as a targeted bond-purchase program.[27]

It needs to be said that the OTM, just as its predecessor known as Securities Market Programme (see Footnote 27), touched upon two related issues at the heart of Europe's single-currency experiment. One is the principle of "market neutrality" whereby the ECB conducts its open-market operations by trading government bonds according to a so-called "capital key" formula determining each country's share in the central bank's bond portfolio so that no single member is being treated differently than its relative size warrants. That principle does not allow the central bank to favor a country disproportionately. And the other prescription is the "no bail-out" clause (Article 125 of the Treaty on the Functioning of the European Union, also known as the Lisbon Treaty) which prohibits countries from taking on debts or expenditures of other countries in the zone. Both of these rules have to do with the insistence of chronic surplus and fiscally frugal nations, especially Germany, not to facilitate the presumed profligacy of the bloc's deficit countries, such as Greece or Italy, hinting at the political tensions reflecting the structural challenge of having two different groups of countries united under a single-currency roof. Ultimately the ECB's targeted bond-buying programs have had to pass muster with both the European Court of Justice as well as Germany's Federal Constitutional Court.

Tackling the second leg of the Eurozone's "doom loop," the banks, proved to be an even more challenging task. When the crisis hit, first during the GFC in 2007/08 and then as a homegrown problem in 2010/11, Europe's banking system was still fragmented into national segments, with most banks more rooted in their long-standing domestic power-elite configurations with local industrialists and government officials than operating supra-nationally within a single financial space which the EU's Single European Act of 1987 was supposed to have created. The Eurozone crisis laid bare the pitfalls of such market segmentation which

[27] The OMT replaced the Securities Market Programme (SMP), launched at the peak of the crisis in May 2010 by the ECB giving itself the power for discretionary purchases of sovereign bonds so as to help bring down unsustainably high yields. Between May 2010 and September 2012 the ECB had used the SMP to buy up to €212.1 billion in mostly Spanish and Italian bonds.

the still nationally oriented regulatory superstructure only compounded. A concerted effort was then made to correct this shortcoming. Still in the midst of the crisis, in 2011, the EU set up the European System of Financial Supervision (ESFS), containing three European Supervisory Authorities (ESAs) responsible for micro-prudential oversight at the European-level—the London-based European Banking Authority (EBA), the Paris-based European Securities and Markets Authority (ESMA), and the Frankfurt-based European Insurance and Occupational Pensions Authority (EIOPA). With Brexit, the EBA was moved to Paris in 2019. In addition, the ESFS contains also a macro-prudential regulatory umbrella responsible for identifying and managing systemic risk in the whole financial system, under the auspices of the ECB and hence also based in Frankfurt, the so-called European Systemic Risk Board (ESRB).

But the reform of banking regulation had to go beyond just imposing a European-level supervisory architecture on top of the national counterparts. Parallel to the financial re-regulation initiatives agreed to globally at the London Summit of the G-20 in April 2009, notably Basel III (see Sect. 4.1.1), the European Union decided to go a step further in response to its own homegrown systemic crisis and launch a so-called Banking Union.[28] This reform aimed to strengthen banking regulation and move it beyond national regulators onto a genuinely federal level.

- The first pillar of the Banking Union was creation in November 2013 of the so-called Single Supervisory Mechanism (SSM) which comprises the ECB and the national banking supervisors for a unified supranational system of banking supervision in the Eurozone. The ECB directly supervises 115 "significant" banks whose combined total amounts to 83 percent of all of nearly 6000 Eurozone banks' assets. These systemically important banks are subjected to tighter

[28] Besides implementing Basel III in the Capital Requirements Directive (CRD) IV, other key EU directives implementing the G-20's London Declaration on Strengthening the Financial System (see Financial Stability Board, 2009 for details) included Solvency II for insurers, the European Market Infrastructure Regulation (EMIR) for stabilization of over-the-counter markets, the Alternative Investment Fund Managers Directive (AIFMD) for hedge funds and other alternative investment vehicles, the Markets in Financial Instruments Directive II (MiFID II) regulating financial markets, and the Undertakings for the Collective Investment in Transferable Securities (UCITS) Directives IV and V for mutual funds.

supervision (of their safety cushions, operations, and risk management), regular stress tests of their resilience in the face of various crisis scenarios, and tougher capital requirements.

- The second pillar of the Banking Union involved setting up in January 2015 the Single Resolution Mechanism (SRM) under the auspices of the ECB to provide a mechanism for "resolving" failing or insolvent banks instead of having them become a burden to the public purse. The ECB is responsible for resolving Europe's top banks under its supervision as well as various cross-border groups while smaller banks are the responsibility of national authorities which still operate under divergent country-specific insolvency laws. The idea behind the SRM is to shield governments from having to bail out banks which in effect removes the threat of a doom loop recurring again. The SRM is supported by a fund (SRF) financed by all Eurozone banks of up to 1 percent of their deposits, amounting eventually to €55 billion (by 2024), with further backing from the European Stability Mechanism (ESM) if and when needed. There are several "bail-in" mechanisms being put in place for the banks' creditors to share in the costs of restructuring weak banks, including loss-sharing arrangements and "contingent convertibles" (i.e. bonds turning into equity under prescribed circumstances) for recapitalization of banks.
- The third pillar, a single European Deposit Insurance Scheme (EDIS) proposed in November 2015, has yet to see the light of day. European bank deposits are insured for up to €100,000 by national deposit guarantee schemes which vary greatly in terms of their funding levels, degrees of administrative competence, and operational procedures. In addition, national regulators have in many countries been inclined to pamper their local banks, treat them like national champions, give them undue preferential treatment, and agree to regulatory forbearance. These biases have resulted in many weak banks continuing to operate without setting aside adequate loan-loss reserves for non-performing loans or restructuring more broadly. European banks tend to have on average higher operating costs and lower returns than their American counterparts. That they perform less well should not surprise, given that they do not have a similarly large integrated (i.e. European) market to serve, yields on European government bonds have hovered near zero or even below for years, and (typically more profitable) investment banking plays a

much smaller role in the EU banking sector. This comparably poor performance, coupled with greater uncertainty about their "true" losses, makes adequate deposit insurance more important, but also more difficult to put in place. The Germans in particular fear of having to bail out weaker, less responsibly managed banks in countries prone to more lax regulation once a union-wide EDIS is in place. Their hesitation to accept the leap from national deposit insurance scheme to a European-level EDIS has led to a deadlock now stretching over five years. More recently there have been intense discussions to put in place a hybrid approach whereby national deposit guarantee schemes and the central fund would coexist. EDIS funds would only kick in once national deposit insurance funds had been exhausted, and other national schemes would have to provide support to the central fund if needed. To the extent that the hybrid model under consideration is a loans-based system, national schemes benefiting from EDIS support would have to reimburse the central fund with interest.[29] While there is a growing sense of urgency to resolve this impasse, not least because of renewed pressure on the solvency of banks in the wake of the Covid shock of 2020, the EU countries will first have to agree on how to move any interim hybrid solution to the end stage of a pan-European EDIS-based system.

Even more fragmented than its banks are Europe's financial markets. The EU's still mostly nationally organized money-, derivative-, bond-, and stock markets are also far less developed and integrated than their American counterparts. Their relative lack of scale and depth has made it more difficult for European companies to get external funding beyond bank loans, a constraint on their growth capacity which surely has contributed to the EU's fairly stagnant economies in recent decades. The constraint weighs especially heavily on innovation, start-ups, as well as small and mid-sized enterprises (SMEs) all of which lack adequate funding channels even though each is crucial for growth and employment. There are many reasons why EU economies remain so bank-centered, ranging from savers' preferences for liquid bank deposits over pension or mutual funds, tax preferences for debtors borrowing from banks compared to issuing

[29] See Valero (2020) and De Guindos (2021) on the current state of debate over the "hybrid model" possibly unblocking the long-standing deadlock over EDIS negotiations.

bonds, a deeply rooted home bias preferring domestic financing arrangements, remaining barriers to cross-border investments, and widespread political disdain for speculators and having finance dominate people's lives. Europe's structural disadvantage of its fragmented and underdeveloped financial markets also limits the euro's international role which would be surely boosted if investors had many more safe and liquid euro-denominated assets to invest in.

In June 2015 EC President Jean-Claude Juncker proposed a Capital Markets Union (CMU) as a five-year action plan for creation of a "single market" for capital across the EU capable of mobilizing an estimated additional €2 trillion into Europe's capital markets over the long haul. The CMU proposal, thought of as a necessary complement to the EU's Banking Union for completion of the Economic and Monetary Union (EMU), consisted of thirty-three specific steps grouped around six major objectives: facilitating cross-border investment by removing a variety of barriers (tax laws, insolvency regimes) and encouraging supervisory convergence; making it easier for companies to enter and raise capital in public markets; boosting venture capital, start-up financing and funding access for SMEs; promoting long-term investment, infrastructure investment, and sustainable finance for climate change mitigation and adaptation; fostering retail investment (e.g. private pension plans); strengthening securitization and covered bonds.[30]

After an initial wave of action, advancing on about twenty of the thirty-three CMU steps proposed, the project stalled even though the Mid-Term Review of 2017 added nine more elements to it. One impediment to further progress came from Brexit, Britain's June 2016 referendum yielding a slim majority in favor of leaving the European Union, which removed the most ardent supporter of CMU while at the same time imposing a significant administrative distraction on the EU's main policymakers having to negotiate a very complex separation. Perhaps most importantly, Britain's exit from the EU deprives the latter of a global financial center, London's City, which renders completion of the CMU on the one hand more urgent than ever while also making the project more difficult to realize. It is still not clear what London's future role will be in the evolving post-Brexit euro-denominated financial-market structure, many aspects of which have yet to be negotiated. Whatever the

[30] See European Commission (2015) for a discussion of the original CMU action plan.

arrangements still to be determined, a significant portion of London's once-dominant market share will likely move to aspiring financial centers on the continent, notably Paris, Amsterdam, Frankfurt, and Luxembourg. The intensifying competition between them also pits their governments against each other. This only reinforces a generalized hesitation among a majority of EU member states to let the full action plan of the CMU get implemented which, if it ever became reality, would greatly dilute the power of their domestic financial regulators to the benefit of EU-wide supranational regulatory authorities like ESMA or EIOPA. In most EU member states financial supervisors and those institutions they supervise have traditionally had close relationships, indicative of "regulatory capture," while local politicians hold on to the widely shared belief that control over domestic finance gives them control over the national economy.

All EU leaders profess to want completion of the CMU project, but only few of them are really willing to accept the concrete steps needed for that to happen. In the meantime, Brexit's removal of London as the EU's financial center has created an opportunity to rethink the supranational dimension of its EU-wide financial structure. Covid's hugely disruptive effects have added urgency to making external financing support for Europe's businesses, notably its SMEs, easier to obtain. Trump's weaponization of the dollar's global dominance, especially his repeated threats of secondary sanctions against European companies dealing with Iran, has reinforced the desire of Europe's leaders to see the euro's international standing strengthened while making their bloc less dependent on the dollar. Squeezed between a more unpredictable United States and an assertive China, the EU has recently committed to a strategic rethink known as "strategic autonomy," carving its own path for which a better structured, more cohesive, supra-nationally supervised and regulated financial system would be an important prerequisite. The EU also has new leadership, under EC President Ursula von der Leyen and President of the European Council Charles Michel, both competent and ambitious when it comes to reviving and repositioning the EU in a more hostile world. Von der Leyen's EC very much wants to complete the banking union and advance the capital markets union. Toward the latter objective the EC launched a trimmed reset of the CMU in September 2020. Its new action plan contains sixteen initiatives, focused on making financing more accessible for European companies in support of a "green, digital, inclusive and resilient recovery," promoting longer-term investment channels for European savers (including private pension plans), and integrating national markets into a genuine single market subject to EU-wide regulation and free cross-border investment flows.[31]

Europe's failure to complete the banking union or make more progress on the capital markets union suggests significant divisions among its politicians and policy-makers. The European Union remains an experiment in the making, with its integration process still being worked on in most policy areas. To keep the EU as decentralized as possible, the "subsidiarity" principle of having whatever policy in question be conducted at the lowest possible level of government rules. Still, turf battles between the EU bureaucracy and national governments over who should be in charge abound, as a combination of crises, geopolitical considerations, reform needs, and thrust toward a "more perfect union" moves once mostly domestic policy issues to becoming a concern best tackled on the federal level. We have clearly seen this process apply to money and banking, more broadly to finance. There are in addition serious divisions among EU members. For one, the Eurozone comprises two different groups, the "core" around Germany and its neighbors (e.g. Austria, Netherlands) inclined to have chronic trade surpluses, to be fiscally frugal, and have strongly anti-inflationary stances, versus the Southern "periphery" countries bordering the Mediterranean prone to twin deficits and somewhat higher inflation. Amidst gradual weakening of the once-solid German–French axis at the center of the EU and Britain's exit, a new coalition of small, sea-bound Eurozone members favoring free trade and fiscal prudence, known as the New Hanseatic League (or Hansa 2.0) and comprising Ireland, Netherlands, the Scandinavian states of Denmark, Sweden and Finland as well as the Baltic States of Estonia, Latvia, and Lithuania, has stepped in to fill the void. Right-wing populists have imposed a more autocratic rule in Poland and Hungary, much to the chagrin of much of the rest of the EU with whom these two governments argue over many thorny issues. Everywhere political polarization has upended long-standing centrist coalition arrangements, making for more volatile politics, greater political instability, and difficult policy-making consensus. Slow growth, compounded by unfavorable demographic trends of rapidly aging populations, add more burden to

[31] See European Commission (2020a) for more details on the new, trimmed-down CMU action plan.

governments. It is against this difficult background that the EU has had to face the intensely deflationary Covid shock. But, once again, it took an acute crisis to concentrate the minds in favor of major reform.

6.3.2 *The EU's Management of the Pandemic*

When the coronavirus hit at the beginning of 2020, it did not take long before it reached Europe's shores and forced extensive lockdowns across the continent by early March. The closing of borders forced by the pandemic has disrupted intra-EU travel and trade while also upending regional supply chains. Still, the Covid-19 crisis has been primarily a national affair, both with regard to its public health aspects as well as having to manage a massive shock to the economy stretching over many months of unprecedented destabilization. Much could be said how this or that government, for better or worse, has coped with the quadrangular balancing acts of this crisis (discussed earlier in Sect. 5.4). With the pandemic coming in waves, governments have recurrently had to pass large spending packages for relief to workers and businesses. In contrast to the US economy laying off a quarter of its workforce at one point or another and losing 22 million jobs during the first few months of the pandemic, a tradition of better job protection in Europe led to so-called "short-time work" (STW) schemes which allowed firms facing temporary economic difficulties to cut hours worked while providing employees income support from the government for hours not worked. These arrangements preserved existing employment contracts even when businesses had to shut down completely during lockdowns.[32] EU governments have also had to mobilize tens or even hundreds of billions for loans and loan guarantees to firms cut off from their normal cash-flow streams by recurrent months-long lockdowns whenever virus transmission accelerated.

To help with these unprecedented government funding injections preserving income for workers and businesses when the economy shut down, the EU had to step up to the plate. Its EC suspended the fiscal pact limiting deficit spending and public debt levels (see Sect. 6.3.1) which, incidentally, will provide a chance for reform streamlining its excessive complexity and perhaps even put in place more realistic targets when the

[32] For more information on those short-term work schemes see Eurofound (2020) and Dias de Silva et al. (2020).

time comes to resume its operation (in 2023?). The EC also suspended existing EU restrictions on state aid so that governments could help keep businesses afloat. And in April 2020, barely a month into the pandemic, the EU passed a €540 billion assistance package of three safety nets—a €100 billion support program to keep people in jobs and businesses running known as SURE (for "Support to mitigate Unemployment Risks in an Emergency") financed for the first time by issue of EU bonds (which have proven highly popular among global investors); a €200 billion support fund from the European Investment Bank for loans to companies; and €240 billion from the European Stability Mechanism in pandemic crisis support to member states following reform of the ESM to widen its use and boost its resources. The EC also mobilized an additional €41 billion from structural funds, its existing multi-year budget, and even some new funds to cope with the public health crisis, for which it provided also an EU-wide coordination and support system known as the Emergency Support Instrument (ESI).[33]

Of course, monetary policy also had to stretch the boundaries of intervention in response to this enormous shock of continent-wide lockdowns (which reduced the EU's real GDP by an unprecedented 16 percent during the first half of 2020). Already in March 2020, when the pandemic first took root in Europe to force the lockdowns, the ECB launched a €750 billion. Pandemic Emergency Purchase Programme (PEPP) of public and private bond purchases, many of which carrying as a result negative market yields, of which it had spent €640 billion. six months later. Since then the ECB has expanded the scope of its PEPP twice, first to €1.35 trillion and then by another €500 billion. to a potential total of €1.85 trillion. to assure that what it describes as "extraordinarily favorable financing conditions" will last well into recovery. In the same vein, the ECB has also launched a €1.5 trillion bank lending program, the third tranche of its Targeted Long-term Refinancing Operations (TLTRO III), where it lends ultra-cheap funds for up to three years to banks at interest rates as low as minus 1 percent. The lending terms of TLTRO III are calibrated so as to make them more favorable for banks demonstrably willing to fund businesses and households. The ECB has also set its deposit rate

[33] For more details on the EU's three safety nets in response to the Covid crisis, see KPMG (2020). The EU's Emergency Support Instrument is discussed in European Commission (2020b).

for banks' excess reserves, the floor rate of the three-rate band under its direct control, at minus 0.5 percent.

The extremely lax monetary policy of the ECB, pulling much of the EU's interest-rate structure deep into negative-yield territory and using bond-buying and bank-funding channels to pump huge doses of liquidity into the financial system, aims at countering deflationary pressures so as to prevent falling into a debt-deflation spiral from which many EU members are not that far away. The great fear across the continent is "Japanification," which refers to Japan's experience with three decades of creeping deflation (since 1990) from which that once-thriving economy has not been able to exit yet. There is related concern of keeping many otherwise unviable firms alive, whose ample access to very cheap funds hides that their balance sheets have been ravaged by the pandemic in terms of running down cash reserves, adding lots of debt, and shrinking working capital, so much weakened that their continued viability is in question. With the EU's corporate sector losing an estimated €720 billion in 2020, about a quarter of all EU businesses entered 2021 having run out of cash and exhausted their working capital. Undercapitalized and excessively leveraged "zombie" companies are bound to slash investment spending to a bare minimum so they preserve the cash needed to survive in the face of high debt servicing charges.

The best way to deal with the deflation threat and bring "zombie" companies back to full life, if they are salvageable, is with stronger growth. This cannot be achieved by monetary policy alone. It needs fiscal stimulus for which national governments do not have enough powder left, given how overstretched the pandemic has rendered them. Recognizing the limits of existing macro-economic stabilization policies, EU leaders spent a good deal of time and effort during mid-2020 to add a fiscal policy dimension to the federal level. In July 2020 they agreed to a €750 billion fund known as the Next Generation EU (NGEU) to help all eligible EU members cope with the damage done to their economies by the Covid crisis and set the stage for a strong post-pandemic recovery with a major effort at modernizing the structure of their national economies.[34] Their agreement on the NGEU recovery fund was part of a comprehensive support package which also contained agreement for a record-large Multi-Annual Financial Framework (MFF) amounting to €1074.3 billion

[34] For details on the NGEU recovery fund I have drawn from European Commission (2021) and European Council (2021).

for the EU's next seven-year budget cycle 2021–2027. At the heart of the NGEU is the €672.5 billion Recovery and Resilience Facility (RRF) of which €312.5 billion are distributed proportionately among EU members as loans and €360 billion as grants, a much more helpful assistance channel for so many of the overindebted national governments within the bloc. In addition, the NGEU also contains a new €50.6 billion regional-policy fund known as ReactEU providing grant transfers to more crisis-affected countries for repair of their public health system and/or in support of green, digital and infrastructure investments disbursed mostly via the European Bank for Reconstruction and Development (EBRD) or European Social Fund (ESF), augmenting existing EU structural funds.[35]

Distribution of NGEU funds is arguably based on need which offers proportionately most aid to the EU members affected worst by the Covid crisis. The disbursement formula takes into consideration, beyond the country's relative wealth and population size as starting point, also the real GDP decline during the pandemic and the rise in unemployment relative to the EU average. This formula makes Italy (€84.8 billion) and Spain (€71.2 billion) the biggest beneficiaries, followed by France (€50.66 billion) and Germany (€47.2 billion), and then Poland (€26.82 billion). But in relative terms smaller countries in Southern and Eastern Europe are bigger beneficiaries. Portugal's expected €13 billion in NGEU funds amount to 6.2 percent of its GDP, and the relative percentages for Romania, Slovakia, Greece, Bulgaria, and Croatia (the largest with nearly 11 percent of GDP) are higher still.

Countries have to submit national investment and expenditure plans detailing how they would spend the NGEU funds over a six-year period. Their plans should detail also the reasoning behind these national priorities as well as the process of consultation with stakeholders. The plans have to set aside 37 percent of the funds allocated for green investments in support of climate change mitigation plans and 20 percent for the digitalization of the domestic economy. The plans have to be approved by the EC and are also subject to evaluative discussion among national governments through the European Council. Besides spelling out the investment

[35] The NGEU framework also allocated €10 billion for a Just Transition Fund to help coal-dependent EU members (especially Poland) deal with the zero-carbon transition, €7.5 billion for rural development, €5.6 billion to InvestEU succeeding EFSI, €5 billion for the EU's research and innovation support fund Horizon Europe, and €1.9 billion to RescEU in support of disaster risk management.

projects to be financed, the national recovery plans submitted also contain commitments to structural supply-side reforms boosting the country's long-term potential growth rate, such as pension and labor protection reforms, renewable energy, modernization of the judiciary and/or public administration, digitalization of business and government, or taxation. There are "do no harm" provisions, notably environmental and social. Which governments must prove to have respected in their plans. Targets and milestones must be adequately specified to be enforceable. Governments also have to clarify how they streamline procedures for effective administration of the plans and dispersal of funds. Most of the funds will go to promote renewable energy, greater energy efficiency (e.g. in buildings), electric vehicles, smart public transport, fiber and 5G networks, digitalization of public administration (including judiciary and healthcare), data cloud capacities, and access to higher education and training. In many countries the combination of such strategic investments and structural reforms will boost long-term growth prospects, with funds being transferred just when recipient countries will have reached sufficient vaccination levels (above 75 percent of adult population) to reopen and thereby launch post-pandemic recovery.

The NGEU recovery plan, while surely motivated by a crisis without precedent, was still a huge achievement for the EU to have reached unanimous agreement on. Apart from long arguments over the fund allocation formula, autocratically inclined leaders of Poland and Hungary objected strenuously for weeks to the NGEU's "rule of law" provisions which allow the EU to suspend funds to countries failing to comply with basic EU rules on democracy. Most importantly, all countries have ratified the crucial "Own Resources Decision" which provides EU members' backing of the European Commission borrowing about €150 billion a year in international bond markets from mid-2021 to the end of 2026 to fund NGEU, both short-term EU-Bills and top-rated long-term EU Bonds issued either through a network of primary dealers or auctions. These EU securities, adding to the agency bonds of the EIB, EBRD, and other smaller EU funds as well as the heavily oversubscribed first batch of EU bonds funding the €100 billion SAFE program, provide for the first time in the Eurozone's existence a federally (EU) issued "safe asset" on a scale large enough to satisfy much of the pent-up global demand for such €-denominated instruments buttressing the international role of the euro as store of value and safe haven. This is an enormous step in the direction of strengthening the euro's world-money role.

6.3.3 *The EU's Broader Quest for "Strategic Autonomy"*

The crisis of the Eurozone a decade ago put a large dent into Europe's ambitions to create a new EU-wide currency capable of challenging the USD's dominance of global finance. In its wake the EUR's world-market share (as measured in the tables presented in Sect. 1.3.2) declined from an approximate 25–28 percent market share in 2008, aggregated across the six international money functions, to a significantly smaller 20–23 percent share by 2015. During the second half of the 2010s the euro's global money role stabilized. Just before the pandemic international investors' confidence had returned even with regard to lower-rated bonds issued by the periphery countries. The EU took some measures to increase the EUR's international use, insisting for instance on invoicing and paying for the bloc's large energy imports in euros while having the ECB build a network of bilateral swap agreements with geographically strategic partners in Eastern Europe, Northern and Western Africa, and Latin America. Finally, Europe's leaders begun to welcome more actively a stronger international role for the euro to make themselves less dependent on the USD. That convergence of sentiment, not so straight forward in light of the euro's likely appreciation in the wake of greater international reserve-currency demand, has had a lot to do with Trump's erratic behavior toward the EU in general, and his painfully targeted threat of punitive action against some of Europe's leading firms and banks in particular. Trump basically threatened them with being cut off from access to the international dollar-based financial system, if they continued trying to salvage the nuclear deal with Iran which he had unilaterally nullified in favor of renewing tough sanctions. Trump's weaponization of the dollar's dominant world-money role made Europeans wish to be less exposed to depending on it. The best way to reduce their dependence on the USD is to enhance the status of the EUR so that a large number of the EU's important partners in the global economy accept dealing with and holding euros.

The EU's renewed interest in promoting the EUR's international role must be put into the broader context of a geopolitical rethink which the new EU leadership has characterized as "strategic autonomy." This new strategy points to a desire by the EU leaders, shared by many heads of state (notably France's Emmanuel Macron and Italy's Mario Draghi), to chart its own course beyond the great-power confrontation between an increasingly isolationist United States and an increasingly assertive China so as not to be drawn into this possibly fateful conflict and instead set forth a positive vision for the world as a third alternative. Important differences in national traditions, social contracts, and elite power structures still shape Europe's nation-states enough to drive them toward divergent institutional practices and policy mixes. Just compare Portugal, Finland, and Hungary—all members of the EU—on any significant policy issue to see prevailing differences. Yet all EU members follow a certain "social market" model of capitalism rooted in a significant role for government as guarantor of income maintenance, as regulator of businesses partial toward "national champions," and as protector of labor and/or citizens. The EU also likes to think of itself as a hugely important, unprecedented experiment in multi-lateral democratic governance pursuing the "rule of law" in key areas of policy-making. As such it believes it can serve as a rules-based model of transparency and cooperation for the rest of the world in such crucial policy areas as trade, competition policy, the digitalization of the economy, climate change, labor protections, and indicative planning.[36]

In sum, the world emerges out of a global pandemic more fragmented and polycentric than it was before. Think of Covid as a multi-faceted crisis, possibly deep and wide enough to be a "crisis of the accumulation regime" (see Sect. 2.2.4) moving us to a new type of capitalism in the face of climate change driven by the acceleration of the zero-carbon transition that awaits us in coming years. We now have three competing power centers, with three different leadership styles and policy models representing their respective variants of capitalism—the United States, the European Union, and China. Their interplay going forward will shape this transition as a triadic configuration.

[36] Initially pushed above all by France's Emmanuel Macron as a necessary reset in EU-US relations following Trump's turn to aggression, the idea of Europe's "strategic autonomy" as a new vector of policy guidance soon became object of intense public debate fueled by think tanks for which European Parliament (2021) lists the most important links.

References

Adrian, T., & Mancini-Griffoli, T. (2019). The rise of digital money. *IMF FinTech Notes* 19/01. https://www.imf.org/en/Publications/fintech-notes/Issues/2019/07/12/The-Rise-of-Digital-Money-47097

Ahmed, S. (2021, April 28). Could China's digital renminbi pose the US dollar a challenge? *Mint*. https://www.livemint.com/opinion/online-views/could-china-s-digital-renminbi-pose-the-us-dollar-a-challenge-11619555545449.html

Brummer, C. (2015, June 22). Renminbi ascending: How China's currency impacts global markets, foreign policy, and transatlantic financial regulation. *Atlantic Council*. https://www.atlanticcouncil.org/in-depth-research-reports/report/renminbi-ascending-how-china-s-currency-impacts-global-markets-foreign-policy-and-transatlantic-financial-regulation/#7

Chatzky, A., & McBride, J. (2020, January 28). China's massive belt and road initiative, council on foreign relations. *Backgrounder*. https://www.cfr.org/backgrounder/chinas-massive-belt-and-road-initiative

Chen, Z., He, Z., & Liu, C. (2020). The financing of local government in China: Stimulus loan wanes and shadow banking waxes. *Journal of Financial Economics, 137*(1), 42–71. https://doi.org/10.1016/j.jfineco.2019.07.009

Cheung, Y.-W., McCauley, R., & Shu, C. (2019). *Geographic spread of currency trading: The renminbi and other EM currencies* (BIS Working Papers No. 806). https://www.bis.org/publ/work806.htm

China Finance 40 Forum. (2020). *Release China's new advantage of the super-large market*. Jingshan Report. http://new.cf40.org.cn/uploads/2020_Jingshan_Report.pdf

Crabtree, J. (2020, December 10). China's radical new vision of globalization. *NOEMA Magazine*. https://www.noemamag.com/chinas-radical-new-vision-of-globalization/

De Guindos, L. (2021, March 18). Banking union—Achievements and challenges. Speech at EC Conference "Strengthening the EU's central bank crisis management and deposit insurance framework". https://www.bis.org/review/r210318d.pdf

Dias de Silva, A., et al. (2020). Short-time work schemes and their effects on wages and disposable income. *ECB Economic Bulletin*, 4/2020. https://www.ecb.europa.eu/pub/economic-bulletin/focus/2020/html/ecb.ebbox202004_06~6b0e718192.en.html

Dollar, D. (2020, October 1). Seven years into China's Belt and Road. *Brookings* Blog. https://www.brookings.edu/blog/order-from-chaos/2020/10/01/seven-years-into-chinas-belt-and-road/

Economist Intelligence Unit. (2020). *Democracy Index 2020: In sickness and in health?* https://www.eiu.com/n/campaigns/democracy-index-2020/?utm_

source=economist-daily-chart&utm_medium=anchor&utm_campaign=democracy-index-2020&utm_content=anchor-1

Eichengreen, B., & Kawai, M. (2014). *Issues for renminbi internationalization: An overview* (ADBI Working Paper, No. 454). Asian Development Bank Institute. http://hdl.handle.net/10419/101261

Eurofound. (2020, May 15). Short-time work. EurWORK Observatory. https://www.eurofound.europa.eu/observatories/eurwork/industrial-relations-dictionary/short-time-work

European Commission. (2015). *Action plan on building a capital markets union.* https://ec.europa.eu/info/publications/2015-action-plan-building-capital-markets-union_en

European Commission. (2020a). *Capital markets union 2020 action plan: A capital markets union for people and businesses.* https://ec.europa.eu/info/business-economy-euro/growth-and-investment/capital-markets-union/capital-markets-union-2020-action-plan_en

European Commission. (2020b). Emergency support instrument. https://ec.europa.eu/info/live-work-travel-eu/coronavirus-response/emergency-support-instrument_en

European Commission. (2021). *Recovery plan for Europe.* https://ec.europa.eu/info/strategy/recovery-plan-europe_en

European Council. (2020). *Investment plan for Europe.* https://www.consilium.europa.eu/en/policies/investment-plan/

European Council. (2021). *A recovery plan for Europe.* https://www.consilium.europa.eu/en/policies/eu-recovery-plan/

European Parliament. (2021). The EU strategic autonomy debate. *Briefing—Think Tanks.* 30.03. https://www.europarl.europa.eu/RegData/etudes/BRIE/2021/690532/EPRS_BRI(2021)690532_EN.pdf

Ferreira Marques, C. (2020, March 16). Oil War May Revive China's Yuan Ambitions. *Bloomberg Opinion.* https://www.bloomberg.com/opinion/articles/2020-03-16/oil-price-war-may-revive-china-s-global-yuan-ambitions

Financial Stability Board. (2009, April 2). *Declaration on strengthening the financial system.* G-20 Summit. https://www.fsb.org/wp-content/uploads/london_summit_declaration_on_str_financial_system.pdf

Financial Stability Board. (2020). *Global monitoring report on non-bank financial intermediation 2020.* https://www.fsb.org/wp-content/uploads/P161220.pdf

Flood, C. (2020, September 27). Beware risks attached to high-yielding China debt. *Financial Times.* https://www.ft.com/content/cf7d70c4-e2ff-4c4a-8cd4-8122276cdee8

Giles, C. (2021, June 1). A new economic era: Is inflation coming back for good? *Financial Times.* https://www.ft.com/content/fe726054-5cc7-4285-9712-e92a21ed6079

Greene, M. (2021, May 6). Joe Biden's experiment could revolutionise economic thinking. *Financial Times*. https://www.ft.com/content/4c7048ee-4336-43f9-9ecb-5718eccec5f1

Greenstein, R. (2021, May 26). Strengthening the Child Tax Credit: What comes next? Brookings *Up Front* blog. https://www.brookings.edu/blog/up-front/2021/05/26/strengthening-the-child-tax-credit-what-comes-next/

Guttmann, R. (2018). *Eco-capitalism: Carbon money, climate finance and sustainable development*. Palgrave Macmillan.

Horowitz, J., Igielnik, R., & Kochhar, R. (2020, January 9). Trends in income and wealth inequality. *Pew Research Center*. https://www.pewresearch.org/social-trends/2020/01/09/trends-in-income-and-wealth-inequality/

Johnson, S. (2019, April 25). Rise of the renminbi is 'story of the next cycle.' *Financial Times*. https://www.ft.com/content/bfe22922-5ab8-11e9-939a-341f5ada9d40

Kawai, M., & Pontines, V. (2016). Is there really a renminbi bloc in Asia? A modified Frankel-Wei approach. *Journal of International Money and Finance, 62*, 72–97. https://doi.org/10.1016/j.jimonfin.2015.12.003

Kogan, R., & Reich, D. (2021, January 21). Introduction to budget "reconciliation." Center on Budget and Policy Priorities. https://www.cbpp.org/research/federal-budget/introduction-to-budget-reconciliation

KPMG. (2020). European Union: Government and institution measures in response to Covid-19. *Insights*. https://home.kpmg/xx/en/home/insights/2020/04/european-union-government-and-institution-measures-in-response-to-covid.html

Krugman, P. (2021, April 1). Bidenomics is as American as Apple Pie. *New York Times*. https://www.nytimes.com/2021/04/01/opinion/biden-infrastructure.html

Kynge, J. (2018, August 7). China's Belt and Road projects drive overseas debt fears. *Financial Times*. https://www.ft.com/content/e7a08b54-9554-11e8-b747-fb1e803ee64e?emailId=5b6db1a9b4713b000461f7cb&segmentId=c393f5a6-b640-bff3-cc14-234d058790ed

Kynge, J., & Wheatley, J. (2020, December 11). China pulls back from the world: Rethinking Xi's 'project of the century'. *Financial Times*. https://www.ft.com/content/d9bd8059-d05c-4e6f-968b-1672241ec1f6

McDowell, D. (2019). The (ineffective) financial statecraft of China's bilateral swap agreements. *Development and Change, 50*(1), 122–143. https://doi.org/10.1111/dech.12474

McMorrow, R., & Riordan, P. (2020, November 16). How China's big tech companies upset Beijing. *Financial Times*. https://www.ft.com/content/72317ec5-5a5c-44ab-8b8b-a752f9792168?emailId=5fb3ba2ce00fb10004f21c44&segmentId=2785c52b-1c00-edaa-29be-7452cf90b5a2

Miner, S. (2016). Renminbi Series Part 1: A Primer on China's Currency. *China Economic Watch*. Peterson Institute for International Economics. https://www.piie.com/blogs/china-economic-watch/renminbi-series-part-1-primer-chinas-currency

Nuttall, C. (2021, June 9). US resets China tech strategy. *Financial Times*. https://www.ft.com/content/0b2f4cbb-be40-4e3a-96ab-954a4f5f6d0e

Office of the United States Trade Representative. (2021, June 10). Remarks of Ambassador Katherine Tai Outlining the Biden-Harris Administration's 'Worker-Centered Trade Policy'. https://ustr.gov/about-us/policy-offices/press-office/press-releases/2021/june/remarks-ambassador-katherine-tai-outlining-biden-harris-administrations-worker-centered-trade-policy

Pop, V., Hua, S., & Michaels, D. (2021, February 8). From lightbulbs to 5G, China battles west for control of vital technology standards. *Wall Street Journal*. https://www.wsj.com/articles/from-lightbulbs-to-5g-china-battles-west-for-control-of-vital-technology-standards-11612722698

Powell, J. (2020, August 27). New economic challenges and the Fed's monetary policy review. Speech at the Federal Reserve Bank of Kansas City Symposium. https://www.federalreserve.gov/newsevents/speech/powell20200827a.htm

Prasad, E. (2017). *Gaining currency: The rise of the renminbi*. Oxford University Press. https://www.gainingcurrency.com/contact/

Rühlig. T. (2020). *Technical standardization, China and the future international order: A European perspective*. Heinrich Böll Stiftung. https://eu.boell.org/en/2020/03/03/technical-standardisation-china-and-future-international-order

Sandbu, M. (2021a, May 20). What is bidenomics? *Financial Times*. https://www.ft.com/content/fb817909-625b-4c0c-a190-78e691f32af9

Sandbu, M. (2021b, January 14). The China challenge. *Financial Times*. https://www.ft.com/content/2924139f-4324-4133-9d18-be3d17ce815a

Simes, D. (2020, August 16). China and Russia ditch dollar in move towards 'financial alliance.' *Financial Times*. https://www.ft.com/content/8421b6a2-1dc6-4747-b2e9-1bbfb7277747

Summers, L. (2021, May 24). The inflation risk is real. *Washington Post*. https://www.washingtonpost.com/opinions/2021/05/24/inflation-risk-is-real/

Szalay, E., & Lockett, H. (2020, October 7). Booming demand for Chinese assets boosts renminbi's global role. *Financial Times*. https://www.ft.com/content/4b4f1aa2-6938-473c-95cf-235478a45976

The White House. (2021a, March 31). FACT SHEET: The American jobs plan. *Briefing Room*. https://www.whitehouse.gov/briefing-room/statements-releases/2021/03/31/fact-sheet-the-american-jobs-plan/

The White House. (2021b, April 28). FACT SHEET: The American families plan. *Briefing Room*. https://www.whitehouse.gov/briefing-room/statements-releases/2021/04/28/fact-sheet-the-american-families-plan/

The White House. (2021c, June 12). FACT SHEET: President Biden and G-7 Leaders Launch Build Back Better World (B3W) Partnership. https://www.whitehouse.gov/briefing-room/statements-releases/2021/06/12/fact-sheet-president-biden-and-g7-leaders-launch-build-back-better-world-b3w-partnership/

Tovar, C., & Mohd Nor, T. (2018). *Reserve currency blocs: A changing international monetary system* (IMF Working Paper WP/18/20). https://doi.org/10.5089/9781484338704.001

Traub, J. (2021, March 17). Biden's 'foreign policy for the middle class' is a revolution. *Foreign Policy*. https://foreignpolicy.com/2021/03/17/bidens-foreign-policy-middle-class-revolution/

US-China Business Council. (2019). Foreign investment law of the People's Republic of China. https://www.uschina.org/sites/default/files/foreign_investment_law_of_the_peoples_republic_of_china_-_unofficial_translation.pdf

Valero, J. (2020, December 8). Commission eyes new proposal to unblock deposit insurance scheme. *EUROACTIV.com*. https://www.euractiv.com/section/banking-union/news/commission-eyes-new-proposal-to-unblock-deposit-insurance-scheme/

Xiaochuan, Z. (2009). Reform the international monetary system. *BIS Review* #41: 1–3. https://www.bis.org/review/r090402c.pdf

Yu. S. (2020, June 21). China's migrant workers spurn cherished 'houkou.' *Financial Times*. https://www.ft.com/content/bb6e6e88-65bc-4742-8d62-d516637ae453?desktop=true&segmentId=d8d3e364-5197-20eb-17cf-2437841d178a#myft:notification:instant-email:content

Zhang, L., et al. (2018, December). *China's high savings: Drivers, prospects, and policies* (IMF Working Papers WP/18/277). https://www.imf.org/en/Publications/WP/Issues/2018/12/11/Chinas-High-Savings-Drivers-Prospects-and-Policies-46437

CHAPTER 7

Cooperation vs. Competition in a World of Adversarial Power Centers

Fifteen years into the downswing phase of capitalism's latest long wave, punctuated by a systemic financial crisis of global proportions, deflationary de-globalization forces, and a pandemic forcing recurrent lockdowns of entire national economies in all five continents, it looks like finally the world economy may soon be on the mend. If and when successful vaccination campaigns will have allowed countries to contain the pandemic enough for recovery, their economies will do so with a lot of pent-up demand, households flush with cash, businesses just having gone through a transformative experience, and extraordinarily stimulative monetary and fiscal policies. The sequence of consecutive crises, culminating in the deadly Covid-19 pandemic, has certainly demolished the accumulation regime driving the previous upswing phase (from 1982 to 2007), that of finance-led capitalism centered on the United States as "buyer of last resort" mediated by the post-Bretton-Woods dollar standard (see Sect. 3.3), and the neoliberal policy regime known as "Washington Consensus" which had sustained it. Both of these are dead, dismantled by the violence of crisis, delegitimized by the pain and suffering thus caused.

We do not yet know whether the forces of reorganization and reform, a good number of which we discussed in Chapters 5 and 6, will be enough to launch a new accumulation regime or whether instead more crisis will be needed for that to happen later. Since the new accumulation regime is

R. Guttmann, *Multi-Polar Capitalism*,
https://doi.org/10.1007/978-3-030-88247-1_7

bound to have the transition to a zero-carbon economy as its centerpiece, a hesitant and slow-moving world locked into excessive greenhouse-gas emissions might unfortunately need more signs of climate crisis before finally willing to undertake the radical changes needed across the planet. Nor do we even know yet whether we are on the cusp of a new long wave which, if true, would give us a couple of decades of more rapid and better-balanced growth as is typically the case during upswing phases. What we do know, however, is that we now live in a polycentric world, dominated by three adversarial power centers whose interaction going forward will shape the answers to these questions. We can already identify several key dimensions of that interaction to point to possible scenarios, policy choices, and looming dangers, a fitting conclusion of a book on multi-polar capitalism filling its last chapter.

7.1 Triadic Configuration

The world lived for seventy years with the United States as dominant superpower, the hegemon behind the *Pax Americana*, its currency as world money, its powerful military at the center of a web of alliances spanning the globe, its economy a magnet for immigrants. The Great Financial Crisis of 2007–2009, caused by an excess of greed and myopia among American bankers, was a major shock to this dollar-centered system, both to its damaged economy and to the reputation of its leaders in finance, business, and politics. The topsy-turvy presidency of Donald Trump, himself a political phenomenon signaling the end of American bipartisanship at the core of its hegemonic control, was yet another shock. During four fateful years at the helm Trump went about dismantling, piece by piece, the institutions and norms of the postwar order the United States had helped create as the *Pax Americana* at the end of World War II. He attacked America's allies and cozied up to its enemies while treating policy and commitment as afterthoughts subject to change by his next tweet. Bent on trade wars and driven by personal animus, Trump forced other leaders to rethink the world and their country's place in it. But his destructive course also left a void, which gave others an opportunity to reposition themselves in the international hierarchy of power relations.

In a tightly connected and inter-dependent world, woven together by media, travel, viruses, and money, a long span of globalization during that upswing phase of finance-led capitalism (1982–2007) has left us with many regional centers in a polycentric world—from Brazil to Japan, from

South Africa to Russia, from Nigeria to Indonesia, and many more in between. They all deserve our attention, not least as active forces trying to shake up that international hierarchy of power relations. Yet there are only two centers possessing the scale and the variety of competencies to pose a challenge to America's dominance. China is an ancient society remaking itself into a new global leader under the Mao-Deng-Xi banner of "socialism with Chinese characteristics." The European Union is a collection of nation-states, with a rich history between them, whose steady deepening of multi-lateral governance and commonly shared policies makes each one of those countries within the EU better off as part of the greater whole than being alone, a factor surely putting in question Britain's post-Brexit experience as go-it-alone power of the past having to find its new niches in a hurry. Both of these centers—China and the EU-27—have each their own variant of capitalism still in the making as a domestic policy project, internally as well as in contradistinction to the other models. And both China and the EU have gone through a lot of reform in the course of the pandemic, with a more determined effort to become less dependent on the United States and the rule of its dollar (see Sects. 6.2 for China and 6.3 for the European Union).

Of course, each center—the United States, China, the European Union—is in the midst of a complicated rebalancing act whose outcome in each case is still too early to foretell. The United States has replaced Trump with Biden and given his Democrats the chance to put in motion a very ambitious and wide-ranging program of reforms going a long way toward putting together the policy framework for a new accumulation regime.[1] But the Democrats have little time before facing again the electorate under far less favorable circumstances (in November 2022). And the still Trump-dominated GOP, no longer the Republican Party of yesteryear, behaves as if the insurrection of January 6, 2021 storming the US Capitol is just a precursor to securing power for autocratic rule irrespective of the precise vote count in 2024. If the central core of that party can take over by illicit means of voter suppression and election subversion, then the United States will be consumed by serious constitutional

[1] Such post-crisis reform periods, as we saw with Roosevelt's New Deal in the 1930s or the Reagan Revolution in the 1980s, play a crucial role in the transition from one accumulation regime to another, a key argument in Régulationists' framing of history's rhythm in terms of long waves (see especially Aglietta, 1976/1979; also more broadly Sects. 2.1 and 2.2).

and political crisis for many years to come. The damage already done to the American body politic and government institutions, compounded by an intense electoral struggle over the next four years possibly turning into a *casus belli*, a situation feeding violent strife if not altogether civil war, may put a serious dent into America's ability to govern itself with forethought. The best outcome, but by no means assured, is that cooler heads prevail, nourished by the possible move out of the pandemic and the broad popularity of Biden's reform proposals.

China will have to cope with its own challenges, starting with the impact of climate change on its vulnerable topography and the demographic challenges of a rapidly aging (huge) population. There are both horizontally intertwined and vertically imposed tensions within a one-party state, which at the same time is also a rather fragmented administrative state, trying to manage a social contract in flux. Chinese households' inter-generationally structured concerns and local roots require a lot of attention and can be best managed with rapid, but also balanced growth—and that is difficult if the top-down direction of restrictive norms outweighs the needed bottom-up initiative of individual or collective ingenuity. Xi's centralized and autocratic rule, built on a personality cult of sorts, will either succeed providing the contours of his "Chinese dream" to sufficiently large numbers of Chinese families or it will force further reforms in the direction of "dual circulation." But the pressures driving that choice can be many, and some of those in the realm of the political (personal liberties, for instance) or the economic (inequality and debt, just to name two forces of destabilization) may be made more serious and/or less easily managed by an excessively centralized autocracy like Xi is putting in place.

President Xi Jinping's rule is legitimized, among several sources of popularity, by China's enhanced international standing as a global leader which appeals to considerable nationalistic sentiments across different demographic and regional groups. But China has taken a beating to its international reputation lately, from its oppression of the Uighur Muslim minority in the western Xinjiang region which China wants to transform into its bridge to the rest of the world along the transportation connectivity tracks of its Belt and Road Initiative to the centralization of control over its (no longer) "one country, two systems" global-financial-center outpost Hong Kong so crucial to the opening of its hitherto closeted financial system on which depends the rise of the yuan (see Sect. 6.2).[2] Worst perhaps is the Xi Administration's unbending refusal to engage the world with an honest, transparent account of the origins of the coronavirus so that we can learn from mistakes in the interest of future prevention. There is a hard-nosed side to China's projection of power on the world stage under Xi, often referred to as "*Wolf Warrior* Diplomacy" (after the popular 2015 political action movie), whose propensity for aggressive response to criticism and pressure may complicate the management of the emerging US-China-EU triadic configuration in years to come.

The European Union, in its integration path somewhere between completing economic and monetary union and figuring out workable contours of political union, depends for both visions as well as competence of day-to-day administration on the quality of its leadership. The triple financial (Eurozone)-political (Brexit)-economic-plus-public health (Covid-19) crisis stretching the entire last decade (2010–2021) has given the EU much impetus for reform. There are a good many transformational projects under way whose outcomes hang in the balance—banking union, capital markets union, fiscal pact reform, recovery program, Green Deal,"Fit For 55" project. Much of this reform program gets shaped by rather intense political turmoil gripping most EU member countries as the traditional political (coalition-centered) landscape underpinning the postwar consensus in favor of a "social market" economy model gets transformed by political polarization between nationalists (on Right and Left) and pro-EU federalists. But the EU has responded to years of crisis and the trauma of the Trump years by working harder to become a more cohesive bloc exerting more power and greater appeal vis-à-vis the rest of the world. Europeans know that theirs can be an attractive model combining democracy and capitalism through a web of social insurance and administrative guidance arrangements. The EU also has a rules-based vision of multi-lateral, perhaps even supranational governance, for which it serves as a case study in motion to the rest of the world looking for

[2] A reeducation campaign has imprisoned a million Uighurs in labor camps across Xinjiang while an influx of Han Chinese into that westernmost province coincides with restructuring this traditionally Muslim region into the gateway of the Belt and Road Initiative. After months of protests by Hong Kong's youth against growing intrusion of Chinese control over its supposedly still semi-autonomous affairs during 2019, China's CCP tightened its grip significantly over the city's administration through imposition of a draconian National Security Law.

negotiated solutions to global challenges. With its experience in patient negotiation and in mastering the intricacies of subsidiarity and governance, the EU can play a leading role in shaping the new order fit for the multi-polar world and its global challenges.

There are obviously other regional centers of great strategic significance, each positioned to play a crucial role here and there in shaping the twenty-first century. There is India, whose population size will shortly surpass China's and whose democracy is under a great deal of stress by partisan rule of the Hindu nationalists, a huge country torn between tradition and modernity. Russia, Iran, Saudi Arabia, Nigeria, each powerfully involved in shaping their region, are all overly dependent on oil or gas and will see their fortunes reshuffled by the mandatory phasing out of fossil fuels during the upcoming zero-carbon transition. Even the United States, suddenly the world's leading oil producer thanks to hydraulic-fracturing ("fracking") technology, will find it difficult to separate from fossil fuels. Canada, Russia, and Brazil are geographically huge countries containing fast approaching tipping points of the climate crisis—the first two facing the thawing of their respectively huge permafrost zones which threatens to release trillions of tons of methane gas, the third containing the world's "lung," the planet's largest carbon sink in the rain forest of the Amazon region.[3] Even BRICS, a regional arrangement of the emerging-market powers Brazil, Russia, India, China, and South Africa, which gave China an early outlet for its efforts at global reach taking hold in the 2000s, has been very much shaped by the commodity super-cycle (see Sect. 4.3.1) and loosened with that cycle's implosion after 2014. As all these aspiring regional power centers get swept up in the upcoming zero-carbon transition's "carbon bubble," their relative re-positioning depends on how that transition plays out.[4]

In the meantime, the United States, EU, and China will figure out the dynamic of such an emerging multi-polar configuration while trying to shape it to their respective advantage. Their bilateral relationships, as

[3] On the climate tipping points see Lenton et al. (2019) and Pearce (2019).

[4] The term "carbon bubble," popularized during 2015 in the run-up to the Paris Climate Agreement, refers to trillions of dollars in stranded assets (e.g. oil refineries, coal-fired plants, fuel-combustion cars) arising from the planned obsolescence of a fossil-fuel-based economy needing to be phased out to achieve carbon neutrality before it is irreversibly too late. See Rubin (2015) or McKibben (2015) for original-use examples of this timely term.

well as the three together on the world stage, will undoubtedly unfold in dialectical fashion, as a multi-layered interplay of competition, coexistence, and cooperation striving for a coherent synthesis. All three are currently in the midst of some kind of half-hearted negotiation with each other—Biden's replacement of Trump's hostility to the EU and NATO with the G-7's "Cornwall Consensus" from June 2021; beginnings of a follow-up dialog over major disagreements on trade, technology transfer, and investment protections between the Biden and Xi governments to move from the incomplete "Phase One" deal of the Trump years (see Sect. 4.4.3) to the "Phase Two" issues yet to be tackled at the heart of the superpower conflict; and the recent (January 2021) EU-China Comprehensive Agreement on Investment (CAI) which has yet to be implemented. Of course, stuck in the triadic configuration of three competing power centers, they can and will exert different degrees of pressure against each other. When there is two against one, the latter gets squeezed into compromise or, going in the opposite direction, finds it necessary to adopt a more aggressive stance of pushing back. We will surely go through our share of nerve-wrecking confrontations and missed opportunities for more constructive dialog, but things are unlikely to deteriorate to the point of war whose costs would simply be unbearably high.

More likely, the three power centers will to some degree feel obliged to cooperate with each other, even if just out of a calculation of self-interest and of survival needs, possibly extending also in relation to other key power centers. Efforts at such coordination of interests are often played out through, or intermingled with, acute competition for the "hearts and minds" of the rest of the world. A good example has been the pursuit of "vaccine diplomacy," as much a matter of competition among pharmaceutical "national champion" giants as it is over prestige of scientific capacity. Yet the global vaccine-distribution effort COVAX remains inadequately funded and provisioned to vaccinate a majority of the world's population, especially those in poorer countries of the Southern hemisphere, in a race with a dangerously mutating virus on the run (see Sect. 5.6.4). There is now pressure on the United States, the EU, and China to contribute more to the global vaccination effort, and it is in their collective interest to banish this global plague.

Just recently there have been three telling examples that a spirit of cooperation can prevail usefully. In March 2021 Biden invited forty heads of state, including even Russia's Vladimir Putin and China's Xi Jinping, for a two-day "Leaders Summit on Climate" to discuss climate policy acceleration.[5] In July 2021 the G-20 nations agreed to a global corporation tax deal, whose 132 signatory states include the world's most important tax havens, to impose an effective global minimum profit tax of 15 percent on multinationals and shift tax collection more to where they actually earn these profits. The three power centers are currently engaged in preparing a meaningful agenda for both the October 2021 meeting of the G-20 in Rome, including a face-to-face meeting between Biden and Xi, and the November 2021 meeting of COP26 on the climate in Glasgow, both of which are crucial moments of consensus-seeking understandings mapping the way forward out of the pandemic and into the zero-carbon transition.

7.2 Redefining Globalization

The interaction dynamic of the centers will be greatly shaped by what the community of nations will do with regard to globalization. We have had a decade of de-globalization trends (see Sect. 4.5), culminating in Trump's trade wars. We will obviously need to move beyond that kind of tit-for-tat imposition of mutually harmful restrictions which end up hurting everybody. Yet we cannot return to the heydays of the world's third globalization wave, during the upswing phase of finance-led capitalism (see Sect. 3.3), when the United States shaped policy worldwide by means of the dollar standard and its "Washington Consensus." That period is gone. So we need to come up with a redefined notion of globalization to which all the major powers can sign on.

Such redefinition should indeed be possible, judging from how America's Biden Administration, the EU under new and more assertive leadership, and China's rebalancing act during Xi's second term have defined "national" interest in a global context. What all these governments have in common is a commitment to an essentially open, unimpeded world economy provided it operates with "fair" rules and in the interest of majorities rather than to the benefit of a few at the expense of many. Biden's vision of a "worker-centric trade policy" and a "foreign policy for the middle class" may help here, giving us needed direction when

[5] For more details on this remarkable gathering of the world's leaders on Zoom to discuss the challenge of climate change and how best to proceed with the goals of the Paris Agreement, see U.S. Department of State (2021).

figuring out what a meaningful upgrade of globalization can possibly look like. One has to start with the realization that globalization creates also losers within national economies who will make their frustrations known one way or another. Their losses tend to be very tangible—bankruptcy, job loss, the urban devastation of deindustrialization—which makes for committed opposition and easy generalization to the point of spreading biases against "free" trade, against immigration, against foreigners deemed unfair.

A second realization points to the built-in inequality of the globalization process when the owners of capital, whether Big Business, wealthy individuals, or leading financial institutions, use their transnational mobility of moving money across borders while labor is locally bound and thus stuck. This mobility advantage has given the owners of capital the ability to escape domestic regulation, taxation, and contractual commitments, while pushing governments desperate for capital into a regulatory-relaxation "race to the bottom." Governments need to realize that they are collectively better off not to be pushed into that trap of unproductive competition, and the July 2021 G-20 global corporation tax deal is a truly important first step in this needed direction of reconsideration. We thus have to make a sharp distinction between globalization and deregulation, keeping in mind that the ideology of the "free market" has often hidden an agenda of the latter behind the fig leaf of positivity connected with the former.[6] The elites of finance-led capitalism and its dollar standard have abused globalization for the sake of deregulation, to escape their fair share of taxation, regulatory restraint, and social responsibility whereupon many among those not given the same privilege have become angry partisans of a nationalist-populist backlash threatening globalization altogether. That backlash is destabilizing politics everywhere, even bringing demagogues to the apex of power. It needs an urgent answer, before it consumes reason and compromise beyond repair. Trump's dangerous four-year term reminds us how urgent that threat has already become!

[6] This distinction between globalization and deregulation, and how those two get confused and obscured for the advantage of the owners of capital able to act transnationally, see the excellent discussion of "new globalization" by Sandbu (2021). His article discusses also the useful suggestions of an international commission headed by Blanchard and Tirole (2021), one former chief economist of IMF and the other 2014 Nobel Prize winner in economics, to deal with the triple challenges of intensifying climate change, inequalities, and demographic aging.

A third imperative when redefining globalization for the twenty-first century has to do with accepting the uniqueness of each nationstate and the society it represents. This is a reciprocal affair, rendered more difficult by the three power centers—the United States, the EU, and China—having different political traditions, economic structures, and policy choices as they represent still sufficiently divergent variants of capitalism. There needs to be acknowledged space for those variants to coexist so that leaders can focus on the common ground rather than have their leadership consumed by the obsessions of "us against them" juxtaposition, competition, and conflict. The tricky part is to recognize each other's deeply held norms, such as environmental protection or labor laws, and arrange whatever international regime is getting constructed around those as a matter of mutual respect. Countries with more deeply held or ambitious public good or social-benefit commitments have the right to insist on those being respected by foreign actors within the domestic space or, if needed, being defended with appropriate restrictions on those not abiding by the same norms and thus reaping comparative advantage from a pure-economic-profit point of view. Today that question is crystalizing rapidly around the vexing question of the "carbon border adjustment mechanism" (CBAM), recently approved by the EU and by the US Democrats trying to pass their $3.5 trillion social-infrastructure program into law. Countries lagging in their climate-mitigation effort should not reap the benefit of lower costs for comparative advantage. Instead, they will have their irresponsibly cheapened imports rendered more expensive by a sort of environmental duty akin to a tax. How we approach this new type of tariff in a global CBAM regime will be one of those crucial moments for the new accumulation regime taking shape.

If I had to think through some collective understandings how to provide for a more attractive globalization framework at the heart of the new international regime underpinning an emerging ecological, yet polycentric accumulation regime, these starting-point principles come to mind:

(1) Gains from trade require flexible and timely reallocation of resources that are now no longer in use because of trade, rather than their prolonged un- or under-employment in wake of displacement. And this rule extends to the revival of spaces left in disuse by deindustrialization. Eventually a city like Pittsburg, Pennsylvania, will have moved from being the center of

the world's leading steel industry to a diversified urban economy excelling in financial services, higher education, high tech, and medicine. But what it takes to get through this transition, and how long it takes, are the key questions looking for answers. Cities need their urban-revival programs just as trade-impacted workers and businesses need their trade adjustment assistance to allow them moving on—the workers into new professions and regions, the businesses reorganized and modernized for renewed competitiveness.

(2) Cross-border investment flows need to be kept open, but also well-recorded, subject to an effective global regulatory regime (see Sect. 3.3.3), and reasonably taxed in balanced fashion. There is surely a need for low-income developing economies to have access to the global savings pool properly channeled through international capital markets that these emerging-market and frontier economies can access under reasonably equitable and stable conditions. One can assume that the three power centers will compete for investment funds while at the same time building their own financial coalitions composing their currency bloc. The Chinese, facing a slow-motion debt crisis ripping through the Belt and Road Initiative and preoccupied with taking control of Hong Kong not least also as a financial center open to the world, are just now beginning to grapple with that aspect of the yuan's internationalization. As different net recipients figure out the currency composition of their activities and balance sheets among dollars, euros, and yuan as well as their exchange-rate regime in relation to those three competing key currencies, the issuers of these competing world-money alternatives will want to stay attractive. Relatively unimpeded international investment flows, preferably subject to well defined inward as well as outward capital controls in case of excessive instability, may also be useful enforcers of competition between the three power centers keeping each one of them striving to be good enough or better.

(3) Reform of the WTO's dispute settlement mechanism (see Sect. 4.4.3), currently in progress and hopefully productive part of a broader rethink of multi-lateral trade policy conduct, might turn it into an effective umpire for the management of trade,

cross-border investments, technology transfer, and even harmonization of competition policy in a polycentric world.[7] This surely requires a transparent, well resourced, rapid, and more equitably balanced assessment-and-sanctioning process so that the WTO can effectively and credibly authorize what barriers and restrictions are justified and which are not. The guiding interest in decision-making should be the balancing of globalization's open-market imperatives and national interest reflecting the public good of protection if there is sufficient justification provided. The WTO should be more powerful, rather than less. But for that to happen, it has to perform adequately well after a reform of streamlining and decide with sufficient balance of objectivity among competing powers.

(4) Countries and private actors exit the pandemic toward recovery with much higher debt levels than before the crisis. This is like having to walk around with a backpack of heavy weights bearing down on you. Debt restructurings, perhaps even debt relief, will possibly become a major policy challenge in need of addressing systematically, without competition from the power centers distorting resolution. The IMF's impending $650 billion issue of new SDRs (see Sect. 5.6.3) may create resources for precisely such a mechanism. But such an initiative, as well as other IMF-directed assistance to members in need, depends on having the biggest, richest countries, precisely those three power centers, reallocate the SDRs they will receive for easy-access use by the poorer members as a means of their support. This would be a logical step, and one that would also show a modicum of cooperation among three power centers for effective global solutions requiring massive redistribution of resources from rich to poor, but clearly also helping the rich in the process over the long run. Making such an important policy reform concerning the SDRs also opens up the possibility for boosting their role greatly in the

[7] The WTO, let us not forget, has already "jurisdiction" over many non-tariff barriers to trade (e.g., anti-dumping duties, subsidies), trade-related investment measures (TRIMS) allowing governments in emerging-market economies to impose conditions on multinational corporations, and trade-related intellectual-property systems (TRIPS) governing technology transfer. It has also begun to focus on the so-called "Singapore Issues" of trade facilitation (see WTO's Bali Agreement of December 2013), transparency in government procurement, trade and investment (aforementioned TRIMS), and competition policy.

emerging tri-polar international monetary system (see Sect. 7.4 below).

(5) Much of the potential for a better globalization process woven into a more balanced international regime depends on broad-based recognition that the collective pursuit of global public goods needs urgent prioritizing for which negotiated solutions will have to be found soon. One such global public good concerns pandemic preparedness, a matter of funds, medical supplies, and pandemic control protocols under the auspices of a reformed, strengthened WHO. Another concerns research and development cooperation, as we have seen in its miraculous potential with regard to the Covid-vaccine and will need to see a lot more of if we are to move beyond the nationalistic, antagonistic "industrial policy" competition we are finding ourselves in right now between the Americans, the Chinese, and the Europeans. In related fashion it is already obvious to most that there will need to be a global regulatory regime for the internet and its concomitant digitalization of the economy/society, notwithstanding China's or for that matter Russia's efforts to build their own top-down-controlled internet segments that can be walled off from the rest of the world. As we are dealing with the digital economy, we will also have to address the challenge of cyber security, including all the way to the regulation of cyber-currencies, lest we let these forces of the dark net provoke warfare in cyberspace and undermine governmental control. Another dangerous technology, nuclear fusion and fission, looms on the horizon in terms of nuclear proliferation which all three power centers have an interest in controlling. Renegotiating a nuclear-control deal with Iran, after Trump's abrogation, is an important test case in that regard, not least also as a model for future containment efforts.

7.3 Zero-Carbon Transition as Vector of a New Accumulation Regime

It is surely tragic that we have waited so long, since the Rio Earth Summit of 1992 when we first discussed the challenge of global warming collectively, to address the need for elimination of greenhouse gasses. We have known for decades that spiking GHG emission levels will make our planet progressively more uninhabitable for the human species. By the time we shall start acting decisively, we will have no choice to do otherwise lest we face catastrophe on a planetary-existential scale. But because we will have waited to act almost beyond the proverbial "last minute," our actions will be more urgent, more radical in nature. Either we all sink beset by conflict, or we face this threat together as we shall all have to bear its consequences. It is quite likely, given the Paris Agreement framework, that eventually intense efforts can steadily help us figure out solutions to a myriad of climate-related problems—from food to finance, from building materials to waste as an energy source, from clean transport to clean air. The global pandemic of 2020–2022 has been an out-of-the-blue trial run of rapidly changing social behavior and massive institutional adjustment on a global scale (see Sect. 5.4), with mixed results and lessons to learn, for the much more durable and encompassing transformation that awaits us.

The prospect of shared catastrophe, manifesting itself year after year more intensely and in a growing number of terrifying events and trends, should make us more likely to want a more productive redefinition of globalization and even pursue these aforementioned global public goods as such. In the face of existential threat, old rulebooks get thrown out. At that point we are becoming rapidly more interested in considering communal survival as perhaps the best option and collective action as the fastest method to get there. We already know what it takes to get out of this problem, the different elements of the zero-carbon transition we are busily designing right now. It is just a question of putting those elements in place, a challenging undertaking of Schumpeterian "creative destruction" where a lot of the costs arise rapidly and before the benefits emerge more gradually. The EU, with its "Green Deal" investment and regulation program (December 2019), its "Green Taxonomy" classification system for sustainable activities (July 2020), and its "Fit for 55" acceleration (July 2021), is way ahead of the others on that question. Its leadership role in the zero-carbon transition may help the EU gain comparative advantages in the construction of the new accumulation regime relative to the United States and/or China. That EU edge may put additional pressure on the United States and on China to do their part toward the zero-carbon transition. China, even though a leader in solar panels, needs to end its heavy reliance on coal which has been the easiest source of expanding its energy supplies in support of its rapid-growth path. Xi has committed to a zero-carbon target by 2060, and that is already a significant first step toward more serious action to come. Biden, too, has made a recent commitment. To make the US carbon neutral as soon as possible, he set a fairly ambitious target of a 50-percent cut (from 2005 levels) by 2030. But Biden's strategy relies exclusively on technology and infrastructure spending, avoiding carbon pricing for fear of causing Americans to get upset at what they would consider to be the equivalent of a substantial tax hike.

As the crisis deepens and the need for urgent action mounts, the zero-carbon transition will take off. But at that (much delayed) point, the transition will already entail a heavy dose of more expensive climate adaptation strategies replacing failed mitigation efforts, heightened financial instability in the wake of more explosive bursts of carbon bubbles or frightfully severe manifestations of climate risks, and massive dislocations of resources triggering large migrations of populations fleeing unsustainable areas of the globe. As we reconnect our economic activity with our natural setting, our embeddedness in nature, and revalue its outcomes within a broader social accounting system rooted in sustainability, we shall change pretty much every aspect of our economic system.

The path to carbon neutrality itself is already pretty well understood. Greenhouse gas emissions need to be priced high enough and along a steadily rising path to internalize the social costs of having become so dependent on them. We need to phase out fossil fuels and replace them with renewables (i.e. solar, wind, biofuels) at the center of our energy mix. Energy efficiency and smart electricity grids are crucial objectives as well. Fuel combustion engines will give way to electric vehicles and eventually even cleaner, more energy-efficient vehicles (e.g. hydrogen). Many industrial processes, especially in steel, cement, and chemicals, will have to be redesigned. Public transport has to be rethought (e.g. jet fuel for airplanes) and expanded (e.g. super-fast trains). Agriculture, at its current "agrobusiness" scale a huge source of methane, has to be reformed back to its organic roots while our eating habits need urgent reconsideration toward a healthier and less environmentally damaging diet. Existing buildings will need to be retrofitted for better insulation as well as more efficient heating and cooling systems, while radical urban architecture is bound to give us much more environmentally friendly structures in the future. Land use and forestry are going to become intense targets for preservation, if not recreation (e.g. campaigns worldwide to plant trees), of carbon sinks. We will want to cut waste, turn it into a source of energy if possible, and make a much greater effort at recycling used materials. A global push into ecosystem services will help us restore some of the damaged environment, or at least give it a try (e.g. plant trees, rebuild the wetlands, stock up fisheries, replenish coral reefs).

We are also bound to engage in a huge global research and development effort about climate change mitigation and adaptation whose results we will want to disseminate as rapidly and widely as possible. Open-source access or knowledge commons will for that purpose replace intellectual property rights in order to socialize innovation away from the pure profit motive. In this regard innovation economist Mariana Mazzucato's (2013) captivating notion of the "entrepreneurial state" promises more relevance in the near future.[8] Governments, with their research labs, support for academic research, subsidies, tax and funding incentives, procurement power, and capacity for coordination bringing together private and public interests, have already proven crucial for key transformative innovations, like the launch of the internet from within the US Pentagon, and will only become more so. They could also build important synergies working and mobilizing their resources together. Right now all three power centers have launched fairly massive "industrial policy" initiatives in boosting their domestic capacities (in competition with each other) in such new growth industries as artificial intelligence, battery technology, electric vehicles, semiconductors, 5-G communication network, strategic metals, and robotics—the EU's Infrastructure Investment Plan (Sect. 6.3.1), Xi's "Made in China 2025" push (Sect. 6.2.1), and the remarkably bipartisan US Innovation and Competition Act of 2021 (Sect. 6.1.6). There will have to be a workable balance between R & D undertaken for profit, for better national capacity in competition with others, and as a global public good or knowledge commons accessible to all those willing to play by widely agreed rules. The latter represents a shared sense of making things work better in the interest of the common good which may have turned into a matter of survival already. The global vaccine-development project against Covid-19, a fascinating case study of public–private as

[8] I recommend Professor Mazzucato's personal web site https://www.marianamazzucato.com for a comprehensive and well-integrated presentation of her most salient arguments rethinking the role of government nationally and in the international economy. They are also brilliantly laid out in her latest book, Mazzucato (2021), which is especially timely as we move toward a new accumulation regime in the making.

well as international cooperation and competition at the same time, is a harbinger of things to come.[9]

The quest is not just for climate-mitigation and -adaptation technologies. There are many other transformative technologies in the works right now, from artificial intelligence linking machines in entirely new ways, to the 5-G telecommunications network platform, to fifth-generation robots with sensory capacities, to blockchain technology rendering obsolete network formation via intermediaries with asymmetric information advantages acting as brokers, nanotechnology shrinking machinery into tiny miniature versions, and quantum computing promising to revolutionize data processing capacity. All these technological advances converge toward radically upgrading and expanding the digital economy on which we, in only three decades of its existence, have already become quintessentially dependent, with all the positive and negative consequences of such a life-dominating and system-shaping dependence.

Right now, the three power centers are already engaged in a kind of high-tech war, whether this concerns the application of the EU's tougher competition policy against America's high-tech giants Microsoft, Apple, Facebook, or Google, America's attacks on leading Chinese high-tech firms (e.g. Huawei, SMIC), and China's nixing of the Qualcomm-NXP merger in apparent retaliation.[10] At the same time, and that too is interesting to observe, all three are also busy revising their respective competition policy approaches to the high tech giants dominating the internet—the EU's Digital Services Act and Digital Markets Act, Biden's remaking of the Federal Trade Commission and Congressional bills, Xi's confrontation with Alibaba's Jack Ma and subsequent anti-trust moves against China's top internet giants. While still in many ways quite different from each other, all three competition policy initiatives aim at the same facets of the emerging digital economy—the fluid structure and monopolistic behavior of these unique high-tech conglomerates, Big Data as a source of value, and individual-freedom protections online. Their convergence is surely not least because of the internet's universality as transformative force. But there may also be more behind such observable convergence of government approach to business practice, a recognition

[9] See Ball (2020) on the notable details of the global vaccine development effort against the Cov-SARS-2 coronavirus.

[10] Perrault and Sacks (2021) make an interesting argument how Biden might best alter Trump's rather blunt launch of a tech war against Chinese high-tech companies.

on both sides that corporate behavior must be part and parcel of a broader social contract and thus also be able to consider wider stakeholder interests. Competition policy, just as corporation taxation, financial disclosure, and accounting rules, will become a matter of multi-lateral regulation in a newly defined globalization regime.

All this radical technological change carries additional social dimensions beyond competition, notably its impact on labor in a potentially unprecedented wave of automation. We already have a "gig economy" of mostly young, nominally "independent contractor"-type of workers paid by assignment, whose supposed degrees of freedom mean only misery when pay is low, benefits are non-existent, and job security is nil. Their fight for rights, fringe benefits, and protections has sparked a bigger push for stronger labor representation and labor law reform in the United States, possibly also in the EU, while China's overworked youngsters dream of working less while worrying about their social mobility. The Covid-19 epidemic has dramatically altered work arrangements, and there will be continued experimentation not least to cut down commuting in the interest of climate-change mitigation. Life-long learning and retraining opportunities, wage insurance, portability of benefits, pensions, a menu of public assistance options, and possibly even universal income benefits for assured minimum income will all become important aspects of a new policy approach toward labor. At the same time higher-wage countries will have an acute interest, part of how globalization should be redefined in a more progressive direction, that lower-wage countries provide appropriate support and protections for their workers. Labor is a global issue, a crucial life aspect of pretty much all humans across the globe. Continuous climate-induced mass migration across the globe, a demographic reshuffling we have not seen for centuries, will also need global burden sharing in the distribution of immigrants and effective integration programs.

There may very well be a chance for profoundly progressive forces growing to a position of influence in the transition's course. Already we see much discussion in Europe about a more collaborative "sharing economy," whether this includes for-profit "platform capitalism" (e.g. Uber, Airbnb) or "commons-based peer-to-peer production" (e.g. Wikipedia). And there is also a concerted effort in the EU to launch the so-called "circular economy" which would replace our current take-make-waste industrial model with a more regenerative production-consumption-reuse model. That change would allow us to decouple growth from the consumption of finite resources as the basis for a new foundation of resource-use (and -reuse) efficiency.[11]

A new accumulation regime, in the best sense of how French Régulation Theory has helped us understand this crucial concept (see Sect. 2.2), also transforms the monetary regime. Finance will push into climate finance. "Green bonds" and other financing instruments for sustainability-driven investments, technologies or products will become a focus of much financial innovation as the world commits to trillions of dollars in worldwide infrastructure and transition investments for at least the next quarter of a century to reach carbon neutrality by mid-century, if not a bit later. The world will learn to live with carbon budgets, obliging us to report our carbon footprint and incentivizing us to live within our apportioned allocations of GHG emissions, as well as generally rising carbon prices linked to those carbon budgets in inverse relation. Beyond an insurance industry having to completely remake itself to cope with the climate crisis descending upon the planet, managing the physical, transition-related, judicial, and reputational risks associated with climate change is going to be a societal challenge of the highest order. We will need very good climate-related financial disclosure practices and sustainability accounting rules in place everywhere. Investors and bank lenders are already busy imposing environmental social governance (ESG) criteria on corporate governance and valuation. ESG in particular will make businesses, and their managers as well as shareholders, more socially conscious of their impact on various stakeholders. There will be continued competition between two different modes of carbon pricing, the "carbon tax" versus the market-based "cap-and-trade" system of emissions permits trading and worldwide carbon offsets. Central banks, grouped together in the Network for the Greening of the Financial System (www.ngfs.net), have begun to rethink their operations and mission in the face of climate change, in terms of risk management, reporting, climate stress tests, financial-stability considerations, and credit reallocation from "brown" to "green" assets.

Of course, the transformation of the monetary regime that we typically experience with the emergence of a new accumulation regime, goes

[11] On the pillars of climate finance, see Guttmann (2018). Benkler (2004) and Stephany (2015) represent those two different dimensions of the "sharing economy." Finally, Ellen MacArthur Foundation (2017) provides us with a good introduction to the "circular economy."

beyond climate finance. It also touches on the international dimension of a globalized system of finance, the international monetary regime. And here we shall likely see the long-standing dollar standard (Sect. 1.4 and Chapter 3) give way, either gradually or brusquely, to an already evolving multi-currency standard with growing world-money shares for both the EUR and the CNY at the expense of the USD. How does such a multi-polar system work?

7.4 The End of the Dollar Standard

We end the book where we started it, discussing the international monetary system. It is possible that the dollar maintains its position of relative dominance, with market shares for its 2 × 4—matrix of world-money functions (see Table 1.1) perhaps a bit lowered to the 40–45 percent range in the aggregate as either euro or yuan or both gain ground. We know (from Sects. 6.2 and 6.3) that both the EU and China have recently accelerated efforts at internationalizing the use and circulation of their currencies into world money as a vector of influence over global affairs. It may also be that the international role of the USD erodes steadily, but in orderly fashion, to a level where there is not that much difference between the dollar-zone, the Eurozone, and/or the yuan bloc. In a recent commentary Nobel Prize winner Paul Krugman (2021) has characterized such a slow end of the dollar standard as basically a non-event, as a slow-motion trend decline without major consequences for either the issuer, the United States, or the rest of the world.[12] If he is correct with his projection, then there is not that much to talk about in this final section.

But there are at least two possible scenarios where the end of the dollar standard and transition to a multi-currency system are going to be more unsettling, if not altogether rocky. One concerns the distinct possibility of domestic political chaos in the United States in the wake of contested elections either in 2022 or, more likely, 2024. The unresolved January 6

[12] Krugman's (2021) argument rests mostly on his claim that being issuer of the currency serving predominantly as world money does not have a lot of meaningful implications, were it not for its ability to borrow at zero interest quite a bit from foreigners holding an inordinate supply of $100 bills for illicit purposes. He thinks neither America's ability to run chronic current-account deficits, given similarly large ones by Australia or Great Britain, nor to borrow cheaply from abroad, looking here at much lower, often altogether negative, yields in Europe, are that big a deal. Losing those advantages would then logically not make much difference either.

insurrection, unresolved because a large percentage of Trump's agitated electoral base holds on to his "Big Lie" of a supposedly stolen 2020 election, has become a blueprint for a power grab by the Republicans. Political instability, to the point of ungovernability of the country, is not at all to be ruled out. Such a situation of civil strife and turmoil will hasten the end of the dollar standard, possibly playing out even amidst major bouts of financial instability such as would unfold with a generalized run out of dollars to what suddenly will appear to look like comparatively "safe" havens in the Eurozone or yuan bloc. United States interest rates could shoot up, either because of inflation premia added on in the wake of a "flight-to-safety" panic, which in turn will hit hard dollar-denominated borrowers at home and abroad.

The other reason is that the United States lags badly behind the EU and even China in taking the necessary steps to launch a meaningful zero-carbon transition. True, Biden has made a big difference, but even his initiatives move the United States only from about zero to perhaps a third where it should be in comparison to the more advanced EU position. Just look at the growth and improved functionality of the EU's Emissions Trading System (ETS). Green parties are gaining ground in many EU member states. By contrast, many Americans either do not consider climate change an imminent problem or they accept it is a problem, but do not want to do much about it. And the Republican leadership, especially as long as it remains tightly controlled by climate denier Trump, does not want to address the issue of climate change at all. Even without political chaos, US climate policy risks stalemate for the foreseeable future. As the zero-carbon transition gains ground everywhere else, America's unwillingness to act will turn away capital, entrepreneurs, and scientists while also possibly burdening the US economy's growth capacity in sudden and unexpected fashion. The United States right now carries a lot of potential "country risk."

Whether suddenly as a matter of "flight out of the dollar" or gradually as a result of the euro's and/or yuan's steady internationalization, the world will eventually have to get used to a multi-currency system where the dollar, the euro, and the yuan vie for international-money status. Both Europeans and Chinese will have to adjust to much higher financial-market volumes of instruments denominated in their respective currencies, including derivatives. Bigger systemic demand for their currencies may well cause lasting upward shifts in exchange- and interest rates which their national economies will have to learn how to live with.

The EU's active leadership role in the rapidly growing $1 trillion global "Green Bond" market, where the euro holds a market-leading 49 percent market share, is an indication that the Europeans are able and willing to make such an increased world-money role of their currency work for them. In early July 2021 the EC even issued a European Green Bond Standard, based on the EU's taxonomy of "green" activities, oversight by ESMA, and verification of "green" project commitments funded by these earmarked bonds. The EGBS should make its €-denominated green bond segment more credible and set the "gold standard" for the rest of the world in an emerging "safe asset" class of great importance to the zero-carbon transition financing environmentally friendly projects, like wind and solar power, resource-efficient housing, or low-carbon transportation infrastructure. China is also pushing hard toward increasing its green bond issues; the United States far less so.[13]

As we move toward a multi-currency system, questions will arise about how the Triffin Dilemma (see Sect. 1.6) will be impacted by such dispersal away from a uniform global money standard. While surely enjoying their seigniorage benefits both as actual pecuniary gains as well as in terms of easier financing conditions for their financial institutions and markets, both ECB as well as PBoC will still have to work through the multi-faceted implications of their currencies gaining global status as world money and thus becoming part of the international liquidity preference (see Sect. 1.1.3). One problem here is that both EU and China have until recently been chronic current-account surplus countries which restricts net outflows of euros or yuan into international circulation, unless more than matched by net capital outflows. The Europeans are quite preoccupied with their intra-zone capital flows, routed through the Eurozone's TARGET2 real-time gross settlement system of payment transfers, and have yet to develop a zone-wide capital-export strategy toward the rest of the world which the EC is beginning to reflect upon.[14] The zero-carbon transition may give Europeans a good opportunity to expand capital exports in the global fight against climate change as a way to

[13] More details on the burgeoning international "green bond" market can be found in Climate Bonds Initiative (2021). See Jessop (2021) on the European Green Bond Standard.

[14] The fascinating "overdraft" arrangement of TARGET2 as the equivalent of an intra-Eurozone payments union is well discussed in European Central Bank (2021).

cement the EU's leadership role in that struggle for advantageous positioning in the international regime that arises with the new accumulation regime discussed here. The Chinese, on the other hand, have always maintained tight controls over capital exports. It still remains unclear how far they will be willing to let go of such controls in the interest of assuring adequate worldwide supplies of yuan.

Looking at the constellation of exchange-rate regimes since the onset of market-determined currency prices in March 1973, the leading currencies have always been allowed to float quite freely against each other, with the exception of the G-5 Plaza Agreement for orderly devaluation of the USD (September 1985–February 1987) and the G-7 Louvre Agreement for exchange-rate coordination (February 1987 until stock-market crash of October 1987). This has even been true for the yuan since August 2015, in the slower "managed-float" sense of its still somewhat controlled, yet already largely market-based currency-price movements (Sects. 4.2.3 and 6.2.4). The \$/€, \$/¥ and €/¥ exchange rates may fluctuate over 20–to–30 percent multi-year price cycles, perhaps occasionally be subject to even larger fluctuations. And each may from time to time be subject to sharp short-term fluctuations of 5–10 percent. But such price volatility should not be confused with "disorderly" market conditions which are rare, likely only during systemic financial crises (see Sect. 4.2.1). While significantly more trade-dependent than they used to be only a few decades ago, all three power centers have large enough domestic economies to absorb even large currency-price fluctuations quite easily. In the meantime, global investors will de facto exercise judgment in their portfolio allocation decisions between the three currencies which should keep each bloc's leaders on their toes and strive hard to compete effectively.

It is quite possible that a multi-currency system may attract even greater short-term portfolio investment flows to exploit exchange-rate or interest-rate movements for gain. Such highly leveraged "hot money" mobilized for speculation purposes tends to create distinct overshoot patterns and may thus contribute to excessive global financial cycles. We have already mentioned the possibility of capital controls (see Sect. 7.2). Speculation may also be constrained by regulation, as with higher margin requirements on currency futures and options. Better still is a financial transactions tax which, even though assessed at a tiny fraction of the total transaction volume, would hit highly leveraged speculators disproportionately hard.[15] Long-standing debates within the EU about best ways to impose such a financial transactions tax should form the basis for what would most usefully apply as a globally imposed tax which ideally also covers other high-frequency trading platforms such as stock-market transactions.

If the coexistence of three competing key currencies should prove inherently too unstable, we can fall back to John Williamson's (1986) proposal for a system of "target zones" which would keep currency-price fluctuations within a prescribed range, of say ± 10 percent, of set rates. Whenever market conditions threaten to push an exchange rate beyond its target-zone floor or ceiling, the central banks in that system launch coordinated currency-market interventions or, if needs be, interest-rate adjustments. If the market threats to the existing target zones persist despite official policy coordination, then central banks concerned may have to re-set the target rates in the middle to move the whole band up or down. They may wish to keep those target rates and their adjustments secret so as to not to provoke speculators to test them and also for better market balance of expectations. These were precisely the arrangements put in place by the one target-zone experiment we actually tried out, the Louvre Agreement in February 1987 (Sect. 3.3.1). The interest-rate hikes on $-denominated bonds needed to keep a weak USD on target helped set off a two-day stock-market crash on Wall Street, the most violent in its checkered history (with the Dow Jones declining by 22 percent on that famous "Black Monday" of October 19, 1987).[16] Apart from the coordinated central bank moves on interest rates or exchange rates, the Louvre Agreement included macro-economic stabilization commitments

[15] The financial transactions tax, also known as "Tobin tax" after its inventor Tobin (1978), could be a tiny fraction of total transaction volume, say 0.5 percent, and still hit speculators like a significant tax of, say, between 10 and 25 percent on their own capital invested. Speculators use highly leveraged currency derivatives contracts which may require 2 percent or 5 percent down-payment. In addition, speculators tend to have very short hold periods and thus rapid turnover, which means they have to pay that tax often, each time they trade.

[16] Pulitzer Prize of 1988 winners Stewart and Hertzberg (1987) wrote a gripping account of the market panic's second day during which United States financial regulators, grouped together informally under the coordinating direction of new Fed Chair Alan Greenspan, used lunch break for a concerted market intervention turning around an otherwise fairly obscure stock-index futures contract that sparked the desired market rebound in the afternoon.

by the G-7 members to cut budget deficits, lower taxes on corporations and individuals, and keep interest rates low. These, however, never bore fruition in the aftermath of that October 1987 stock-market crash having rapidly dissipated whatever earlier willingness for such policy coordination, implying a deeper level of cooperation, had existed. While the crash shook the accord, the dollar started a solid recovery during 1988 to calm frayed global financial markets.

If we ever had good enough reason to return to the idea of target zones between USD, EUR, and CNY, as the institutional core of a multi-player coordination game, we will need to do better than we did thirty-five years ago. Once freed of the uniformly biased prescriptions of the Reagan Revolution's neo-conservative "Washington Consensus" in favor of fiscal austerity, supply-side tax cuts, and monetary accommodation, we can take a deeper look at the required financial-sector rebalancing adjustments in the respective $[X - M = (S - I) + (T - G)]$ configurations of the three power centers. Exchange rates depend on the $X - M$ trade balance, which in turn is determined by the private and public sectors' net savings positions. The tricky part is to orchestrate simultaneous policy-driven adjustments between chronic-deficit and chronic surplus countries which the latter do not have to sign on to and may not want to for loss- of-competitiveness fears. Chronic-deficit countries have to made market-mediated or policy-driven adjustments in their external, public, and private-sector balances lest they want persistent imbalances to explode into crisis triggering crisis-induced adjustments. Those tend to be more brutal, yet also more rapid than the other two adjustment modes via markets or policy mix. Chronic surplus countries, on the other hand, do not face such a prospect of crisis from sheer inaction and therefore are not obliged to consider action proactively as a matter of crisis avoidance. And they will hesitate to commit to balance adjustments meant to cut their external surpluses. How can we then assure adequate symmetry between these two opposite groups?

One strategy facilitating such symmetric coordination games is to use an institutional anchor, the IMF's Special Drawing Rights (SDRs), and build on that pillar. The SDR is a synthetic currency basket containing weighted back-up allocations of USD, EUR, CNY, JPY, and GBP on which holders of SDRs can draw from if so desired. The allocations of basket currencies backing up such a drawing right come from reallocations of reserves, in the case of the United States from its Treasury's

Exchange Stabilization Fund. If large enough, those allocations may ultimately require parliamentary approval. Widespread opposition in the US Congress has always restrained how large an issue of SDRs the IMF can get away with, while the United States maintains a more general veto right over this potential supranational competitor to the dollar as world money. Most of the time, at least so far, SDRs are not drawn but used instead for reserve purposes or to settle official payment obligations among IMF members. Even at this still limited stage of their usage, it makes sense to have SDRs become the denomination anchor for all exchange rates. As the weighted average of all five international currencies, the SDR is a more stable numeraire than any of the bilateral movements between different constituent elements in its basket would be. That is true for both exchange rates and interest rates.

Beyond serving simply as price anchor, the SDRs may well deserve wider use in the direction of an organized supranational international monetary system. Right now, in the waning months of 2021, we are at the cusp of imagining such wider applicability of SDRs for the multi-polar capitalism we are transitioning to. There is the $650 billion issue of new SDRs, of course, followed by discussion how we can reshuffle the allocation beyond the normal formula to steer them to the debtor countries in greatest need. Both developments are without precedent, hence worthy of note. However, this may just be the beginning. We can move quite radically beyond that simply by relaxing the issue conditions for SDRs. Since only a fraction of SDRs is drawn from in exchange with basket currencies, it should be possible to have SDRs no longer backed by earmarked basket-currency reserves. Instead we can have open-ended currency swap lines between the IMF and the five basket-constituent central banks which kick in whenever responding to drawing right requests of conversion, part of an endogenous money creation process centered on elastic IMF-issue of SDRs. Such elastic two-tiered issue of a new supranational international money form paves the way for turning SDRs into full-bodied world money along all eight international-money functions in the 2 × 4 matrix (see Table 1.1 in Sect. 1.2) getting redenominated in SDRs. We can have SDR-denominated bonds, stocks, fund-transfer systems, and price formation. This may well happen gradually, and in direct competition with the dollar, euro, or yuan. The SDR basket can, after all, work both ways, in this case having the SDRs soak up excess dollars, euros, or yuan in substitution accounts at the IMF allowing national currencies to be replaced over time by supranational currency. Such a gradual transformation toward full-bodied SDRs as world money recalls Keynes' 1943 Bancor Plan (see Sect. 3.1). For that to be a realistic prospect in coming years, the international monetary system's centripetal forces must become strong enough to push centralization toward SDRs. Such centripetal forces may arise with funding the zero-carbon transition on a global scale, launching large-scale restructuring of debts via swaps, pandemic preparedness, or the rest of the world tiring of the United States and China stuck in an unproductive, even dangerous new Cold War.

The time has come to think globally, act locally, work cooperatively!

References

Aglietta, M. (1976/1979). *A theory of capitalist regulation: The US experience*. Verso Books. First published in French as *Régulation et crises du capitalisme*.

Ball, P. (2020). The lightning-fast quest for COVID vaccines – And what it means for other diseases. *Nature*. https://www.nature.com/articles/d41586-020-03626-1. Accessed 18 Dec.

Benkler, Y. (2004). Sharing nicely: On Shareable Goods and the emergence of sharing as a modality of economic production. *Yale Law Review, 114*(2), 273–358. https://doi.org/10.2307/4135731

Blanchard, O., & Tirole, J. (2021). The major future economic challenges. *France Stratégie*. https://www.strategie.gouv.fr/english-articles/major-future-economic-challenges-olivier-blanchard-and-jean-tirole. Accessed 7 July 2021.

Climate Bonds Initiative. (2021). Explaining green bonds. *CBI Market Intel*. https://www.climatebonds.net/market/explaining-green-bonds. Accessed 6 July 2021.

Ellen MacArthur Foundation. (2017). What is the circular economy? https://www.ellenmacarthurfoundation.org/circular-economy/what-is-the-circular-economy. Accessed 16 September 2019.

European Central Bank. (2021). What is TARGET2? https://www.ecb.europa.eu/paym/target/target2/html/index.en.html. Accessed 20 March 2021.

Guttmann, R. (2018). *Eco-capitalism: Carbon money, climate finance and sustainable development*. Palgrave Macmillan.

Jessop, S. (2021). Explainer: EU throws weight behind new standard for green bonds. Reuters. *Sustainable Business* blog. https://www.reuters.com/business/sustainable-business/eu-throws-weight-behind-new-standard-green-bonds-2021-07-06/. Accessed 6 July.

Krugman, P. (2021). Wonking out: The greenback rules. So what? *New York Times*. https://www.nytimes.com/2021/05/28/opinion/us-dollars-currency.html. Accessed 28 May.

Lenton, T., Rockström, J., Gaffney, O., Rahmstorf, S., Richardson, K., Steffen, W., & Schellnhuber, H. J. (2019). Climate tipping points – Too risky to bet against. *Nature*. https://www.nature.com/articles/d41586-019-03595-0. Accessed 27 Nov.

Mazzucato, M. (2013). *The Entrepreneurial state: Debunking public vs. private sector myths*. London.

Mazzucato, M. (2021). *Mission economy: A moonshot guide to changing capitalism*. Harper Business.

McKibben, B. (2015). Exxon, Keystone and the turn against fossil fuels. *The New Yorker*. http://www.newyorker.com/news/news-desk/exxon-keystone-and-the-turning-tide-on-fossil-fuels. Accessed 6 Nov.

Pearce, F. (2019). As climate change worsens, a cascade of tipping points looms. *YaleEnvironment360*. https://e360.yale.edu/features/as-climate-changes-worsens-a-cascade-of-tipping-points-looms. Accessed 5 Dec.

Perrault, M., & Sacks, S. (2021). A Sharper, Shrewder U.S. Policy for Chinese Tech Firms. *Foreign Affairs*. https://www.foreignaffairs.com/articles/united-states/2021-02-19/sharper-shrewder-us-policy-chinese-tech-firms. Accessed 19 Feb.

Rubin, J. (2015). *The carbon bubble: What happens to us when it bursts*. Penguin Random House. https://www.penguinrandomhouse.com/books/240901/the-carbon-bubble-by-jeff-rubin/

Sandbu, M. (2021). Globalisation's coming renaissance. *Financial Times*. https://www.ft.com/content/7b844dbe-0805-43ce-ba4e-a1fc579fb63b. Accessed 1 July.

Stephany, A. (2015). *The business of sharing: Making it in the new sharing economy*. Palgrave Macmillan.

Stewart, J. B., & Hertzberg, D. (1987). How the stock market almost disintegrated a day after the crash: Credit dried up for brokers and especially specialists until fed came to rescue. *Wall Street Journal*. https://www.wsj.com/articles/SB119256599114260941. Accessed 20 Nov.

Tobin, J. (1978). A proposal for international monetary reform. *Eastern Economic Journal, 4*(3–4), 153–159. https://econpapers.repec.org/article/eejeeconj/v_3a4_3ay_3a1978_3ai_3a3-4_3ap_3a153-159.htm

U.S. Department of State. (2021). Leaders Summit on Climate. https://www.state.gov/leaders-summit-on-climate/. Accessed 13 May 2021.

Williamson, J. (1986). *Target zones and the management of the dollar* (Brookings Papers on Economic Activity No. 1:1986), 165–174. https://www.brookings.edu/wp-content/uploads/1986/01/1986a_bpea_williamson.pdf

Index

R. Guttmann, *Multi-Polar Capitalism*,
https://doi.org/10.1007/978-3-030-88247-1

D

The manufacturer's authorised representative in the EU is Springer Nature Customer Service Centre GmbH, Europaplatz 3, 69115 Heidelberg, Germany. If you have any concerns regarding our products, please contact ProductSafety@springernature.com

Printed and bound by CPI Group (UK) Ltd, Croydon, CR0 4YY
30/09/2026
02225499-0013